2nd Edition

The Official Guide to

FINANCING
YOUR MBA

P9-DHQ-946

Author	Bart Astor
Advisory Panel	Ursula E. Kaiser Director of Financial Aid Administration Graduate School of Business Stanford University
	Shari Holmer Lewis Assistant Dean, Director of the MBA Program College of Business Administration University of Illinois at Chicago
	Alice Murphey Director of Financial Aid Stern School of Business New York University
Consulting Editor	James W. Schmotter Dean College of Business and Economics Lehigh University
Managing Editor	Nancy W. Ballard
Copy Editor	Sarah A. Dallam

Inquiries regarding this publication should be directed to:
Graduate Management Admission Council, P.O. Box 6106, Princeton, New Jersey 08541-6106.

Inclusion of a program in this book does not imply Graduate Management Admission Council (GMAC) recommendation nor does omission imply GMAC disapproval. The individual schools are solely responsible for the accuracy of the information in their descriptions. Program listings are free of charge and are provided by the GMAC as a service to schools and prospective graduate management students.

Other publications of the Graduate Management Admission Council:

- *The Official Guide for GMAT Review*
- *The Official Guide to MBA Programs*
- *The Official Software for GMAT Review*

Contents

Preface

The Graduate Management Admission Council (GMAC) presents *The Official Guide to Financing Your MBA* to help you understand the complex issues involved in the financing of graduate management education. A companion to two other GMAC publications, *The Official Guide to MBA Programs* and *The Official Guide for GMAT Review*, this book will guide you through the maze of financial options and strategies available to help M.B.A. students pay for their education. By understanding this information, you will be better able both to select and to afford the graduate school of management that most suits your academic needs and budget. Although often complex and technical, these options and strategies make it possible for tens of thousands of M.B.A. students to attend the institutions of their choice each year.

The Graduate Management Admission Council (GMAC) is an organization of graduate business and management schools. The Council provides information to schools and prospective students to help both make reasoned choices in the admission process. It provides a forum for the exchange of information through research, educational programs, and other services among the broad constituency of individuals and institutions concerned with management education. It sponsors the Graduate Management Admission Test (GMAT), and it also sponsors a comprehensive student loan program called "MBA LOANS" designed to meet the specific educational financing needs of graduate level business students.

The Council has three basic objectives:

1. To enhance the management admission process,

2. To broaden knowledge about management education,

3. To promote the highest standards of professional practice in the administration of management education programs and related activities.

GMAC Member Schools

Arizona State University
College of Business

Babson College
Graduate School of Business

Baruch College
School of Business and Public Administration

Baylor University
Hankamer School of Business

Boston College
The Wallace E. Carroll Graduate School of Management

Boston University
School of Management

Bowling Green State University
College of Business Administration

Brigham Young University
Marriott School of Management

California State University, Long Beach
College of Business Administration

Carnegie Mellon University
Graduate School of Industrial Administration

Case Western Reserve University
Weatherhead School of Management

Clark Atlanta University
School of Business Administration

College of William and Mary
School of Business Administration

Columbia University
Columbia Business School

Cornell University
Johnson Graduate School of Management

Dartmouth College
Amos Tuck School of Business Administration

DePaul University
The Charles H. Kellstadt Graduate School of Business

Duke University
The Fuqua School of Business

East Carolina University
School of Business

Emory University
Goizueta School of Business

Florida State University
College of Business

George Mason University
School of Business Administration

Georgetown University
School of Business

Georgia Institute of Technology
School of Management

Georgia Southern University
College of Business Administration

Georgia State University
College of Business Administration

Hofstra University
School of Business

Howard University
School of Business

Indiana University (Bloomington)
Graduate School of Business

INSEAD
The European Institute of Business Administration

Kent State University
Graduate School of Management

Lehigh University
College of Business and Economics

London Business School

Louisiana Tech University
College of Administration and Business

Marquette University
College of Business Administration

Massachusetts Institute of Technology
Sloan School of Management

Michigan State University
Eli Broad Graduate School of Management

New York University
Stern School of Business

Northeastern University
Graduate School of Business Administration

Northwestern University
J. L. Kellogg Graduate School of Management

The Ohio State University
College of Business

Old Dominion University
College of Business and Public Administration

Pennsylvania State University
The Smeal College of Business Administration

Purdue University (West Lafayette)
Krannert Graduate School of Management

Rensselaer Polytechnic Institute
School of Management

Rollins College
Crummer Graduate School of Business

Rutgers, The State University of New Jersey
Graduate School of Management

San Francisco State University
School of Business

Seton Hall University
W. Paul Stillman School of Business

Southern Methodist University
Edwin L. Cox School of Business

Stanford University
Graduate School of Business

Suffolk University
School of Management

Syracuse University
School of Management

Temple University
School of Business and Management

Texas A&M University
Graduate School of Business

Texas Christian University
M. J. Neeley School of Business

Tulane University
A. B. Freeman School of Business

The University of Alabama
Manderson Graduate School of Business

University of Arizona
Karl Eller Graduate School of Management

University at Buffalo (State University of New York)
School of Management

University of California, Berkeley
Walter A. Haas School of Business

University of California, Irvine
Graduate School of Management

University of California, Los Angeles
John E. Anderson Graduate School of Management

University of Central Florida
College of Business Administration

University of Chicago
Graduate School of Business

University of Cincinnati
College of Business Administration

University of Colorado at Boulder
Graduate School of Business Administration

University of Connecticut (Storrs)
School of Business Administration

University of Delaware
College of Business and Economics

University of Denver
Graduate School of Business

University of Florida
Graduate School of Business

University of Georgia
Terry College of Business

University of Hawaii at Manoa
College of Business Administration

University of Houston
College of Business Administration

University of Illinois at Chicago
College of Business Administration

University of Illinois at Urbana-Champaign
College of Commerce and Business Administration

University of Iowa
School of Management

The University of Kansas
School of Business

University of Kentucky
College of Business and Economics

University of Maryland
College of Business and Management

University of Miami
School of Business Administration

The University of Michigan
The Michigan Business School

University of Minnesota
Curtis L. Carlson School of Management

University of Missouri—Columbia
College of Business and Public Administration

University of Missouri—St. Louis
School of Business Administration

The University of North Carolina at Chapel Hill
Kenan-Flagler Business School

University of Notre Dame
College of Business Administration

University of Oklahoma
College of Business Administration

University of Oregon
Graduate School of Management

University of Pennsylvania
The Wharton School (Graduate Division)

University of Pittsburgh
Joseph M. Katz Graduate School of Business

University of Rhode Island
College of Business Administration

University of Richmond
Richard S. Reynolds Graduate School

University of Rochester
William E. Simon Graduate School of Business
  Administration

University of San Francisco
McLaren College of Business

University of South Carolina
College of Business Administration

University of South Florida
College of Business Administration

University of Southern California
Graduate School of Business Administration

The University of Tennessee, Knoxville
College of Business Administration

The University of Texas at Austin
Graduate School of Business

The University of Tulsa
College of Business Administration

University of Utah
David Eccles School of Business

University of Virginia
Darden Graduate School of Business Administration

University of Washington
Graduate School of Business Administration

University of Wisconsin—Madison
Graduate School of Business

University of Wisconsin—Milwaukee
School of Business Administration

Vanderbilt University
Owen Graduate School of Management

Virginia Commonwealth University
School of Business

Virginia Polytechnic Institute and State University
The R. B. Pamplin College of Business

Wake Forest University
Babcock Graduate School of Management

Washington State University
College of Business and Economics

Washington University (St. Louis)
John M. Olin School of Business

Yale University
Yale School of Organization and Management

1
Pursuing an M.B.A.: The Choices Involved

Graduate Management Degrees: How Important and Why?

Over the past two decades, the M.B.A.[1] degree has grown in both popularity and impact. From 5,000 M.B.A. graduates in 1965, the number increased to 31,000 in 1973, 65,000 in 1979, and nearly 79,000 in 1991. These large numbers of degree holders increase the competition for management positions and permit employers to use increasing selectivity in hiring new talent. As a result, prospective M.B.A. candidates must become equally selective in the choice of both school and program to make certain they will receive the most value possible from the educational institution they choose, not just for their first jobs but for their entire careers.

This choice is complicated not only by the tremendous growth of new M.B.A. programs that has taken place in the U.S. since 1960 but also by an apparent decline in the popular appeal of graduate management education. While potential M.B.A. candidates can today

choose a graduate program in management from any of about 900 different institutions, the numbers of those taking the Graduate Management Admission Test (GMAT) has declined by 13 percent since 1991. Magazine articles questioning the degree's value and future have become common.

Yet, to paraphrase Mark Twain, reports of the death of graduate management education are greatly exaggerated. Business schools everywhere are reforming their curricula to respond to the challenges of their environment. And the M.B.A. remains a credential whose value can be measured directly in high starting salaries, exciting career mobility, and entry into attractive career tracks. For roles in some industries—invest-ment banking and management consulting, to name two—the M.B.A. has become the most common credential for entry. Lawyers, engineers, and liberal arts graduates are, of course, still hired by firms in these industries, but far less frequently than M.B.A.s. In

other industries, holders of the degree have quicker access to "fast track" management development programs that prepare them for organizational leadership. Others may enter such tracks, but the common assumption is that the prior education of M.B.A.s makes them especially well qualified for the challenges of upper-level management.

Contrary to today's often negative press, the job market continues to reward M.B.A.s. Evidence of direct recognition of the economic value of the degree is most apparent in the starting salaries its holders command. According to the College Placement Council's September 1993 *CPC Salary Survey*,[2] annual salary offers for M.B.A.s with nontechnical degrees and no experience averaged $36,513; those with technical undergraduate degrees had beginning offers of $40,980. The equivalent averages for nontechnical and technical bachelor's degree holders with two to four years of experience and an M.B.A. were $49,165 and $54,286, respectively. The average starting

---

[1] Graduate management degrees have many different names and focuses. For convenience, the term M.B.A. will be used throughout this volume to refer to all graduate management programs.

[2] The *CPC Salary Survey* is an annual study of beginning salary offers made to graduating students during the recruiting period September through June.

salary for holders of the bachelor's degree in business in 1993 was $24,555.

In considering an M.B.A., however, you should remember the limitations of starting salary as the sole indicator of value for the degree or for a particular school. Geography and local costs of living influence salaries, with the highest paying jobs usually found in those living areas with the highest costs of living—primarily the Northeast, the mid-Atlantic and Pacific states, and abroad. Whatever the location, some new M.B.A.s will start significantly below or above the average salary range. The fact is that differences in individual starting salaries are the result of many factors. Among them are:

- the type of industry, its location, whether it is in the public or private sector, its size, and its profitability;

- the job applicant's M.B.A. academic concentration, academic standing, work experience, age, and individual characteristics;

- the recruiting pattern of the school attended and employers' perception of that school.

Remember, too, that in pursuing an M.B.A. you are making a *long-term* investment in yourself as a human resource. Do not be overly influenced by today's job market or current popular perceptions of graduate management education. Both can change. The investment you are making is for your entire career, not just your first job.

Finally, do not let financial aid concerns *alone* be the factor that determines whether or not you pursue an M.B.A. The reality of student financial aid today is that most American students can find the resources they need to attend some graduate management school somewhere. The questions that this book addresses regarding how much you should spend, and borrow, for an M.B.A. education are of a practical nature and will probably be important in helping you choose *between* programs.

Some Questions to Ask About Investing in a Graduate Management Education

Investment is the key word, for to qualify for the opportunities afforded by the M.B.A. degree, you must be willing to expend both time and money. If you are enrolled in a full-time program, you will sacrifice two years of income and also often pay substantial costs in tuition and fees. If you pursue part-time study, the costs will be different, but no less real, especially if you have a family or a demanding job. As the pages that follow will show, a wide array of sources of financial assistance are available to those pursuing the degree.

*Can I **really** afford it?* Some M.B.A. programs can cost up to $35,000 per year for tuition and living costs, in addition to forgone earnings. Although many less expensive alternatives are available and avenues of financial support are plentiful, the decision to pursue graduate education is still one of the biggest financial commitments you will make in the decade after you graduate from college.

Will it be necessary to borrow? On average, M.B.A. students attending full-time programs graduate owing as much as $25,000 to $35,000. Indeed, it is not uncommon for M.B.A. graduates to accumulate student loan debts of more than $50,000.

The average total indebtedness of M.B.A. graduates has been, in fact, increasing in recent years. Financial aid allocated to M.B.A. students tends to include a larger proportion of loans than it does scholarships and grants as compared to undergraduate financial aid. Not only is the cost of attending graduate management school rising, but M.B.A. students are today entering graduate programs owing more because of higher borrowing levels during their undergraduate years.

Most universities assume that M.B.A. graduates will secure jobs that pay well. Hence, they often do not provide much financial support in the form of fellowships or assistantships. Normally such awards are reserved for doctoral and master's-level students in research oriented academic programs. Occasionally, however, demands for teaching support in large undergraduate business programs can produce teaching assistantships for selected M.B.A. students. The availability of these opportunities depends upon the university and is most typical in large public institutions.

Are high levels of student loan debt a problem? If an M.B.A. increases your earning power to a level that will allow you to pay off your student loans easily, a high level of debt is obviously not a problem. Likewise, if the degree opens doors to careers that are rewarding and attractive, worry about debt levels will probably be minimal.

If, on the other hand, your level of debt forces you to make specific career choices simply to pay off these debts, it is a problem. If the demands of debt repayment force you to evaluate all employment opportunities in terms of the immediate cash they will provide, you may find yourself passing up interesting opportunities that may actually be more rewarding over the longer term. Such choices can be

How to Use This Book

Use this book

1. as a "hands-on" guide: with detailed plans, timetables, tips, and personal guidance;

2. as a workbook: including worksheets for personal use;

3. as a reference text: with information on individual graduate schools of management, scholarships, loan programs, and other forms of assistance;

4. as a sourcebook: with referrals to other sources of information that will help you finance your M.B.A.

a prescription for unhappiness, underachievement, and career burnout. In short, some levels of debt can be too much debt.

How will projected debt levels affect my choice of a graduate management school? If you have a choice of graduate management schools to attend, your decision will likely be influenced by the level of debt each alternative requires. The chapters of this book on financial aid, cost of attendance, and financial aid packaging will help you weigh the issue of debt in deciding which school to attend. In addition, Chapter 14 describes the policies and alternatives of 300 graduate schools of management. For more detailed information about these and other schools, see *The Official Guide to M.B.A. Programs*, also published by the GMAC. Above all, when deciding which school to attend, do not rule out any institution on cost alone until you have evaluated the financial aid package each school is offering you. You may be pleasantly surprised.

We have tried to make this book practical and as relevant as possible to the concerns of applicants for financial aid. The next two chapters provide overviews of both the issues surrounding financial aid and the various matters you must consider in paying for an M.B.A. The following chapters are more specific, covering the sources of financial aid, how cost of attendance and financial need are determined, how schools package financial aid, and how students must plan and budget in order to successfully finance their education. Special information on debt management and credit and a special caution for international students are provided. Finally, Chapters 14 and 15 give information on the availability of financial aid at hundreds of graduate schools of management and on sources of outside scholarships.

We mean this to be a "hands-on" guide to the sometimes confusing world of financial aid. We use concrete examples wherever possible and offer strategies and tips to help you budget and plan. We also provide specific information about individual graduate schools of management and lists of organizations that award scholarships to M.B.A. students, as well as a detailed, step-by-step guide to applying for financial aid. Worksheets and tables of statistics are included for you to use in determining your ability to afford an M.B.A. program. Use these worksheets and tables and don't be overwhelmed by the mass of specific information in the chapters ahead. All of the information will not be relevant to you, but make sure you identify and remember all that is. Make notes in the margins. Dog ear the corners of key pages. Highlight or circle items you will refer to again. Apply the rules of thumb we present here to your own personal situation. And above all, be realistic in assessing both your personal aspirations and financial resources.

Timeliness of the Information in This Book

Many aspects of the financial aid policies and practices of individual schools, lenders, government agencies, and other important players in the financing of higher education can change in a relatively short time, even yearly. This edition of *The Official Guide to Financing Your M.B.A.* is being released in the summer of 1994, and many of the examples are directed specifically toward readers who plan to begin their graduate management education in the fall of the 1995-96 academic year.

The Higher Education Act that governs the federal financial aid programs must be authorized every several years. The latest reauthorization occurred in July 1992. In between major reauthorizations, Congress and the Department of Education continue to refine the provisions of the legislation. This book incorporates the most recent revisions at the time of publication. The financial aid office at the schools to which you are applying can provide you with updates. Costs for tuition and other expenses will increase each year. As a general rule, however, the basic concepts that follow on financial planning, budgeting, and debt management should remain current and relevant.

The graduate management schools listed in Chapter 14 require the Graduate Management Admission Test of substantially all applicants for their master's degree programs. All such schools were invited to submit information about their financial aid policies and practices; only the schools responding to this invitation are included.

2

An Introduction to Financial Aid

Sources of Financial Aid

The concept of financial aid—money provided to students to bridge the gap between a student's personal resources and the costs of an academic program—has become an important element in American higher education since World War II. Before the 1940s, most financial aid was institutional and merit based and allocated in small amounts to students judged especially deserving or attractive by faculty and other administrators—for example, brilliant mathematicians, needy children of graduates, or football stars. Little attention was given to the broader concept of financial aid as a vehicle to expand access to higher education.

Federal Government

The situation changed after World War II. Most historians of education regard the Servicemen's Readjustment Act of 1944 or "GI Bill," which provided financial support for veterans, as the first example of direct U.S. federal government aid that fundamentally widened access to higher education. Further expansion of that policy came in the wake of the Soviet launch of Sputnik in 1957, when the U.S. sought to encourage the study of science and engineering by making college easier to afford with the National Defense Student Loans. In the early 1960s, individual government aid programs were created; these were ultimately combined in the Higher Education Act of 1965. Since then, federal government involvement in the financing of higher education through direct grant programs and the provision or guarantee of student loans has become an important element in the nation's educational policy as well as in the personal budgets of individual students.

- The federal government is the largest single source of student financial aid.

- Aid is authorized through the Higher Education Act of 1965, amended 1992 (Title IV).

- More than half of the total student population of American colleges and universities receives federal assistance.

- Federal programs include mostly loans and work-study programs; very little direct grant aid is available for graduate students.

State Governments

State governments provide substantial financial resources for higher education.

- Most support comes through reduced tuition for state residents at public colleges and universities. The average tuition and fees for state residents at publicly supported graduate schools of management are substantially less than the average tuition and fees at private institutions.

- Most states have grant programs, but graduate students are often not eligible.

- To qualify for state aid, you must be a state resident. Definitions of residency vary from state to state. You should inquire about residency requirements at individual financial aid offices.

- Many state agencies serve as the loan guarantee agency for federally guaranteed student loans (for example, the Federal Stafford Loans).

Graduate Management Schools
Public and private schools use their own institutional funds to provide support for students.

- Graduate management schools collectively offer hundreds of millions of dollars of their own funds—on the basis of need, merit, or both—to enable students to attend.

- Many schools award grants, scholarships, and fellowships.

- Some schools offer institutional loan programs.

- School-funded work opportunities exist on many campuses.

Organizations Outside of Higher Education
Additional sources of financial support to students include foundations, agencies, clubs, and fraternal organizations (see Chapter 15).

Organizations outside of higher education award both need-based and merit-based aid in the form of scholarships, grants, and loans, usually in open competitions, or they make awards to students who meet special requirements in their backgrounds or career aspirations (e.g., residents of a given city or region, members of particular ethnic communities, or students willing to commit themselves to a particular career).

Scholarship search firms can help locate these sources of financial aid, but their services are often not worth the price they charge applicants. Sources of financial assistance of the kind described above are listed in books available in school and public libraries; often experienced financial aid adminis-

trators can provide even better information—at no cost.

Private Lenders (usually financial institutions)
As the providers of capital for federally guaranteed student loans and private education loans, private lenders lend more than $1 billion per year to M.B.A. students.

Employers
Employers are an important source of financial support through direct tuition reimbursement or attractive loans to employees as well as sponsorship of students in Executive M.B.A. programs. In addition, corporations donate money to individual graduate schools of management for scholarships and loans.

- Employee educational benefits are often reserved for employees

who have worked at the firm for a particular period of time.

- Amounts of these awards are often based on one's academic performance and progress; this gift or loan aid may be taxable in some cases.

- One of the most serious commitments a firm can make to an employee is to sponsor him or her in an Executive M.B.A. program; accepting such sponsorship implies a commitment from the employee as well.

Philosophies and Principles That Shape Financial Aid Policies

Several broad philosophies have guided the development of financial aid policy at both the state and

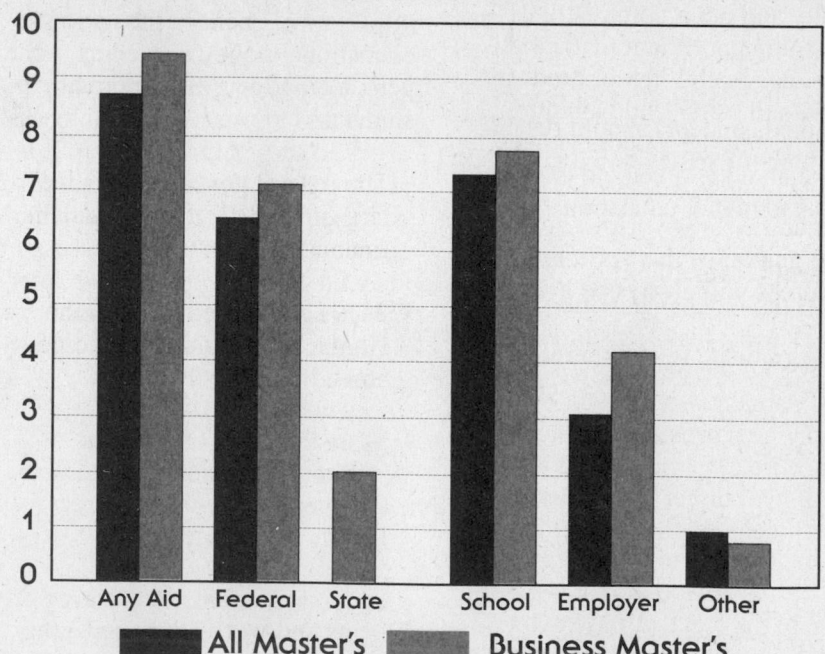

Sources of Financial Aid for Master's Degree Students

Average Aid (Thousands)

Legend: ■ All Master's   ▨ Business Master's

X-axis categories: Any Aid, Federal, State, School, Employer, Other

Source: U.S. Department of Education, National Center for Education Statistics (1990)

federal levels in the decades since World War II. Foremost among these is the concept of *family contribution*, the idea that the primary responsibility for paying for higher education rests with students and their families, to the extent they are financially able. Attention to the ideas of *objectivity* and *timeliness* are also important. The former asserts that a family's ability to pay should be objectively evaluated and the latter that a family's current (not past or anticipated future) financial status should be used to evaluate its ability to pay for higher education.

The application of additional philosophical concepts connected with financial aid—those of *access* and *choice*—is shaped by the values and missions of institutions. Although most leaders of American graduate management education agree in general with these principles, some would argue that the economic realities of higher education sometimes make them impossible to uphold in all cases. The concept of *access* holds that all students should have an opportunity to attend an institution of higher education if eligible for admission. The idea of *choice* goes a step further by asserting that once accepted, students should be able to attend the graduate management school of their choice regardless of their ability to pay. However, there is no guarantee that sufficient aid resources will always be available.

Most graduate schools of management do seek to provide the necessary financial assistance to as many as possible of their accepted applicants. But increased competition for limited resources leaves growing numbers of graduate schools of management unable to meet the financial need of all accepted students. It is important that you obtain candid information

from each school at which you have been accepted before making a final decision about where to enroll.

Types of Financial Aid

Financial aid can come in the form of grants with no conditions attached (often referred to as "free money"); loans that you must repay at a later date; and wages for services performed, for instance as a research assistant, campus security guard, or part-time library clerk. Free money is awarded on the basis of financial need, students' "merit," or a combination of the two.

Although defined differently on different campuses, the concepts of *need* and *merit* are crucial in the awarding of financial aid. Need-based aid takes into consideration a family's financial ability to pay for higher education. For the most part, federal and state student assistance programs and the most attractive loan programs—are based on need. Merit-based aid may be based on the assessment of the attractiveness of a student when measured against others who have been offered admission. Some institutional scholarships offered by graduate schools of management are merit-based and are specifically intended to enroll those believed to be the best potential students and alumni, no schools offer such awards to all accepted. Criteria used in assessing students for merit-based and other non-need-based grant aid vary from school to school. Among the most common are past academic performance and future potential to achieve high grades; interest in fields of study especially important to the school; demonstrated achievements in specific activities in prior educational or work settings; and ethnicity or national origin. Because such awards, the most attractive on any campus,

require neither repayment nor the performance of services, competition for them is keen. Only a small percentage of entering M.B.A. students receive such non-need-based scholarship or grant aid.

Educational loans differ from private commercial loans in one important respect: the amount one can borrow with a commercial loan is generally based on the borrower's ability to repay; the amount one can borrow with an educational loan is often based primarily on the cost of the education you seek. Eligibility for need-based loans is derived by comparing the cost of education with your family's resources whereas the amount one can borrow through non-need-based loan programs such as the Federal Unsubsidized Stafford Loan and through private lenders such as the MBA LOANS Tuition Loan Program (TLP) is based solely on the cost of education. Both need-based and non-need-based loans have maximum loan limits. The distinction between need-based and non-need-based aid programs varies among graduate schools of management. For example, the award of particular types of aid—say, assistantships—may be need-based at one school and non-need-based at another.

Financial Responsibility

Under federal and state financial aid policies, you and your family have the primary responsibility for paying for your education. The amount of your contribution is based on your family size and your financial resources.

As a graduate student, you are considered independent when applying for federal aid; your parents' income is not included in the evaluation process. In distributing their own school-based aid,

TABLE 2.1	Types of Financial Aid

Self-Help Aid
Definition: money you must earn or pay back later

Federal College Work-Study
State Work-Study
Federal Perkins Loans
Federal Subsidized and
   Unsubsidized Stafford Loans
Institutional loans
Graduate assistantships (research, teaching,
   resident)
Private employment
Corporate sponsorship
Employee benefits
Private loans

Gift Aid
Definition: free money

Federal grants
State grants
Institutional grants,
   scholarships,
   and fellowships
Private fellowships or
   scholarships
Tuition waivers
Tuition reductions

such as scholarships, some schools will consider your parents' financial status or expect your parents to contribute toward your education even though you are considered independent by federal eligibility standards.

Many M.B.A. students have had experience with financial aid during their prior educational experiences.

While many of the rules, policies, and procedures of undergraduate financial aid apply to aid awarded for M.B.A. programs, there are some differences as well. Table 2.2 outlines the differences.

TABLE 2.2	Differences between Graduate and Undergraduate Financial Aid
UNDERGRADUATE AID	**GRADUATE AID**
1. Most students are considered dependent on parents; parental/student/spouse resources are included in determining federal eligibility.	1. All graduate students are considered independent; parental resources are excluded in determining federal eligibility.
2. There is widespread eligibility for grant programs, including Federal Pell Grants and Federal Supplemental Educational Opportunity Grants (SEOG).	2. There is limited availability of grant aid (students are not eligible for Federal Pell Grants or Federal Supplemental Educational Opportunity Grants).
3. Governments are most committed to access and are concerned about increasing debt levels.	3. Governments are less concerned with access and with the increasing debt level.
4. Schools try to minimize the level of debt.	4. Schools are concerned about debt, but most financial aid is still through loans.
5. Schools offer a great deal of their own scholarship and grant money to attract students.	5. Schools offer less grant and scholarship aid to attract students; more loans, work, and assistantships are offered.
6. Most students attend full time and are not able to pay their own way.	6. More than half of the M.B.A. students nationwide attend part time and are self-supporting.
7. Undergraduate budgets are lower.	7. Graduate student budgets are usually higher due to higher living expenses; also, at many schools, tuition is higher.
8. All financial aid is usually administered by one central office.	8. Aid may be administered by different offices: the business school, the central financial aid office, or a combination of the two.

3

Paying for Your M.B.A.: An Overview

The chapters that follow cover the nuts and bolts of financial aid, defining and describing various options and financial strategies that can help you pay for your M.B.A. This chapter provides an overview of these options and strategies and suggests the appropriate times to employ them. Some of the strategies must be used long before enrollment or even application for admission if they are to be effective. Others can be used during the months between acceptance and enrollment; others during the program itself; and still others after graduation.

You should start to plan how you will finance your M.B.A. well in advance of your application. Research the various programs and options you can use to pay your costs. Weigh your alternatives carefully and make short-term decisions that complement your earlier long-range plans. During the years of your program, you should budget carefully, control your expenses, and take advantage of all possible avenues of financial support. After graduation, manage your debts responsibly. Undertaking the financing of your M.B.A. with this longer term viewpoint will

not reduce its costs, but it will ensure that you have examined all possibilities for financial assistance and have followed strategies that will help make your approach effective.

Long-Term Preparation

If you are contemplating beginning your graduate management education in two or three years, you have an opportunity in the interim to undertake a variety of sensible strategies that will make the financing of your degree easier to manage. The earlier this planning begins the better. Even during the years of your undergraduate program, you can take actions that will pay off later. Following are some strategies to consider.

Minimize your debt and increase your ability to borrow. If you are currently enrolled in a degree program, try to control your borrowing. Loan programs limit the total amount students may borrow for all of their educational programs. High levels of prior student debt could well limit the amount you can borrow for your M.B.A. and thus narrow your choice of schools. In addition, institutional

and private loan programs often base the amount they will lend on your anticipated debt levels at graduation. By limiting the amount of your prior educational loans, your ability to borrow from both federal and private loan sources will be preserved. As early as possible, you should begin to reduce your debt, especially credit card debt. This common consumer debt carries the worst credit terms available. A high balance on your credit card will mean you have to make large monthly payments that will not only affect your ability to pay tuition and other costs after enrollment but also may limit the amount you can borrow from other, more economical sources. In addition, schools do not include discretionary costs such as consumer debt when determining your need for aid. If you have large car payments, consider changing cars. The more loans you have paid off and the smaller your personal debts, the better your chances to borrow all the funds you need for your M.B.A. Continue this debt reduction up until the very day you enroll.

Manage your remaining debt. Examine the terms of any current educational loans including interest rates and deferment options and evaluate the relative attractiveness of paying down the loan versus placing your funds in an interest-bearing investment. In general, the interest rates and other terms of federal student loans make them relatively attractive.

Build up your savings. Try to plan ahead as early as possible by introducing a new and strict discipline into your personal finances. Determine whether or not you can pay for an M.B.A. with your present assets and decide what adjustments you must make to more effectively budget for your education. Consider also whether the services of a professional financial planner will be of help to you in achieving your goals. Arrange any investments you have to take advantage of compound interest. But, above all, simply save as much as you can. Once you have made a commitment to returning to graduate school, immediately begin to live a student life-style.

Approaching Financial Issues Strategically during the Year before Enrollment

Carefully research all of your options. In the year before you intend to begin your M.B.A., examine the various alternatives for paying tuition and other costs at the graduate schools of management you are considering. Learn about the financial aid policies of these schools and compare costs. Since most will permit you to borrow under federal loan programs if you demonstrate need, find out how much scholarship or other free money they award. If the schools award merit scholarships, try to identify their criteria and apply

to those that are most appropriate. Use financial aid offices or library reference sources to explore outside scholarships for which you might have special eligibility. Check to see if your parents' employers provide financial support for children of employees.

Evaluate realistically your options for financing if you do *not* receive a scholarship. Since most M.B.A. programs have relatively small allocations for grants of free money and use these sparingly, you should plan for the contingency of financing your entire education through savings, loans, and earnings. This may narrow the range of institutions you can realistically consider.

If you are employed, consider the alternative of part-time study. Check the catalogues of the schools in your region to see if they offer programs that meet your educational needs. Talk to your company's personnel office to learn more about any educational benefits available to study for an M.B.A. Find out if you have worked long enough at your present company to be eligible for such benefits. Evaluate the commitments you may have to make to receive such benefits and their impact on the career you plan. A requirement of several years with your current employer after graduation may make this support less attractive to you. If you are well into a management career and happy with your employer, consider the possibility of an Executive M.B.A. program, if such an alternative exists in your area. If this possibility seems realistic, have some candid conversations with your supervisor and your colleagues about their view of its suitability for you.

Attend to all the details. Know the application *deadlines* at the gradu-

ate schools of management that interest you and *don't miss them.* Prepare all the necessary materials to apply for financial aid when you prepare your applications for admission. For full-time programs beginning in the fall, prepare the materials at least 10 months in advance. Request financial aid application forms as early as possible. For fall enrollment, many schools require that you apply for financial aid no later than January 31. After you have been admitted to a graduate school of management, you will be required to submit financial aid transcripts from all schools you have attended previously. Prepare your income tax return in a timely fashion; some graduate schools of management may ask you to provide documentation of your earnings.

Make sure you apply for *all* forms of financial aid for which you are eligible. If you have served in the armed forces, make sure you are aware of all benefits offered to veterans. If you are applying to a public university, make sure you know the implications of residency for your tuition charges. Enlist aid from family members if possible, but be aware that this support may affect your institutional aid package.

What to Do after Acceptance and after Enrollment

Weigh your options. If you have been offered admission and financial aid at more than one graduate school of management, use the methodological frameworks in this book (Chapter 9) to compare financial aid packages. Consider both short- and long-term costs and benefits; assess realistically your ability to afford the various programs. Do not expect to be able to alter your packages substantially by bargaining with financial aid offices unless your financial situation changes. Most M.B.A. programs have fairly rigid financial aid policies and large applicant pools; individual applicants usually have little leverage for changing what has already been decided.

After you have made your decision about where to enroll, find out whether the school offers a tuition prepayment plan (described in Chapter 6). Usually such plans help with budgeting and provide a good investment opportunity. Do not plan to use credit cards to pay tuition and fees unless you are absolutely certain that you will have the funds to pay off the debt within a month. Avoid finance charges whenever possible.

Don't neglect personal financial management during your enrollment. Develop a sound and sensible budget. (Chapters 7 and 10 of this book provide some hints and frameworks to help with this.) Maintain strict personal discipline about finances and immediately contact your financial aid office if emergencies or other problems arise. If these are genuine and outside of your control, direct help may be available.

Consider working part time. If your financial aid package includes Federal College Work-Study funds, you should definitely take advantage of that opportunity. In any case, after you have determined the demands that academic work will make on your time, you might consider part-time work. Such employment can not only reduce the amount of money you borrow but also provide useful professional contacts with professors or other administrators. Do not, however, try to maintain a substantial commitment to outside work while

attending an M.B.A. program full time. Your classroom work will suffer, and the return on the investment you are making in yourself will be reduced. Be aware that some graduate schools of management actively discourage full-time students from working, even part time, during the first year of study.

If work is a possibility, stay in touch with your school's placement office or other administrators to arrange for both part-time and summer jobs. In searching for the latter, evaluate seriously the salary you need to generate savings for the academic year ahead. This requirement may mean that some possibilities are eliminated, but do not underestimate the importance of the professional contacts and experience that some low-paying summer jobs can provide. Remember, you are making a long-term investment.

Find out about any possibilities for further funding that your financial aid office's policies permit. Some schools reward distinguished academic performance by increasing merit scholarships after the first year. Some employment opportunities—for example teaching assistantships—may become available only after a student has demonstrated his or her academic talents. Policies such as these can improve the financial aid packages awarded for the second year or later stages of an M.B.A. program. Make sure you know if they apply to you.

Your Responsibilities after Graduation

Repay your loan. Because of the substantial indebtedness most students incur, they continue paying for their M.B.A.s long after they graduate. Fortunately, M.B.A.s continue to land positions that pay well and enable them to repay their

student loans. It is very important to your career and your personal financial standing to avoid loan defaults. Chapters 11 and 12 provide advice on ways to help ensure that you will be able to meet your commitments.

Immediately after graduation, make sure that you take advantage of grace periods and other opportunities to defer loan payments. Certain loan programs allow you to make low payments at the beginning of your repayment period and increase the size of the payments over time. This approach prevents you from being overburdened with debt during the period right after school when your salary is at its lowest and when you may have a lower disposable income due to the costs associated with establishing yourself in a new job and possibly a new location as well.

If you do find yourself having problems with your loan repayment arrangements, speak with the lender or loan servicer. Most lenders and servicers can work out a solution, at least temporarily. And do not forget the key strategy of loan consolidation in managing debt. This important concept is discussed in Chapter 11.

4

The Application Process

Applying for financial aid can be complicated and repetitive. We suggest that you follow the steps below exactly as they are given. Attempting shortcuts can be tricky and may cost you money.

Step 1: Learn about the deadlines.

Financial aid deadlines, which differ from school to school, are usually publicized in catalogues and other materials schools distribute. You do not have to be admitted before you apply for financial aid.

If you are planning to enroll in the fall term, many schools require that you apply for financial aid by January 31. *DO NOT apply for need-based aid before January 1.*

Sometimes priority for scholarships is given to applicants whose financial aid forms are submitted by an established deadline. You should note that the deadlines for outside scholarships and institutional fellowships and assistantships may not be the same as for need-based financial aid. These deadlines are usually listed in the brochures and other literature available

from the graduate schools of management and the sponsoring agencies, and deadlines for applying for many such awards are given in Chapters 14 and 15 of this book.

Important: Applying after the deadline can severely limit your aid or your eligibility for scholarship and grant aid. Yet even if the deadline has passed, you should apply. It is possible that a late application will receive consideration. A deadline may be given only to ensure that there will be time to process your application before school starts.

Step 2: Obtain the correct financial aid application forms.

To apply for any government-sponsored aid programs, you must file the Free Application for Federal Student Aid (FAFSA). To apply for state or institutional aid, you may be required to file additional applications. Most schools will send you the required forms upon request or will include them in the admissions packet. Schools usually also list the required forms in their brochures.

Note: Some schools have developed their own required forms that supplement the national forms. These may be for any aid, or for one particular type of aid (scholarships, for example). Further, most loan programs have additional applications that must be completed and submitted to the financial aid office.

Important: Financial aid applications are used for establishing financial need and are not loan application forms, which are used later in the process. Do not complete any loan applications until you have been awarded a loan by the school or have determined that you will need a private loan. Also, do not submit a loan application to a school until you are sure you will be enrolling there.

Step 3: Complete the financial aid application(s).

Complete *all* questions on the financial aid application(s). Use actual figures where possible. Use estimates of your income and assets when it is stated on the form that you may do so if you do not have actual figures.

Most applicants do not have their exact income figures when completing the financial aid application since it is usually due before Internal Revenue Service (IRS) W-2 Forms are sent out. However, you should be able to determine your earned income total from your last pay stub(s) of the year. Try to make your estimates reasonable. Most schools will ask you to verify the data later on.

Incomplete applications could delay the process or make you ineligible for programs that make awards on a first-come, first-served basis. Many schools insist that their application be completed with accurate information by the stated deadlines in order for you to receive a financial aid award. Other schools will make a tentative award that can be changed if the estimated information proves to be incorrect.

If there are individual questions that you do not know how to answer, call the financial aid office and ask for advice. Do not leave questions unanswered.

Make a photocopy of the financial aid application to retain for your records.

Step 4: Send the application(s).
Send your completed application(s) to the address(es) listed on the form(s).

Send your application by first class mail. Do not use registered mail, special delivery, or an overnight mail service, as this could actually delay processing. If payment is required, make sure you include the correct fee.

If you are applying to your state agency for financial aid, check with the state agency to see if you have to fill out another application.

Step 5: Receive Student Aid Report (SAR)
The Federal processor will send you a Student Aid Report (SAR) summarizing the information from your FAFSA.

Review the SAR for accuracy. Read it carefully and take any required action.

Keep this document in a safe place. Federal aid cannot be processed without it.

Most schools require original SARs. If you are applying for financial aid at more than one school, contact the processor to obtain additional originals.

Step 6: Submit documents as required.
Send an original SAR to each school.

After the institutions have received your documents, the financial aid office may contact you and ask for additional information.

Be prepared to send to the graduate school(s) of management to which you have been admitted copies (not originals) of the following:

- A signed and dated copy of your entire income tax return, including W2s, or a statement that you were not required to file. If you will not have the tax return done by the time the school requires it, contact the school for alternatives.

- Documentation of any non-taxed income you received (e.g., disability insurance, veterans benefits, and welfare).

- Any other documentation that is appropriate for your specific income information (e.g., unusual medical expenses, special considerations, disability expenses).

- Documentation of scholarships awarded to you by outside organizations.

Some schools will request further documentation. Do not send additional documents unless the schools ask for them; it will only cause confusion and delay. The following are examples of documents some schools request:

- a copy of your parents' income tax return,

- bank statements and other proof of assets,

- loan documents, proof of child support, and alimony payments.

Important: When sending documentation to schools, be certain your name and social security number appear on every page.

Step 7: Request Financial Aid Transcripts.
A Financial Aid Transcript is a record of financial aid you received at a school. Before disbursing any aid, graduate schools of management are required by law to have a Financial Aid Transcript from every college or university you have ever attended, regardless of whether you received aid.

Write to the financial aid office at the schools you have attended and request that each one send a Financial Aid Transcript to every M.B.A. school to which you have been admitted.

Important: Remember that the Financial Aid Transcript is different from an academic transcript and is required before you can receive any aid. There is no charge for a Financial Aid Transcript.

Step 8: Review your financial aid award(s)—your "package(s)."

After you are admitted, you will receive a financial aid award letter from each graduate management school to which you have been accepted. The award letter will show the amount of each type of financial aid (loans, scholarships, etc.) you have been awarded.

If you have been admitted to and received financial aid awards from more than one school, you should compare the awards to see which offer is best for you. Refer to Chapter 9 for a discussion on comparing financial aid packages.

Each school generates its own award letter, and each is different. Some award letters spell out everything; some letters are brief and give estimates. Some schools award Federal Stafford Loans and private loans; some schools simply refer you to these programs. Some schools include a detail of your budget and your calculated family contributions; some do not. If you have any questions about your award, call the financial aid office.

Step 9: Submit your loan applications.

The award letter should indicate your eligibility for loans. If you have been awarded a loan, you will also need to fill out the appropriate loan applications and promissory notes.

If your award includes a Federal Perkins Loan or a Federal Direct Stafford Loan, the school will supply the additional forms you need and will keep track of all the paper work. For those loans, the government supplies the funds, and the school is the lender.

If you have been awarded a Federal Stafford Loan or if you are borrowing a non-government subsidized loan from MBA LOANS or another private lender, you must locate a lender and complete a loan application (see Chapter 5).

Complete the top portion of the loan application and submit it to the financial aid office at the school you will be attending. The school will complete its portion and will either send it directly to the lender you specify or give it back to you for you to send to the lender.

Check with the school about how early you can start the loan application process. Allow sufficient time for loan processing. Federal Stafford Loans and private loans can take 8 to 12 weeks from the time you apply to the date of disbursement. You will generally have sufficient time to apply for one of these loans after you have received your financial aid award letter from the school.

Step 10: Receive your loan disbursements.

Lenders send loan checks directly to the school. The checks are either payable to you or co-payable to you and the school. You may use the money to pay for any costs related to your education, including living expenses.

Most loan programs require that the total amount for the year be divided among two or three disbursements. Each loan program has its own regulations regarding the timing of disbursements.

Important: If the timing of the disbursement(s) will cause a hardship, speak to someone in the financial aid office. In unusual circumstances, you may be able to get an emergency loan.

Step 11: Apply for in-school deferments.

If you have previously borrowed under either the Federal Perkins, Federal Stafford Loan, or Federal SLS program, you are eligible for a deferment while you are enrolled in school. However, you must apply to the lender or loan servicer for a deferment.

When you enroll, have the registrar complete an in-school deferment form. (Many schools will not certify your enrollment until you actually begin classes.) Deferment forms are available from the lender or loan servicer. Be sure to continue your loan payments until you have been notified that your deferment has been granted by the lender. You must complete an in-school deferment form for each year you are enrolled.

Step 12: Apply for the second year's financial aid.

Remember that you must reapply every year for financial aid. After January 1 of the first year in your M.B.A. program, complete a new application. Do the same in each succeeding year in which you will be enrolled.

Note: Continuing students may have different deadlines and forms than entering students, so check with the financial aid office to make sure you have the correct information and materials.

To apply for the second year's financial aid, repeat steps 1 through 10 above.

5
Financial Aid Programs

In this chapter, the major financial assistance programs are listed. Additional sources of aid are listed in Chapter 6, Chapter 15, and Appendix A. The text reflects information available at the time of publication. The financial aid offices at the schools to which you are applying can provide you with any updates.

Eligibility Criteria for Federal Financial Aid

To be eligible for federal financial aid, you

- must be a U.S. citizen or an eligible non-citizen (permanent resident; non-citizen national; and certain residents of the Trust Territory of the Pacific Islands and Micronesia),

- must be enrolled at least half time in an eligible institution for the purpose of obtaining a degree,

- must have financial need on the basis of a need analysis system approved by the Secretary of Education,

- may not be in default on any Title IV Higher Education Act (HEA) loan, may not have borrowed in excess of loan limits, or may not owe a refund on any Title IV HEA grant,

- must certify that the money will be used solely for expenses related to attendance at the school,

- must certify either that you are registered with Selective Service or that, for a specific reason, are not required to be registered,

- must be maintaining satisfactory academic progress, as defined by the school.

Grants, Scholarships, and Fellowships

Definition: Grants, scholarships, and fellowships ("free money") are awards you do not have to earn or repay.

Institutions and other organizations have a variety of objectives in awarding gift aid including: 1) meeting a portion of the financial need of students and limiting student indebtedness, 2) recruiting and attracting the best students, and 3) helping schools meet enrollment goals. These objectives cannot always be achieved because of limited resources.

Institutional Grants

Most schools offer gift aid. The criteria for awarding this money varies according to institutional policy.

- Grants can be need-based, merit-based, or a combination of the two.

- Grants may be limited to full-time students.

- Grants may be in the form of tuition waivers or tuition reductions.

- Often, separate applications are required for scholarships, fellowships, and tuition waivers.

Private, higher-cost business schools tend to have more gift aid available than lower-cost, publicly supported business schools. This aid can sometimes help to offset their higher costs. To attract the most desirable students and to meet the admissions objectives of quality and diversity, many schools offer merit-based aid. Institutional gift aid is highly competitive. Be certain to apply by stated deadlines.

State Grants

State grants to individual M.B.A. students are very limited and not available in all states.

- You must be a resident of the state to qualify.

- Most programs require that you attend a school in the state.

For further information, check with the financial aid office at the school(s) to which you are applying or contact the appropriate state agency listed in Appendix E.

Federal Grants

The availability of federal grants is extremely limited. Most federal grant aid is for undergraduate students (graduate students are not eligible for Federal Pell Grants or Federal Supplemental Educational Opportunity Grants).

Some federal sources of grant aid are listed in Chapter 6, "Other Forms of Financing," and Chapter 15, "Scholarship Opportunities."

Work Programs

Definition: Work programs are financial aid programs under which you earn a salary or stipend.

Federal College Work-Study (CWS)

- CWS funds are federal money given to and matched by the school.

- Not all schools have CWS funds available for graduate students.

- CWS funds are earned through employment.

- CWS is a need-based program; eligibility is determined using the Federal Methodology of need analysis (see Chapter 8).

- The institution decides who receives CWS awards and the amount you will receive.

You may earn only up to the amount of Federal College Work-Study funds awarded and may choose from a variety of jobs, both on and off campus. Off-campus jobs usually involve work that is in the public interest, although schools may also have agreements with employers in the private sector. Schools may award CWS in conjunction with a graduate assistantship.

State Work-Study Programs

A few states offer work programs for graduate students similar to the Federal College Work-Study program, but their availability is very limited. Financial aid offices often provide information about state work programs.

Part-Time Employment

- If you are receiving need-based financial aid, you must inform the financial aid office if you have a part-time job. Your income may reduce the amount of aid you receive.

- Placement offices at most schools will assist you in locating a job.

- Jobs can be either on or off campus.

- Financial aid offices or placement offices will provide you with information about part-time employment.

- Some graduate schools of management strongly discourage you from working while enrolled in a full-time program.

Graduate Assistantships

Graduate teaching or research assistantships can be extremely limited and very competitive. Often they require a separate application.

Many schools offer students the opportunity to teach undergraduate students or to perform research for which they earn a stipend or a tuition reduction or waiver. Although such awards are most commonly made to Ph.D. or research-oriented master's level students, M.B.A. students can sometimes obtain them. Chances of doing so are usually best at large universities with undergraduate business programs.

Resident assistantships are sometimes available. Many schools pay graduate students a stipend to live in an undergraduate dormitory and serve as an advisor. Room and board is generally waived. Resident assistantships are usually awarded through a campus housing office with a separate selection process. Special application procedures are usually involved, and students with experience in residence halls as undergraduates usually have an advantage in securing such assistantships.

For further information on teaching, research, or resident assistantships, check with the financial aid office or admissions office at the school you wish to attend.

Loan Programs

Definition: Loan programs provide aid that you must pay back. Repayment begins either while you are still attending school or after you have left. Loans constitute the largest source of financial assistance for M.B.A. students.

Each loan program has its own terms. Depending on the program, the lender can be either a private bank, savings institution, or the school itself. Some loans are subsidized by the federal or state government, some loans require immediate repayment, and some loans require a history of good credit. The following are the primary loan programs available to most graduate management students.

Federal Perkins Loan

The Federal Perkins Loan program is authorized by the Higher Education Act, Title IV; loans are awarded by individual schools. These loans were formerly called National Direct Student Loans (NDSLs).

- A Federal Perkins Loan is a need-based loan; eligibility is determined according to Federal Methodology (see Chapter 8).

- The interest rate is 5 percent.

- For most students, repayment begins six months after graduation.

- The cumulative maximum is $30,000 including undergraduate and previous graduate Federal Perkins Loans.

- There is an annual limit of $5,000 for graduate students. Some institutions will establish lower maximums.

Not all schools have Federal Perkins Loan funds. Each participating school determines who is awarded a Federal Perkins Loan.

How the Federal Perkins Loan Program Works:

Each participating school has a sum to award from a federal government allocation, school matching funds, and money paid back to the school by previous borrowers. Eligibility for a Federal Perkins Loan is determined using Federal Methodology. The amount of the loan is determined by the school, and loans are made to the most needy students first. Borrowers sign a promissory note stating their agreement to repay the loan. The promissory note also lists the borrower's rights and responsibilities. Borrowers repay the school, although many schools employ outside agencies to assist with billing and collection.

Repayment:

The amount of your monthly payment depends on the total amount borrowed and the maximum number of months allowed for repayment. The maximum amount of time to repay your Federal Perkins Loans is 10 years, and new Federal Perkins Loan borrowers must pay at least $40 per month.

Under certain special circumstances — extended illness or unemployment, for example — borrowers may make special arrangements to pay a lesser amount or to extend the payment period. If you have already begun repayment of a previous Federal Perkins Loan/ NDSL, you can defer payments while you are attending graduate school, although you *must* apply for this deferment.

Table 5.1 shows how to estimate your monthly payments.

Grace Period:

Federal Perkins Loan borrowers are granted a grace period after they either have completed their schooling or are no longer attending at least half time. During a grace period, no repayment is necessary and no interest accrues. Grace periods do not count towards determining the 10-year maximum repayment period. If you receive a Federal Perkins Loan, your grace period is six months.

If you previously received either a Federal Perkins or National Direct Student Loan, different rules may apply, particularly if you are already in the repayment period or received a deferment. Check with the school from which you borrowed, either at the billing, collection, or bursar's office, about grace periods.

Deferments:

Under certain circumstances, borrowers may be able to postpone or defer payments of their Perkins Loans. Whereas a grace period may be automatic, deferments are *not*. Borrowers must apply for one by completing a deferment form available through the school from which they borrowed. A list of deferments for Perkins Loan borrowers appears in Table 5.2.

Cancellations:

All of your loan will be canceled if you die or become permanently disabled.

All or a portion of your loan may be canceled if you:

- teach handicapped children,

- teach in a *designated* elementary or secondary school that serves low-income students,

- work in a specified Head Start program or serve as a VISTA or Peace Corps Volunteer.

Refer to your promissory note for additional cancellation provisions.

The Department of Defense will repay a portion of your student loan if you serve in certain selected specialties of the U.S. Army, the Army Reserves, the Army National Guard, or the Air National Guard. Check with an armed services recruiting officer for further information.

A Federal Perkins Loan is one of the most attractive loan programs because of its low interest rate, excellent repayment terms, and deferment options. Therefore, be certain to apply by the school's deadline.

Federal Subsidized Stafford Loan

The Federal Stafford Loan Program was formerly called the Guaranteed Student Loan Program (GSL).

* Need-based, eligibility for loans is determined in accordance with Federal Methodology (see Chapter 8).

* Loans are made by an outside lender of the student's choice.

* Loans are insured by a "guarantee agency" in each state (or a national agency) and reinsured by the federal government.

* The 1994-95 maximum loan per year for graduate students is $8,500.

* The cumulative maximum is $65,500 including prior educational loans.

* The interest rate is variable based on the 91-day Treasury Bill rate plus 3.1 percent, with a cap of 8.25 percent.

* An origination fee of 3.0 percent and an insurance fee of up to 1.0 percent are both deducted from net proceeds.

* There is a grace period of six months before repayment begins.

How the Federal Stafford Loan Program Works:

Students complete the FAFSA (see Chapter 4) to determine loan eligibility. Once a school awards a loan, you must file a separate loan application (available from a lender) with the school you will be

---

TABLE 5.1 — Calculating Your Monthly Loan Repayment

MONTHLY PAYMENTS FOR A $1,000 LOAN*

Rate	60 Months	120 Months	180 Months	240 Months	300 Months
5%	$18.87	$10.61	$ 7.91	$ 6.60	$ 5.85
6%	19.33	11.10	8.44	7.16	6.44
7%	19.80	11.61	8.99	7.75	7.07
8%	20.28	12.13	9.56	8.36	7.72
9%	20.76	12.67	10.14	9.00	8.39
10%	21.25	13.22	10.75	9.65	9.09
11%	21.74	13.77	11.37	10.32	9.80
12%	22.24	14.35	12.00	11.01	10.53
13%	22.75	14.93	12.65	11.72	11.28
14%	23.27	15.53	13.32	12.44	12.04
16%	24.32	16.75	14.69	13.91	13.59
18%	25.39	18.02	16.10	15.43	15.17
20%	26.49	19.33	17.56	16.99	16.78

*Minimum monthly payment may apply regardless of the loan amount.

Use Table 5.1 to calculate virtually any monthly payment on a level-payment loan for the five payback periods shown (60, 120, 180, 240, and 300 months). For example, suppose you had a $5,000 loan at 8 percent for 10 years (120 months). As the table shows, the monthly payment for a $1,000 loan would be $12.13. Therefore, the monthly payment for a $5,000 loan would be $12.13 times 5, or $60.65.

To determine the monthly payment of a $13,500 loan at 10.9 percent for 15 years, find the monthly payment for 11 percent ($11.37) and subtract the monthly payment for 10 percent ($10.75). That yields $.62, or the monthly payment for 1 percent. Multiply $.62 by .9 (i.e., the .9 in 10.9), which equals $.56 (rounded off). Add $.56 to $10.75, which equals $11.31. That is the monthly payment for a $1,000 loan at 10.9 percent for 15 years. Now multiply $11.31 by 13.5 to find the monthly payment on a $13,500 loan, or $152.69. (Note: this method yields an approximation that is within pennies of the actual monthly payment.) If your loan accrues deferred interest that is capitalized, be sure to add the accrued interest to the original principal before calculating the payments.

To determine your total interest paid, multiply your monthly payment times the number of months and subtract the original principal. For example, on the $13,500 loan at 10.9 percent for 15 years, multiply the monthly payment of $152.69 times 180 months to get the total repayment of $27,484.20. Then subtract the original principal of $13,500 to determine the total interest paid of $13,984.20.

TABLE 5.2 — Student Loan Deferments

REASON FOR DEFERMENT OF REPAYMENT	FEDERAL PERKINS LOAN	FEDERAL SUBSIDIZED STAFFORD LOAN (OR GSL)	FEDERAL SUPPLEMENTAL LOANS FOR STUDENTS (SLS) AND FEDERAL UNSUBSIDIZED STAFFORD LOAN
NEW BORROWERS (THOSE WHOSE FIRST LOAN DISBURSEMENT WILL BE MADE ON OR AFTER JULY 1, 1993; INCLUDES PREVIOUS BORROWERS WHOSE PRIOR LOANS ARE COMPLETELY PAID)			
At least half-time enrollment in postsecondary school or graduate program	Yes	Yes	Yes, principal only; interest still accrues
Conscientiously seeking, but unable to find, full-time employment	Yes, for up to 36 months	Yes, for up to 36 months	Yes, principal only up to 36 months; interest still accrues
Economic hardship	Yes, for up to 36 months	Yes, for up to 36 months	Yes, principal only up to 36 months; interest still accrues
Community service	While engaged in activity	No	No
Study in an approved graduate fellowship program or in a rehabilitation training program for disabled people	Yes	Yes	Yes, principal only; interest still accrues
PREVIOUS BORROWERS (THOSE WHO HAVE OUTSTANDING BALANCES ON LOANS FIRST DISBURSED PRIOR TO JULY 1, 1993)			
Half-time enrollment in post-secondary school or graduate program	Yes, of both principal and interest	Yes, principal and interest (if first loan after July 1, 1987)	Yes, principal only; interest still accrues
Full-time enrollment at a school participating in Stafford Loan and SLS	Yes, principal and interest	Yes, principal and interest	Yes, principal only; interest still accrues
Enrolled in internship, residency, graduate fellowship program, or rehabilitation program for disabled borrowers	Up to lender; interest may accrue; 24 months for internship and residency	Principal and interest; up to 24 months for internship and residency	Principal only; interest still accrues; up to 24 months for internship and residency
Active duty in the U.S. armed forces or National Oceanic and Atmospheric Administration Corps, or officer in the Commissioned Corp of the U.S. Public Health Service	Yes, for up to 36 months	Yes, for up to 36 months	Principal only up to 36 months; interest still accrues
Volunteer in Peace Corp, ACTION program, or a comparable service	Yes, for up to 36 months	Yes, for up to 36 months	Principal only up to 36 months; interest still accrues
Temporary total disability or unable to work because caring for temporarily totally disabled spouse or dependent	Yes, for up to 36 months	Yes, for up to 36 months	Principal only up to 36 months; interest still accrues
Conscientiously seeking, but unable to find, full-time employment in the U.S.	Up to lender, but interest still accrues	Yes, for up to 24 months	Principal only up to 24 months; interest still accrues
Pregnant or caring for newborn or newly adopted child	Up to 6 months but cannot be gainfully employed	Up to 6 months but cannot be gainfully employed	Principal only up to 6 months; cannot be gainfully employed
Mother with preschool age children, entering or reentering work force, paid no more than $1 more than minimum hourly wage	Up to 12 months	Up to 12 months	Principal only up to 12 months
Full-time teacher in public or nonprofit private elementary or secondary school in a designated teacher shortage area	Portion of loan may be cancelled for each year of service	Up to 36 months	Principal only for up to 36 months

attending. The school certifies that you are eligible and have need. The school submits the loan application to a lender you have chosen.

When you borrow, you will sign a promissory note agreeing to repay the loan according to the terms outlined in the note. A sample loan application and promissory note are included as Appendix B.

Note: The Federal *Direct* Stafford Loan Program has different application procedures. See the description later in this chapter.

Finding a Lender:

Many banks, savings and loans, credit unions, and some schools themselves participate in the Federal Stafford Loan program. MBA LOANS, a program sponsored by the Graduate Management Admission Council is a participating lender. If you need help finding a lender, check with the school(s) you wish to attend.

If you previously borrowed under the Federal Stafford or Guaranteed Student Loan programs, consider using the same lender if possible. Doing so should prevent your having to make separate loan payments to different lenders once you begin repayment. In order to use the same lender, you must be a resident of, and continue to have an address in, the state in which you previously borrowed. If this is not the case, locate a new lender who uses the guarantee agency in the state where the graduate school of management you will be attending is located.

Interest Rates:

Interest is variable based on the 91-day Treasury Bill rate plus 3.1 percent, with a cap of 8.25 percent.

Other Charges:

Lenders charge an *origination fee* of 3 percent, which will be deducted from the proceeds of the loan. This money is sent to the federal government to help offset the cost of subsidizing the loans. The deduction does *not* reduce the amount you must repay.

Lenders also charge an *insurance fee* of up to 1.0 percent, which will be deducted from the proceeds of the loan. This money is used to insure loans and to offset administrative costs incurred by the guarantee agency. This deduction does not reduce the balance owed.

Once the lender approves your loan, you will receive a notice of disclosure and guarantee from the lender. This legal document will indicate the fees the lender will deduct and the resulting amounts of the loan checks.

Repayment:

The amount of your monthly payment depends on the total amount you borrowed and the number of months in the repayment schedule. Table 5.1 shows how to estimate your own monthly payment, total payments, and interest paid.

You must pay at least $50 per month, and the loan must be repaid within 10 years. Under certain circumstances — extended illness or unemployment, for example — you may make special arrangements to make a smaller payment or to extend the payment period. There is no prepayment penalty.

Grace Period:

If your interest rate on a previous loan is either 8 or 9 percent *and you have not already used a grace period,* you do not have to begin repaying your Federal Stafford

Loan until six months after you have graduated, leave school, or drop below half-time enrollment status. If your interest rate is 7 percent, repayment begins 9 to 12 months after you have graduated, leave school, or drop to less than half-time status. Variable interest rate Federal Stafford loans provide a six-month grace period.

Deferments:

Under certain circumstances, you may be able to postpone payments of your Federal Stafford Loan. However, even if you meet the criteria, a deferment is not automatic; you must apply through your lender. A complete list of deferments for the Federal Stafford Loan program is included in Table 5.2, Student Loan Deferments.

Cancellations:

The only provisions for total cancellation of a Federal Stafford Loan are death or permanent disability.

Partial cancellation of loans is available in some cases if you become a teacher, a nurse, or if you perform community service. Details are given on your promissory note.

Federal Unsubsidized Stafford Loans for Middle Income Students

The Federal Unsubsidized Stafford Loan Program provides non-need-based loans guaranteed by the federal government.

- The maximum loan for a graduate student is $18,500, minus any amount borrowed under the Federal Subsidized Stafford Loan Program.

- The cumulative maximum is $138,500, including any amounts borrowed under the Federal Stafford Loan Program.

- You must apply for a Federal Subsidized Stafford Loan first.

- Interest is based on the 91-day Treasury Bill plus 3.1 percent, adjusted annually.

- The maximum interest rate is 8.25 percent.

- A combined origination and insurance fee of 3.0 percent and a guarantee fee of up to 1.0 percent are subtracted from the loan proceeds.

- Repayment of principal begins six months after you graduate or cease to be enrolled at least half time.

- You may either pay interest during periods of enrollment or request an in-school deferment of interest. Deferred interest still accrues and is capitalized.

How the Federal Unsubsidized Stafford Loan Program Works:

The Federal Unsubsidized Stafford Loan, in combination with any other aid you receive, may not exceed the cost of education as determined by the school. Under certain circumstances, an institution may allow a student to borrow under this program to offset the calculated family contribution (see Chapter 8).

To apply for a Federal Unsubsidized Stafford Loan, you must complete the FAFSA. Once the school has awarded this loan, you must complete a separate Stafford application available from a lender. This application can be used for both the Federal Subsidized Stafford and the Federal Unsubsidized Stafford Loan programs. If you do not qualify for a Federal Subsidized Stafford Loan, you may still apply for a Federal Unsubsidized Stafford Loan.

Note: The Federal *Direct* Stafford Loan Program has different application procedures. See the description later in this chapter.

Finding a Lender:

Many banks, savings and loans, and credit unions, and some schools themselves, participate in the Federal Unsubsidized Stafford Loan Program. MBA LOANS, a program sponsored by the Graduate Management Admission Council is a participating lender. If you need help finding a lender, check with the school(s) you wish to attend.

If you previously borrowed under the Stafford or Guaranteed Student Loan programs, consider using the same lender if possible. Doing so should prevent your having to make separate loan payments to different lenders once you begin repayment. In order to use the same lender, you must be a resident of, and continue to have an address in, the state in which you previously borrowed. If this is not the case, locate a new lender who uses the guarantee agency in the state where the graduate school of management you will be attending is located.

Interest Rates:

The Federal Unsubsidized Stafford Loan is a variable rate loan program. Interest rates are adjusted annually. The interest rate will be 3.1 percent plus the bond equivalent rate of 91-day Treasury Bills auctioned at the final auction held prior to June 1. This rate cannot exceed 8.25 percent.

Other Charges:

Lenders will charge a combined *origination* and *guarantee fee* of up to 4.0 percent, which will be deducted from the proceeds of the loan. This money is sent to the federal government to help offset

the cost of default claims and to reduce the cost of special allowances, if any. The deduction does *not* reduce the amount you must repay.

Once the lender approves your loan, you will receive a notice of disclosure and guarantee from the lender. This legal document will indicate the fees the lender will deduct and the resulting amounts of the loan checks.

Repayment:

The amount of your monthly payment depends on the total amount you borrowed, the number of months in the repayment schedule, and whether you elected to pay interest during school or defer interest payments.

Repayment of principal begins six months after you graduate or cease to be enrolled at least half time. Interest may be paid monthly or quarterly while you are in school, or you may elect to defer payment. If you defer interest payments, interest will accrue and will be capitalized no more frequently than quarterly.

You must pay at least $50 per month once you begin repayment of principal and interest, and the loan must be repaid within 10 years. There is no prepayment penalty.

Grace Period:

You do not have to begin repayment of principal until six months after you graduate or cease to be enrolled at least half time. Interest does accrue and is capitalized unless you choose to pay the interest while in school.

Deferments:

Under certain circumstances, you may be able to postpone payments of your Federal Unsubsidized

Stafford Loan. Deferment options will be listed on your promissory note. However, even if you meet the criteria, a deferment is not automatic; you must apply through your lender.

Cancellation:

The only provisions for total cancellation of an Unsubsidized Stafford Loan are death or permanent disability of the borrower.

Institutional Loan Programs

- Institutional loan programs are private loan programs offered by schools themselves.

- They are not offered by many schools.

- These loan programs may have attractive terms and competitive interest rates.

Because each school's program is different, and not all schools offer a loan program, you should check with the financial aid office about availability. The staff of the financial aid office will be able to assist you in evaluating the program. See Chapter 6 and Appendix A for additional loan programs.

Federal Direct Student Loan

The Federal Direct Student Loan is a loan program authorized by Congress in 1993 that will be phased in over a five-year period. For the 1994-95 academic year, 105 schools will participate in the program. The number of schools will increase through 1998-99. The program consists of two programs for which graduate students are eligible: the Federal Direct Stafford Loan (FDSL) and the Federal Direct Unsubsidized Stafford Loan (FDUSL). The program is very similar to the Federal Stafford Loan Program, except that the school will award the loans instead of an outside lender.

Developing a Borrowing Strategy

1. Choose the right lender:
- services its own loans or sells entire portfolio to one secondary market
- uses one loan servicing agency with one billing statement
- offers life of loan servicing, regardless of whether the loan is sold to a secondary market
- participates in the Federal Loan Consolidation Program
- offers deferment of interest payments
- offers toll-free phone number
- offers repayment options
- offers forbearance
- offers a family of loans if needed
- will intercede with the guarantor or servicer on your behalf

2. Shop for the best terms (particularly with private loans):
- lowest interest rate
- uses the least volatile index to determine the interest rate for variable rate private loans (the more the index changes, the more likely your interest will be higher)
- interest capitalized as infrequently as possible (the more often interest is capitalized, the more your principal grows, and the more you end up repaying)
- longest grace period before payments are required
- number of deferments offered
- lowest guarantee and insurance fees required
- least effect on your income tax

3. Find alternatives to debt:
- part-time employment
- full-time employment/part-time schooling
- cooperative education program
- loan repayment assistance programs
- accelerated study, which may lower your total cost
- assistance from your family

- Loans are both need based (Federal Direct Stafford Loan) and non-need based (Federal Direct Unsubsidized Stafford Loan).

- Loans are made by the university and guaranteed by the federal government.

- The maximum loan per year is $18,500. The maximum need-based FDSL portion is $8,500. The maximum non-need-based FDUSL portion is $18,500 minus the amount of the FDSL eligibility.

- The cumulative maximum for graduate students, including prior Federal Direct Loans, is $138,500: $65,500 for Federal Direct Stafford Loans and $73,000 in Unsubsidized Direct Loans.

- The interest rate is variable based on the 91-day Treasury Bill. For loan periods beginning on or after July 1, 1994, the rate is the 91-day T-Bill plus 3.1 percent, capped at 8.25 percent. For loan periods beginning on or after July 1, 1995, the rate is the 91-day T-Bill plus 2.5 percent, capped at 8.25 percent.

- An origination fee of 4 percent is deducted from the loan proceeds.

- Loan proceeds are first credited towards tuition and fees. If you live in school housing, room and board will also be paid. Any remaining loan amount will be disbursed to you in check form.

How the Federal Direct Student Loan Program Works:

Students complete the federally approved financial aid application (see Chapter 4) to determine loan eligibility. The school will determine your eligibility. You will receive a promissory note that will list your rights and responsibilities as a borrower. You will be required to sign this note stating your intent to repay the loan. The Department of Education will contract with a loan servicer to whom you will repay your loan.

Interest Rates:

The interest rate will vary, depending on when you borrow the funds. For loan periods beginning on or after July 1, 1994, the interest rate is the 91-Day Treasury Bill rate plus 3.1 percent, but the loan will not exceed 8.25 percent. For loan periods beginning on or after July 1, 1995, the interest rate is the 91-Day Treasury Bill rate plus 2.5 percent, not to exceed 8.25 percent.

Other Charges:

The federal government charges a 4 percent origination fee, which will be deducted from your loan proceeds.

Repayment:

The amount of your monthly payment depends on the total amount borrowed and the number of months in the repayment schedule. There are four repayment plans for the Direct Loans. The standard repayment requires a fixed payment per month for a maximum of 10 years. There is a $50 per month minimum payment. The extended repayment plan is similar to the standard repayment plan, but is for periods longer than 10 years. The graduated repayment plan allows you to make lower payments early in the repayment schedule and increasing payments later in the process. The income contingent repayment plan allows payments based on your adjusted gross income. All of these options are described in the promissory note you will sign.

Grace Period:

You do not have to begin repayment until six months after you graduate or cease to be enrolled at least half time. For the unsubsidized program, interest continues to accrue and is capitalized, unless you choose to pay the interest while in school.

Deferments:

Under certain circumstances, you may be able to postpone payments of your Federal Direct Student Loans. During the deferment period, the Department of Education will pay the interest on Federal Direct Stafford Loans. Interest will accrue on the Federal Direct Unsubsidized Loans. Deferments are available for at least one-half-time enrollment at a postsecondary institution, unemployment or economic hardship (up to three years), and for study in an approved graduate fellowship or rehabilitation training program.

6
Other Forms of Financing

Government sponsored student loans, institutional scholarships and grants, personal earnings, and family contributions account for the bulk of the money used to pay for graduate business education. However, other sources of funding are available. Many of these sources are targeted for specific groups and are limited in amount and eligibility. Some private and public sources of scholarships to which you must apply separately and for which there are specific eligibility criteria are listed in Chapter 15, "Scholarship Opportunities."

Private Loan Programs

Commercial Lender Loans
Many commercial lenders, as well as some Federal Stafford lenders, offer private loans to students and their families. The terms, maximum amounts, interest rates, fees charged, and repayment options of the loans vary. You should evaluate carefully the terms of each program before borrowing. Financial aid offices can be helpful in evaluating the terms and may know the experience previous borrowers have had with a particular lender. In most instances, federally guaranteed loans have the most attractive terms.

The Graduate Management Admission Council has worked closely with industry experts to develop two outstanding loan programs to serve graduate business students. First, MBA LOANS provides both the Federal Stafford Loans and the privately funded Tuition Loan Program (TLP) for students enrolled in traditional graduate business programs. And, second, the Executive MBA LOANS program is available to students enrolled in executive M.B.A. programs who prefer to bypass the federal financial aid process. Specific provisions of the MBA LOANS and Executive MBA LOANS programs include:

MBA LOANS — Tuition Loan Program
How the Tuition Loan Program works:

Students who have a satisfactory credit history may borrow Tuition Loan Program (TLP) funds to help meet graduate school expenses. TLP may be used to offset your calculated family contribution. You may use the MBA LOANS application materials available either in school financial aid offices or by contacting MBA LOANS directly at:

1-800-366-6227

Eligibility Criteria:

- You must be enrolled as a graduate student at least half time in an approved business school. Not all graduate business schools are eligible for the TLP.

- You must be a citizen or national of the U.S. or a permanent resident without conditions and with proper evidence of eligibility. All permanent resident borrowers are required to obtain a credit-worthy cosigner who is a U.S. citizen.

- You must meet credit-ready criteria (i.e., the absence of adverse credit information).

- You must apply for federal financial aid and if eligible, submit an application for a Federal Stafford Loan before applying for the TLP.

- You may not be in default on any student loan or owe a refund on any student financial aid.

Loan Limits:

The annual maximum TLP limit is $15,000, and the total TLP limit is $30,000. The aggregate unpaid educational loan limit from all sources is $70,000. The minimum loan amount for first-time borrowers is $1,000, and the minimum for continuing borrowers is $500.

Interest Rate:

The interim period rate is variable, adjusted quarterly to the coupon equivalent average of the 13-week U.S. Treasury Bill rate plus 3.25 percent. During repayment, the variable rate is adjusted quarterly and is the coupon equivalent average of the 13-week U.S. Treasury Bill rate plus 3.4 percent.

Interest Payment:

Interest accrues while you are in school. It is deferred until six months after you graduate or your status drops below half time. Interest is capitalized and added to principal at repayment. There is no penalty for early repayment.

Origination Fee:

There is no origination fee for a TLP.

Insurance Fee:

An insurance premium is deducted from the loan proceeds. The amount of the fee varies:

• 7.5 percent for loans that are cosigned; or

• 7.5 percent at disbursement, plus an additional 2.5 percent added at repayment for loans without a cosigner.

Repayment:

Repayment begins six months after you graduate or your status drops to less than half time, or three years after the date of the first TLP disbursement. You have a maximum of 12 years to repay. There are two repayment options: the standard repayment terms are 12 years of interest and principal; the alternative payment terms are one year of interest only and 11 years of interest and principal payments. There is no penalty for prepayment.

Grace period:

You have a grace period of six months after you graduate or your status drops below half time. During this time, you do not have to make payments. However, interest continues to accrue and is added to the principal at repayment.

Forbearance:

Under special circumstances, the lender may grant you a forbearance of principal. During this time, interest continues to accrue. During the period of forbearance, the lender may ask you to make interest payments if you are able. You must apply directly to MBA LOANS for forbearance.

Cancellation:

There is no provision for cancellation of a TLP.

Executive MBA LOANS
How the Executive MBA LOANS Program Works:

The Executive MBA (EMBA) LOANS Program has been developed specifically for those students enrolled in Executive M.B.A. programs who wish to bypass the federal student financial aid process. You can obtain EMBA LOANS application materials either from school financial aid offices or by contacting EMBA LOANS directly at:

1-800-366-6227

Eligibility Criteria:

• You must not have applied and will not apply for any Federal Title IV student financial aid during this enrollment period.

• You must be enrolled in an approved executive, fully employed, part-time, or other nontraditional, graduate business program at least half time. Not all graduate business schools are eligible for the EMBA LOANS program.

• You must be a citizen or national of the U.S. or a permanent resident without conditions and with proper evidence of eligibility. All permanent resident borrowers are required to obtain a credit-worthy cosigner who is a U.S. citizen.

• You must meet credit-worthy criteria for EMBA LOANS as determined by the lender.

• You may not be in default on any student loan or owe a refund on any student financial aid.

Loan Limits:

The annual maximum for EMBA LOANS is the cost of education as determined by EMBA LOANS. The annual minimum is $1,000. The aggregate limit is the cost of education.

Interest Rate:

The interest rate is variable and is adjusted quarterly to the coupon equivalent average of the 13-week U.S. Treasury Bill rate plus 3.5 percent.

Interest Payment:

Interest accrues while you are in school. It is deferred until six months after you graduate or your status drops below half time. Interest is capitalized and added to principal at repayment. There is no penalty for early repayment.

Origination Fee:

There is no origination fee for EMBA LOANS.

Insurance Fee:

An insurance premium of 6.5 percent is deducted from the loan proceeds.

Repayment:

Repayment begins six months after you graduate or your status drops to less than half time, or three years after the date of the first EMBA LOANS disbursement. You have a maximum of 12 years to repay. There are two repayment options: the standard repayment terms are 12 years of interest and principal; the alternative payment terms are one year of interest only and 11 years of interest and principal payments. There is no penalty for pre-payment.

Grace Period:

You have a grace period of six months after you graduate or your status drops below half time. During this time, you do not have to make payments. However, interest continues to accrue and is added to the principal at repayment.

Forbearance:

Under special circumstances, the lender may grant you a forbearance of principal. During this time, interest continues to accrue. During the period of forbearance, the lender may ask you to make interest payments if you are able. You must apply directly to EMBA LOANS for forbearance.

Cancellation:

There is no provision for cancellation of EMBA LOANS.

Home Equity Loans

Many commercial lenders offer home equity loans, some at very attractive rates with extended payment periods. In addition, the interest on such loans may be tax deductible. However, these lenders do not offer grace periods, nor do they offer the deferment provisions offered with many educational loans. Furthermore, at the time you draw the funds, some lenders of home equity loans will recheck your ability to repay the loan. If you qualified based on your employment and have stopped working full time in order to attend school, you may no longer qualify for the loan. Because there may be tax consequences involved with a home equity loan, students are encouraged to check with a tax advisor before determining whether a home equity loan is appropriate.

If you are considering a home equity loan, you should also make certain you will be able to maintain your loan payments while you are enrolled in school. If payments become a problem, you may be jeopardizing your home ownership.

Other Assistance

Employee Educational Benefits

As a general rule, the larger the company, the more likely it is to offer some educational payments as part of its benefits package. However, there are also many small firms that provide tuition assistance to employees. There are also some companies that offer tuition benefits to children and/or spouses of employees. Such benefits are especially important for those who are contemplating part-time M.B.A. study. They tend to be of less help for full-time M.B.A. enrollment.

To evaluate whether such educational benefits can be of help to you, do some checking around. If you are currently working, check with your employer's personnel department to see whether the company offers tuition benefits. Ask your parents to check with the personnel department of their employers to see whether they participate in a tuition benefit program for children of employees. And check with your tax advisor about potential tax consequences of receiving educational benefits or tuition reimbursement from an employer.

Timing of reimbursement can present cash flow problems for some part-time students. Most companies reimburse employees after the completion of courses. Schools, on the other hand, nearly all require payment of tuition when courses begin. Since some private graduate schools of management can charge as much as $2,000 per course, and company reimbursement can take up to five or six months after initial enrollment, cash flow can indeed be an issue. Personal financial planning is obviously in order in this situation.

Executive M.B.A. Programs

About 100 schools offer Executive M.B.A. programs. Participants are generally practicing managers with five or more years of professional experience and records of significant accomplishment or leadership promise. The employer is making an investment in such employees by sponsoring them in an Executive M.B.A. program and paying the school directly for all educational expenses. The employer also commits to giving employees participating in Executive M.B.A. programs time off during working hours to attend classes. Students maintain full-time managerial responsibilities while completing the program. Because the curriculum is specially designed for students with work experience, the program can be either shorter or longer than a regular M.B.A. program.

In today's uncertain economy, some notes of caution about Executive M.B.A. programs are in order. Support for participants in such programs can be eliminated or reduced when a company experiences financial difficulty. In addition, if you are laid off or terminated from the company, your enrollment in the program may end, or you may have to pay for the program yourself. In exploring the Executive M.B.A. option, it is important to ascertain your employer's criteria for sponsorship and its policy on continuing commitment to those who begin such programs.

College and University Tuition Benefits

Many colleges and universities offer tuition benefits to employees and their children by permitting them to enroll for a reduced tuition rate or even for no tuition at all. Some institutions have established alliances with other colleges and universities to permit employees or children of employees to take courses or pursue degree programs there at similarly reduced tuition rates.

If you, your spouse, or your parents are employed by a college or university, check with its personnel office about this possibility. As with company tuition benefits, there are apt to be restrictions.

Veterans' Educational Benefits

A large source of federal educational assistance comes from benefits to veterans. These benefits are government entitlements, and you do not have to show need to claim them.

There are three major programs under which veterans and current enlistees can get educational assistance. These are all listed in Table 6.1. If you entered active duty before 1977, check with your local Veterans Administration (VA) office to determine if you are eligible for any benefits.

State Residency Benefits

Your status as the resident of a state can in itself make you eligible for financial assistance. The tuition and fees for state residents at state-supported universities can be substantially lower than for non-residents. This savings can be as much as $10,000 per year.

Qualifications for state residency vary considerably from state to state. In most states, you must have lived in the state for at least one full year to be considered a resident. Documents such as rent receipts, checking accounts, and voter registration cards are required to prove residency. If you are contemplating attending a state-supported school, explore the specific requirements for becoming a state resident. These can often work to your advantage. For instance, occasionally a school will immediately grant state residency to graduate assistants. The admissions office or registrar usually can help you with such specific policies regarding residency.

Interstate Financial Aid

Interstate Reciprocal Agreements:

Some states have reciprocal tuition agreements through which public colleges and universities charge the resident tuition rate to residents of other states that reciprocate. If you will be attending a publicly supported school in a neighboring state, check to see if such a reciprocal tuition agreement exists for residents of your state.

Regional Tuition Agreements:

There are also two regional interstate agreements that can benefit students in business-related programs.

The New England Regional Student Program is for New England residents who enroll in one of four specific master's degree business programs at a public university in another New England state because their state public university does not offer the program. Students enrolled in one of these programs pay the in-state resident tuition plus 50 percent. There are no other conditions, and there is no separate application. A general M.B.A. program is not one of the four, but the master's degree programs in Accounting; Hotel, Restaurant and Travel Administration; Manufacturing Management; and Organizational Management are included. For information about this arrangement, inquire at the graduate admissions office of the participating New England university or call The New England Board of Higher Education at (617) 357-9620.

The Western Regional Graduate Program, sponsored by the Western Interstate Commission for Higher Education (WICHE), applies to residents of one of 14 participating western states who enroll in a "distinctive" master's degree program in another western state because their state public university does not offer the program. Again, a general M.B.A. is not one of the programs, but the master's degree in fields such as taxation, hotel administration, or organizational development are included. Participants in this program pay the in-state tuition rate rather than the nonresident tuition rate. For further information, call WICHE at (303) 541-0210.

TABLE 6.1 Veterans' Benefits

	SURVIVORS'/DEPENDENTS' EDUCATIONAL ASSISTANCE PROGRAM (DEAP), CHAPTER 35	POST-VIETNAM ERA VETERANS' EDUCATIONAL ASSISTANCE PROGRAM (VEAP), CHAPTER 32	MONTGOMERY G.I. BILL—ACTIVE DUTY, CHAPTER 30 (NEW G.I. BILL)
Eligible	Child or spouse of veteran who died or is permanently disabled as a result of active service (spouse eligibility extends for 10 years) children 18 to 26 years old	Entered service between January 1, 1977, and June 30, 1985 Enrolled in VEAP before April 1, 1987 Completed two years of active duty Served continuously for 181 days Received honorable discharge	Entered service after June 30, 1985 Completed two years of active duty Received $100 per month reduction in military pay for 12 months
Maximum term	Forty-five months, including undergraduate school	Up to 36 months, including undergraduate school	Up to 36 months including undergraduate school
Rate	Monthly amount fixed by government	Voluntary May contribute $25-$100 per month Government matches 2:1	Varies based on the length of service Depends upon enrollment status

Tuition Payment Plans

There are several privately sponsored tuition payment plans for students or their parents to help manage school expenses. Some are listed in Appendix A.

A tuition payment plan is generally a form of payment by installment. Three to five months prior to enrollment, students and/or their families begin paying the year's tuition and any expenses for which the school bills. Payments are usually extended for a period of 10 months, with no interest or finance charge added. There is often a small application fee of approximately $50.

Adequate resources and a good credit rating are needed to qualify for a tuition payment plan. If you have savings, continue to work during school, or have a working spouse, this may be an appropriate option for you.

Many sponsors of these payment plans also offer loan programs with competitive interest rates that extend the tuition payments over an even longer period.

Tuition Prepayment Plans/ Tuition Guarantees

Recently, much attention has been given by the media to tuition prepayment plans or tuition guarantees. Also called "tuition futures," a handful of M.B.A. schools currently offer them.

Under a school-sponsored tuition prepayment plan, you pay future tuition by making one large payment sufficient to cover, with a reasonable adjustment for inflation, the tuition for the entire program. You make the payment either far in advance or at the beginning of the first year. The school guarantees that even as costs rise, you will not have to pay any more for your tuition.

In addition to school-sponsored tuition prepayment plans, some states have considered legislation that would set up tuition futures for its publicly supported graduate schools of management. These programs would be similar to those at individual schools except that your lump sum payment would apply to any publicly supported business school in the state.

Whether or not a school-sponsored or state-sponsored tuition prepayment plan is an appropriate choice for you depends upon your financial situation, choice of school, state of residency, and other financing options. Consider the plans carefully and check with an accountant or your tax advisor before entering into any agreement.

You can learn if the school you are planning to attend offers such plans by inquiring at either the admissions or financial aid office.

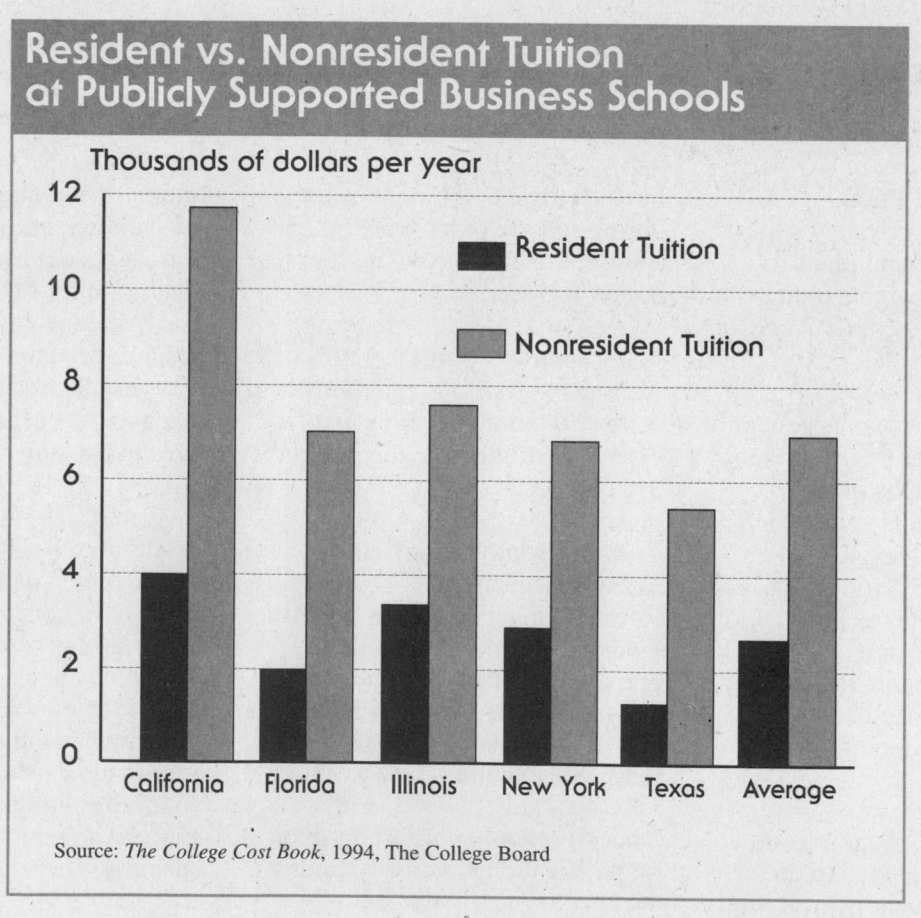

Resident vs. Nonresident Tuition at Publicly Supported Business Schools

Thousands of dollars per year

Source: *The College Cost Book*, 1994, The College Board

7

The Cost of Attendance

The cost of attendance is the amount of money needed to pay for one year of school at a modest, but adequate, standard of living. It is also referred to as the student expense budget. This total cost of attending a graduate school of management includes direct costs such as tuition, fees, and books, as well as living expenses and other indirect costs.

Student Expense Budgets

Student expense budgets are fixed amounts developed by each school. They are based upon average, reasonable costs, and reflect the amount of money needed by the average student. Student budgets generally do not accommodate individual needs and preferences. They may not include as much as you are used to or as much as you would like, especially if you have been out of undergraduate school and working for several years.

In nearly all cases, however, if an individual arrives at an M.B.A. school relatively free of obligations (with the exception of prior educational loans), the standard student budget will provide the resources necessary to make it through school. If you have special

expenses, such as unusual medical bills, you should speak with the financial aid administrator.

Direct Costs

Tuition and Fees:

Fixed tuition and fees are charged to students carrying the same academic work load.

Required Fees:

The required fees include only student fees required of *all* students in a given category. Fees for rental or purchase of equipment, materials, or supplies must be required of all students in the same course of study in order to be included in the student's budget.

Books and Supplies:

The amount required for books and supplies is determined by each graduate school of management. The figure is generally based on an average cost that takes into account the textbooks and supplies required of all students in the same program. The cost of a computer or word processor can only be included if the school requires *all* students in the program to purchase one.

Indirect Costs

Room and Board:

The allowance for room and board costs, whether you are living in school housing, with your parents, or in your own apartment or house, is generally based on an average, reasonable budget. Most schools conduct surveys to determine the actual living costs in the area.

Under the regulations governing federal financial aid programs, only the student's expenses are included in the expense budget. Your spouse's and/or dependent children's living expenses are accounted for in the calculation of your family contribution. Refer to the income protection allowance in Chapter 8, "Determining Your Financial Need."

Transportation:

The cost of travel between your residence and the school and any travel costs that are required for completing a course of study are included. The cost of purchasing a car is *not* included.

Personal Expenses:

The average cost of such items as clothing, laundry, grooming aids, insurance, and recreation is included.

Child Care:

This allowance, as determined by the school, is intended to cover reasonable expenses incurred for child care so that you can attend school. The amount is based on the number and ages of your children.

Summer Costs:

Standard budgets take into account the actual period of enrollment, which for full-time M.B.A. programs is generally only the nine-month academic year. However, a school may include costs associated with summer enrollment using a 12-month budget. This includes both the direct and indirect expenses listed above.

Disabled Student Expenses:

This allowance, as determined by the school, is for expenses relating to a disability. These include any required special services, transportation, equipment, and supplies.

Loan Origination and Insurance Fees:

These fees are charged by lenders for borrowing money. The origination fee represents prepaid interest and is sent to the federal government to help offset the cost of subsidizing the loan. The insurance fee is the guaranty agency's insurance premium, which helps cover the costs of administering the loan. Lenders deduct both fees from the proceeds of the loan. As a result, the amount you owe, and are required to repay, will be larger than the amount of the checks you actually receive. Many schools add these fees to the student budgets, or provide enough money in the financial aid package to cover the additional costs.

Miscellaneous:

If there are extenuating circumstances, the financial aid office may take into account other expenses or increase individual elements used in the standard budgets. These additional expenses must be well documented, and decisions can only be made on a case-by-case basis.

TABLE 7.1		Factors Used to Determine Cost of Attendance
	ELEMENT	**DESCRIPTION**
Direct costs	Tuition	Fixed tuition charged by the school
	Fees	Student fees required of *all* graduate business students carrying the same number of credits
	Books and supplies	The average cost as determined by each school
Indirect costs	Living expenses	Room and board
	Transportation	Commuting costs and any other required travel costs
	Personal expenses	Clothing, laundry, grooming aids, insurance, recreation, etc.
	Child care	Expenses for child care, i.e., day care
	Summertime costs	All costs associated with summertime enrollment
	Disabled student expenses	Any additional expenses resulting from a disability
	Loan fees	Fees charged by lenders in order to borrow funds
	Miscellaneous	Other expenses related to extenuating circumstances

SAMPLE STUDENT BUDGET

NINE MONTHS; SINGLE, NO DEPENDENTS

Fixed Expenses	Academic Year	Monthly
Rent or mortgage payment	$ 3,600	$ 400
Utilities (gas, electric, phone)	900	100
Insurance (homeowners/renters, fire, health, but not auto)	270	30
Child care/child support	n/a	
TOTAL FIXED EXPENSES	$ 4,770	$ 530

Flexible Expenses	Academic Year	Monthly
Food and household goods	$ 1,575	$ 175
Books and supplies	630	70
Personal (including laundry, cleaning, toiletries, and entertainment)	1,800	200
Transportation (car expenses including gas/oil, repairs, parking, license, insurance, etc.; or fare for public transportation)	900	100
Medical and dental expenses (as needed)	0	0
TOTAL FLEXIBLE EXPENSES	$ 4,905	$ 545

	Academic Year	Monthly
TOTAL EXPENSES (FIXED + FLEXIBLE)	$ 9,675	$ 1,075
+ Tuition and Fees	$ 10,000	
= TOTAL COST OF ATTENDANCE	$ 19,675	

Note: Some expenses must be paid quarterly or semiannually and should be considered in terms of cash flow.

YOUR STUDENT BUDGET

NINE MONTHS

	Academic Year	Monthly
Fixed Expenses		
Rent or mortgage payment	$_____	$_____
Utilities (gas, electric, phone)	_____	_____
Insurance (homeowners/renters, fire, health, but not auto)	_____	_____
Child care/child support	_____	_____
TOTAL FIXED EXPENSES	$_____	$_____
Flexible Expenses		
Food and household goods	$_____	$_____
Books and supplies	_____	_____
Personal (including laundry, cleaning, toiletries, and entertainment)	_____	_____
Transportation (car expenses including gas/oil, repairs, parking, license, insurance, etc.; or fare for public transportation)	_____	_____
Medical and dental expenses	_____	_____
TOTAL FLEXIBLE EXPENSES	$_____	$_____
TOTAL EXPENSES (FIXED + FLEXIBLE)	$_____	$_____
+ Tuition and Fees	_____	
= TOTAL COST OF ATTENDANCE	$_____	

8

Determining Your Financial Need

A specific definition of need is used to determine eligibility for financial assistance:

> **Definition of Need**
>
> Cost of Attendance
> − Family Contribution
> _____
> = Student's Financial Need

To determine educational financial need, schools must know your calculated family contribution (FC). Once this figure is established, it is subtracted from the student expense budget for the period of attendance. The result is the student's financial need as determined for that school.

Family Contribution

The family contribution is derived from a formula developed by the federal government that measures a family's ability to pay for the education of its members. This is true whether the family consists of just you or you, your spouse, and/or your dependents.

The family contribution is derived objectively from financial data supplied by you and your family and uses standards applied uniformly to all families. These standards are applied under what is known as the Federal Methodology (FM) of need analysis, the formula used to determine eligibility for most federal financial aid programs, which has been written into law by the Congress of the United States. For non-federal aid programs, including school-based and state aid programs, other need analysis formulas may be used at the discretion of the state or school. These formulas also use objective standards applied uniformly to all families.

How Your Family Contribution Is Determined to Establish Eligibility for Federal Funds

Elements Used:

- Total income from the previous calendar year (also called *base year*—see below)

- Current assets

- Taxes and other financial obligations

- Asset protection for retirement

- Number of family members

- Number of family members attending school

- Costs associated with employment

- An income protection allowance for basic living expenses (see definition below)

Base Year Income:

To determine the family contribution under the Federal Methodology, the income for the calendar year preceding the year of enrollment is used. For a student enrolling in the 1995-96 academic year, the 1994 calendar year income is used.

Income Protection Allowance:

The Income Protection Allowance is an allowance for basic living expenses not included in the standard student budget. The amount of this allowance varies by family size and number enrolled at least half time in postsecondary education. In the 1994-95 calculation tables, a single student has an allowance of $3,000; a married student, with no dependents other than a spouse and whose spouse is not a student, has an allowance of $6,000. For students with dependent children, the amount varies based on family size. A married student with one dependent child whose spouse is not in school will have an income protection allowance of $13,490.

Employment Allowance:

For married students and single parents, the need analysis formula includes an employment allowance. For married students, the allowance is 35 percent of the lower of the two incomes, up to $2,500. For single parents, the allowance is 35 percent of the student's income, up to $2,500.

Asset Protection Allowance:

The need analysis formula includes an asset protection allowance, based on your age and marital status (see Table 8.5). If you are age 26 or older, this allowance is subtracted from your assets, and a portion of the remaining assets is used in the calculation.

Formula Variations and Professional Judgment:

Schools are permitted to revise individual figures used in the Federal Methodology based on information supplied by the student. These revisions must be made on a case-by-case basis and must be based on extenuating circumstances such as the loss of a job or a change in the family size.

Use of the Federal Methodology
Following are three examples of need analyses using the Federal Methodology formula for the 1994-95 academic year. The first involves a student who is single with no dependents and is just out of college, the second involves a single student with no dependents who has been in the work force for several years, and the third is a student who is married and has dependents. You can use these analyses/worksheets to help estimate your FC for 1994-95. They can also serve as a guide for estimating your FC in future years. The references to line items on the U.S. income tax forms 1040, 1040A, and 1040EZ are current as of the 1993 tax year. The line references may change in subsequent years.

Note: Elements used in the calculations vary according to the family's status, so not all elements appear in all calculations.

To understand how a school determines the amount of funds you will be expected to contribute, it is important to look at a number of factors: the student budget, your family size, how many people in your family will be enrolled in school, and your income and assets. Student budgets are always based on a single student's costs, regardless of marital status or family size. The size of your family and the number of people in your family enrolled in school will determine the amount of your income protection allowance; your age and your marital status will determine your asset protection allowance (see Tables 8.3 and 8.5).

The calculations in the following examples show the amount the federal government will expect you to contribute towards your education. These calculations must be used if the school offers you federal aid. All of the examples use base year income; some schools may use different income figures, especially if you and/or your spouse do not expect to work during the academic year. Schools may use yet another set of calculations to determine your contribution for school-funded fellowships and loans. You may want to check with your school(s) to see if they use different calculations for different kinds of aid.

As you complete the calculations on the following pages, we suggest that you compare the amount of funds you will be expected to contribute using the federal methodology with the money that you actually will have available to you. Under the federal methodology, you are expected to contribute only a portion of your income and assets for your education. Assuming that you have resources, you can use the remaining "untapped" portion of your income and/or assets to supplement your living expense budget or to reduce your borrowing.

In Example 1, the student has an income of $8,800; taxes and the income protection allowance of $3,000 are subtracted leaving $4,303 in available income. The contribution from income is calculated at 50 percent, leaving $2,151 in untapped income. The student has $8,000 in assets; there is no asset protection allowance because the student is under age 25. The contribution from assets is calculated at 35 percent, leaving $5,200 in untapped assets. The calculated contribution is $4,952.

In Example 2, the student's income is $24,200, the income protection allowance is $3,000, and the untapped income is $7,717. This student's assets are $2,000, which is less than the asset protection allowance of $6,200 for a 29 year old, so all of the assets are protected and there is no contribution from assets. The calculated contribution is $7,718.

In Example 3, the family has income of $46,600, the income protection allowance for a family of four with one member in college is $16,670, and the employment allowance is $2,500. The family's assets of $1,000 are less than the asset protection allowance of $6,400, so all of the assets are protected, and there is no income supplement from assets. The total contribution is calculated using a sliding scale of percentages based on the level of adjusted available income. Untapped income in this case is $12,348. The calculated contribution is $4,075.

It is important to remember that untapped funds from income and assets will be available only as long as you have these resources. You should also note that students in multi-year programs may be expected to bring untapped assets with them into succeeding years of study. Your eligibility for financial aid in future years may be based in part on your initial level of assets, even if you have already depleted those funds.

If you plan to use untapped resources to reduce your loans or to increase your standard of living beyond the typical student budget, we recommend that you talk to your school financial aid administrator to determine if your strategy will jeopardize your ability to finance your education in future years.

CALCULATING FAMILY CONTRIBUTION TO DETERMINE
ELIGIBILITY FOR FEDERAL AID—EXAMPLE 1

This worksheet may be used for a student, single or married, with no dependents other than spouse.

Description: Twenty-four years old, single, no dependents, just graduated from college, lives in California, works part time during the school year and full time during the summer, filed an IRS 1040. No financial aid or parental contribution received in the preceding year.

Conclusion: A family contribution of $4,952 has been calculated.

		Example	You
1.	Total base year wages, salaries, and tips (1040 item 7, 1040A item 7, 1040EZ item 2)	$ 8,400	$_____
2.	Taxable interest income (1040 item 8a, 1040A item 8a, 1040EZ item 3)	400	_____
3.	Dividend income (1040 item 9, 1040A item 9)	0	_____
4.	Other taxable income (e.g., refunds, alimony, capital gain, business/farm income, unemployment, etc.) (1040 items 10-22, 1040A items 10-13)	0	_____
5.	Total taxable income (add lines 1-4)	8,800	_____
6.	Adjustments to taxable income (IRA, KEOGH, interest penalties, alimony paid) (1040 item 30, 1040A item 15C)	0	_____
7.	Adjusted gross income (AGI) (line 5 minus line 6)	8,800	_____
8.	Child support paid	0	_____
9.	Financial aid income reported on tax return	0	_____
10.	Total UNTAXED income and benefits (welfare, child support received, social security, taxed deferred pension/savings plan, etc.; **do not include VA benefits**)	0	_____
11.	**TOTAL INCOME** (line 7 minus line 8, minus line 9, plus line 10)	$ 8,800	$_____
12.	U.S. income tax liability (NOT the amount withheld) (1040 item 53, 1040A item 27, 1040EZ item 8)	414	_____
13.	State and other taxes (see Table 8.1)	440	_____
14.	Social Security (FICA) (see Table 8.2)	643	_____
15.	Income Protection Allowance (see Table 8.3)	3,000	_____
16.	**TOTAL ALLOWANCES** (add lines 12-15)	$ 4,497	$_____
17.	Available income (line 11 minus line 16)	4,303	_____
18.	**TOTAL CONTRIBUTION FROM AVAILABLE INCOME** (50% of line 17; may be negative)	$ 2,152	$_____
19.	Cash, savings, checking accounts	8,000	_____
20.	Real estate (other than primary residence) and investments; current value minus amount owed	0	_____
21.	Business and farm (other than family farm on which family resides; see Table 8.4)	0	_____
22.	**TOTAL NET ASSETS** (add lines 19-21)	$ 8,000	$_____
23.	Asset protection allowance (from Table 8.5)	0	_____
24.	Discretionary net worth (line 22 minus line 23)	8,000	_____
25.	**CONTRIBUTION FROM ASSETS** (line 24 times 35% or zero, whichever is greater)	$ 2,800	$_____
26.	**CALCULATED FAMILY CONTRIBUTION** (add lines 18 and 25; if negative, enter zero)	$ 4,952	$_____

CALCULATING FAMILY CONTRIBUTION TO DETERMINE ELIGIBILITY FOR FEDERAL AID—EXAMPLE 2

This worksheet may be used for a student, single or married, with no dependents other than spouse.

Description: Twenty-nine years old, single, no dependents, lives in Massachusetts, leaving full-time employment to attend school full time, filed an IRS 1040. No financial aid or parental contribution received in the preceding year.

Conclusion: A family contribution of $7,718 has been calculated.

	Example	You
1. Total base year wages, salaries, and tips (1040 item 7, 1040A item 7, 1040EZ item 2)	$ 24,000	$_____
2. Taxable interest income (1040 item 8a, 1040A item 8a, 1040EZ item 3)	200	_____
3. Dividend income (1040 item 9, 1040A item 9)	0	_____
4. Other taxable income (e.g., refunds, alimony, capital gain, business/farm income, unemployment, etc.) (1040 items 10-22, 1040A items 10-13)	0	_____
5. Total taxable income (add lines 1-4)	24,200	_____
6. Adjustments to taxable income (IRA, KEOGH, interest penalties, alimony paid) (1040 item 30, 1040A item 15C)	0	_____
7. Adjusted gross income (AGI) (line 5 minus line 6)	24,200	_____
8. Child support paid	0	_____
9. Financial aid income reported on tax return	0	_____
10. Total UNTAXED income and benefits (welfare, child support received, social security, taxed deferred pension/savings plan, etc.; **do not include VA benefits**)	0	_____
11. **TOTAL INCOME** (line 7 minus line 8, minus line 9, plus line 10)	$ 24,200	$_____
12. U.S. income tax liability (NOT the amount withheld) (1040 item 53, 1040A item 27, 1040EZ item 8)	2,719	_____
13. State and other taxes (see Table 8.1)	1,210	_____
14. Social Security (FICA) (see Table 8.2)	1,836	_____
15. Income Protection Allowance (see Table 8.3)	3,000	_____
16. **TOTAL ALLOWANCES** (add lines 12-15)	$ 8,765	$_____
17. Available income (line 11 minus line 16)	15,435	_____
18. **TOTAL CONTRIBUTION FROM AVAILABLE INCOME** (50% of line 17; may be negative)	$ 7,718	$_____
19. Cash, savings, checking accounts	2,000	_____
20. Real estate (other than primary residence) and investments; current value minus amount owed	0	_____
21. Business and farm (other than family farm on which family resides; see Table 8.4)	0	_____
22. **TOTAL NET ASSETS** (add lines 19-21)	$ 2,000	$_____
23. Asset protection allowance (from Table 8.5)	6,200	_____
24. Discretionary net worth (line 22 minus line 23)	−4,200	_____
25. **CONTRIBUTION FROM ASSETS** (line 24 times 35% or zero, whichever is greater)	$ 0	$_____
26. **CALCULATED FAMILY CONTRIBUTION** (add lines 18 and 25; if negative, enter zero)	$ 7,718	$_____

CALCULATING FAMILY CONTRIBUTION TO DETERMINE
ELIGIBILITY FOR FEDERAL AID—EXAMPLE 3

This worksheet may be used for a student with dependents other than spouse.

Description: Married, 2 children, 28 years old, resident of Kansas. Worked full-time for eight months, part-time for four months while attending school full time. Spouse works full time. They own their home, worth $80,000 with an outstanding mortgage of $70,000, filed an IRS 1040A.

Conclusion: A family contribution of $4,075 has been calculated.

	Example	You
1. Student's base year wages, salaries, and tips (1040 item 7, 1040A item 7)	$ 22,500	$_____
2. Spouse's wages, salaries, and tips (1040 item 7, 1040A item 7)	24,000	_____
3. Taxable interest income (1040 item 8a, 1040A item 8a)	100	_____
4. Dividend income (1040 item 9, 1040A item 9)	0	_____
5. Other taxable income (e.g., refunds, alimony, capital gain, business/farm income, unemployment, etc.) (1040 items 10-22, 1040A items 10-13)	0	_____
6. Total taxable income (add lines 1-5)	46,600	_____
7. Adjustments to taxable income (IRA, KEOGH, interest penalties, alimony paid) (1040 item 30, 1040A item 15c)	0	_____
8. Adjusted gross income (AGI) (line 6 minus line 7)	46,600	_____
9. Child support paid	0	_____
10. Financial aid income reported on tax return	0	_____
11. Total UNTAXED income and benefits (welfare, child support received, social security, tax deferred pension/savings plan, etc.; **do not include VA benefits**)	0	_____
12. **TOTAL INCOME** (line 8, minus line 9, minus line 10, plus line 11)	$ 46,600	$_____
13. U.S. income tax liability (NOT the amount withheld) (1040 item 53, 1040A item 27)	4,654	_____
14. State and other taxes (Table 8.1)	2,796	_____
15. Social Security (FICA) (see Table 8.2)	3,557	_____
16. Employment allowance (see Table 8.2)	2,500	_____
17. Income Protection Allowance (see Table 8.3)	16,670	_____
18. **TOTAL ALLOWANCES** (add lines 13-17)	$ 30,177	$_____
19. **AVAILABLE INCOME** (line 12 minus line 18)	$ 16,423	$_____
20. Cash, savings, checking accounts	1,000	_____
21. Real estate (other than primary residence) and investments; current value minus amount owed	0	_____
22. Business and farm (other than family farm on which family resides; see Table 8.4)	0	_____
23. **TOTAL NET ASSETS** (add lines 20-22)	$ 1,000	$_____
24. Asset protection allowance (from Table 8.5)	6,400	_____
25. Discretionary net worth (may be negative) (line 23 minus line 24)	− 5,400	_____
26. Income supplement from assets (line 25 times 12%; if line 25 is negative, enter zero)	0	_____
27. Adjusted available income (line 19 plus line 26)	16,423	_____
28. **TOTAL CONTRIBUTION** (line 27 times the percentage from Table 8.6; if line 27 is negative, enter zero)	$ 4,075	$_____

For future years, these tables will change.

TABLE 8.1 — Allowances for State and Other Taxes

	Students with Dependents Other than Spouse Total Income		Students with No Dependents Other than Spouse Total Income		Students with Dependents Other than Spouse Total Income		Students with No Dependents Other than Spouse Total Income
	Less than $15,000	$15,000 or more	Any Amount		Less than $15,000	$15,000 or more	Any Amount
Alabama	5%	4%	3%	Missouri	6%	5%	3%
Alaska	3	2	0	Montana	8	7	5
American Samoa	4	3	2	Nebraska	8	7	4
Arizona	6	5	3	Nevada	3	2	0
Arkansas	6	5	4	New Hampshire	7	6	1
California	8	7	5	New Jersey	8	7	3
Canada	4	3	2	New Mexico	6	5	4
Colorado	7	6	4	New York	11	10	7
Connecticut	6	5	2	North Carolina	8	7	5
Delaware	8	7	5	North Dakota	6	5	2
District of Columbia	10	9	7	Northern Marianas	4	3	2
Federated States of Micronesia	4	3	2	Ohio	8	7	5
Florida	4	3	1	Oklahoma	6	5	4
Georgia	7	6	4	Oregon	10	9	6
Guam	4	3	2	Palau	4	3	2
Hawaii	8	7	6	Pennsylvania	7	6	3
Idaho	7	6	5	Puerto Rico	4	3	2
Illinois	6	5	2	Rhode Island	9	8	4
Indiana	6	5	4	South Carolina	8	7	5
Iowa	8	7	5	South Dakota	4	3	0
Kansas	7	6	4	Tennessee	3	2	0
Kentucky	7	6	5	Texas	3	2	0
Louisiana	4	3	2	Utah	8	7	3
Maine	9	8	5	Vermont	8	7	4
Marshall Islands	4	3	2	Virgin Islands	4	3	2
Maryland	9	8	6	Virginia	8	7	4
Massachusetts	9	8	5	Washington	4	3	0
Mexico	4	3	2	West Virginia	6	5	4
Michigan	9	8	4	Wisconsin	10	9	5
Minnesota	9	8	6	Wyoming	3	2	0
Mississippi	5	4	3	Not reported /other	4	3	2

TABLE 8.2   Allowances against Income

ALLOWANCE FOR SOCIAL SECURITY TAXES	
FICA Wages: $1-$57,600	7.65% of income by each wage earner (maximum $4,406.40 per wage earner)
FICA Wages: $57,601 or more	$4,406.40 + 1.45% of income earned above $57,600, up to $135,000 by each wage earner (maximum of $5,529 per wage earner)
EMPLOYMENT ALLOWANCE	
Married	Lesser of $2,500 or 35% of the earned income of the student or spouse with the lesser earned income
Single parent (surviving spouse or head of household)	Lesser of $2,500 or 35% of student's earned income
Single (no dependents)	Zero

TABLE 8.3   Income Protection Allowance

Students with Dependents Other than Spouse

FAMILY SIZE (INCLUDING STUDENT)	NUMBER IN COLLEGE				
	1	2	3	4	5
2	$10,840	$ 8,980			
3	13,490	11,650	$ 9,800		
4	16,670	14,810	12,970	$11,110	
5	19,660	17,810	15,970	14,110	$12,270
6	23,000	21,150	19,300	17,450	15,600

For each additional family member, add $2,600.
For each additional college student, subtract $1,840.

Students with No Dependents Other than Spouse

Single	$3,000
Married; spouse is also student	$3,000
Married; spouse is not student	$6,000

TABLE 8.4	Table for Business or Farm Adjustments
IF THE NET WORTH (NW) OF A BUSINESS OR FARM IS:	**THE ADJUSTED NET WORTH IS:**
less than $1	$0
$1 to $75,000	40% of NW
$75,001 to $230,000	$30,000 + 50% of NW over $75,000
$230,001 to $385,000	$107,500 + 60% of NW over $230,000
$385,001 or more	$200,500 + 100% of NW over $385,000

TABLE 8.5 Asset Protection Allowance

IF YOUR AGE IS:	THEN YOUR ASSET PROTECTION ALLOWANCE IS:	
	Single	**Married**
25 or under	$ 0	$ 0
26	1,500	2,100
27	3,100	4,300
28	4,600	6,400
29	6,200	8,600
30	7,700	10,700
31	9,200	12,900
32	10,800	15,000
33	12,300	17,200
34	13,900	19,300
35	15,400	21,500
36	16,900	23,600
37	18,500	25,800
38	20,000	27,900
39	21,600	30,100
40	23,100	32,200
41	23,500	33,000
42	24,100	33,900
43	24,500	34,700
44	25,100	35,400
45	25,600	36,300
46	26,200	37,200
47	26,900	38,500
48	27,500	39,400
49	28,000	40,500
50	28,700	41,500
51	29,400	42,800
52	30,300	43,900
53	31,000	45,300
54	31,800	46,700
55	32,500	47,900
56	33,500	49,400
57	34,300	50,900
58	35,300	52,500
59	36,300	54,400
60	37,200	56,000
61	38,200	58,100
62	39,300	59,800
63	40,400	61,900
64	41,800	64,100
65 or over	42,900	66,300

TABLE 8.6	Assessment from Adjusted Available Income (AAI) (students with dependents other than spouse)
IF ADJUSTED AVAILABLE INCOME (AAI) IS:	**THEN THE ASSESSMENT IS:**
Less than − $3,409	− $750
− $ 3,409 to + 9,700	22% of AAI
$ 9,701 to 12,200	$2,134 + 25% of AAI over $ 9,700
$12,201 to 14,600	$2,759 + 29% of AAI over $12,200
$14,601 to 17,100	$3,455 + 34% of AAI over $14,600
$17,101 to 19,600	$4,305 + 40% of AAI over $17,100
$19,601 or more	$5,305 + 47% of AAI over $19,600

9

Financial Aid Packaging

Awarding aid to individual students involves three steps.

Step 1: The student applies for financial assistance.

Step 2: Financial need is established by the graduate school(s) of management:

School Cost of Attendance

− Calculated Family Contribution

= Student's Financial Need

Step 3: The financial aid office prepares an award package. Packaging is a complex process, based on many variables. Most schools rely on a combination of financial aid programs to meet your need. Although some grant funds are available, most schools expect you to use loans, earnings, and outside monies to help finance the cost of your education.

On the average, graduates from private graduate schools of management leave school owing $25,000 to $35,000, including loans to finance prior education. More and more students graduate with debts in excess of $50,000.

Graduates from publicly supported graduate schools of management leave school owing considerably less, particularly if their prior educational debt was low. The average graduate from a publicly supported business school owes $15,000 to $20,000 including previous educational loans.

Packaging Strategies

Graduate schools of management have different strategies regarding aid packaging, which they use to achieve the following goals:

• to minimize the use of loans for the neediest students

• to recruit the most attractive students

• to maximize limited grant monies

• to budget school resources

You should understand packaging strategies in order to understand your award, to compare different packages, and to understand the real cost of completing an M.B.A. program. Following are three examples of strategies graduate schools of management use to

package students' financial aid awards:

1. Grants and scholarships (gift aid) are awarded to recruit attractive candidates. The size of the award may be based on:

   • academic excellence (grades, scores on tests, rank in class, or specific talent);

   • institutional enrollment goals (ethnicity, national origin, and state of residency); or

   • a combination of need and merit.

2. Grant aid up to a set maximum is awarded to students before other forms of financial assistance. Remaining financial need is met through self-help programs (i.e., loans and work).

3. The self-help programs are awarded first, up to a set maximum. Remaining need is met through grant aid. With this approach, the neediest students do not graduate with proportionally greater debt.

Use of Outside Aid

Scholarships or grants students receive from outside sources are treated differently by different graduate schools of management. For students receiving any need-based aid, including federal funds, the total amount you receive from *all* sources cannot exceed the cost of attendance. Some schools use outside aid to replace the self-help portion of your package. Other schools lower their own grant aid or loans, or a combination of the two, when students receive outside scholarships. You must inform the school of any outside aid you receive.

Use of Parental Contribution

Some graduate schools of management calculate a parental contribution for all students, even though graduate students are classified independent by Federal Methodology. These schools consider a parental contribution in awarding institutional grants or loans. You may be permitted to borrow funds to meet this parental expectation.

Use of Assets

Many prospective students have assets that are not included when eligibility for federal funds is being determined. However, schools may consider assets such as home equity and retirement funds when evaluating your financial strength and eligibility for institutional aid.

Replacing Loan Origination and Insurance Fees

Since schools recognize that there are fees associated with borrowing from federal programs, they will often increase the amount of loan eligibility to the extent possible (up to maximum loan amount) to provide you with the full amount required for direct and indirect educational costs.

The total amount of the loan cannot exceed the loan maximum or the individual student's amount of eligibility. Borrowers are responsible for repaying the entire amount, even the portion subtracted for origination and insurance fees.

For example, if a student demonstrated eligibility and applied for a $5,000 loan, the student could receive as little as $4,600 after origination and insurance fees are deducted. In order to meet the student's full eligibility, the school might increase the loan amount so that the total loan disbursements would be the full $5,000.

Student Options

Although the bulk of most M.B.A. students' packages will be loans, it is possible for you to request that a Federal College Work-Study award be given in lieu of a portion of the loan or that you be permitted to work for the amount of loan awarded. Be aware, however, that not all schools have Federal College Work-Study funds. Check with the financial aid office.

On some institutional or supplemental financial aid applications, you are given the option of stating a preference for either loans, work, or both. This preference is given as much consideration as possible. If no choice appears on the application and you have a preference for work versus a loan, write or call the financial aid office directly.

Important: You should take into consideration the recommendations from the institution about working while in graduate school. Many schools discourage full-time, first-year students from working at all during the school year because of the heavy course load, the rigors of the curriculum, and the benefits of full participation in academic and other group activities.

School Packaging Policies

You should contact the financial aid office if you have concerns about your package. Administrators in that office should be able to explain the school's packaging policy and provide you with further details about any appeals process.

Appeals

If you feel your award or calculated contribution is not appropriate for your circumstances, you may appeal the decision on the amount of the contribution, the amount of your financial aid award, or the denial of eligibility for aid. However, you must base this appeal on legitimate reasons that can be documented. At some schools, the appeal process can be quite complicated, involving a committee made up of faculty, students, and administrators to whom you must make formal, written requests. At others, the appeal process is simpler. And at some schools, no appeal is possible.

Requests to alter your student expense budget or to change any of the elements used in the need analysis formula may be granted if the expense is not discretionary and can be documented, if the need analysis formula does not take into account relevant facts, or if there has been a significant and substantial change in your financial picture.

Requests to change Federal Perkins and/or Federal Stafford Loans to Federal College Work-Study

Tips for Comparing Financial Aid Packages

1. Do not assume that the package offering the highest amount of grant aid is the most attractive financial aid award. Rather, add up the total self-help aid offered. You may find, to your surprise, that you would graduate from a high-cost business school with less debt than a low-cost school. Or, the reverse could be true.

2. Compare the calculated expected family contribution. A school offering more grant aid while expecting a greater family contribution could prove to be less attractive financially. If you need to borrow funds in order to provide a high expected family contribution you could graduate with more debt.

3. Look at the expected family contribution to see whether a parent contribution is expected. Also, compare the amounts of the expected student contribution. Some schools require a minimum amount, regardless of the calculated contribution. You may need to borrow additional funds to provide either of these amounts.

4. How realistic is the budget used to determine your package? If it is low and you are permitted to increase your budget because your expenses are higher, chances are you will have to borrow or earn more to meet that additional need.

5. If a school is located some distance from you, your travel costs could be high. A budget revision for this additional expense would probably entail borrowing or earning more and may require an appeal.

6. Compare the different loans within the financial aid package. Borrowing a smaller amount from a loan program with less attractive terms could end up costing more than a larger loan from a more attractive program.

7. Similarly, borrowing smaller amounts from multiple loan programs may end up costing more in the long run than borrowing a larger amount from one program. Although in certain instances a borrower can combine payments by consolidating loans, the terms for a consolidated loan may end up being less attractive. Refer to Chapter 12, "Debt Management and Loan Repayment," for more information on loan consolidation.

8. Find out if packages for second-year students remain consistent with first-year packages. Some schools award more grant aid to first-year students, while other schools increase the grant aid in the second year.

9. Remember that the short-term financial cost of an M.B.A. is but one criterion to consider in choosing a school. If a given school meets all of your educational needs and you are convinced it can launch you on an exciting career, a significant upfront investment may, over the long term, turn out to be a bargain.

awards are often approved if funds are available. Although schools typically discourage additional borrowing, it may be possible to borrow funds from private loan programs to replace an expected contribution. For the most part, requests for additional grant aid are rarely approved unless they are based on a change in the information originally reported. Schools give serious consideration to packaging policies and guidelines, and altering policies or making exceptions without clear justification is not done capriciously.

Comparing Financial Aid Packages

If you apply for aid at a number of graduate management schools, you may receive award letters with significantly different packages. Comparing these awards is difficult unless the schools are identical in every other way (e.g., program content, size, and location), which is unlikely.

Ideally, decisions as significant as which M.B.A. program to attend should not be based solely on short-term costs, but on a variety of criteria. Some students may place the greatest emphasis on academic and professional criteria, while others may place heavy emphasis on the financial aid award. When comparing packages, try to equate as best you can the true financial impact of your different options.

Sample Packages

Following are sample financial aid packages awarded to three different first-year M.B.A. students. The construction of the awards has been based on a business school packaging survey, and each is a combination of several real schools' policies and costs. Six samples are provided for each student—three for private, high-cost graduate schools of management and three for lower-cost, publicly supported schools. A brief analysis of the awards is also provided.

Remember that these packages are samples and do not indicate what your financial aid award will actually be. They are provided strictly for informational purposes and for guidance in financing your M.B.A.

SAMPLE GRADUATE MANAGEMENT SCHOOL FINANCIAL AID PACKAGES — STUDENT 1

Full-time student, single or married with no dependents

Description: Twenty-four years old, single with no dependents, just graduated from college, lives in California, will work part time during the school year and full time during the summer

PRIVATE GRADUATE SCHOOLS OF MANAGEMENT

	School 1	School 2	School 3
Tuition and Fees	$12,800	$19,300	$16,700
Living Expenses	9,670	11,600	8,500
Total Cost	$22,470	$30,900	$25,200
Family Contribution	$ 4,952	$ 4,952	$ 4,952
Need	$17,518	$25,948	$20,248
Sample Package			
Institutional Scholarship	$ 2,000	$ 7,448	$ 5,000
State Grant	0	0	0
Federal Perkins Loan	1,500	0	0
Federal Subsidized Stafford Loan	8,500	8,500	8,500
Federal Unsubsidized Stafford Loan	5,518	10,000	5,000
Federal College Work-Study	0	0	1,748
Total Package	$17,518	$25,948	$20,248

ANALYSIS OF SAMPLE FINANCIAL AID PACKAGES—STUDENT 1

School 1:

This school uses the base year income to determine the student's contribution. A small institutional scholarship is offered along with a combination of three federal loan programs. Although the tuition and fee cost of this institution is relatively low for a private institution, the borrowing is relatively high. In this package, the student will have loans totalling $15,518.

School 2:

This school also uses the base year income to determine the student's contribution. The packaging policy of this school determines that the student be offered the maximum Federal Subsidized Stafford Loan and the maximum Federal Unsubsidized Stafford Loan before any scholarship assistance is awarded. The student is offered the highest scholarship in this package, but the student will have to borrow the maximum amount available from the federal loan programs—$18,500—to meet the financial need.

School 5:

This school also uses the base year income to determine the student's contribution, but the slightly higher cost of education and the lack of a scholarship make this a less attractive package. The student is being required to borrow under both the Federal Subsidized Stafford Loan and the Federal Unsubsidized Stafford Loan programs. Total borrowing would be $9,998.

	School 4	School 5	School 6
Tuition and Fees	$ 1,850	$ 3,350	$ 7,100
Living Expenses	9,670	11,600	8,500
Total Cost	$11,520	$14,950	$15,600
Family Contribution	$ 4,952	$ 4,592	$ 4,952
Need	$ 6,568	$ 9,998	$10,648
Sample Package			
Institutional Scholarship	$ 0	$ 0	$ 1,148
State Grant	0	0	1,000
Federal Perkins Loan	1,000	0	0
Federal Subsidized Stafford Loan	4,068	8,500	8,500
Federal Unsubsidized Stafford Loan	0	1,498	0
Federal College Work-Study	1,500	0	0
Total Package	$ 6,568	$ 9,998	$10,648

School 6:

Although this school is publicly supported, the tuition and fees are comparable to some private schools. The student is only required to borrow $8,500 under the Federal Subsidized Stafford Loan program. With the scholarship and the state grant offered, this is an attractive package.

School 3:

This school also uses the base year to calculate the student's contribution. This example demonstrates a school with relatively low living expenses. The required borrowing by the school is $13,500, which is less than the required borrowing at School 1, even though the total budget at this school is higher. The school offers Federal College Work-Study, which can be used to pay living expenses but not tuition and fees. If the student chooses not to work and requests additional borrowing, the total loans would increase to $15,255, which is still less than the amount of borrowing required at School 1 and School 2.

School 4:

This publicly supported school has a low cost of education. They use the base year income to determine the student's contribution. Because of the low cost of this school, no institutional money is available. Instead, the school offers Federal Perkins Loans and Federal College Work-Study funds to its M.B.A. students. The student only has to borrow $4,068 in Federal Subsidized Stafford Loan to meet the financial need. If the student chose to decline the Federal College Work-Study, the total borrowing would be only $6,568. This is an attractive package.

SAMPLE GRADUATE MANAGEMENT SCHOOL FINANCIAL AID PACKAGES — STUDENT 2

Full-time student, single or married with no dependents

Description: Twenty-nine years old, single with no dependents, lives in Massachusetts, leaving full-time employment to attend school full time

PRIVATE GRADUATE SCHOOLS OF MANAGEMENT

	School 1	School 2	School 3
Tuition and Fees	$12,800	$19,300	$16,700
Living Expenses	9,670	11,600	8,500
Total Cost	$22,470	$30,900	$25,200
Family Contribution	$ 7,718	$ 7,718	$ 7,718
Need	$14,752	$23,182	$17,482
Sample Package			
Institutional Scholarship	$ 0	$ 9,350	$ 2,000
State Grant	0	0	1,200
Federal Perkins Loan	0	3,000	0
Federal Subsidized Stafford Loan	8,500	8,500	8,500
Federal Unsubsidized Stafford Loan	6,252	2,332	3,782
Federal College Work-Study	0	0	2,000
Total Package	$14,752	$23,182	$17,482

ANALYSIS OF SAMPLE FINANCIAL AID PACKAGES—STUDENT 2

School 1:

This school uses base year income to determine the student's contribution. No institutional scholarship is included since the school packages the maximum in federal loans before offering any institutional scholarship. With the contribution of $7,718, this student does not need anything other than federal loans. Although the tuition and fee costs of this school are relatively low for a private institution, the borrowing is relatively high. In this package, the student will have loans totalling $14,752.

School 2:

This school uses the base year income to determine the student's contribution. The packaging policy of this school determines that the student be offered a Federal Subsidized Stafford Loan before any scholarship assistance is awarded. The student is offered the highest scholarship in this package but will still have to borrow $13,832 to meet the financial need.

	School 4	School 5	School 6
Tuition and Fees	$ 1,850	$ 3,350	$ 7,100
Living Expenses	9,670	11,600	8,500
Total Cost	$11,520	$14,950	$15,600
Family Contribution	$ 7,718	$ 7,718	$ 7,718
Need	$ 3,802	$ 7,232	$ 7,882
Sample Package			
Institutional Scholarship	$ 0	$ 0	$ 2,000
State Grant	0	1,500	0
Federal Perkins Loan	0	0	0
Federal Subsidized Stafford Loan	3,802	5,732	5,882
Federal Unsubsidized Stafford Loan	0	0	0
Federal College Work-Study	0	0	0
Total Package	$ 3,802	$ 7,232	$ 7,882

School 3:

This school also uses the base year to calculate the student's contribution. The borrowing required is $12,282. In this example, the student has been offered assistance through several different programs. The grants through the institution and the state equal $3,200 along with some Federal College Work-Study money. These reduce the amount of borrowing and make this package more attractive than the one offered by School 1, even though the total costs of School 3 are higher. If the student chose to decline the work study, the borrowing would increase to $14,282.

School 4:

This publicly supported school has a low cost of education. They use the base year income to determine the student's contribution. Because of the low educational cost, no institutional scholarships are available. Students are eligible to borrow under the federal loan programs to meet their financial need. In this example, the student only needs to borrow $3,802 in Federal Subsidized Stafford Loan. This is an attractive package.

School 5:

This school also uses the base year income to determine the student's contribution, but the student has qualified for a state grant. This state grant offsets the higher tuition at this institution making those costs equivalent to School 4, but the higher cost of living will force the student to borrow more money than was required at School 4. Total borrowing would be $5,732.

School 6:

Although this school is publicly supported, the tuition and fees are comparable to some private schools. Although the tuition charges are higher at this school than at School 5, the lower cost of living keeps the borrowing about the same. The scholarship makes this an attractive package. The student should confirm that the scholarship will be renewed for the second year of the program.

Full-time student, married with dependents other than spouse

Description: Twenty-eight years old, married with two children, lives in Kansas, worked full time for eight months, part time for four months while attending school full time, spouse works full time, they own their own home worth $80,000 with an outstanding mortgage of $70,000.

PRIVATE GRADUATE SCHOOLS OF MANAGEMENT

	School 1	School 2	School 3
Tuition and Fees	$12,800	$19,300	$16,700
Living Expenses	9,670	11,600	8,500
Total Cost	$22,470	$30,900	$25,200
Family Contribution	$ 4,075	$ 4,075	$ 4,075
Need	$18,395	$26,825	$21,125
Sample Package			
Institutional Scholarship	$ 2,500	$ 8,325	$ 4,700
State Grant	0	0	1,000
Federal Perkins Loan	1,395	0	2,000
Federal Subsidized Stafford Loan	8,500	8,500	8,500
Federal Unsubsidized Stafford Loan	6,000	10,000	4,925
Federal College Work-Study	0	0	0
Total Package	$18,395	$26,825	$21,125

ANALYSIS OF SAMPLE FINANCIAL AID PACKAGES—STUDENT 3

School 1:

Although this school's tuition is the lowest of the private schools, the borrowing is relatively high. The school does not offer much institutional scholarship money, instead depending on the student's ability to borrow through the federal loan programs. With this package, the student will be borrowing $15,895.

School 2:

This school uses the base year contribution as the basis of the financial aid package. The packaging philosophy of this institution is to make the student borrow the maximum amount in the federal loan programs and then make up the remainder in institutional scholarship funds. Although this package includes the largest scholarship, it also requires the highest level of borrowing, $18,500. In the second year of the program, the family contribution should decrease because of the lower income of the student, and the institutional scholarship funding should increase. The student should verify the expectation for the second year.

Married Students versus Single Students

When offering their own aid from their own funds, schools may use a budget that reflects your marital status and family size. However, if the school is offering you a federal loan, it will be based on the single student budget regardless of your marital status. This government regulation often confuses married students. It is easy to assume that families are treated unfairly since it appears that families must live on the same budget as single students. This is not the case. When calculating your expected contribution, schools make an allowance against your income that varies according to the size of your family. Therefore, the amount a married student must contribute is lower than that of a single student with the same income. (See the calculations of family contribution in Chapter 8).

	School 4	School 5	School 6
Tuition and Fees	$ 1,850	$ 3,350	$ 7,100
Living Expenses	9,670	11,600	8,500
Total Cost	$11,520	$14,950	$15,600
Family Contribution	$ 4,075	$ 4,075	$ 4,075
Need	$ 7,445	$10,875	$11,525
Sample Package			
Institutional Scholarship	$ 0	$ 0	$ 2,000
State Grant	0	750	0
Federal Perkins Loan	0	0	0
Federal Subsidized Stafford Loan	7,445	8,500	8,500
Federal Unsubsidized Stafford Loan	0	1,625	1,025
Federal College Work-Study	0	0	0
Total Package	$ 7,445	$10,875	$11,525

School 5:

The relatively high cost of living at this institution gives the student a substantially higher need even though the tuition and fee charges are only $1,500 more than at School 4. Even though the student is offered a state grant to attend this institution, the low amount of the grant coupled with the higher budget will compel this student to borrow $10,125. This package does not seem as attractive as the package offered by School 4.

School 6:

This relatively high cost, publicly supported business school uses base year to calculate the student contribution. Since the tuition is substantially higher than that of most other public schools, this school offers some institutional scholarship assistance to its students. The result is a loan total of $9,525. Even with double the tuition and fees of School 5, the total loans are lower.

School 3:

This school uses the base year contribution to calculate the student's financial need. It offers the student a variety of financial aid programs in the package. The borrowing level of $15,425 is the lowest of the three private schools.

School 4:

This school uses the base year to calculate the student contribution. Because of the overall low cost of this institution, only federal loans are offered to meet a student's financial need. The total loan awarded is $7,745 in the Federal Subsidized Stafford Loan program. This is an attractive package.

Worksheet for Comparing
Your Graduate Management School
Financial Aid Packages

	School 1	School 2	School 3
Tuition and Fees	$	$	$
Living Expenses			
Total Cost			
Family Contribution			
Need	$	$	$
Sample Package			
Institutional Scholarship	$	$	$
State Grant			
Federal Perkins Loan			
Federal Subsidized Stafford Loan			
Federal Unsubsidized Stafford Loan			
Federal College Work-Study (CWS)			
Other			
Total Package	$	$	$

10
Financial Planning and Budgeting

This chapter provides concrete advice on planning and on budgeting your financial resources in order to make the best possible use of the funds you save or borrow for your M.B.A. education. Apply the principles described here to your own financial situation. Complete the worksheets and ask yourself hard questions. If you do, the pages ahead can be of great practical value. They will not only help you develop a financial plan, a map to guide you toward your financial future, but they will also introduce you to budgeting, the basis of carrying out this financial plan.

Developing Your Financial Plan

Step 1: Establish your financial goals and determine your costs.

Using the figures you developed for your student budget in Chapter 7, forecast below the total cost of the first year of your business school education. Include all costs, not just tuition. If you are married and/or have dependents, include the living expenses of your family when determining your total costs.

Add the costs for all the years of your program. If possible, use the actual tuition for the institution you will be attending. You can use Table 10.1, Inflation Factors, to predict how much both tuition and living expenses will increase over time.

Make sure you use a realistic budget within which you can live while attending graduate business school. Costs may vary greatly by location. The expense budgets used by the school to determine eligibility for financial aid reflect costs for the area.

Cost of Attendance

Year 1 $ _____

Year 2 $ _____

Additional Years $ _____

Total $ _____

Step 2: Evaluate your income.

Estimate your total after tax income for all the years you will be in business school: $ _____

Subtract your total after tax income from the total cost in Step 1: $ _____

The balance is the amount you will need to make up using your net worth and other resources.

Step 3: Evaluate your financial strength.

Use the worksheet on the following page to determine your net worth.

Calculate the value of all your assets:
    cash, bank accounts, stocks and bonds, trusts, real estate, and business and personal property

Subtract all liabilities:
    money owed on your assets, all loans, and credit card balances

Principles of
Educational Financial Planning

1. The earlier you start saving for your graduate management education, the more funds you will accumulate, the more interest you will earn on your savings, and the less you will have to borrow.

2. Compounding of interest increases a base amount over time. Compounding of interest has two effects on your finances: it multiplies the money you save, but it also increases the amount you owe on money you borrow. (Savings at 8 percent interest double in value in nine years. Total repayment on a loan at 8 percent paid back over 20 years is equal to double the amount of the original loan.)

3. The more you extend the repayment period of your educational loans, the smaller your monthly payments, but the more total interest you pay.

4. It is important to note that inflation may increase or reduce the relative value of your savings or payments. (If you take out a loan at 5 percent interest and inflation averages 7 percent while you are repaying it, the money you received from the loan is worth more than the money you will pay back.)

TABLE 10.1 Inflation Factors

Inflation will affect the cost of business school. The rate of college inflation for the last 5 years, according to The College Board, averaged 8% per year. The Consumer Price Index is an approximate indicator of the inflation on your living expenses. The average rate of the CPI over the past five years was 4.3%. To calculate the cost of each year of school, multiply the tuition and fees for your first year of school by the appropriate inflation factor. Then multiply your living expenses times the appropriate factor. Add the two figures together to get the cost of your second year of business school. Repeat the procedure for any subsequent years of school.

YEAR IN BUSINESS SCHOOL	INFLATION FACTORS	
	TUITION AND FEES	LIVING EXPENSES
1	1.00	1.00
2	1.08	1.04
3	1.17	1.09
4	1.26	1.14
5	1.36	1.19
6	1.47	1.24
7	1.59	1.29
8	1.72	1.35
9	1.86	1.41
10	2.01	1.47

The difference is your net worth. Compare this figure with the amount from Step 2, the balance you need from net worth to pay for your education.

Step 4: Structure your financial plan.

Ask yourself the following questions:

1. Can I pay for my education from my income?

2. Is my net worth sufficient to cover any difference? (If not, you will need to supplement your income and assets with financial aid and other outside resources.)

3. If my net worth is sufficient, can I liquidate my assets to pay for my education?

4. How do I reposition my assets to optimize both the income I earn and the availability of my other assets to pay for my education?

5. Should I seek the advice of an expert?

Step 5: Develop strategies to meet your goals.

The answers to the questions in Step 4 will help you determine how to meet your goals.

1. If you can meet your expenses using just your income, you will still need to live on a carefully planned budget and use your time well. This may well be the case for many students pursuing graduate management study on a part-time basis. You may still be eligible for financial assistance and should apply for whatever is available.

2. If your assets are not sufficient to pay for your graduate management education, it will be important that you apply for all assistance available. Note that the calculated family contribution used to determine eligibility for financial aid does not include all assets used in the net worth model. Most schools do *not* require that you liquidate all of your assets.

3. If you will be using your assets to help pay for your education, the money must be readily available when you need it. You will have to carefully plan how much money you will need at any one particular time. Your cash flow will be critical. Map out the schedule for your entire graduate business education, month by month. Determine when you will need to make large payments for tuition, books, and other expenses. Unless you are planning to use a home equity loan to help pay for your education, consider that the equity in your home, if you own one, is not available. Keep in mind that liquidation of certain assets may carry penalties and have tax implications.

4. If you are making your assets available for your educational costs, you will want to ensure that you are receiving the maximum return with the highest possible level of safety for the principal. You will have to focus on short-term investments since you will not have the luxury of waiting out fluctuations in markets. At the same time, short-term investments may require numerous transaction fees, which could eat into your profit. Finally, the safety of the principal is important for you to complete your education.

5. If you have considerable assets or a complicated financial situation, you may want to enlist the services of a professional: a financial planner, a tax accountant, or a lawyer.

Net Worth Worksheet

ASSETS

Checking Accounts	$ _____
Savings Accounts	_____
Money Market Accounts	_____
Certificates of Deposit	_____
IRA/Retirement Accounts	_____
Life Insurance Cash Value	_____
Bonds	_____
Mutual Funds	_____
Stocks	_____
Trusts	_____
Receivables (money owed you)	_____
Home Value	_____
Other Real Estate	_____
Automobiles	_____
Other Personal Property (antiques, jewelry, etc.):	
_____	_____
_____	_____
TOTAL ASSETS	$ _____

LIABILITIES

Home Mortgage	$ _____
Other Mortgages	_____
Automobile Loans	_____
Credit Card Balances	_____
Installment Accounts	_____
Contracts (money borrowed)	_____
Taxes owed (income, property)	_____
Miscellaneous:	
_____	_____
_____	_____
TOTAL LIABILITIES	$ _____
TOTAL ASSETS	$ _____
LESS LIABILITIES	_____
NET WORTH	$ _____

Note: This net worth model is to be used for financial planning purposes, not for determining eligibility for financial aid. Your total net worth may not necessarily coincide with the calculated family contribution as determined in Chapter 8, "Determining Your Need." Your total net worth includes all your assets; the calculated family contribution does not. The net worth model does not in any way suggest that you should liquidate any assets, but it does include them all in your total net worth. With the net worth model, credit card balances and automobile loans are also deducted as liabilities; you should be aware that many graduate schools of management will not include these balances in determining need.

11

Debt Management and Loan Repayment

Q. What is an appropriate amount to borrow to get my M.B.A.?

A. Only the amount you need and will be able to afford to repay when you begin repayment.

Although this may seem an obvious answer to the question, the reality can be more complicated. Of course an educational loan is an investment in your future ability to earn a higher salary. Of course it makes sense to borrow for your education only if you are reasonably sure you will be able to pay it back later. And of course it makes sense to borrow for your education only if the loan does not severely limit your career choices.

But how much is too much? How can you tell when your borrowing is reaching an amount that threatens your ability to pay it back and constrains your career choices? Completing the worksheets and studying the tables in this chapter will help you answer these complex questions.

Debt Management: The Three Steps

Step 1: Estimate your salary.
Using Table 11.1, Average Starting Annual Salary Offers, or, the average starting salaries reported by your school of choice as a guide, estimate your annual starting salary upon graduation from graduate business school. Divide by 12 and fill in your expected monthly salary on the worksheet.

Step 2: Calculate your monthly net income.
Calculate how much you will take home after taxes are withheld. Subtract the applicable federal tax (approximately 22 percent of wages), social security/FICA tax (7.65 percent of wages), and state and local taxes (approximately 6 percent of wages). This yields your monthly net income.

Step 3: Estimate your monthly budget.
Prepare an estimated monthly budget and compare it with your monthly net income. The sample budgets on the worksheet that follows are provided to assist you.

TABLE 11.1	Average Starting Annual Salary Offers to Graduate Business Degree Candidates	
GRADUATE DEGREE	**1992**	**1993**
M.B.A. (nontechnical undergraduate degree)		
1 year or less experience	$35,734	$36,513
1-2 years of experience	44,911	44,326
2-4 years of experience	49,287	49,165
over 4 years of experience	50,972	50,637
M.B.A. (technical undergraduate degree)		
1 year or less experience	41,313	40,980
1-2 years of experience	48,884	52,278
2-4 years of experience	55,249	54,286
over 4 years of experience	56,298	56,040
Accounting	31,259	30,284
Economics and Finance	36,677	35,275
Labor/Industrial Relations	31,597	30,837
Management Information Systems	34,780	36,155
Marketing/Marketing Management	39,508	40,104

Source: College Placement Council, *CPC Salary Survey*, September 1993

Worksheet 1: Monthly Net Income

	Sample M.B.A. 1 (based on $38,000 per year)	Sample M.B.A. 2 (based on $48,000 per year)	You
(1) Expected Monthly Salary	(1) $ 3,167	(1) $ 4,000	(1) $_____
(2) Less Taxes:			
Federal (22% of wages)	(2) −697	(2) −880	(2) −_____
FICA (7.65% of wages)	−242	−306	−_____
State (6% of wages)	−190	−240	−_____
(3) Equals Monthly Net Income	(3) $ 2,038	(3) $ 2,574	(3) $

Worksheet 2: Budgets

Fixed Expenses	Sample M.B.A. 1	Sample M.B.A. 2	You
Rent or Mortgage Payment	$ 650	$ 800	$_____
Utilities (gas, electric, phone)	100	100	_____
Insurance (homeowners/renters, fire, health, life, but not auto)	50	50	_____
Child Care/Child Support	n/a	n/a	_____
Car Loan ($12,000 car, 20% down, 10% loan for 48 months)	243	243	_____
Car Expenses (gas/oil, repairs, parking, license, insurance, etc.) or Fare for Public Transportation	150	150	_____
Student Loans			
Federal Stafford Loan ($18,500 @ 8%)*	224	224	_____
Private Loan ($8,000 @ 9%)*	101	101	_____
TOTAL FIXED EXPENSES	$ 1,518	$ 1,668	$

Flexible Expenses			
Food and Household Goods	$ 180	$ 200	$_____
Lunch (weekdays)	100	120	_____
Personal (including laundry, cleaning, toiletries, etc.)	50	60	_____
Clothing	75	100	_____
Entertainment/Recreation	80	120	_____
Emergency Fund (6% of gross)	190	240	_____
TOTAL FLEXIBLE EXPENSES	$ 675	$ 840	$
TOTAL EXPENSES (FIXED + FLEXIBLE)	$ 2,193	$ 2,508	$
TOTAL NET INCOME (after taxes)	$ 2,038	$ 2,574	$
TOTAL DISCRETIONARY INCOME	($ 155)	$ 66	$

---

* A fixed interest rate is assumed for projections. Federal Stafford is now a variable interest rate loan. Some private loans may have variable interest rates as well.

Summary of Sample Budgets

M.B.A. 1

With a salary of $38,000 per year and a reasonable to low-cost life style, student loan payments ($325 per month) and car payments ($243 per month) are higher than can be managed comfortably with this budget.

M.B.A. 2

Even a $48,000 salary and a more generous budget (although hardly extravagant) yield barely enough per month to get by comfortably. The discretionary portion of a $48,000 income does not leave much margin for error.

In reviewing the amounts shown on the sample budgets and income worksheet, there are a number of points you need to keep in mind.

Although the budgets include a six percent emergency fund, they do not contain start-up costs for living in a new home, including first and last months' rent, security deposit, and the purchase of furniture and household goods. The budgets do take into account the purchase of clothing needed for a new job, however, by including a clothing allowance of $75-$100 per month. With this modest amount, clothes would have to be purchased gradually. Two or three months of the budgeted amount could be saved and combined toward a purchase, or payments could be spread out over several months with the use of a credit card. It is important to remember, however, that the credit card option raises the total cost of the purchase because of finance charges, often at a rate of 18 to 20 percent per year, if the entire balance of the account is not paid monthly.

In calculating the car payment, a 20 percent down payment was used. If a smaller down payment is made or if the car is more expensive, the monthly payment will rise. Whether additional costs can be accommodated here or anywhere else in the budget will depend on the salary level and overall allocation of expenses. By saving $50 per month on rent, perhaps by sharing an apartment, it may be possible to afford a somewhat more expensive car or simply to meet student loan payments and other expenses.

TABLE 11.2	Lender Standards for Borrowing		
INCOME YEARLY (MONTHLY)	MAXIMUM TOTAL RECURRING MONTHLY PAYMENT	MAXIMUM SUGGESTED HOUSING PAYMENT[1]	TOTAL AVAILABLE FOR CAR AND STUDENT LOAN AND OTHER RECURRING DEBT[2]
$20,000 ($1,667)	$ 600	$ 466	$ 133
$25,000 ($2,083)	750	583	167
$30,000 ($2,500)	900	700	200
$35,000 ($2,917)	1,050	817	233
$40,000 ($3,333)	1,200	933	267
$45,000 ($3,750)	1,350	1,050	300
$50,000 ($4,166)	1,500	1,167	333
$55,000 ($4,583)	1,650	1,283	367
$60,000 ($5,000)	1,800	1,400	400

Source: AmeriFederal Savings Bank

[1] In order to qualify for a mortgage, monthly housing costs generally cannot exceed 28 percent of gross income. Monthly housing costs include principal, interest, homeowners insurance, and real estate taxes.

[2] Recurring debts plus monthly housing costs should not exceed 36 percent of gross income. Recurring debts include all revolving credit and consumer loans.

It is often helpful to calculate average weekly, or even daily, amounts for particular expenses from the monthly budget. The sample budget for M.B.A. 1 lists $80 per month for entertainment and recreation, approximately $20 per week. This amount can then be compared to the cost of a proposed activity, such as attendance at a movie or concert, including ticket, parking or transportation, refreshments, etc. Similarly, M.B.A. 1 has a daily budget of $5 per day for weekday lunches. If this amount is not adequate, it is important to trim expenses in other areas of the budget to control expense and debt levels.

Recommended Debt Levels

Loan counselors and other professionals recommend that monthly payments towards all debts be no more than 15 percent of gross income. This amount includes all credit card debts but not the cost of housing (rent or mortgage). The figure of 15 percent is a maximum manageable level; a reasonable range would be 8-10 percent of gross income for debt payments. Table 11.2, Lender Standards for Borrowing, shows suggested maximum amounts of debt at various income levels.

For Sample M.B.A. 1 shown above, monthly payments towards loans total $568 (including the car loan).

TABLE 11.3	Debt Management Repayment Guide			
AMOUNT OF EDUCATIONAL AND CONSUMER LOANS[1]	YEARS IN REPAY-MENT	MONTHLY PAYMENT[2]	MINIMUM MONTHLY INCOME[3]	MINIMUM ANNUAL INCOME[3]
$ 5,000	10	$ 63	$ 420	$ 5,040
10,000	10	126	840	10,080
15,000	10	190	1,267	15,200
20,000	10	253	1,687	20,240
25,000	10	316	2,106	25,280
30,000	10	380	2,533	30,340
35,000	10	443	2,953	35,440
40,000	10	506	3,373	40,480
45,000	10	570	3,800	45,600
50,000	10	633	4,220	50,640
$20,000	20	$179	$1,193	$14,320
25,000	20	225	1,500	18,000
30,000	20	270	1,800	21,600
35,000	20	314	2,093	25,120
40,000	20	360	2,400	28,800
45,000	20	405	2,700	32,400
50,000	20	450	3,000	36,000

Adapted from *Financing Your Law School Education* with permission of Law School Admission Services, Inc.

(1) includes all loans and debt, including student loans, car loans every 5 years, and revolving credit

(2) average of 9% interest

(3) 15% of monthly gross income available for all loan payments

That equals just under 18 percent of gross, more than can be handled with that budget.

For Sample M.B.A. 2, the monthly payments towards loans of $568 (including the car loan) equal just over 14 percent. This amount is below the maximum manageable level, which makes the loan payments feasible.

The tables and graphs that follow can serve as a rough guide for determining the total amount you can afford to borrow. Remember, these amounts include all debts, including car loans, student loans, and revolving credit payments. Table 11.3, Debt Management Repayment Guide, shows the *minimum* monthly salary required to repay loans of various amounts based on an allocation of 15 percent of monthly gross income to loan repayment. It is very likely that at the lower income levels listed, a larger proportion of monthly income would be needed to cover basic living expenses, and that 15 percent for debt repayment at those income levels might be unrealistically high.

Salary Increases

In determining how much you can afford to borrow, you must also take into consideration how your salary will increase over time. The graphs that follow assume a starting salary of $38,000 in 1997, the year you might begin work after receiving your M.B.A. The figures also assume a 5 percent increase in salary per year, a car loan of $9,600 at 10 percent every four years, no other loans or revolving credit payments, and a maximum manageable loan payment level of 15 percent.

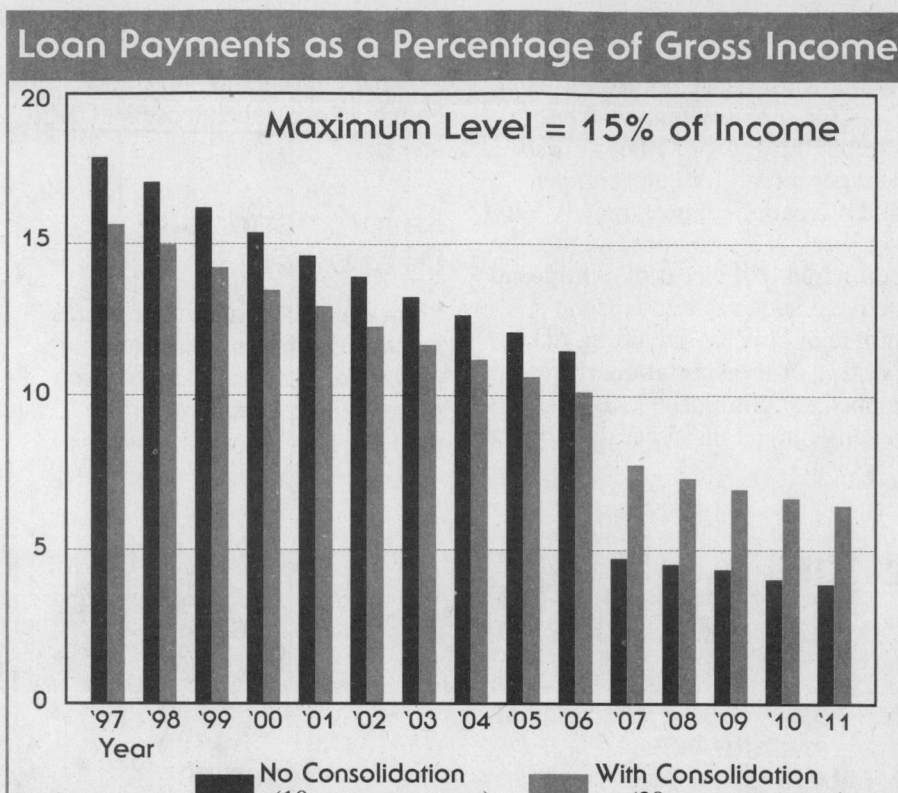

Loan Payments as a Percentage of Gross Income

Maximum Level = 15% of Income

No Consolidation (10-year repayment)   With Consolidation (20-year repayment)

$38,000 starting salary; 5% growth/year; $18,500 federal loan; $8,000 private loan; $9,600 car loan every 5 years

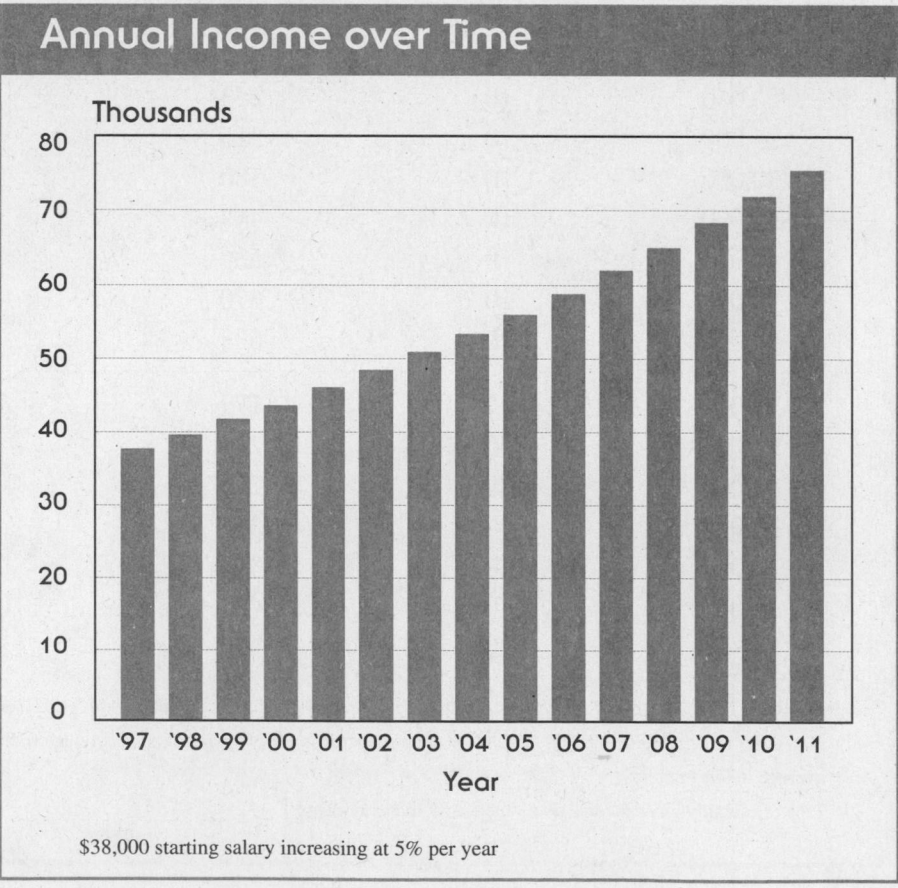

Annual Income over Time

$38,000 starting salary increasing at 5% per year

Relationship of Debt Level to Career Choice

The realities shown in these graphs lead to the following question: How will the level of debt I assume for my graduate management education influence my career choices?

If your loan payments will be more than you can afford, you must either increase your income or reduce your monthly loan payments. To increase your monthly income, you may have to decline a job offer you otherwise would like to accept because the pay is too low, or you may have to accept a job offer because the salary is more than you can make anywhere else. Either way, your job decision will be based almost exclusively on the salary offered. To reduce your monthly loan payments, one alternative is loan consolidation. The best option of course is to avoid incurring high educational debt and consumer debt initially.

Meeting Your Obligations

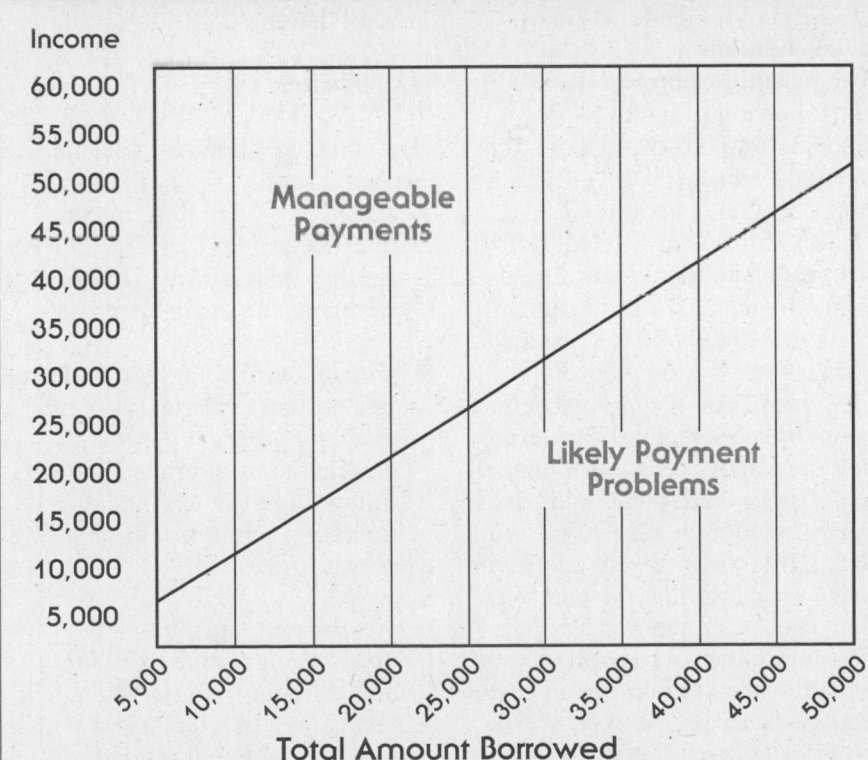

Income

Total Amount Borrowed

Amount borrowed includes all loans and debt; average interest of 9% per year; 15% of monthly gross income available for all loan payments

Loan Payments as a Percentage of Income

As the graph at the left clearly shows, the debt level of Sample M.B.A. 1, with an annual starting salary of $38,000, does not reach the maximum manageable debt level of 15 percent until the fourth year of repayment. Even at higher income levels, an average amount of student and car debt means delaying any additions to savings or enhancements to lifestyle for five years.

Federal Loan Consolidation

Under federal loan consolidation, a borrower combines several federal loans into one larger loan, typically with an extended repayment period. The new interest rate is the weighted average of the rates of the consolidated loans.

There are several advantages to loan consolidation. One large loan with a longer repayment period is less of a drain on your resources and easier to manage than several smaller loans with shorter repayment periods. The monthly payment amount on one large loan with a longer repayment period is less than the monthly payment amount on several smaller loans with shorter repayment periods. And even if the total loan repayment period is not extended, monthly payments may be reduced if one or more of the consolidated loans is small and subject to a minimum monthly payment. Keeping records of multiple loan repayments also is more complex and can lead to neglecting one of the loans, causing a delinquency.

There are disadvantages to loan consolidation as well. First, the total interest paid is higher if the loan repayment period is longer.

Second, the interest rate on some low-interest loans increases when consolidated.

If the M.B.A. students referred to in the samples in this chapter consolidated their Federal Subsidized and Unsubsidized Stafford Loans, the combined total would still equal $18,500. The private loan cannot be consolidated. At 8 percent with a 20-year repayment period, the consolidated payment is $155 per month, as compared with $224 per month for the 10 year repayment period. The result is a $69 reduction in the monthly loan payment and a total monthly debt burden of $499 (including car and private loan payments).

After loan consolidation, the total of all loan payments (including the car and private loans) would equal 16 percent of Sample M.B.A. 1's gross income of $3,167 per month. This would still leave no discretionary income and would eat into the 6 percent emergency fund. However, if no long-term credit card debts were incurred, the payments would be manageable until the salary increased enough to cover the payments in just two years' time. For Sample M.B.A. 2, loan consolidation would mean reducing total monthly debt payments from just over 14 percent of gross income to a more manageable 12 percent. The difference that loan consolidation would make is obvious.

The savings in lower monthly payments resulting from loan consolidation must be weighed against the impact of the increased amount of interest paid during an extended repayment period. Without consolidation of the Stafford Loans, the M.B.A. graduates in the example would pay $224 a month for 10 years, for a total of $26,880, with $18,500 of principal on the loan and $8,380 in interest. With loan consolidation, the Sample

TABLE 11.4	Federal Consolidated Loan Repayment Periods
TOTAL STUDENT LOAN DEBT	**MAXIMUM REPAYMENT PERIOD**
Less than $ 7,500	10 years
$ 7,500 to 9,999	12 years
10,000 to 19,999	15 years
20,000 to 39,999	20 years
40,000 to 59,999	25 years
60,000 or more	30 years

M.B.A.s would pay $155 a month for 20 years for a total of $37,200, with $18,500 for the principal on the loan and $18,700 in interest. With consolidation, the M.B.A.s would end up repaying more than twice the amount of their original loans. Borrowers should carefully consider the price for lower monthly payments resulting from loan consolidation.

Qualifying for Federal Loan Consolidation

The federally approved loan consolidation program allows students who borrowed under the Federal Perkins (NDSL), Federal Stafford (GSL), Federal SLS, or Health Professions Student Loans to consolidate these loans into one loan. To qualify for this program, you must already be in repayment or in a grace period preceding repayment. You may not be delinquent by more than 90 days. And you must apply for a consolidation loan from a lender that holds one of the outstanding loans being consolidated. If none of these lenders will make the consolidation loan, you may choose another lender. You may consolidate any or all of your federal loans; if you have a Federal Perkins Loan at 5 percent, you do not have to consolidate it with other loans at higher rates.

Interest Rate

The method for determining the interest rate for a federally approved consolidated loan is mandated by the government. The rate is a weighted average of all eligible loans, rounded up to the nearest whole percent.

Fees

No insurance premium or application fee may be charged for loan consolidation.

Deferments

The repayment of principal of Federal Consolidated Loans may be deferred for a variety of reasons. During a period of deferment, interest continues to accrue and must be paid regularly. Deferments of principal are available if:

- you are enrolled at least half time in a post-secondary school or graduate program; or you are enrolled in an approved graduate fellowship or rehabilitation training program for disabled persons;

- you are temporarily totally disabled; or unable to secure employment because you are taking care of a temporarily totally disabled dependent;

- you are seeking but unable to find full-time employment.

Repayment Period

The number of years you take to repay your consolidation loan depends on the total amount of your student loan debt including all private educational loans. Table 11.4 lists the number of years you may choose. At least half of the total educational debt used to determine the length of your repayment period must be federal loans (Perkins, Stafford, SLS, or Health Professions Student Loans).

Note that the table shows *maximum* time limits. Choose the shortest repayment period you can afford. This minimizes the amount of interest paid over the life of your loan. Generally, a 15-year repayment period is preferable, if the payments are manageable.

Prepayment of Consolidated Loans

You may prepay all or a portion of your consolidation loans at any time without penalty. Prepayment reduces the amount of interest you will pay over the life of the loan.

Suggested Strategies

Consolidate your loans to get relief early in your career when your salary is at its lowest. Then, if possible, double up on your payments as your ability to repay increases with your income.

You may consider excluding the lower interest Federal Perkins Loan, and consolidate only the more costly loan programs. Remember, though, that multiple payments will be required.

More Debt Management Ideas

Alternative Payment Plans

Interest Only Payments:

You pay only the interest for a period of one to two years. As a result, your monthly payment is lower. Presumably, your salary will have increased enough to cover both the principal and interest payments necessary to pay off the loan once the interest-only period is over. Although you pay more total interest on the loan, the payments are more affordable early in your career when your salary is at its lowest. Only a few lenders offer this option for student loans.

Graduated Payments:

Initially, you pay only the interest or you pay interest plus a small amount towards principal. The monthly payments gradually increase in succeeding years. This option has not been widely available but must be offered to people who are new borrowers and whose first loan disbursement is made on or after July 1, 1993.

Prepayment of Student Loans

All federal loans and most other student loans permit paying off the complete loan at any point without penalty. Thus, to whatever extent possible after you graduate, direct any excess cash towards paying off those of your loans with the highest interest rates.

Family Financing: Gifts and Loans

Although M.B.A. students are defined as independent for federal student financial aid purposes, many families are still willing to help, particularly if the money reduces a student's total debt and does not replace grant dollars. You must judge both your own family's willingness and your own feelings about accepting such support.

One alternative that can provide a useful compromise is a private loan. Some family members are more willing to provide loans than outright gifts. Such loans can be structured with more attractive terms than a bank loan, such as no origination fees, no payments for a number of years, or lower interest rates. For example, you can offer to pay a higher interest rate than your relative's money will earn in a savings account but lower than the interest rate for one of the student loan programs.

Early Graduation

You may be able to reduce your total indebtedness by completing your education more quickly than scheduled. For example, you may take one or two extra courses during the year. At some graduate schools of management, this reduces the number of terms in which full time enrollment is necessary, thereby allowing you to begin working sooner. Make sure this is possible at your school before pursuing this option. Many M.B.A. programs have full-time residency requirements that are seldom waived. If you will be graduating mid-year, you should consult your career placement office about the relative availability of jobs.

Part-time Attendance

Another option, if the school permits, is to enroll part time for a term or for the entire program. This allows more time to earn money to pay the costs of your M.B.A. and thus reduces the amount of money you must borrow. Remember, however, that to qualify for any federal financial assistance, you must be enrolled at least half time.

This normally equals six credits per term, or about two courses. If you attend less than half time, you will have to start paying off your loans.

Loan Forgiveness Programs

To encourage graduates to take jobs in public service or to take positions in areas where there may be a great need but for which the pay is low, a few schools have started Loan Forgiveness Programs (also called Loan Repayment Assistance Programs).

In these programs, if, after graduation, your total income is less than a specified amount, the school reimburses you for all or a portion of your student loan payments made during the year. The terms of loan forgiveness programs vary from school to school, and the income requirement may change annually.

Loan forgiveness programs are a relatively new, but growing, concept. When you are considering which graduate school of management to attend, check the Schools-at-a-Glance table in this book to see which schools sponsor Loan Forgiveness Programs (or Loan Repayment Assistance Programs).

Employer Signing Bonuses

In select cases, an employer will offer you a signing bonus if you agree to work for the company after you graduate. Similarly, an employer may agree to either partially or completely repay your student loans if you guarantee employment with them for one to two years. Or, they may increase your starting salary to cover your student loan payments for as long as you work there. These benefits are individually negotiated between

you and the employer. Keep them in mind when you are weighing various offers. You should also be aware that accepting a signing bonus before you graduate may affect your financial aid for the year.

Questions and Answers about Loan Repayment

Q. To whom do I direct my student loan payments?

A. That depends on who is the lender. If you borrowed under the Federal Perkins Loan or Federal Direct Stafford Loan programs, the lender is the school itself. In this case, you pay the school or its loan servicer.

The lender for a Federal Stafford Loan, Federal SLS, or private loan is a bank, savings and loan, credit union, or other similar institution. In this case, you will pay the lender directly or pay its loan servicer.

Q. What are loan servicers, or billing agencies?

A. Many lenders and schools contract with an outside agency to oversee the payment of loans. Borrowers send payments to a billing agency rather than to the lender.

Q. What is the secondary loan market?

A. Lenders often sell their loans to other lenders. This is referred to as the secondary market, and it effectively puts more capital into the market. Occasionally loans are sold even before the first payment is made. Secondary markets often use loan servicers to collect loans.

For many borrowers, the sale of their loan has no effect since none of the terms of the loan change. An effect is felt only when a lender sells two or more of your loans to different secondary markets, or only sells some loans and keeps the remaining ones. In this instance, you may have to make multiple monthly payments to different loan servicers, the sum total of which may be greater than the amount required for one larger loan.

You should ask about a lender's policy about selling your loans in the secondary markets. If possible, choose a lender that keeps your portfolio or sells only to one secondary market.

Q. Other than by reading my loan promissory note, is there any way I can learn about my rights and responsibilities?

A. Schools are required to meet with all federal loan borrowers prior to disbursement to discuss the terms of the loan and the borrower's rights and responsibilities. These are called entrance interviews.

Schools also are required to conduct exit interviews with these borrowers. The exit counseling is done either just before graduation or, if that is not possible, through the mail. In both entrance and exit counseling, the school reviews the terms of your loans and explains your rights and responsibilities, deferments, refinancing, loan consolidation options, and your obligation to repay your loans.

Q. What is a deferment?

A. A deferment allows you to postpone loan payment for a specified period of time. A deferment is granted when you meet certain criteria established under the terms of the loan promissory note.

Deferments on principal and interest payments for the federal loan programs (Stafford, SLS, and Perkins Loans) may be granted for:

- enrollment in school at least half time;

- unemployment;

- economic hardship.

For borrowers with outstanding debt whose first disbursement was made prior to July 1, 1993, additional deferment categories exist (refer to Table 5.2, Student Loan Deferments).

Deferments are granted only at the discretion of the lender. For most non-federal loans (e.g., MBA LOANS), only the principal can be deferred. Interest continues to accrue and either must be paid regularly or capitalized at the end of the deferment period.

Remember, deferments are not automatic. You should not assume that your lender knows you are enrolled in school, even if you are applying for a new student loan from the same lender. Generally, you must file an official deferment form with each lender before a deferment is granted. You must file for deferment for each year you are in school.

Q. What is forbearance?

A. Forbearance is a type of deferment granted by the lender when you are willing, but temporarily unable, to repay because of financial difficulties. The loss of a job or temporary disability are examples of such difficulties.

When you are granted forbearance, the lender may allow you to temporarily stop making payments, reduce the amount you have to pay each month, or extend the time for making payments. Lenders may grant forbearance of principal, interest, or both, but the borrower is still responsible for any interest that accrues.

You must make special arrangements with the lender to be granted forbearance. Most lenders prefer to set up an interest-only repayment schedule so that the principal does not increase and the lender's costs are covered during the forbearance period.

Rules for Loan Repayment

1. Always communicate with the lender or the loan servicer about any repayment difficulties before your payment is due.

2. Always notify your lender or loan servicer in writing of any change in address, name, or enrollment status (the terms of the loan usually require notification about such change within 30 days).

12

Questions and Answers: Credit and Credit Reporting

Q. What is a credit history?

A. A credit history, also called a credit report, is a list of all your previous debts and repayment histories. Included in this list are any loans, mortgages, and credit cards. In addition, some credit histories reflect rent due or similar financial obligations.

Q. Who keeps my credit history?

A. Your credit history is kept by a credit bureau. There are three major credit bureaus in this country:

Equifax Credit Information
  Services (CBI)
P.O. Box 740241
Atlanta, Georgia 30374
(800) 685-1111
or your local telephone directory

Trans Union Systems
111 West Jackson Boulevard
Chicago, Illinois 60604
(312) 408-1050
or your local telephone directory

TRW Information Systems and
  Services
505 City Parkway West
Orange, California 92613-6230
(800) 682-7654
or your local telephone directory

To obtain information about your credit history, you are advised to contact a credit bureau office in your local area rather than calling the national offices listed above.

Q. Why is a good credit history important?

A. A history of good credit will enable you to qualify for loans to finance your education.

A record of consistent repayment of loans demonstrates your credit worthiness for future indebtedness. This includes buying a car, renting or buying a house, or applying for additional credit cards.

A credit history that demonstrates inconsistency in payments or unwillingness to repay debts can create a significant barrier to financing your graduate management education. If your credit history indicates that your commitment to repay is questionable, your loan application may be denied.

Lenders have the right and the responsibility to deny a loan if there is an indication that a borrower will not repay. Note

that students already in default on previous federal Title IV loans (Perkins, Stafford, or SLS) are not eligible to receive any additional loans.

Q. Should I obtain a copy of my credit report?

A. For most students, it is not necessary to have a copy of your credit report. However, if you have ever been denied credit, or if you occasionally miss a monthly payment or pay late on a credit card or loan, you should definitely get a copy. Federal legislation allows you to have one free report per year. In addition, borrowers who are denied credit are entitled, by law, to receive a free copy of the report on which the denial was based. The request must be made within 30 days of the denial. There may be a small charge for any additional credit reports you request.

Q. Where can I obtain a copy of my credit report?

A. Each of the major credit bureaus carries information

about borrowers nationwide. Unfortunately, the bureaus do not always coordinate their information, and it is possible to have a clean report from one and a record of bad credit from another.

Q. Which bureau should I use?

A. Call the bank that issued the credit card you use most often, or call the holder of your mortgage. Ask which credit bureau it reports to, and start there. If you notice that the report does not reflect all of the credit you have, probably another bureau will have the missing information.

Q. Can I get a loan if I have no credit history?

A. It depends on the loan program.

For Federal Perkins Loans and Federal Stafford Loans, no credit report will be required and you do not need previous credit. If you have demonstrated need, based on the federal criteria, you are eligible unless you are in default on a Federal Title IV student loan (Perkins, Stafford, or SLS Loan) or a previous institutional loan.

For private student loans and commercial loans, almost all lenders require credit reports. If a lender is unable to determine your commitment to repay by inspecting your credit history, the lender may deny the loan. If you have never established credit, the lender may request that you find a cosigner.

Q. May a lender deny my loan application because of my previous debts?

A. Lenders may deny any loan because of an adverse credit

Definitions of Adverse Credit

Delinquent   scheduled loan payment not made by the date required

Bad Credit   student borrower delinquent for 90 days on any financial obligation

Default   failure to make required installment payments for a specified period.

for Federal Stafford and Federal SLS Loans:
failure to make installment payments for 180 days (for loans repayable in monthly installments) or 240 days (for loans repayable in less frequent installments)

for Federal Perkins Loan:
failure to make payments for 120 days (for monthly repayment schedules) or 180 days (for payments scheduled less frequently)

history. However, a lender cannot deny a federally guaranteed student loan because of an already high debt burden. The regulations governing the loan programs determine the maximum amount you can borrow. For commercial loans, or for one of the private student loan programs such as MBA LOANS, a lender will usually consider your total debt burden in determining your eligibility.

Q. What is debt burden?

A. Your debt burden is the total amount of money you owe. Lenders are increasingly concerned about students who are overburdened with student debt and are therefore unable to repay their loans. You are overburdened when the payment required for all outstanding debts exceeds a predetermined percentage of your income. The exact percentage is determined by the lender,

although there are industry standards connected with various types of loans. Refer to Table 11.2, Lender Standards for Borrowing.

If you do not meet the minimum income standard to obtain a loan, you may still qualify by having a cosigner who does meet the standard.

Q. What if my loan application is denied? May I appeal the decision?

A. If you are denied a loan based on a bad credit history, you may appeal the lender's decision. However, you must prove that you meet the lender's credit criteria. If your credit report is wrong, the creditor reporting the misinformation must clarify the discrepancy in writing. You must supply all supporting documentation to the lender before a successful appeal can be made.

Q. What is considered adverse credit?

A. Adverse credit is generally considered to be a delinquency of 90 days. However, many lenders will deny a loan if, in the preceding two years, you have been delinquent for just 60 days, more than once. Adverse credit includes nonpayment of mortgages, student loans, credit card balances, car payments, and even rent and telephone bills if the delinquency was serious enough to be reported to a credit bureau. To qualify for private student loans, you must clear up any adverse credit before enrolling in school. Paying off a delinquency in order to qualify for a student loan will not necessarily erase the history of adverse credit. Since guarantors place emphasis on the last 12 to 24 months of your credit history, you may have to postpone enrollment.

Q. What happens if my student loan is delinquent?

A. If you are delinquent in repaying a student loan, even before your loan is officially in default, lenders take certain steps to ensure repayment.

Within the first 30 days of a delinquency, the lender, or a loan servicer acting on behalf of the lender, tries to make contact with you to reestablish repayment.

If the lender is unsuccessful in contacting you or if the delinquency continues, the lender may submit your name to a credit bureau.

Two to three months after your payment is overdue, the loan may be assigned to a collection agency.

If you have moved and cannot be located, the lender will attempt to find your new address using records from your school, the department of motor vehicles, and other organizations.

You are not eligible for additional student loans while you are delinquent on a prior loan. If you are planning to apply for additional loans, notify the lender with whom you are delinquent and find out what steps you need to take. Although a large initial payment and subsequent consistent, timely payments may be sufficient evidence to qualify you for an additional student loan in some states, other states may require 12 consecutive payments or payment of the entire balance before considering you for an additional loan.

Q. How do I pay off a delinquent loan?

A. To pay off a delinquent loan, contact the creditor and make satisfactory arrangements to repay.

Q. What happens if I default on my student loan?

A. If you default on your loan, this will be reported to a credit bureau, which may prevent you from obtaining any subsequent credit. You may also be sued for payment, and your wages may be garnished, that is, a portion of your wages will automatically be deducted to pay for your defaulted loan. In addition, your bank accounts and personal property may be seized, and any tax refunds you may be expecting may be offset by the amount of the loan. Finally, your loan can be "accelerated,"

that is, your lender may demand that the entire balance of the loan be paid immediately rather than in payments over time; and all costs associated with collecting your loan will be added to your obligation.

The most critical time in default prevention is in the early stages of repayment. Once most people establish a payment routine, they usually maintain it, except under unusual circumstances.

Q. Can my lender use a collection agency?

A. Many lenders contract with collection agencies to prevent delinquent loans from going into default. Collection agencies have the authority to negotiate different payment schedules than the one originally established. The agency generally requests an initial large payment as "good faith" money, and then regular monthly payments. Collection agencies earn a percentage of the money they collect and are usually willing to work out an acceptable arrangement.

Remember, once a loan is delinquent, the lender may accelerate the loan and demand immediate payment of the entire balance, including any collection costs. And once a collection agency is involved, your repayment schedule must be renegotiated.

13

Realities Facing International Students in U.S. Graduate Management Schools

Most of the material in this book describes financing options that are, by and large, available only to U.S. citizens and permanent residents. If you are from a foreign country and plan to study in a U.S. graduate management school, you will find far fewer sources of financial aid. You will also face special financial requirements before you are even permitted to enter the U.S. as a student.

It is important to remember that the cost of attending a graduate school of management in the U.S. includes more than just tuition.

Costs to Consider

Admission Application Fees
Most schools charge a fee to apply to the school. This is true for both international students and residents of the U.S. The amount ranges from $25 to $90 and must be paid at the time of application. The fee is neither refundable nor applicable to tuition charges.

Travel
Travel to and from the United States is almost always the responsibility of the student.

Tuition and Fees
Usually tuition and fees for each term must be paid in full at registration. Occasionally, a school will permit a student to pay the full amount in several payments. International students generally pay the nonresident tuition rate at publicly supported institutions. Be prepared to pay the entire cost of tuition, fees, and books at the beginning of each term.

Living Expenses
The cost of housing and food and other expenses in the United States are among the highest in the world. The budgets included in this book give average amounts. In large metropolitan areas, costs can be significantly higher.

Medical Expenses
Most schools have a health service facility for minor illnesses or accidents. The school often charges an annual fee for this service. Dental work is generally not included in this service. Medical costs in the U.S. are high; an office visit to a physician is often $50 or more. An overnight stay in a hospital costs more than $500 per night.

Health Insurance
Most schools require you to carry health insurance to cover costs in the event of accident or illness. The cost of this insurance for a single student ranges from $300 to $500 or more per year.

Summer Expenses
International students often cannot find work during the summer break. The U.S. Immigration and Naturalization Service only grants permission to work under extraordinary circumstances and only if you entered the U.S. with a visa that allows you to work. When preparing your budget, assume you will not be able to earn any money during the summer. Plan to have sufficient funds to cover all living expenses for the entire period of time you will be in the United States.

Certification of Sufficient Funds

To obtain either an F-1 or J-1 student visa, you must certify that you have sufficient funds to finance at least the first year of study. Although a graduate management program may decide that you are a suitable candidate for admission, the institution may not grant formal admission or issue a Certificate of Eligibility for a visa until you prove that you have sufficient funds for your entire M.B.A. education, not just the first year. As a general rule, U.S. graduate schools of management provide very little financial assistance to international students. In addition, United States govern-

ment aid for international students is virtually nonexistent. Therefore, it is important for you to obtain funds from your own resources, including from your own government.

Most graduate schools of management describe clearly in their catalogs the financial aid policies

they apply to international students. Applicants from overseas should take these policies seriously no matter how discouraging they may be. In American culture, there are rarely opportunities to negotiate such institutional policies. The schools mean what they say.

14
Graduate Schools of Management

This chapter contains specific information about graduate schools of management located in the United States and is divided into two sections. The first section is the "Schools at a Glance" chart, which provides some basic information about whether schools have graduate assistantships, various types of gift aid, and other financing options. The chart is arranged in alphabetical order by state so that you can locate schools in the regions in which you are interested. The school descriptions that follow contain more detailed information about each school including enrollment, cost of attendance, financial aid available, and the percentage of students receiving aid. The school descriptions are arranged in alphabetical order by school name. Addresses for correspondence with the schools are also given.

The Graduate Management Admission Test (GMAT) is used by about 900 graduate management schools throughout the world. About 600 schools in the United States require GMAT scores from each applicant. All of the schools that require the GMAT of substantially all of their applicants were invited to provide financial aid information for this book. Three hundred and eighty-five

schools chose to submit information. Because the information was provided by the schools themselves, the Graduate Management Admission Council (GMAC) cannot guarantee its accuracy.

The information in this chapter was collected through a survey of the schools. For the "Schools at a Glance" chart, the schools were asked to respond "Yes," "No," or "Not Applicable" to the following questions:

1. Do you offer graduate assistantships, including research, teaching, and resident?

2. Do you waive or reduce tuition for students awarded assistantships?

3. Are any types of assistantships awarded to incoming first-year students?

4. Do you offer any gift aid, including scholarships, grants, and fellowships, based solely on MERIT (other than federal or state funds)?

5. Do you offer any gift aid, including scholarships, grants, and fellowships, based solely on NEED (other than federal or state funds)?

6. Do you offer any gift aid, including scholarships, grants, and fellowships, that gives preference to members of minority groups?

7. Do you offer any gift aid, including scholarships, grants, and fellowships, that gives preference to women?

8. Do you offer a tuition/fee payment plan?

9. Do you offer any financial aid for courses taken at your school during the summer term?

10. Do you assist students in locating paid summer jobs/ internships?

11. Do you offer a cooperative education program?

12. Do you offer a loan forgiveness program?

Standards for Reporting Admission Statistics

Introduction

All schools supplying data for this book were asked to follow these guidelines, adopted by the GMAC in 1993, to provide graduate management schools with standards for reporting statistical information about graduate management program applicants, persons offered admission, and matriculants. Standardizing the reporting of such information allows prospective students and other interested persons to make valid inferences and comparisons.

Statistical Reporting Standards

1. Citizens and permanent residents of the United States are reported as domestic applicants, persons offered admission, and matriculants. All other applicants, persons offered admission, and matriculants are reported as international.

2. Geographic areas listed by domestic applicants, persons offered admission, and matriculants as permanent residence are reported according to the following Graduate Management Admission Test registration boundaries:

Northeast
Maine, Vermont, New Hampshire, Massachusetts, Connecticut, New Jersey, New York, Rhode Island

Mid-Atlantic
Pennsylvania, Maryland, Virginia, West Virginia, District of Columbia, Delaware

South
North Carolina, South Carolina, Kentucky, Tennessee, Georgia, Florida, Alabama, Arkansas, Louisiana, Mississippi

Midwest
Wisconsin, Missouri, Kansas, Iowa, Minnesota, Nebraska, Michigan, Ohio, Indiana, North Dakota, South Dakota, Illinois

Southwest
Colorado, Arizona, Texas, Oklahoma, New Mexico

West
California, Hawaii, Washington, Oregon, Alaska, Montana, Idaho, Utah, Nevada, Wyoming

Possessions and Territories
American Samoa, Palau, Guam, Puerto Rico, Virgin Islands

3. Racial and ethnic designations for domestic applicants follow U.S. Census terms: White; Black/African-American; American Indian, Aleut/Eskimo; Asian or Pacific Islander; Hispanic (which includes persons of Mexican, Puerto Rican, Cuban, and Central or South American heritage).

4. The number of male, female, minority, international, and other subgroup applicants, persons offered admission, and matriculants are reported as a percentage of the category total.

5. Full-time work experience is calculated in increments of one year and includes only postbaccalaureate experience. Work experience in excess of one-half year is rounded up to the next whole number.

6. GMAT scores include all persons in each category reported: applicants, persons offered admission, and matriculants. GMAT scores are reported as a percentage of category total and are distributed in the following score ranges: below 400; 400-490; 500-590; 600-690; and 700 and above.

7. Average (mean) undergraduate grade point averages reported include all persons in each reported category of applicants, persons offered admission, or matriculants, and are reported on a 4.0 scale.

8. Full-time and part-time classifications are determined in accordance with the definitions established by the U.S. Department of Education in connection with eligibility for federal student aid.

9. Full-time and part-time information should be reported separately.

10. Statistical descriptions of applicants and persons offered admission include total annual number of applicants who complete applications, without regard to special demographic, academic, or geographic circumstances unless explicitly specified otherwise.

11. Statistical descriptions of matriculants include all matriculants, and specify the total number of such matriculants without regard to special demographic, ethnic, academic, or geographical circumstances unless explicitly specified otherwise.

12. The total number of applicants reported to have been offered admission includes those who were offered or requested deferred admission and those offered conditional admission. If persons offered admission choose to defer matriculation, they are considered to have refused their offers of admission.

✔ Yes
– Not applicable

Institution	Graduate Assistantships (Research, Teaching, Resident)			Gift Aid (Scholarships, Grants, and Fellowships)				Other Options					Page Number
	Available	Tuition Waivers/Reductions	Available for First-Year Students	Awarded Based on MERIT	Awarded Based on NEED	Preference for Minorities	Preference for Women	Tuition/Fee Payment Plan	Aid for Summer Programs	Paid Summer Jobs/Internships	Cooperative Education Program	Loan Forgiveness Program	
ALABAMA													
Auburn University	✔	✔	✔				–			✔	–		112
Troy State University	✔		✔	✔				✔					232
University of Alabama, The	✔	✔	✔	✔		✔		✔	✔	✔	✔	–	235
ALASKA													
University of Alaska Anchorage	✔	✔	✔	✔				✔	✔		✔		235
University of Alaska Fairbanks	✔	✔	✔	✔				✔	✔				236
ARIZONA													
American Graduate School of International Management	✔	✔	✔	✔		✔		✔	✔	✔			108
Arizona State University	✔	✔	✔	✔		✔	✔	✔	–	✔			110
Arizona State University West	✔	✔	✔	✔	✔	✔	✔		✔	✔			111
Grand Canyon University		–		✔			✔						159
Northern Arizona University	✔	✔	✔	✔	✔	✔	✔		✔	✔			192
University of Arizona	✔	✔	✔	✔	✔	✔	✔	✔		✔	✔		237
ARKANSAS													
University of Arkansas	✔	✔	✔	✔		✔			✔				237
U. of Arkansas at Little Rock	✔	✔	✔	✔	✔	✔	–	✔	✔	✔			238
U. of Central Arkansas	✔		✔					✔					242
CALIFORNIA													
Azusa Pacific University								✔					113
California Lutheran University	✔	✔	✔	✔	✔			✔	✔				123
California Polytechnic State U., San Luis Obispo	✔		✔	✔		✔	✔	✔		✔	✔		123
California State U., Chico	✔		✔	✔	✔	✔	✔	✔		✔	✔		124
California State U., Dominquez Hills		–						✔					124
California State U., Fullerton	✔					✔	✔	✔		✔	✔		125
California State U., Long Beach	✔		✔	✔	✔	✔		✔					125
California State U., Northridge													126
California State U., Stanislaus	✔			✔					✔		✔		126
Chapman University	✔		✔	✔				✔	✔	✔	✔		131
Claremont Graduate School, The	✔			✔	✔	✔		✔	✔	✔			132
College of Notre Dame	✔			✔	✔	✔	✔	✔	✔				136
Holy Names College		–						✔					161
Humboldt State University	✔			✔	✔	✔	✔		✔				162
La Sierra University	✔		✔	✔	✔		✔	✔	✔				171
Loyola Marymount University	✔	✔	✔	✔		✔	✔	✔		✔			176
Monterey Institute of Int'l. Studies	✔		✔	✔	✔	✔		✔	✔				185
Pepperdine University	✔	✔	✔	✔		✔		✔	–	✔			200
San Francisco State University	✔		✔		✔	✔	✔	✔					217
Santa Clara University	✔	✔	✔		✔	✔		✔	✔	✔			217

	Graduate Assistantships (Research, Teaching, Resident)					Gift Aid (Scholarships, Grants, and Fellowships)				Other Options			
	Available	Tuition Waivers/Reductions	Available for First-Year Students	Awarded Based on MERIT	Awarded Based on NEED	Preference for Minorities	Preference for Women	Tuition/Fee Payment Plan	Aid for Summer Programs	Paid Summer Jobs/Internships	Cooperative Education Program	Loan Forgiveness Program	Page Number
Stanford University		–	–	✔	✔	✔		✔	–	✔		✔	223
United States Int'l. University	✔		✔			✔		✔	✔	✔			234
U. of California, Berkeley	✔	✔	✔	✔			✔	✔	✔		✔		240
U. of California at Davis	✔	✔	✔	✔	✔		✔	✔	✔	✔			240
U. of California, Irvine	✔		✔		✔			✔	✔	✔			241
U. of California, Los Angeles	✔	✔	✔	✔	✔	✔	✔	✔	✔	✔			241
U. of California, Riverside	✔	✔	✔					✔		✔	✔		242
University of La Verne	✔		✔	✔				✔	✔				253
University of the Pacific	✔	✔	✔	✔	✔	✔		✔	✔	✔			268
University of San Diego	✔	✔		✔	✔			✔	✔	✔			272
University of San Francisco	✔	✔	✔			✔		✔		✔			273
University of Southern California		–		✔	✔			✔		✔			275
Woodbury University		–						✔	✔	✔			296
COLORADO													
Colorado State University	✔	✔	✔	✔		✔	✔			✔	✔		138
U. of Colorado at Boulder	✔	✔	✔	✔	✔	✔			✔	✔			245
University of Denver	✔	✔	✔	✔				✔	✔	✔			247
University of Southern Colorado	✔			–	–	–	–	✔					276
CONNECTICUT													
Fairfield University								✔		✔			148
Quinnipiac College	✔	✔	✔					✔					203
University of Bridgeport	✔	✔	✔					✔	✔	✔			239
University of Connecticut	✔	✔	✔	✔		✔		✔	✔	✔	✔		245
Yale University	✔		✔	✔	✔			✔	–	✔		✔	298
DELAWARE													
Goldey-Beacom College	✔	✔			✔			✔	✔	✔	✔		157
University of Delaware	✔	✔	✔	✔	✔	✔		✔		✔	–	–	247
DISTRICT OF COLUMBIA													
American University, The	✔	✔	✔	✔		✔		✔	✔	✔	✔		109
George Washington U., The	✔		✔	✔		✔		✔	✔	✔	✔		154
Georgetown University	✔	✔	✔	✔		✔	✔	✔	–	✔			155
Howard University	✔	✔	✔	✔			✔		✔	✔			161
FLORIDA													
Barry University	✔	✔	✔					✔		✔	✔		115
Embry-Riddle Aeronautical U.	✔	✔	✔				✔	–	✔		✔	–	147
Florida Atlantic University	✔	✔	✔			✔			✔		✔		149
Florida Institute of Technology	✔	✔	✔		–	–	✔		✔		–		150
Florida International University				✔	✔	✔		✔		✔			150
Florida State University	✔	✔	✔	✔	✔	✔			✔	✔			151
Jacksonville University				✔	✔	✔			✔	✔			168
Rollins College	✔	✔	✔	✔				✔		✔			207
Saint Leo College		–							✔	✔	✔		213

✔ Yes
– Not applicable

	Graduate Assistantships (Research, Teaching, Resident)				Gift Aid (Scholarships, Grants, and Fellowships)			Other Options					
	Available	Tuition Waivers/Reductions	Available for First-Year Students	Awarded Based on MERIT	Awarded Based on NEED	Preference for Minorities	Preference for Women	Tuition/Fee Payment Plan	Aid for Summer Programs	Paid Summer Jobs/Internships	Cooperative Education Program	Loan Forgiveness Program	Page Number
Stetson University	✔		✔										225
University of Central Florida	✔	✔	✔			✔			✔	✔	✔		243
University of Florida	✔	✔	✔	✔		✔		–	✔				248
University of Miami	✔	✔	✔	✔		✔	✔		✔				256
University of South Florida	✔	✔	✔	✔		✔				✔			275
GEORGIA													
Albany State College													108
Augusta College	✔	✔	✔	✔	✔	✔	✔		✔	✔		✔	113
Berry College	✔		✔				✔						118
Clark Atlanta University	✔	✔		✔		✔	✔		✔	✔			133
Emory University	✔		✔	✔		✔		✔	✔	✔			148
Georgia College	✔	✔	✔		✔	✔	✔		✔	✔	✔		155
Georgia Institute of Technology	✔	✔	✔			✔	✔		✔	✔			156
Georgia Southern University	✔	✔	✔			✔	✔		✔				156
Georgia State University	✔	✔	✔	✔	✔	✔			✔	✔			157
Southern College of Technology	✔	✔	✔						✔				220
University of Georgia	✔	✔	✔	✔		✔			✔	✔			249
West Georgia College	✔	✔	✔						✔		✔		291
HAWAII													
Chaminade U. of Honolulu			✔				✔	✔	✔				131
University of Hawaii at Manoa	✔	✔		✔					✔	✔	–		249
IDAHO													
Boise State University	✔	✔	✔	✔			✔		✔				119
Idaho State University	✔	✔	✔					✔	✔				162
ILLINOIS													
Bradley University	✔	✔	✔	✔		✔		✔	✔	✔	✔		121
Governors State University	✔	✔	✔	✔		✔		✔	✔	✔			158
Illinois Benedictine College	✔	✔	✔		–				✔				163
Illinois Institute of Technology	✔	✔	✔				✔	✔	✔				163
Illinois State University	✔	✔	✔	✔	✔	✔	✔	✔	✔	✔	✔		164
Lake Forest Graduate School of Management, The	–	–	–	–	–	–	–	✔	✔	–	–	–	172
Lewis University	–	–	–				ı	✔	✔	–	–		174
North Central College		–	✔	✔	–	–	✔	✔	✔		✔		188
North Park College		–	–	✔				✔	✔				189
Northeastern Illinois University	✔	✔	✔	✔				✔	✔	✔			190
Northern Illinois University	✔	✔	✔	✔		✔			✔		✔		192
Northwestern University			✔	✔	✔	✔	✔	✔		✔			194
Rockford College	–	–	–	–	–	–		✔	✔	✔			207
Roosevelt University	✔	✔	✔		✔	✔		✔	–				208
Rosary College	✔	✔	✔		✔			✔	✔				208
Saint Xavier College	✔	✔		–	✔	✔	–	✔		✔	✔	–	215

– 97 –

✔ Yes
– Not applicable

	Available	Tuition Waivers/Reductions	Available for First-Year Students	Awarded Based on MERIT	Awarded Based on NEED	Preference for Minorities	Preference for Women	Tuition/Fee Payment Plan	Aid for Summer Programs	Paid Summer Jobs/Internships	Cooperative Education Program	Loan Forgiveness Program	Page Number
	Graduate Assistantships (Research, Teaching, Resident)			**Gift Aid (Scholarships, Grants, and Fellowships)**				**Other Options**					
Southern Illinois University at Carbondale	✔	✔	✔	✔	✔	✔		✔	✔	✔			221
Southern Illinois University at Edwardsville	✔	✔	✔	✔	✔			✔	✔		✔		221
University of Chicago		–	–	✔				✔	✔	✔			244
University of Illinois at Chicago	✔	✔		✔		✔		✔	✔	✔			250
University of Illinois at Urbana–Champaign	✔	✔	✔	✔		✔		✔	✔	✔			251
INDIANA													
Ball State University	✔	✔	✔	✔	✔		✔	✔		✔	✔		115
Butler University		–	–					✔		✔	✔		122
Indiana State University	✔	✔	✔	✔		✔	✔	✔	✔		✔		164
Indiana University	✔	✔	✔			✔	✔		–	✔			165
Indiana University Northwest	✔	✔	✔					✔	✔	–			165
Indiana University–Purdue University Fort Wayne	✔	✔	✔	–	–	–	–	✔	✔	✔			166
Indiana University South Bend													166
Purdue University	✔	✔		✔		✔		✔	✔				203
Saint Francis College	✔	✔	✔	✔	✔		✔	✔					212
University of Notre Dame			–	✔		✔		–		✔			266
University of Southern Indiana		–	–					✔	✔	✔	✔		276
IOWA													
Iowa State University	✔	✔	✔	✔		✔	✔	✔		✔			168
Maharishi International U.		–	–	✔				–	✔				178
St. Ambrose University		✔	✔					✔	✔	✔	✔		210
University of Iowa, The	✔	✔	✔	✔	✔	✔	✔	✔	✔	✔			251
University of Northern Iowa	✔		✔	✔		✔	✔				✔		266
KANSAS													
Fort Hays State University	✔	✔	✔	✔				–					152
Friends University								✔					153
Kansas State University	✔	✔	✔	✔		✔	✔		✔				169
Pittsburg State University	✔	✔	✔	✔				✔	✔				201
University of Kansas	✔	✔	✔			✔	✔			✔			252
Wichita State University, The	✔	✔	✔		✔	✔		✔					294
KENTUCKY													
Bellarmine College		✔	✔					✔	✔	✔			117
Eastern Kentucky University	✔	✔	✔			✔		✔	✔	✔	✔	✔	145
Morehead State University	✔	✔	✔	✔		✔	✔	✔	✔	✔	✔	✔	185
Murray State University	✔	✔	✔					✔		✔	✔		186
Northern Kentucky University	✔		✔	✔				✔	✔	–			193
University of Kentucky	✔	✔	✔	✔		✔	✔	✔	✔	✔			252

– 98 –

✔ Yes
– Not applicable

	Graduate Assistantships (Research, Teaching, Resident)			Gift Aid (Scholarships, Grants, and Fellowships)					Other Options				
	Available	Tuition Waivers/Reductions	Available for First-Year Students	Awarded Based on MERIT	Awarded Based on NEED	Preference for Minorities	Preference for Women	Tuition/Fee Payment Plan	Aid for Summer Programs	Paid Summer Jobs/Internships	Cooperative Education Program	Loan Forgiveness Program	Page Number
LOUISIANA													
Louisiana Tech University	✔		✔				✔	✔					175
Loyola University	✔	✔	✔				✔		✔				176
Nicholls State University	✔	✔	✔					✔			–		188
Northeast Louisiana University	✔	✔	✔										189
Southeastern Louisiana University	✔	✔	✔				✔	✔	✔				220
Tulane University	✔			✔		✔	✔		✔	✔			232
U. of Southwestern Louisiana	✔	✔	✔						✔				278
MAINE													
Thomas College								✔					231
University of Maine	✔	✔	✔			–	–	✔	✔		–		253
University of Southern Maine	✔		✔		✔			✔	✔				277
MARYLAND													
Loyola College in Maryland	✔	✔	✔		✔			✔	✔				175
Mount Saint Mary's College	✔	✔	✔					✔	✔				186
Salisbury State University	✔	✔	✔		✔		✔	✔	✔				216
University of Baltimore	✔	✔	✔	✔		✔		✔	✔	✔	–		238
University of Maryland	✔	✔	✔	✔		✔		✔		✔	✔		254
MASSACHUSETTS													
Anna Maria College		–						✔	✔		–		109
Assumption College		–	–										112
Babson Grad. School of Business	✔	–	✔	✔		✔		✔	✔	✔			114
Bentley College	✔	✔	✔	✔	✔	✔	✔	✔	✔	✔	✔	✔	118
Boston College	✔	✔	✔	✔		✔			✔	✔			120
Boston University	✔		✔	✔	✔	✔	✔	✔	✔				120
Clark University	✔	✔	✔	✔		✔	✔	✔	✔				134
Massachusetts Institute of Technology	✔	✔	✔		✔			✔	–	✔	–		181
Northeastern University (Grad. School of Business)	✔	✔	✔	✔	✔	✔		✔		✔			191
Northeastern University (Grad. School of Prof. Acctg.)	✔	✔	✔	✔	✔	✔		✔		✔	✔		191
Salem State College	✔	✔	✔	✔	✔			✔	✔	✔			215
Simmons College			✔	✔	✔	✔	✔	✔	✔				219
Suffolk University	✔	✔	✔	✔	✔	✔	✔	✔	✔	✔			226
U. of Massachusetts, Amherst	✔	✔	✔	✔	✔	✔		–	✔				255
U. of Massachusetts Boston	✔	✔	✔						✔		–		255
U. of Massachusetts Dartmouth	✔	✔	✔					✔					256
Western New England College		–		–	–	–	–	✔					293
Worcester Polytechnic Institute	✔							✔		–	✔		297
MICHIGAN													
Central Michigan University	✔	✔	✔	✔	✔	✔		✔					130

✔ Yes
– Not applicable

	Graduate Assistantships (Research, Teaching, Resident)			Gift Aid (Scholarships, Grants, and Fellowships)				Other Options					
	Available	Tuition Waivers/Reductions	Available for First-Year Students	Awarded Based on MERIT	Awarded Based on NEED	Preference for Minorities	Preference for Women	Tuition/Fee Payment Plan	Aid for Summer Programs	Paid Summer Jobs/Internships	Cooperative Education Program	Loan Forgiveness Program	Page Number
Eastern Michigan University	✔	✔	✔	✔	✔	✔			✔	✔			145
Grand Valley State University	✔	✔	✔					✔	✔				159
Lake Superior State University		–	–					✔	✔	✔			172
Lawrence Technological U.		–						✔	✔	✔			173
Madonna University								✔					177
Michigan State University	✔	✔	✔	✔	✔	✔	✔	✔	–	✔			183
Michigan Technological U.	✔	✔	✔					✔		✔	✔		183
Oakland University	✔	✔	✔	✔		✔			✔	✔			194
University of Detroit Mercy	✔	✔	✔	✔	✔	✔	✔	✔	✔	✔			248
University of Michigan		–	–			✔	✔	✔	✔	✔	–		257
University of Michigan–Dearborn		–	–			✔	✔	✔	✔	✔	✔	✔	257
Wayne State University	✔	✔	✔	✔		✔	✔		✔	✔	✔		290
MINNESOTA													
St. Cloud State University	✔	✔	✔										211
University of Minnesota	✔	✔	✔	✔		✔			✔				258
MISSISSIPPI													
Millsaps College	✔	✔	✔	✔	✔	✔		✔	✔	✔			184
University of Mississippi	✔	✔	✔	✔		✔		✔	✔				258
U. of Southern Mississippi, The	✔	✔						✔	✔				277
William Carey College	✔	✔	✔	✔									296
MISSOURI													
Central Missouri State University	✔	✔	✔	✔	✔	✔	✔	✔	✔	✔			130
Drury College								✔					141
Northeast Missouri State U.	✔	✔	✔										190
Northwest Missouri State U.	✔	✔	✔	✔	✔			✔		–	–	–	193
Saint Louis University	✔	✔	✔					✔		✔	✔		214
U. of Missouri–Columbia	✔	✔	✔	✔	✔	✔	✔	✔	✔	✔			259
U. of Missouri–Kansas City	✔	✔		✔	✔		✔		✔				259
U. of Missouri–St. Louis	✔	✔	✔	✔		✔	✔	✔	✔	✔	✔		260
Washington University	✔		✔	✔	✔	✔			✔				289
MONTANA													
University of Montana	✔	✔		✔		✔		✔		✔	✔		260
NEBRASKA													
University of Nebraska at Kearney	✔	✔	✔										261
University of Nebraska–Lincoln		–		✔	✔	✔	✔		✔	✔			261
University of Nebraska at Omaha	✔	✔	✔			✔	✔		✔	–			262
NEVADA													
University of Nevada, Las Vegas	✔	✔	✔	✔				✔	✔				262
NEW HAMPSHIRE													
Dartmouth College		–	–	✔	✔			–	✔				140
Plymouth State College	✔	✔	✔										201
University of New Hampshire	✔	✔	✔	✔		✔		✔	✔	✔			263

Yes ✔
Not applicable −

	Graduate Assistantships (Research, Teaching, Resident)			Gift Aid (Scholarships, Grants, and Fellowships)				Other Options					
	Available	Tuition Waivers/Reductions	Available for First-Year Students	Awarded Based on MERIT	Awarded Based on NEED	Preference for Minorities	Preference for Women	Tuition/Fee Payment Plan	Aid for Summer Programs	Paid Summer Jobs/Internships	Cooperative Education Program	Loan Forgiveness Program	Page Number
NEW JERSEY													
Fairleigh Dickinson University	✔	✔	✔	✔		−		✔					149
Montclair State University	✔	✔	✔					✔	✔	✔			184
Rider University	✔	✔						✔					206
Rowan College of New Jersey	✔	✔	✔					✔					209
Rutgers, The State University of New Jersey	✔	−	✔	✔	✔	✔		✔	✔	✔			209
Seton Hall University	✔	✔	✔		✔	✔		✔	✔	✔	✔		218
NEW MEXICO													
College of Santa Fe, The	✔	−	✔				✔	✔			✔		137
Eastern New Mexico University	✔	✔	✔	✔		✔	✔	✔					146
New Mexico State University	✔	✔	✔		✔	✔	✔	✔	✔	✔	✔	✔	187
NEW YORK													
Adelphi University	✔	✔	✔				✔		−				107
Baruch College	✔		✔					✔					116
Canisius College													128
Clarkson University	✔	✔	✔	✔		✔		✔					134
College of Insurance, The	✔	✔	✔	✔	✔	✔		✔	✔	✔			136
College of Saint Rose, The	✔	✔	✔					✔	✔				137
Columbia University				✔	✔	✔		✔					139
Cornell University				✔		✔	✔	✔		✔			139
Dowling College	✔	✔	✔	✔	✔			✔	✔	✔	✔		140
Fordham University	✔	✔	✔	✔		✔	✔	✔	✔	✔			151
Hofstra University	✔	✔	✔	✔	✔		✔	✔	✔				160
Iona College	✔	✔	✔			✔		✔	✔				167
Manhattan College		−		✔			✔		✔				178
Marist College	✔			✔				✔	✔			−	179
Mercy College	✔	✔	✔				✔	✔	✔				182
New York University	✔	✔			✔	✔		✔					187
Pace University	✔	✔	✔	✔	✔	✔	✔	✔	✔	✔	✔		198
Rensselaer Polytechnic Institute	✔	✔	✔	✔	✔	✔	✔			✔	✔		205
Rochester Institute of Technology	✔	✔	✔	✔	✔	✔		✔	✔	✔	✔	−	206
Sage Graduate School	✔	✔	✔	✔			✔	✔	✔				210
St. Bonaventure University	✔	✔	✔	−	−	−	−	✔	✔				211
St. John's University	✔	✔	✔	✔				✔	✔	✔			212
State University of New York at Binghamton	✔	✔	✔	✔	✔	✔		✔		✔			224
State University of New York at Oswego	✔	✔		✔		✔		✔	✔				224
Syracuse University	✔	✔	✔	✔		✔		✔	✔				226
Union College	✔	✔	✔	✔		✔		−	✔	✔			233

✔ Yes
– Not applicable

	Graduate Assistantships (Research, Teaching, Resident)			Gift Aid (Scholarships, Grants, and Fellowships)				Other Options					
	Available	Tuition Waivers/Reductions	Available for First-Year Students	Awarded Based on MERIT	Awarded Based on NEED	Preference for Minorities	Preference for Women	Tuition/Fee Payment Plan	Aid for Summer Programs	Paid Summer Jobs/Internships	Cooperative Education Program	Loan Forgiveness Program	Page Number
University at Albany– State University of New York	✔	✔	✔	✔	✔	✔		✔	✔	✔		✔	236
University at Buffalo, State University of New York	✔	✔	✔	✔		✔			✔				239
University of Rochester	✔		✔	✔		✔	✔	✔	✔	✔			271
NORTH CAROLINA													
Appalachian State University	✔	✔	✔	✔		✔		✔	✔				110
Campbell University		–	–					✔					127
Duke University			✔		✔			✔	–	✔			142
East Carolina University	✔		✔					✔			✔		143
Elon College		–		✔				✔	✔	✔			147
University of North Carolina at Chapel Hill			✔		✔				✔				263
University of North Carolina at Charlotte, The	✔	✔	✔					✔	✔	✔			264
University of North Carolina at Greensboro, The	✔	✔	✔	✔		–	–	✔	✔				264
University of North Carolina– Wilmington	✔		✔	✔			✔		✔				265
Wake Forest University			✔	✔	✔	✔	✔	✔	–	✔			288
Western Carolina University	✔	✔	✔	✔		–	–	✔	✔				292
NORTH DAKOTA													
University of North Dakota	✔	✔	✔	✔	–	✔		✔				–	265
OHIO													
Ashland University	✔	✔						✔					111
Baldwin-Wallace College		–	–	–	–	–	–	✔	✔				114
Bowling Green State University	✔	✔	✔	✔		✔		✔	✔	✔	✔		121
Capital University								✔					128
Case Western Reserve University	✔	✔	✔	✔		✔			✔				129
Cleveland State University	✔	✔	✔					✔	✔	✔	✔		135
John Carroll University	✔	✔	✔	–	–	–	–	✔		–	–	–	169
Kent State University	✔	✔	✔	✔		✔		✔	✔				170
Miami University	✔	✔	✔			✔		✔					182
Ohio State University, The	✔	✔	✔	✔		✔		✔		✔			195
Ohio University													195
Tiffin University		–	–					✔	✔	✔			231
University of Akron, The	✔	✔	✔	✔	✔	✔	✔	✔					234
University of Cincinnati	✔	✔	✔	✔		✔		✔	✔				244
University of Dayton	✔	✔	✔	✔				✔	✔				246
Wright State University	✔	✔	✔	✔		✔		✔	✔	–	–		297
Xavier University	✔	✔	✔	✔	✔			✔	✔				298
Youngstown State University	✔	✔	✔	✔				✔	✔	✔	✔		299

Yes: ✔
Not applicable: –

	Graduate Assistantships (Research, Teaching, Resident)			Gift Aid (Scholarships, Grants, and Fellowships)				Other Options					
	Available	Tuition Waivers/Reductions	Available for First-Year Students	Awarded Based on MERIT	Awarded Based on NEED	Preference for Minorities	Preference for Women	Tuition/Fee Payment Plan	Aid for Summer Programs	Paid Summer Jobs/Internships	Cooperative Education Program	Loan Forgiveness Program	Page Number
OKLAHOMA													
Oklahoma State University	✔	✔	✔	✔		✔		✔	–	✔			196
Oral Roberts University	✔		✔	✔		✔		✔		✔			197
University of Central Oklahoma	✔	✔	✔	✔	✔	✔	✔	✔	✔	✔		✔	243
University of Oklahoma	✔	✔	✔	✔		✔		✔	✔				267
University of Tulsa, The	✔	✔	✔	✔		✔		✔	✔	✔			281
OREGON													
Oregon State University	✔	✔	✔	✔	✔	✔	✔	✔		✔			197
Portland State University	✔	✔	✔					✔	✔	✔			202
Southern Oregon State College	✔	✔	✔	✔	✔			✔	✔				222
University of Oregon	✔	✔		✔	✔	✔		✔		✔			267
University of Portland								✔	✔	✔	✔		269
Willamette University	✔		✔	✔		✔		✔		✔			295
PENNSYLVANIA													
Bloomsburg University	✔	✔	✔					✔	✔	✔			119
California University of Pennsylvania	✔	✔	✔					✔		✔			127
Carnegie Mellon University	✔	✔		✔	✔	✔	✔	✔	✔	✔			129
Clarion U. of Pennsylvania	✔	✔	✔			✔		✔					133
Drexel University	✔	✔	✔	✔				✔	✔		✔		141
Duquesne University	✔	✔	✔					✔	✔				142
Eastern College	✔	✔	✔	✔	✔	✔		✔	✔		✔		144
Gannon University	✔	✔	✔		✔				✔	✔			153
Indiana U. of Pennsylvania	✔	✔	✔	✔		✔		✔	✔	✔			167
Kutztown University	✔	✔	✔					✔	✔	✔			170
La Salle University	✔	✔	✔	✔	✔	✔		✔	✔	✔			171
Lehigh University	✔	✔	✔	✔		✔		✔	✔	✔			174
Marywood College			✔		–	–		✔	✔	✔	✔		181
Penn State	✔	✔	✔	✔		✔		✔	✔	✔			198
Penn State Erie		–	✔		✔			✔	✔				199
Penn State Harrisburg	✔	✔	✔	✔		✔	✔	✔					199
Philadelphia College of Textiles and Science	✔	✔	✔	✔				✔			✔		200
Point Park College	✔	✔	✔	✔	✔			✔	✔	✔			202
Saint Joseph's University	✔	✔	✔					✔					213
Temple University	✔	✔	✔			✔	✔	✔	✔	✔	✔		227
University of Pittsburgh				✔	✔	✔	✔	✔	✔	✔			268
University of Scranton	✔	✔	✔					✔					273
Waynesburg College								✔	✔				290
Wharton School, The (University of Pennsylvania)	✔		✔	✔	✔	✔	✔	✔		✔			294
Widener University	✔	✔						✔	✔				295

✔ Yes
– Not applicable

	Graduate Assistantships (Research, Teaching, Resident)			Gift Aid (Scholarships, Grants, and Fellowships)				Other Options					
	Available	Tuition Waivers/Reductions	Available for First-Year Students	Awarded Based on MERIT	Awarded Based on NEED	Preference for Minorities	Preference for Women	Tuition/Fee Payment Plan	Aid for Summer Programs	Paid Summer Jobs/Internships	Cooperative Education Program	Loan Forgiveness Program	Page Number
RHODE ISLAND													
University of Rhode Island	✔	✔	✔		✔			✔	✔	✔	✔	✔	270
SOUTH CAROLINA													
Clemson University	✔	✔	✔	✔		✔		✔	✔				135
Francis Marion University	✔		✔			✔		✔					152
University of South Carolina	✔	✔	✔	✔		✔		✔	✔				274
SOUTH DAKOTA													
University of South Dakota	✔	✔	✔					✔	✔				274
TENNESSEE													
Belmont University	✔	✔	✔					✔	✔	✔	–		117
Christian Brothers University	–	–						✔		✔			132
East Tennessee State University	✔	✔	✔	✔		✔			✔				143
Tennessee State University	✔	✔	✔										227
Tennessee Technological U.	✔	✔	✔		✔				✔	✔	–		228
Union University	✔	✔	✔				✔	✔	✔	✔			233
University of Tennessee at Chattanooga, The	✔	✔	✔	✔	✔	✔	✔	✔	✔	✔		✔	278
U. of Tennessee, Knoxville	✔	✔	✔	✔	✔	✔	✔	✔	✔				279
U. of Tennessee at Martin, The	✔		✔		✔			✔		✔			279
Vanderbilt University	–		✔	✔	✔			–	✔				287
TEXAS													
Abilene Christian University	✔	✔	✔	✔	✔			✔		✔			107
Baylor University	✔	✔	✔					✔	✔				116
East Texas State U. at Texarkana		–		✔	✔	✔	✔	✔	✔				144
Lamar University	✔	✔	✔	✔	✔			✔	✔	✔			173
Rice University		–	✔		✔			✔	✔	✔			205
Sam Houston State University	✔	✔	✔					✔					216
Southern Methodist University	✔	✔	✔	✔	–			✔	✔				222
Southwest Texas State University		–	–	✔	✔	✔		✔	✔				223
Stephen F. Austin State U.	✔							✔	✔				225
Texas A & M University	✔	✔	✔	✔		✔		✔	✔	✔	✔	–	228
Texas A & M University–Corpus Christi	✔		✔	✔	✔			✔	✔				229
Texas Christian University	✔	✔	✔	✔		✔	✔	✔	✔				229
Texas Southern University	✔	✔	✔					✔	✔				230
Texas Tech University	✔	✔	✔	✔	✔	✔	✔	✔	✔				230
University of Dallas	✔	✔						✔	✔	✔	✔		246
University of Houston	✔	✔	✔	✔		✔			✔	✔			250
U. of Mary Hardin-Baylor								✔					254
University of St. Thomas	✔	✔			✔			✔	✔				272
U. of Texas at Arlington, The	✔	✔	✔	✔				✔	✔	✔	✔		280
University of Texas at Austin, The	✔	✔	✔	✔	✔	✔		✔	✔	✔			280

✔ Yes
– Not applicable

	Graduate Assistantships (Research, Teaching, Resident)							Gift Aid (Scholarships, Grants, and Fellowships)		Other Options			
	Available	Tuition Waivers/Reductions	Available for First-Year Students	Awarded Based on MERIT	Awarded Based on NEED	Preference for Minorities	Preference for Women	Tuition/Fee Payment Plan	Aid for Summer Programs	Paid Summer Jobs/Internships	Cooperative Education Program	Loan Forgiveness Program	Page Number
University of Texas at Tyler, The			✔	✔	✔	✔	✔		✔	✔			281
West Texas A & M University	✔	✔	✔	✔	✔	✔	✔	✔	✔	✔	✔		291
UTAH													
Brigham Young University	✔		✔	✔	✔	✔	–	✔	✔	–			122
University of Utah	✔	✔	✔	✔	✔	✔	✔						282
Utah State University	✔	✔	✔	✔	✔	✔	✔		✔	✔			286
VIRGINIA													
College of William & Mary	✔	✔	✔	✔	✔	✔	✔		✔				138
George Mason University	✔	✔	✔	✔		✔		✔	✔	✔	–	–	154
Hampton University	✔	✔	✔		✔			✔		✔			160
Lynchburg College in Virginia								✔					177
Marymount University	✔	✔	✔					✔	✔				180
Old Dominion University	✔	✔	✔	✔		✔		✔	✔	✔			196
Radford University	✔		✔	✔				✔	✔				204
Regent University		–	✔	✔	✔	–		✔	✔	–	✔		204
Shenandoah University	✔	✔	✔	✔				✔	✔	✔			219
University of Richmond	✔		✔					✔					271
University of Virginia			✔	✔	✔	✔	✔		✔				282
Virginia Commonwealth U.	✔	✔	✔			✔	✔	✔					287
Virginia Polytechnic Institute and State University	✔		✔	✔		✔		✔		✔	✔		288
WASHINGTON													
Eastern Washington University	✔	✔	✔	✔		✔			✔				146
Gonzaga University	✔	✔	✔	–	✔			✔	✔				158
Saint Martin's College								✔					214
Seattle University	✔		✔		✔	✔		✔	✔	✔		✔	218
University of Washington	✔	✔	✔	✔	✔	✔			✔				283
Washington State University	✔	✔	✔			✔			✔		–	–	289
Western Washington University	✔	✔	✔	✔									
WEST VIRGINIA													
Marshall University	✔	✔	✔	✔		✔		✔	✔				180
West Virginia University	✔	✔	✔	✔		✔		✔			–		292
WISCONSIN													
Marquette University	✔	✔	✔	✔		✔	✔	✔	✔	✔			179
U. of Wisconsin–Eau Claire	✔		✔				✔	✔					283
U. of Wisconsin–Madison	✔	✔	✔	✔		✔	✔		✔	✔			284
U. of Wisconsin–Milwaukee													284
U. of Wisconsin–Oshkosh	✔	✔	✔			✔	✔						285
U. of Wisconsin–Whitewater	✔	✔	✔			✔		✔	✔				285
WYOMING													
University of Wyoming	✔	✔	✔			✔	✔	✔	✔				286

	Graduate Assistantships (Research, Teaching, Resident)			Gift Aid (Scholarships, Grants, and Fellowships)				Other Options					
	Available	Tuition Waivers/Reductions	Available for First-Year Students	Awarded Based on MERIT	Awarded Based on NEED	Preference for Minorities	Preference for Women	Tuition/Fee Payment Plan	Aid for Summer Programs	Paid Summer Jobs/Internships	Cooperative Education Program	Loan Forgiveness Program	Page Number
PUERTO RICO													
University of Puerto Rico	✔	✔	✔	✔	✔			✔	✔	✔			269
University of Puerto Rico, Mayaguez Campus	✔	✔	✔					✔	✔	✔			270

ABILENE CHRISTIAN UNIVERSITY
College of Business Administration

Abilene, Texas 79699
Telephone: 800-888-0228
915-674-2593

Total Enrollment (1993-94)	Full-Time	Part-Time
	13	24

Cost of Attendance (1993-94)		
Academic Year		
Standard Course Load per Semester/Term		
(credit hours/units)	12	6
Semesters/Terms per Academic Year	2	
Tuition and Fees	$5,736	$2,868
Living Expenses	$4,810	$4,610
Summer Term		
(R = Required, O = Optional, N = None)	R	O
Standard Course Load	6	3
Tuition and Fees	$1,434	$ 717

Financial Aid Available	Deadline (fall starts)	Awarded to Full-Time	Part-Time
Gift Aid	Rolling	Yes	Yes
Federal College Work-Study	Rolling	Yes	Yes
Federal Perkins Loans	Rolling	Yes	Yes
Federal Stafford Loans	Rolling	Yes	Yes
School-Based Loans	NA	No	No
Outside and Private Loans	NA	No	No
Graduate Assistantships	Rolling	Yes	No

Percentage of Students Receiving Aid	Full-Time	Part-Time
All students	92%	32%

ADELPHI UNIVERSITY
Schools of Business

South Avenue
Garden City, New York 11530
Telephone: 516-877-4669

Total Enrollment (1993-94)	Full-Time	Part-Time
	90	815

Cost of Attendance (1993-94)		
Academic Year		
Standard Course Load per Semester/Term		
(credit hours/units)	12	6
Semesters/Terms per Academic Year	2	2
Tuition and Fees	$6,250	$375/cr.; $150 fee
Living Expenses	$5,500	NA
Summer Term		
(R = Required, O = Optional, N = None)	O	O
Standard Course Load	12	6-12
Tuition and Fees	$4,500	$375/cr.; $ 75 fee

Financial Aid Available	Deadline (fall starts)	Awarded to Full-Time	Part-Time
Gift Aid	NA	No	No
Federal College Work-Study	NA	No	No
Federal Perkins Loans	May	Yes	Yes (6+ credits)
Federal Stafford Loans	May	Yes	Yes (6+ credits)
School-Based Loans	NA	No	No
Outside and Private Loans	NA	No	No
Graduate Assistantships	May	Yes	No

ALBANY STATE COLLEGE
MBA Program

504 College Drive
Albany, Georgia 31705
Telephone: 912-430-4770

Total Enrollment (1993-94)	Full-Time	Part-Time
	30	30

Cost of Attendance (1993-94)		
Academic Year		
Standard Course Load per Semester/Term		
(credit hours/units)	10	5
Semesters/Terms per Academic Year	3	3
Tuition and Fees		
Resident	$ 500	$193
Nonresident	$1,250	$560
Living Expenses	NA	NA
Summer Term		
(R = Required, O = Optional, N = None)	O	O
Standard Course Load	10	5
Tuition and Fees		
Resident	$ 500	$193
Nonresident	$1,250	$560

Financial Aid Available	Deadline (fall starts)	Awarded to Full-Time	Part-Time
Gift Aid	NA	No	No
Federal College Work-Study	NA	No	No
Federal Perkins Loans	NA	No	No
Federal Stafford Loans	NA	No	No
School-Based Loans	NA	No	No
Outside and Private Loans	NA	No	No
Graduate Assistantships	NA	No	No

Percentage of Students Receiving Aid	Full-Time	Part-Time
All students	0%	0%

THE AMERICAN GRADUATE SCHOOL OF INTERNATIONAL MANAGEMENT

15249 North 59th Avenue
Glendale, Arizona 85306-6000
Telephone: 602-978-7130

Total Enrollment (1993-94)	Full-Time
	1,415

Cost of Attendance (1993-94)	
Academic Year	
Standard Course Load per Semester/Term	
(credit hours/units)	12-15
Semesters/Terms per Academic Year	2
Tuition and Fees	$15,800
Living Expenses	$ 8,300
Summer Term	
(R = Required, O = Optional, N = None)	O
Standard Course Load	9-12
Tuition and Fees	$ 5,790

Financial Aid Available	Deadline (fall starts)	Awarded to Full-Time
Gift Aid	March 1	Yes
Federal College Work-Study	April 1	Yes
Federal Perkins Loans	April 1	Yes
Federal Stafford Loans	April 1	Yes
School-Based Loans	NA	No
Outside and Private Loans	April 1	Yes
Graduate Assistantships	April 1	Yes

Percentage of Students Receiving Aid	Full-Time
All students	70%
Minority students	25%
Women students	29%
International students	2%

THE AMERICAN UNIVERSITY
Kogod College of Business Administration

4400 Massachusetts Avenue, N.W.
Washington, D.C. 20016
Telephone: 202-885-1913
       800-ANAUMBA

Total Enrollment (1993-94)	Full-Time	Part-Time
	293	250

Cost of Attendance (1993-94)		
Academic Year		
Standard Course Load per Semester/Term		
(credit hours/units)	12-15	6
Semesters/Terms per Academic Year	3	3
Tuition and Fees	$534	$534
Living Expenses	Information not available	
Summer Term		
(R = Required, O = Optional, N = None)	O	O
Standard Course Load	6	6 (average)
Tuition and Fees	$534	$534

Financial Aid Available	Deadline (fall starts)	Awarded to Full-Time	Awarded to Part-Time
Gift Aid	February 1	Yes	No
Federal College Work-Study		No	No
Federal Perkins Loans	March 1	Yes	No
Federal Stafford Loans	March 1	Yes	No
School-Based Loans		No	No
Outside and Private Loans		No	No
Graduate Assistantships	April 1	Yes	No

Percentage of Students Receiving Aid	Full-Time	Part-Time
All students	20%	

ANNA MARIA COLLEGE
Graduate Business Programs

Sunset Lane
Paxton, Massachusetts 01612-1198
Telephone: 508-849-3347
       508-849-3348

Total Enrollment (1993-94)	Full-Time	Part-Time
	120	130

Cost of Attendance (1993-94)		
Academic Year		
Standard Course Load per Semester/Term		
(credit hours/units)	6	6
Semesters/Terms per Academic Year	5	5
Tuition and Fees	$5,940	$5,940
Living Expenses	$ 600	$ 600
Summer Term		
(R = Required, O = Optional, N = None)	O	O
Standard Course Load	2-6	2-6
Tuition and Fees	$ 579	$ 30

Financial Aid Available	Deadline (fall starts)	Awarded to Full-Time	Awarded to Part-Time
Gift Aid	NA		
Federal College Work-Study	NA		
Federal Perkins Loans	NA		
Federal Stafford Loans		Yes	Yes
School-Based Loans	NA		
Outside and Private Loans		Yes	Yes
Graduate Assistantships	NA		

Percentage of Students Receiving Aid	Full-Time	Part-Time
All students	10%	10%
Minority students	10%	10%
Women students	10%	10%
International students	10%	10%

APPALACHIAN STATE UNIVERSITY
John A. Walker College of Business

Thelma C. Raley Hall
Boone, North Carolina 28608
Telephone: 704-262-2922

Total Enrollment (1993-94)	Full-Time	Part-Time
	64	48

Cost of Attendance (1993-94)		
Academic Year		
Standard Course Load per Semester/Term		
(credit hours/units)	9	<9
Semesters/Terms per Academic Year	2	2
Tuition and Fees		
Resident	$ 744	$ 289 (3-5 hrs.)
		$ 486 (6-8 hrs.)
Nonresident	$3,777	$1,806 (3-5 hrs.)
		$2,760 (6-8 hrs.)
Living Expenses	$3,000	
Summer Term		
(R = Required, O = Optional, N = None)	R	
Standard Course Load	6	
Tuition and Fees		
Resident	$ 486	
Nonresident	$2,760	

Financial Aid Available	Deadline (fall starts)	Awarded to Full-Time	Part-Time
Gift Aid	Rolling	Yes	NA
Federal College Work-Study	NA	No	No
Federal Perkins Loans	NA	No	No
Federal Stafford Loans	Rolling	Yes	
School-Based Loans	NA	No	No
Outside and Private Loans	NA	No	No
Graduate Assistantships	May 31	Yes	NA

Percentage of Students Receiving Aid	Full-Time	Part-Time
All students	50%	
Minority students	100%	
Women students	50%	
International students	75%	

ARIZONA STATE UNIVERSITY
College of Business Administration

MBA Program
Box 874906
Tempe, Arizona 85287-4906
Telephone: 602-965-3332

Total Enrollment (1993-94)	Full-Time	Part-Time
	127	90

Cost of Attendance (1993-94)		
Academic Year		
Standard Course Load per Semester/Term		
(credit hours/units)	12	6
Semesters/Terms per Academic Year	3	3
Tuition and Fees		
Resident	$1,778	$ 5,196
Nonresident	$7,284	$10,702
Living Expenses	$5,000	NA
Summer Term		
(R = Required, O = Optional, N = None)	O	O
Standard Course Load	6-12	6
Tuition and Fees		
Resident	$93/cr. hr.	Varies
Nonresident	$93	Varies

Financial Aid Available	Deadline (fall starts)	Awarded to Full-Time	Part-Time
Gift Aid	NA		
Federal College Work-Study	Rolling	Yes	Yes
Federal Perkins Loans	Rolling	Yes	No
Federal Stafford Loans	Rolling	Yes	Yes
School-Based Loans	NA	No	No
Outside and Private Loans	Rolling		Yes
Graduate Assistantships	Rolling	Yes	No

Percentage of Students Receiving Aid	Full-Time	Part-Time
All students	75%	10%
Minority students	95%	100%
Women students	80%	0%
International students	90%	0%

ARIZONA STATE UNIVERSITY WEST
Business Programs

4701 West Thunderbird Road
P.O. Box 37100
Phoenix, Arizona 85069-7100
Telephone: 602-543-6239

Total Enrollment (1993-94)	Full-Time	Part-Time
	25	225

Cost of Attendance (1993-94)		
Academic Year		
Standard Course Load per Semester/Term		
(credit hours/units)	9	5
Semesters/Terms per Academic Year	2	2
Tuition and Fees		
Resident	$ 889	$ 562
Nonresident	$3,642	$2,070
Living Expenses	$7,760	$7,410
Summer Term		
(R = Required, O = Optional, N = None)	O	O
Standard Course Load	9	5
Tuition and Fees	$93/cr.hr.	$93/cr.hr.

Financial Aid Available	Deadline (fall starts)	Awarded to Full-Time	Awarded to Part-Time
Gift Aid	March 1	Yes	Yes
Federal College Work-Study	March 1	Yes	Yes
Federal Perkins Loans	March 1	Yes	No
Federal Stafford Loans	March 1	Yes	Yes
School-Based Loans	NA	Yes	Yes
Outside and Private Loans	NA	NA	NA
Graduate Assistantships	NA	Yes	Yes

Percentage of Students Receiving Aid	Full-Time	Part-Time
All students	2%	50%

ASHLAND UNIVERSITY

401 College Avenue
Ashland, Ohio 44805
Telephone: 419-289-5214

Total Enrollment (1993-94)	Full-Time	Part-Time
	50	475

Cost of Attendance (1993-94)		
Academic Year		
Standard Course Load per Semester/Term		
(credit hours/units)	9	3-6
Semesters/Terms per Academic Year	3	3
Tuition and Fees	$ 255	$ 255
Living Expenses	$7,000	
Summer Term		
(R = Required, O = Optional, N = None)	O	O
Standard Course Load	9	3-6
Tuition and Fees	$ 255	$ 255

Financial Aid Available	Deadline (fall starts)	Awarded to Full-Time	Awarded to Part-Time
Gift Aid	None	Yes	No
Federal College Work-Study	NA	No	No
Federal Perkins Loans	NA	No	No
Federal Stafford Loans	None	Yes	Yes
School-Based Loans	NA	No	No
Outside and Private Loans	NA	No	No
Graduate Assistantships	None	Yes	No

Percentage of Students Receiving Aid	Full-Time	Part-Time
All students	3%	3%

ASSUMPTION COLLEGE

500 Salisbury Street
P.O. Box 15005
Worcester, Massachusetts 01615-0005
Telephone: 508-752-5615

Total Enrollment (1993-94)	Full-Time	Part-Time
	3	111

Cost of Attendance (1993-94)		
Academic Year		
Standard Course Load per Semester/Term		
(credit hours/units)	9	6
Semesters/Terms per Academic Year	2	2
Tuition and Fees		
Resident	$9,540	$3,180
Nonresident		
Living Expenses	NA	NA
Summer Term		
(R = Required, O = Optional, N = None)	O	O
Standard Course Load		

Financial Aid Available	Deadline (fall starts)	Awarded to Full-Time	Part-Time
Gift Aid	NA	No	No
Federal College Work-Study	NA	No	No
Federal Perkins Loans	July 1	Yes	Yes
Federal Stafford Loans	July 1	Yes	Yes
School-Based Loans	NA	No	No
Outside and Private Loans	NA	No	No
Graduate Assistantships	NA	No	No

AUBURN UNIVERSITY
College of Business, Graduate Programs

415 West Magnolia Avenue, Suite 563
Auburn, Alabama 36849
Telephone: 205-844-4060

Total Enrollment (1993-94)	Full-Time	Part-Time
	147	109

Cost of Attendance (1993-94)		
Academic Year		
Standard Course Load per Semester/Term		
(credit hours/units)	10-15	5-9
Semesters/Terms per Academic Year	4	4
Tuition and Fees		
Resident	$ 650	$ 110
Nonresident	$1,950	$ 330
Living Expenses (room & board only)	$1,260	$1,260
Summer Term		
(R = Required, O = Optional, N = None)	O	O
Standard Course Load	10-15	5-9
Tuition and Fees		
Resident	$ 650	$ 110
Nonresident	$1,950	$ 330

Financial Aid Available	Deadline (fall starts)	Awarded to Full-Time	Part-Time
Gift Aid	NA	No	NA
Federal College Work-Study	NA	No	No
Federal Perkins Loans	April 15	Yes	NA
Federal Stafford Loans	Rolling	Yes	NA
School-Based Loans	None	Yes	NA
Outside and Private Loans	NA	NA	NA
Graduate Assistantships	Rolling	Yes	No

Percentage of Students Receiving Aid	Full-Time	Part-Time
All students	20%	
Minority students	20%	
Women students	20%	
International students	20%	

AUGUSTA COLLEGE

2500 Walton Way
Augusta, Georgia 30904-2200
Telephone: 706-737-1565

Total Enrollment (1993-94)	Full-Time	Part-Time
	80	75

Cost of Attendance (1993-94)

Academic Year		
Standard Course Load per Semester/Term		
(credit hours/units)	10 hrs.	5 hrs.
Semesters/Terms per Academic Year	4	4
Tuition and Fees		
Resident	$ 455	$ 263
Nonresident	$1,225	$ 464
Living Expenses	$9,486	$9,242
Summer Term		
(R = Required, O = Optional, N = None)	O	O
Standard Course Load	2	1
Tuition and Fees	$ 455	$ 263
Resident	$1,225	$ 464
Nonresident		

Financial Aid Available

	Deadline (fall starts)	Awarded to Full-Time	Part-Time
Gift Aid	NA	Yes	Yes
Federal College Work-Study	NA	Yes	Yes
Federal Perkins Loans	NA	Yes	Yes
Federal Stafford Loans	NA	Yes	Yes
School-Based Loans	NA	Yes	Yes
Outside and Private Loans	NA	Yes	Yes
Graduate Assistantships	NA	Yes	Yes

AZUSA PACIFIC UNIVERSITY
School of Business & Management

901 East Alosta, Box 7000
Azusa, California 91702
Telephone: 818-812-3037

Total Enrollment (1993-94)	Full-Time	Part-Time
	37	70

Cost of Attendance (1993-94)

Academic Year		
Standard Course Load per Semester/Term	12	9
(credit hours/units)		
Semesters/Terms per Academic Year	3	3
Tuition and Fees	$ 325	$ 325
Living Expenses	$5,000	$5,000
Summer Term		
(R = Required, O = Optional, N = None)	O	O
Standard Course Load	12	9
Tuition and Fees	$ 325	$ 325

Financial Aid Available

	Deadline (fall starts)	Awarded to Full-Time	Part-Time
Gift Aid	NA		
Federal College Work-Study	NA		
Federal Perkins Loans	January 1	Yes	Yes
Federal Stafford Loans	January 1	Yes	Yes
School-Based Loans	NA		
Outside and Private Loans	NA		
Graduate Assistantships	NA		

Percentage of Students Receiving Aid	Full-Time	Part-Time
All students	80%	

BABSON GRADUATE SCHOOL OF BUSINESS

Office of Graduate Admission
Nichols P.O. Box 57310
Babson Park, Massachusetts 02157-0310
Telephone: 617-239-4317
800-488-4512

Total Enrollment (1993-94)	Full-Time	Part-Time
	335	1,222

Cost of Attendance (1993-94)		
Academic Year		
Standard Course Load per Semester/Term		
(credit hours/units)	16	6
Semesters/Terms per Academic Year	2	3
Tuition and Fees	$17,000	$8,225
Living Expenses	$12,200	$ 375
Summer Term		
(R = Required, O = Optional, N = None)	O	O
Standard Course Load		6
Tuition and Fees	$ 6,580	$3,290

Financial Aid Available	Deadline (fall starts)	Awarded to Full-Time	Part-Time
Gift Aid	Same as admissions deadline	Yes	No
Federal College Work-Study	Same as admissions deadline	Yes	No
Federal Perkins Loans	Same as admissions deadline	Yes	No
Federal Stafford Loans	Same as admissions deadline	Yes	Yes
School-Based Loans	NA		
Outside and Private Loans	None	Yes	Yes
Graduate Assistantships	Same as admissions deadline	Yes	No

Percentage of Students Receiving Aid	Full-Time	Part-Time
All students	47%	4%
Minority students	53%	8%
Women students	49%	5%
International students	12%	0%

BALDWIN-WALLACE COLLEGE

275 Eastland Road
Berea, Ohio 44017
Telephone: 216-826-2108

Total Enrollment (1993-94)	Full-Time	Part-Time
		419

Cost of Attendance (1993-94)		
Academic Year		
Standard Course Load per Semester/Term		
(credit hours/units)	12	5
Semesters/Terms	3 quarters/6 terms	
Tuition and Fees	NA	$ 252
Living Expenses	NA	$1,000/mo.
Summer Term		
(R = Required, O = Optional, N = None)		
Standard Course Load	Same as above	
Tuition and Fees		
Resident		
Nonresident		

Financial Aid Available	Deadline (fall starts)	Awarded to Full-Time	Part-Time
Gift Aid		No	No
Federal College Work-Study		No	No
Federal Perkins Loans		No	No
Federal Stafford Loans	NA	Yes	Yes
School-Based Loans		No	No
Outside and Private Loans	NA	Yes	Yes
Graduate Assistantships		No	No

Percentage of Students Receiving Aid	Part-Time
All students	30%

BALL STATE UNIVERSITY
College of Business

Whitinger Building
Muncie, Indiana 47306
Telephone: 317-285-1931

Total Enrollment (1993-94)	Full-Time	Part-Time
	46	212

Cost of Attendance (1993-94)		
Academic Year		
Standard Course Load per Semester/Term		
(credit hours/units)	9-12	3-6
Semesters/Terms per Academic Year	3	3
Tuition and Fees		
Resident	$ 4,200	$2,876
Nonresident	$10,092	$5,988
Living Expenses	$ 3,756	$3,756
Summer Term		
(R = Required, O = Optional, N = None)	O	O
Standard Course Load	9-12	3-6
Tuition and Fees	Included in above figures	
Resident		
Nonresident		

Financial Aid Available	Deadline (fall starts)	Awarded to Full-Time	Part-Time
Gift Aid	February 15	Yes	No
Federal College Work-Study	NA	No	No
Federal Perkins Loans	NA	No	No
Federal Stafford Loans	Rolling	Yes	Yes
School-Based Loans	NA	No	No
Outside and Private Loans	Varies	Yes	Yes
Graduate Assistantships	March 1	Yes	No

Percentage of Students Receiving Aid	Full-Time	Part-Time
All students	76%	NA
Minority students	2%	NA
Women students	21%	NA
International students	17%	NA

BARRY UNIVERSITY
Andreas School of Business

11300 NE Second Avenue
Miami, Florida 33161
Telephone: 305 899-3500

Total Enrollment (1993-94)	Full-Time	Part-Time
	25	325

Cost of Attendance (1993-94)		
Academic Year		
Standard Course Load per Semester/Term		
(credit hours/units)	9	6
Semesters/Terms per Academic Year	3	3
Tuition and Fees	$340	$340
Living Expenses	Varies	Varies
Summer Term		
(R = Required, O = Optional, N = None)	O	O
Standard Course Load	9	6
Tuition and Fees	$340	$340

Financial Aid Available	Deadline (fall starts)	Awarded to Full-Time	Part-Time
Gift Aid	NA	No	No
Federal College Work-Study	NA	No	No
Federal Perkins Loans	NA	No	No
Federal Stafford Loans	Rolling	Yes	Yes
School-Based Loans	NA	No	No
Outside and Private Loans	Rolling	Yes	Yes
Graduate Assistantships	Rolling	Yes	No

Percentage of Students Receiving Aid	Full-Time	Part-Time
All students	1%	30%

BARUCH COLLEGE

155 East 24th Street
New York, New York 10010
Telephone: 212-447-3775

Total Enrollment (1993-94)	Full-Time	Part-Time
	636	1,853

Cost of Attendance (1993-94)		
Academic Year		
Standard Course Load per Semester/Term		
(credit hours/units)	12	6
Semesters/Terms per Academic Year	2	2
Tuition and Fees		
Resident	$1,675	$ 145
Nonresident	$2,925	$ 250
Living Expenses	$8,764	$8,764
Summer Term		
(R = Required, O = Optional, N = None)	O	O
Standard Course Load	6	3
Tuition and Fees		
Resident	$ 145	$ 145
Nonresident	$ 250	$ 250

Financial Aid Available	Deadline (fall starts)	Awarded to Full-Time	Awarded to Part-Time
Gift Aid		No	No
Federal College Work-Study	May 1	Yes	Yes
Federal Perkins Loans	May 1	Yes	Yes
Federal Stafford Loans	May 1	Yes	Yes
School-Based Loans		No	No
Outside and Private Loans		No	No
Graduate Assistantships	May 1	Yes	No

Percentage of Students Receiving Aid	Full-Time	Part-Time
All students	36%	6%

BAYLOR UNIVERSITY
Hankamer School of Business

P.O. Box 98001
Waco, Texas 76798
Telephone: 817-755-3718

Total Enrollment (1993-94)	Full-Time	Part-Time
	250	0

Cost of Attendance (1993-94)	
Academic Year	
Standard Course Load per Semester/Term	
(credit hours/units)	12
Semesters/Terms per Academic Year	3
Tuition and Fees	$5,700
Living Expenses	$7,776
Summer Term	
(R = Required, O = Optional, N = None)	O
Standard Course Load	12
Tuition and Fees	$2,800

Financial Aid Available	Deadline (fall starts)	Awarded to Full-Time	Awarded to Part-Time
Gift Aid	May 1	Yes	No
Federal College Work-Study	May 1	Yes	Yes
Federal Perkins Loans	May 1	Yes	Yes
Federal Stafford Loans	May 1	Yes	Yes
School-Based Loans	May 1	Yes	Yes
Outside and Private Loans	NA	No	No
Graduate Assistantships	May 1	Yes	Yes

Percentage of Students Receiving Aid	Full-Time	Part-Time
All students	54%	36%
Minority students	58%	50%
Women students	55%	67%
International students	55%	60%

BELLARMINE COLLEGE
W. Fielding Rubel School of Business

2001 Newburg Road
Louisville, Kentucky 40205
Telephone: 502-452-8240

Total Enrollment (1993-94)	Full-Time	Part-Time
	8	255

Cost of Attendance (1993-94)	
Academic Year	
Standard Course Load per Semester/Term	
(credit hours/units)	6
Semesters/Terms per Academic Year	3
Tuition and Fees	$3,276
Living Expenses	Varies
Summer Term	
(R = Required, O = Optional, N = None)	O
Standard Course Load	6
Tuition and Fees	$1,638

Financial Aid Available	Deadline (fall starts)	Awarded to Full-Time	Awarded to Part-Time
Gift Aid	NA	Yes	Yes
Federal College Work-Study	NA	No	
Federal Perkins Loans	NA		
Federal Stafford Loans	None	Yes	Yes
School-Based Loans	NA		
Outside and Private Loans	NA		
Graduate Assistantships	NA	Yes	Yes

BELMONT UNIVERSITY
Jack C. Massey School of Business

1900 Belmont Boulevard
Nashville, Tennessee 37212-3757
Telephone: 615-386-4574

Total Enrollment (1993-94)	Part-Time
	238

Cost of Attendance (1993-94)	
Academic Year	
Standard Course Load per Semester/Term	
(credit hours/units)	7
Semesters/Terms per Academic Year	3
Tuition and Fees	$9,387
Living Expenses	NA
Summer Term	
(R = Required, O = Optional, N = None)	O
Standard Course Load	7 hrs.
Tuition and Fees	$3,129

Financial Aid Available	Deadline (fall starts)	Awarded to Part-Time
Gift Aid	NA	No
Federal College Work-Study	NA	No
Federal Perkins Loans	NA	No
Federal Stafford Loans	March 15	Yes
School-Based Loans	NA	No
Outside and Private Loans	March 15	Yes
Graduate Assistantships	Rolling	Yes

Percentage of Students Receiving Aid	Part-Time
All students	25%

BENTLEY COLLEGE
Graduate School of Business

175 Forest Street
Waltham, Massachusetts 02154-4705
Telephone: 617-891-2108
800-442-4723

Total Enrollment (Fall 1992)	Full-Time	Part-Time
	285	1,918

Cost of Attendance (1993-94)		
Academic Year		
Standard Course Load per Semester/Term	4	2
(credit hours/units)		
Semesters/Terms per Academic Year	2	2
Tuition and Fees	$1,530/course	$1,530/course
	$32.50 fee	$15 fee
Living Expenses	$6,000-10,000	$1,000-12,000
Summer Term		
(R = Required, O = Optional, N = None)	O	O
Standard Course Load	2	1
Tuition and Fees	$1,530/course	$1,530/course
	$15 fee	$15 fee

Financial Aid Available	Deadline (fall starts)	Awarded to Full-Time	Part-Time
Gift Aid	March 15	Yes	Yes
Federal College Work-Study	March 15	Yes	Yes
Federal Perkins Loans	March 15	Yes	Yes
Federal Stafford Loans	March 15	Yes	Yes
School-Based Loans	NA		
Outside and Private Loans	No deadline	Yes	Yes
Graduate Assistantships	March 15	Yes	No

BERRY COLLEGE

5024 Mount Berry Station
Mount Berry, Georgia 30145-5024
Telephone: 706-236-1751

Total Enrollment (1993-94)	Full-Time	Part-Time
	2	40

Cost of Attendance (1993-94)		
Academic Year		
Standard Course Load per Semester/Term		
(credit hours/units)	9	NA
Semesters/Terms per Academic Year	3	NA
Tuition and Fees	$2,412	$268/hour
Living Expenses	$9,350	$9,350
Summer Term		
(R = Required, O = Optional, N = None)	O	O
Standard Course Load	9	NA
Tuition and Fees	$2,412	$268/hour

Financial Aid Available	Deadline (fall starts)	Awarded to Full-Time	Part-Time
Gift Aid	NA	No	No
Federal College Work-Study	April 1	Yes	No
Federal Perkins Loans	April 1	Yes	No
Federal Stafford Loans	April 1	Yes	Yes
School-Based Loans	NA	No	No
Outside and Private Loans	NA	No	No
Graduate Assistantships	NA	Yes	Yes

Percentage of Students Receiving Aid	Full-Time	Part-Time
All students	0%	5%
Minority students	0%	0%
Women students	0%	2.5%
International students	0%	0%

BLOOMSBURG UNIVERSITY
College of Business

109 Waller Administration Building
Bloomsburg, Pennsylvania 17815
Telephone: 717-389-4015

Total Enrollment (1993-94)	Full-Time	Part-Time
	22	69

Cost of Attendance (1993-94)		
Academic Year		
Standard Course Load per Semester/Term		
(credit hours/units)	9	3-6
Semesters/Terms per Academic Year		
Tuition and Fees		
Resident	$1,477	$164
Nonresident	$2,598	$289
Living Expenses	$4,700	$450
Summer Term		
(R = Required, O = Optional, N = None)	O	O
Standard Course Load	6	6
Tuition and Fees		
Resident	$ 164	$164
Nonresident	$ 289	$289

Financial Aid Available	Deadline (fall starts)	Awarded to Full-Time	Part-Time
Gift Aid		Yes	
Federal College Work-Study	March 15	Yes	Yes
Federal Perkins Loans	March 15	Yes	Yes
Federal Stafford Loans		Yes	Yes
School-Based Loans			
Outside and Private Loans		No	No
Graduate Assistantships		Yes	

Percentage of Students Receiving Aid	Full-Time
All students	24%
Minority students	3%
Women students	5%
International students	11%

BOISE STATE UNIVERSITY

1910 University Drive B310
Boise, Idaho 83725
Telephone: 208-385-1126
        800-824-7017

Total Enrollment (1993-94)	Full-Time	Part-Time
	29	174

Cost of Attendance (1993-94)		
Academic Year		
Standard Course Load per Semester/Term		
(credit hours/units)	9	3
Semesters/Terms per Academic Year	3	2
Tuition and Fees		
Resident	$2,126	$95/cr.
Nonresident	$5,176	$95/cr.
Living Expenses		
Summer Term		
(R = Required, O = Optional, N = None)	O	O
Standard Course Load	3	3
Tuition and Fees	$95/cr.	$95/cr.

Financial Aid Available	Deadline (fall starts)	Awarded to Full-Time	Part-Time
Gift Aid	March 1	Yes	Yes
Federal College Work-Study	March 1	Yes	Yes
Federal Perkins Loans	March 1	Yes	Yes
Federal Stafford Loans	March 1	Yes	Yes
School-Based Loans	None	Yes	Yes
Outside and Private Loans	None	Yes	Yes
Graduate Assistantships	March 1	Yes	Yes

BOSTON COLLEGE
The Wallace E. Carroll Graduate School of Management

Lyons Hall Room 210
Chestnut Hill, Massachusetts 02167
Telephone: 617-552-3920

Total Enrollment (1993-94)	Full-Time	Part-Time
	157	438

Cost of Attendance (1993-94)		
Academic Year		
Standard Course Load per Semester/	1st yr.-31 cr. hrs.	6 cr. hrs.
Term (credit hours/units)	2nd yr.-24 cr. hrs.	
Semesters/Terms per Academic Year	2	2
Tuition and Fees	$17,794	$6,888
Living Expenses		
Summer Term		
(R = Required, O = Optional, N = None)	O	O
Standard Course Load	3 cr. hrs.	3 cr. hrs.
Tuition and Fees	$1,722	$1,722

Financial Aid Available	Deadline (fall starts)	Awarded to Full-Time	Awarded to Part-Time
Gift Aid	March 1	Yes	No
Federal College Work-Study	April 15	Yes	No
Federal Perkins Loans	April 15	Yes	Yes
Federal Stafford Loans	April 15	Yes	Yes
School-Based Loans	April 15	No	No
Outside and Private Loans	April 15	Yes	Yes
Graduate Assistantships	March 1	Yes	No

Percentage of Students Receiving Aid	Full-Time	Part-Time
All students	30%	NA

BOSTON UNIVERSITY
Graduate School of Management

685 Commonwealth Avenue
Boston, Massachusetts 02215
Telephone: 617-353-2670

Total Enrollment (1993-94)	Full-Time	Part-Time
	586	939

Cost of Attendance (1993-94)		
Academic Year		
Standard Course Load per Semester/Term		
(credit hours/units)	15	8
Semesters/Terms per Academic Year	2	2
Tuition and Fees	$17,600	$ 8,788
Living Expenses	$11,310	$11,310
Summer Term		
(R = Required, O = Optional, N = None)	O	O
Standard Course Load	8	8
Tuition and Fees	$ 4,344	$ 4,344

Financial Aid Available	Deadline (fall starts)	Awarded to Full-Time	Awarded to Part-Time
Gift Aid	March 15	Yes	Yes
Federal College Work-Study	March 15	Yes	No
Federal Perkins Loans	March 15	Yes	No
Federal Stafford Loans	June 1	Yes	Yes
School-Based Loans	June 1	Yes	Yes
Outside and Private Loans	June 1	Yes	Yes
Graduate Assistantships	March 15	Yes	Yes

Percentage of Students Receiving Aid	Full-Time	Part-Time
All students	67%	45%

BOWLING GREEN STATE UNIVERSITY
College of Business Administration

Graduate Studies in Business
Bowling Green, Ohio 43403
Telephone: 800-247-8622

Total Enrollment (1993-94)	Full-Time	Part-Time
	95	190

Cost of Attendance (1993-94)		
Academic Year		
Standard Course Load per Semester/Term		
(credit hours/units)	12	6
Semesters/Terms per Academic Year		
Tuition and Fees		
Resident	$2,314	$ 651-$1,194
Nonresident	$4,400	$1,248-$2,496
Living Expenses	$6,300	$6,000
Summer Term		
(R = Required, O = Optional, N = None)	O	O
Standard Course Load	9	6
Tuition and Fees		
Resident	$1,926	$1,284
Nonresident	$3,807	$2,538

Financial Aid Available	Deadline (fall starts)	Awarded to Full-Time	Part-Time
Gift Aid	March 1	Yes	
Federal College Work-Study	March 1	Yes	
Federal Perkins Loans	March 1	Yes	Yes
Federal Stafford Loans	March 1	Yes	Yes
School-Based Loans	March 1	Yes	Yes
Outside and Private Loans	March 1		
Graduate Assistantships	March 1	Yes	

Percentage of Students Receiving Aid	Full-Time	Part-Time
All students	63%	5%
Minority students	98%	3%
Women students	70%	5%
International students	90%	NA

BRADLEY UNIVERSITY
College of Business Administration

Peoria, Illinois 61625
Telephone: 309-677-2253

Total Enrollment (1993-94)	Full-Time	Part-Time
	30	147

Cost of Attendance (1993-94)		
Academic Year		
Standard Course Load per Semester/Term		
(credit hours/units)	9	3
Semesters/Terms per Academic Year	2+	2+
Tuition and Fees		
Resident	$281/hr. (up to 7)	same
Nonresident	$351/hr. (7.5 or more)	same
Living Expenses	$5,000	NA
Summer Term		
(R = Required, O = Optional, N = None)	O	O
Standard Course Load	6	3
Tuition and Fees	$281/hr.	$281/hr.

Financial Aid Available	Deadline (fall starts)	Awarded to Full-Time	Part-Time
Gift Aid	March 1	Yes	Yes
Federal College Work-Study	March 1	No	No
Federal Perkins Loans	March 1	Yes	Yes
Federal Stafford Loans	May 1	Yes	Yes
School-Based Loans	March 1	No	No
Outside and Private Loans	March 1	Yes	Yes
Graduate Assistantships	April 1	Yes	Yes

Percentage of Students Receiving Aid	Full-Time	Part-Time
All students	85%	10%

BRIGHAM YOUNG UNIVERSITY
Marriott School of Management

730 Tanner Building
Provo, Utah 84602
Telephone: 801-378-6824

Total Enrollment (1993-94)	Full-Time	Part-Time
	228	102

Cost of Attendance (1993-94)		
Academic Year		
Standard Course Load per Semester/Term		
(credit hours/units)	15	9
Semesters/Terms per Academic Year	2	3
Tuition and Fees		
Resident (LDS Member)	$4,200	$350/hr.
Nonresident (Non-LDS Member)	$6,300	$350/hr.
Living Expenses		
Summer Term		
(R = Required, O = Optional, N = None)	N	R
Standard Course Load		
Tuition and Fees		$350/hr.

Financial Aid Available	Deadline (fall starts)	Awarded to Full-Time	Part-Time
Gift Aid	April	Yes	No
Federal College Work-Study	NA	No	No
Federal Perkins Loans	NA	No	No
Federal Stafford Loans	March 1	Yes	Yes
School-Based Loans			No
Outside and Private Loans	NA	No	No
Graduate Assistantships	Arranged on need basis (March 1-fall)	Yes	No

Percentage of Students Receiving Aid	Full-Time
All students	35%
Minority students	NA
Women students	50%
International students	65%

BUTLER UNIVERSITY
College of Business Administration

4600 Sunset Avenue
Indianapolis, Indiana 46208
Telephone: 317-283-9221

Total Enrollment (1993-94)	Full-Time	Part-Time
	46	376

Cost of Attendance (1993-94)		
Academic Year		
Standard Course Load per Semester/Term		
(credit hours/units)	12 hrs.	6 hrs.
Semesters/Terms per Academic Year	3	3
Tuition and Fees	$230/cr. hr.	$230/cr. hr.
Living Expenses	$5,000	
Summer Term		
(R = Required, O = Optional, N = None)	O	O
Standard Course Load	6 hrs.	3 hrs.
Tuition and Fees	$230/cr.hr.	$230/cr.hr.

Financial Aid Available	Deadline (fall starts)	Awarded to Full-Time	Part-Time
Gift Aid	NA		
Federal College Work-Study	NA		
Federal Perkins Loans	NA		
Federal Stafford Loans	NA		
School-Based Loans	June 1	Yes	Yes
Outside and Private Loans	June 1	Yes	Yes
Graduate Assistantships	NA		

CALIFORNIA LUTHERAN UNIVERSITY

60 West Olsen Road
Thousand Oaks, California 91360
Telephone: 805-493-3125

Total Enrollment (1993-94)	Full-Time	Part-Time
	400	22

Cost of Attendance (1993-94)

	Full-Time	Part-Time
Academic Year		
Standard Course Load per Semester/Term		
(credit hours/units)	8	4
Semesters/Terms per Academic Year	2	2
Tuition and Fees	$2,520	$315/unit
Living Expenses	$6,784	$6,136
Summer Term		
(R = Required, O = Optional, N = None)	O	O
Standard Course Load	8	4
Tuition and Fees		
Resident	Same as above	
Nonresident		

Financial Aid Available

	Deadline (fall starts)	Awarded to Full-Time	Part-Time
Gift Aid	September 1, January 15	Yes	No
Federal College Work-Study	NA	No	
Federal Perkins Loans	NA	No	
Federal Stafford Loans	September 1, January 15	Yes	Yes
School-Based Loans		No	No
Outside and Private Loans	September 1, January 15	Yes	Yes
Graduate Assistantships	August 1, December 1	Yes	Yes

Percentage of Students Receiving Aid	Full-Time	Part-Time
All students	14%	1%
Minority students	.1%	.1%
Women students	.1%	.03%
International students	.04%	0%

CALIFORNIA POLYTECHNIC STATE UNIVERSITY, SAN LUIS OBISPO
Graduate Management Programs, College of Business

San Luis Obispo, California 93407
Telephone. 805-756-2285

Total Enrollment (1993-94)	Full-Time	Part-Time
	100	15
	(Students are not formally admitted on a part-time basis)	

Cost of Attendance (1993-94)

	Full-Time	Part-Time
Academic Year		
Standard Course Load per Semester/Term		
(credit hours/units)	16	NA
Semesters/Terms per Academic Year	3	NA
Tuition and Fees		
Resident	$ 1,869	NA
Nonresident	$ 9,741	NA
Living Expenses	$10,000	
Summer Term		
(R = Required, O = Optional, N = None)	R (EMP program only)	
Standard Course Load	8	
Tuition and Fees		
Resident	$ 623	
Nonresident	$3,247	

Financial Aid Available

	Deadline (fall starts)	Awarded to Full-Time
Gift Aid	March 2	Yes
Federal College Work-Study	March 2	Yes
Federal Perkins Loans	March 2	Yes
Federal Stafford Loans	March 2	Yes
School-Based Loans	March 2	Yes
Outside and Private Loans	March	Yes
Graduate Assistantships	September 1	Yes

Percentage of Students Receiving Aid	Full-Time	Part-Time
All students	65%	NA
Minority students	NA	NA
Women students	65%	NA
International students	20%	NA

CALIFORNIA STATE UNIVERSITY, CHICO
Business Graduate Programs

Chico, California 95929
Telephone: 916-898-4425

Total Enrollment (1993-94)	Full-Time	Part-Time
	35	15

Cost of Attendance (1993-94)

Academic Year		
Standard Course Load per Semester/Term		
(credit hours/units)	9-12	3-6
Semesters/Terms per Academic Year	2	2
Tuition and Fees		
Resident	$891 +	$588 +
	$246/unit	$246/unit
Nonresident	$891 +	$588 +
	$246/unit	$246/unit
Living Expenses	$8,000	$8,000
Summer Term		
(R = Required, O = Optional, N = None)	N	N
Standard Course Load		
Tuition and Fees		
Resident		
Nonresident		

Financial Aid Available

	Deadline (fall starts)	Awarded to Full-Time	Awarded to Part-Time
Gift Aid	April 15	Yes	No
Federal College Work-Study	March 1	Yes	No
Federal Perkins Loans	March 1	Yes	No
Federal Stafford Loans	March 1	Yes	No
School-Based Loans	March 1	Yes	No
Outside and Private Loans	April 15	Yes	No
Graduate Assistantships	August 1	Yes	No

Percentage of Students Receiving Aid	Full-Time	Part-Time
All students	40%	0%
Minority students	1%	0%
Women students	12%	0%
International students	6%	0%

CALIFORNIA STATE UNIVERSITY, DOMINGUEZ HILLS
School of Management

1000 East Victoria Street
Carson, California 90747
Telephone: 310-516-3465

Total Enrollment (1993-94)	Full-Time	Part-Time
	43	117

Cost of Attendance (1993-94)

Academic Year		
Standard Course Load per Semester/Term		
(credit hours/units)	9	3-6
Semesters/Terms per Academic Year	2	2
Tuition and Fees		
Resident	$1,616	$1,010
Nonresident	$246/unit	$246/unit
Living Expenses	$6,500	$5,500
Summer Term		
(R = Required, O = Optional, N = None)	O	O
Standard Course Load	3-6 units	3-6 units
Tuition and Fees	$112/unit	$112/unit
Resident		
Nonresident		

Financial Aid Available

	Deadline (fall starts)	Awarded to Full-Time	Awarded to Part-Time
Gift Aid	April 30	Yes	Yes
Federal College Work-Study	July 1	Yes	Yes
Federal Perkins Loans	July 1	Yes	Yes
Federal Stafford Loans	March 1	Yes	Yes
School-Based Loans	NA	No	No
Outside and Private Loans	Open	Yes	Yes
Graduate Assistantships	NA	No	No

Percentage of Students Receiving Aid	Full-Time	Part-Time
All students	5%	5%
Minority students	20%	20%
Women students	20%	20%
International students	75%	0%

CALIFORNIA STATE UNIVERSITY, FULLERTON
School of Business Administration and Economics

Fullerton, California 92634
Telephone: 714-773-2211

Total Enrollment (1993-94)	Full-Time	Part-Time
	20	336

Cost of Attendance (1993-94)		
Academic Year		
Standard Course Load per Semester/Term		
(credit hours/units)	7 + units	0-6 units
Semesters/Terms per Academic Year	2	2
Tuition and Fees		
Resident	$1,624	$1,018
Nonresident	$7,528	$3,970
Living Expenses	$8,200-$9,500	$8,200-$9,500
Summer Term		
(R = Required, O = Optional, N = None)	O	O
Standard Course Load	3	3
Tuition and Fees		
Resident	$ 509	$ 509
Nonresident	$1,247	$1,247

Financial Aid Available	Deadline (fall starts)	Awarded to Full-Time	Part-Time
Gift Aid	February 28	Yes	Yes
Federal College Work-Study	October 1	Yes	Yes
Federal Perkins Loans	March 2	Yes	Yes
Federal Stafford Loans	Rolling	Yes	Yes
School-Based Loans	Varies	Yes	Yes
Outside and Private Loans	Varies	Yes	Yes
Graduate Assistantships	Varies	Yes	Yes

Percentage of Students Receiving Aid	Part-Time
All students	4%
Minority students	30%
Women students	40%

CALIFORNIA STATE UNIVERSITY, LONG BEACH
College of Business Administration

1250 Bellflower Boulevard
Long Beach, California 90840
Telephone: 310-985-1797

Total Enrollment (1993-94)	Full-Time	Part-Time
	85	520

Cost of Attendance (1993-94)		
Academic Year		
Standard Course Load per Semester/Term		
(credit hours/units)	9	6
Semesters/Terms per Academic Year	2	2
Tuition and Fees		
Resident	$ 804	$ 501
Nonresident	$3,018	$1,977
Living Expenses	$8,000	$8,000
Summer Term		
(R = Required, O = Optional, N = None)	O	O
Standard Course Load	12	6
Tuition and Fees	$1,800	$ 900

Financial Aid Available	Deadline (fall starts)	Awarded to Full-Time	Part-Time
Gift Aid	April 30	Yes	Yes
Federal College Work-Study	April 30	Yes	Yes
Federal Perkins Loans			
Federal Stafford Loans			
School-Based Loans	April 30	Yes	Yes
Outside and Private Loans			
Graduate Assistantships		Yes	Yes

CALIFORNIA STATE UNIVERSITY, NORTHRIDGE
School of Business Administration and Economics

18111 Nordhoff Street
Northridge, California 91330-8245
Telephone: 818-885-2467

Total Enrollment (1993-94)	Full-Time	Part-Time
	50	400

Cost of Attendance (1993-94)		
Academic Year		
Standard Course Load per Semester/Term		
(credit hours/units)	9-12	3-6
Semesters/Terms per Academic Year	2	2
Tuition and Fees		
Resident	$1,692	$1,064
Nonresident	$6,116	$3,164
Living Expenses	$9,350	$9,350
Summer Term		
(R = Required, O = Optional, N = None)	N	O
Standard Course Load		3
Tuition and Fees		$ 318

Financial Aid Available	Deadline (fall starts)	Awarded to Full-Time	Part-Time
Gift Aid			
Federal College Work-Study			
Federal Perkins Loans			
Federal Stafford Loans			
School-Based Loans			
Outside and Private Loans			
Graduate Assistantships			

CALIFORNIA STATE UNIVERSITY, STANISLAUS

Master of Business Administration
801 W. Monte Vista Blvd.
Turlock, California 95382
Telephone: 209-667-3074

Total Enrollment (1993-94)	Full-Time	Part-Time
	25	125

Cost of Attendance (1993-94)		
Academic Year		
Standard Course Load per Semester/Term		
(credit hours/units)	9	6
Semesters/Terms per Academic Year	3	3
Tuition and Fees		
Resident	$1,000	$ 540
Nonresident	$5,000	$3,500
Living Expenses	$8,000	NA
Summer Term		
(R = Required, O = Optional, N = None)	O	O
Standard Course Load	6	6
Tuition and Fees		
Resident	$ 600	$ 600
Nonresident	$ 600	$ 600

Financial Aid Available	Deadline (fall starts)	Awarded to Full-Time	Part-Time
Gift Aid		Yes	No
Federal College Work-Study		Yes	No
Federal Perkins Loans		No	No
Federal Stafford Loans		Yes	No
School-Based Loans		No	No
Outside and Private Loans		No	No
Graduate Assistantships		Yes	No

Percentage of Students Receiving Aid	Full-Time
All students	10%
Minority students	10%
Women students	8%

CALIFORNIA UNIVERSITY OF PENNSYLVANIA
Business and Economics Department

250 University Avenue
California, Pennsylvania 15419-1394
Telephone: 412-938-4371

Total Enrollment (1993-94)	Full-Time	Part-Time
	40	62

Cost of Attendance (1993-94)		
Academic Year		
Standard Course Load per Semester/Term		
(credit hours/units)	12	3-6
Semesters/Terms per Academic Year	3	3
Tuition and Fees		
Resident	$1,477	$164/cr. hr.
Nonresident	$2,598	$289/cr. hr.
Living Expenses	$5,300	$5,300
Summer Term		
(R = Required, O = Optional, N = None)	R	O
Standard Course Load	9-12	3-6
Tuition and Fees		
Resident	$157/cr.	$157/cr.
Nonresident	$233/cr.	$233/cr.

Financial Aid Available	Deadline (fall starts)	Awarded to Full-Time	Part-Time
Gift Aid	NA		
Federal College Work-Study	NA	No	No
Federal Perkins Loans	NA	No	No
Federal Stafford Loans	Rolling	Yes	Yes
School-Based Loans	NA	No	No
Outside and Private Loans	NA	No	No
Graduate Assistantships	Rolling	Yes	

Percentage of Students Receiving Aid	Full-Time
All students	50%
Minority students	60%
Women students	65%
International students	40%

CAMPBELL UNIVERSITY
Lundy-Fetterman School of Business

Graduate Admissions Office
P.O. Box 546
Buies Creek, North Carolina 27506
Telephone: 800-334-4111

Total Enrollment (1993-94)	Part-Time
	343

Cost of Attendance (1993-94)	
Academic Year	
Standard Course Load per Semester/Term	
(credit hours/units)	6
Semesters/Terms per Academic Year	2
Tuition and Fees	$145/sem. hr.
Living Expenses	NA
Summer Term	
(R = Required, O = Optional, N = None)	R
Standard Course Load	3 semester hrs.
Tuition and Fees	$145/sem. hr.

Financial Aid Available	Deadline (fall starts)	Awarded to Full-Time	Part-Time
Gift Aid	NA	No	No
Federal College Work-Study	NA	No	No
Federal Perkins Loans	Rolling	Yes	No
Federal Stafford Loans	Rolling	Yes	Yes
School-Based Loans	NA	No	No
Outside and Private Loans	NA	No	No
Graduate Assistantships	NA	No	No

Percentage of Students Receiving Aid	Part-Time
All students	10%
Minority students	35%
Women students	10%
International students	0%

CANISIUS COLLEGE
Richard J. Wehle School of Business

2001 Main Street
Buffalo, New York 14208
Telephone: 716-888-2140

Total Enrollment (1993-94)	Full-Time	Part-Time
	10	500

Cost of Attendance (1993-94)		
Academic Year		
Standard Course Load per Semester/Term		
(credit hours/units)	12	6
Semesters/Terms per Academic Year	3	3
Tuition and Fees	$375/cr.hr.	$375/cr.hr.
Living Expenses		
Summer Term		
(R = Required, O = Optional, N = None)	O	O
Standard Course Load		
Tuition and Fees	$375/cr.hr.	$375/cr.hr.
Resident		
Nonresident		

Financial Aid Available	Deadline (fall starts)	Awarded to Full-Time	Awarded to Part-Time
Gift Aid	Rolling	Yes	Yes
Federal College Work-Study	NA	No	No
Federal Perkins Loans	NA	No	No
Federal Stafford Loans	Rolling	Yes	Yes
School-Based Loans	NA	No	No
Outside and Private Loans	NA	No	No
Graduate Assistantships	None	Yes	Yes

CAPITAL UNIVERSITY
Graduate School of Administration

2199 East Main Street
Columbus, Ohio 43209
Telephone: 614-236-6679

Total Enrollment (1993-94)	Part-Time
	310

Cost of Attendance (1993-94)	
Academic Year	
Standard Course Load per Semester/Term	
(credit hours/units)	6-7 cr.
Semesters/Terms per Academic Year	3
Tuition and Fees	$230/cr.hr.
Living Expenses	
Summer Term	
(R = Required, O = Optional, N = None)	O
Standard Course Load	6-7 cr.
Tuition and Fees	$230/cr.hr.

Financial Aid Available	Deadline (fall starts)	Awarded to Full-Time	Part-Time
Gift Aid	NA		
Federal College Work-Study	NA		
Federal Perkins Loans	NA		
Federal Stafford Loans	NA		
School-Based Loans	NA		
Outside and Private Loans	NA		
Graduate Assistantships	NA		

CARNEGIE MELLON UNIVERSITY
Graduate School of Industrial Administration

Schenley Park
Pittsburgh, Pennsylvania 15213
Telephone: 412-268-7581

Total Enrollment (1993-94)	Full-Time	Part-Time
	397	156

Cost of Attendance (1993-94)		
Academic Year		
Standard Course Load per Semester/Term		
(credit hours/units)		
Semesters/Terms per Academic Year	2	3
Tuition and Fees	$19,600	$14,860
Living Expenses	$ 8,500	$ 7,050
Summer Term		
(R = Required, O = Optional, N = None)	O	R
Standard Course Load	36	24
Tuition and Fees	$ 9,800	$ 4,920
Resident		
Nonresident		

Financial Aid Available	Deadline (fall starts)	Awarded to Full-Time	Part-Time
Gift Aid	May 1	Yes	No
Federal College Work-Study	May 1	Yes	No
Federal Perkins Loans	May 1	Yes	No
Federal Stafford Loans	July 1	Yes	Yes
School-Based Loans	NA	No	No
Outside and Private Loans	NA	Yes	No
Graduate Assistantships	NA	Yes	No

Percentage of Students Receiving Aid	Full-Time	Part-Time
All students	64%	26%
Minority students	100%	0%
Women students	49%	35%
International students	0%	0%

CASE WESTERN RESERVE UNIVERSITY
Weatherhead School of Management

310 Enterprise Hall
10900 Euclid Avenue
Cleveland, Ohio 44106-7235
Telephone: 216-368-2030

Total Enrollment (1993-94)	Full-Time	Part-Time
	340	641
	(includes 73 EMBA students)	

Cost of Attendance (1993-94)		
Academic Year		
Standard Course Load per Semester/Term		
(credit hours/units)	15	6
Semesters/Terms per Academic Year	2	2
Tuition and Fees	$16,700	$696/cr. hr.
Living Expenses	$ 9,180	$ 8,870
Summer Term		
(R = Required, O = Optional, N = None)	O	O
Standard Course Load	3-12	3 hrs.
Tuition and Fees	$ 8,350	$696/cr.hr.

Financial Aid Available	Deadline (fall starts)	Awarded to Full-Time	Part-Time
Gift Aid	March 15	Yes	Yes
Federal College Work-Study	Rolling deadline (6-8 wks. to process)	Yes	No
Federal Perkins Loans	Rolling	Yes	No
Federal Stafford Loans	Rolling	Yes	Yes
School-Based Loans	Dependent on needs analysis outcome	Yes	No
Outside and Private Loans	Rolling	Yes	Yes
Graduate Assistantships		No	No

Percentage of Students Receiving Aid	Full-Time	Part-Time
All students	85%	5-10%
Minority students	100%	5-10%
Women students	90%	5-10%
International students	5-10%	5-10%

CENTRAL MICHIGAN UNIVERSITY
College of Business Administration

Grawn Hall
Mount Pleasant, Michigan 48859
Telephone: 517-774-3150

Total Enrollment (1993-94)	Full-Time	Part-Time
	119	401

Cost of Attendance (1993-94)		
Academic Year		
Standard Course Load per Semester/Term		
(credit hours/units)	12	6
Semesters/Terms per Academic Year	2	2
Tuition and Fees		
Resident	$2,808	$1,404
Nonresident	$5,574	$2,787
Living Expenses	$3,836	
Summer Term		
(R = Required, O = Optional, N = None)	O	O
Standard Course Load	12	6
Tuition and Fees		
Resident	$2,808	$1,404
Nonresident	$5,574	$2,787

Financial Aid Available

	Deadline (fall starts)	Awarded to Full-Time	Awarded to Part-Time
Gift Aid	February 6	Yes	No
Federal College Work-Study	March 1	Yes	Yes
Federal Perkins Loans	March 1	Yes	No
Federal Stafford Loans	March 1	Yes	Yes
School-Based Loans	NA	No	No
Outside and Private Loans	NA	No	No
Graduate Assistantships	March 1	Yes	No

Percentage of Students Receiving Aid	Full-Time	Part-Time
All students	30%	0%
Minority students	0%	0%
Women students	NA	0%
International students	20%	0%

CENTRAL MISSOURI STATE UNIVERSITY
College of Business and Economics

Dockery Hall 108C
Warrensburg, Missouri 64093
Telephone: 816-543-8571

Total Enrollment (1993-94)	Full-Time	Part-Time
	70	60

Cost of Attendance (1993-94)		
Academic Year		
Standard Course Load per Semester/Term		
(credit hours/units)	12	6
Semesters/Terms per Academic Year	2	2
Tuition and Fees		
Resident	$3,000	$1,500
Nonresident	$5,000	$2,500
Living Expenses	$6,650	$6,350
Summer Term		
(R = Required, O = Optional, N = None)	O	O
Standard Course Load	6	3
Tuition and Fees		
Resident	$ 750	$ 375
Nonresident	$1,200	$ 600

Financial Aid Available

	Deadline (fall starts)	Awarded to Full-Time	Awarded to Part-Time
Gift Aid	April 15	Yes	Yes
Federal College Work-Study	April 15	Yes	Yes
Federal Perkins Loans	April 15	Yes	Yes
Federal Stafford Loans	April 15	Yes	Yes
School-Based Loans	NA	No	No
Outside and Private Loans	Varies	Yes	Yes
Graduate Assistantships	April 1	Yes	Yes

Percentage of Students Receiving Aid	Full-Time	Part-Time
All students	55%	55%
Minority students	70%	70%
Women students	55%	55%
International students	10%	10%

CHAMINADE UNIVERSITY OF HONOLULU
School of Business

3140 Waialae Avenue
Honolulu, Hawaii 96816
Telephone: 808-739-4604

Total Enrollment (1993-94)	Full-Time	Part-Time
	100	118

Cost of Attendance (1993-94)

Academic Year		
Standard Course Load per Semester/Term		
(credit hours/units)	6	3
Semesters/Terms per Academic Year	4	4
Tuition and Fees	$5,280	$2,640
Living Expenses		
Summer Term		
(R = Required, O = Optional, N = None)		
Standard Course Load		
Tuition and Fees		
Resident		
Nonresident		

Financial Aid Available

	Deadline (fall starts)	Awarded to Full-Time	Part-Time
Gift Aid	August 15	Yes	Yes
Federal College Work-Study	August 15	Yes	Yes
Federal Perkins Loans	August 15	No	No
Federal Stafford Loans	August 15	Yes	Yes
School-Based Loans	August 15	No	No
Outside and Private Loans	August 15	No	No
Graduate Assistantships	August 15	No	No

CHAPMAN UNIVERSITY
School of Business and Economics

333 North Glassell
Orange, California 92666
Telephone: 714-997-6786

Total Enrollment (1993-94)	Full-Time	Part-Time
	160	98

Cost of Attendance (1993-94)

Academic Year		
Standard Course Load per Semester/Term		
(credit hours/units)	9	3-6
Semesters/Terms per Academic Year	18	3-17
Tuition and Fees	$ 375	$375
Living Expenses	$15,000	NA
Summer Term		
(R = Required, O = Optional, N = None)	O	O
Standard Course Load	6	3
Tuition and Fees	$ 375	$375

Financial Aid Available

	Deadline (fall starts)	Awarded to Full-Time	Part-Time
Gift Aid	FCFS*	Yes	Yes
Federal College Work-Study	FCFS	No	No
Federal Perkins Loans	FCFS	No	No
Federal Stafford Loans	FCFS	Yes	Yes
School-Based Loans	FCFS	No	No
Outside and Private Loans	FCFS	No	No
Graduate Assistantships	FCFS	Yes	Yes

* FCFS: First come first served

CHRISTIAN BROTHERS UNIVERSITY

650 East Parkway South
Memphis, Tennessee 38104
Telephone: 901-722-0317

Total Enrollment (1993-94)	Full-Time	Part-Time
		125

Cost of Attendance (1993-94)		
Academic Year		
Standard Course Load per Semester/Term		
(credit hours/units)	9-12	3-6
Semesters/Terms per Academic Year	3	3
Tuition and Fees	$265/hr.	$265/hr.
Living Expenses	NA	NA
Summer Term		
(R = Required, O = Optional, N = None)	O	O
Standard Course Load	9-12	3-6
Tuition and Fees	$265/hr.	$265/hr.

Financial Aid Available	Deadline (fall starts)	Awarded to Full-Time	Part-Time
Gift Aid	NA		
Federal College Work-Study	NA		
Federal Perkins Loans	NA		
Federal Stafford Loans		Yes	Yes
School-Based Loans	NA		
Outside and Private Loans	NA		
Graduate Assistantships	NA		

Percentage of Students Receiving Aid	Part-Time
All students	10%

THE CLAREMONT GRADUATE SCHOOL
The Peter F. Drucker Graduate Management Center

925 North Dartmouth Avenue
Claremont, California 91711
Telephone: 909-621-8073

Total Enrollment (1993-94)	Full-Time	Part-Time
	95	115

Cost of Attendance (1993-94)		
Academic Year		
Standard Course Load per Semester/Term		
(credit hours/units)	16	8
Semesters/Terms per Academic Year	3	3
Tuition and Fees	$15,850	$710/unit
Living Expenses	$11,345	NA
Summer Term		
(R = Required, O = Optional, N = None)	O	O
Standard Course Load	16	8
Tuition and Fees	$710/unit	$710/unit
Resident		
Nonresident		

Financial Aid Available	Deadline (fall starts)	Awarded to Full-Time	Part-Time
Gift Aid	April 30	Yes	Yes
Federal College Work-Study	April 30	Yes	No
Federal Perkins Loans	April 30	Yes	Yes
Federal Stafford Loans	April 30	Yes	Yes
School-Based Loans	NA	No	No
Outside and Private Loans	April 30	Yes	Yes
Graduate Assistantships	April 30	Yes	No

Percentage of Students Receiving Aid	Full-Time	Part-Time
All students	49%	25%
Minority students	64%	21%
Women students	58%	33%
International students	14%	13%

CLARION UNIVERSITY OF PENNSYLVANIA
Master of Business Administration

302 Still Hall
Clarion, Pennsylvania 16214
Telephone: 814-226-2605

Total Enrollment (1993-94)	Full-Time	Part-Time
	40	18

Cost of Attendance (1993-94)		
Academic Year		
Standard Course Load per Semester/Term		
(credit hours/units)	9	3-6
Semesters/Terms per Academic Year	2	2
Tuition and Fees		
Resident	$1,817	$ 164/cr.
Nonresident	$2,938	$ 259/cr.
Living Expenses	$1,701	$1,701
Summer Term		
(R = Required, O = Optional, N = None)	N	O
Standard Course Load	9	3-6
Tuition and Fees		
Resident	$164/cr.	$164/cr.
Nonresident	$259/cr.	$259/cr.

Financial Aid Available	Deadline (fall starts)	Awarded to Full-Time	Awarded to Part-Time
Gift Aid			
Federal College Work-Study			
Federal Perkins Loans	August 1	Yes	Yes
Federal Stafford Loans	August 1	Yes	Yes
School-Based Loans			
Outside and Private Loans			
Graduate Assistantships	August 1	Yes	Yes

Percentage of Students Receiving Aid	Full-Time	Part-Time
All students	40%	40%
Minority students	100%	100%
Women students	40%	40%
International students	40%	40%

CLARK ATLANTA UNIVERSITY

James P Brawley Drive at Fair Street
Atlanta, Georgia 30314
Telephone: 404-880-8479

Total Enrollment (1993-94)	Full-Time
	170

Cost of Attendance (1993-94)	
Academic Year	
Standard Course Load per Semester/Term	
(credit hours/units)	15
Semesters/Terms per Academic Year	2
Tuition and Fees	$9,270
Living Expenses	$4,700
Summer Term	
(R = Required, O = Optional, N = None)	O
Standard Course Load	9
Tuition and Fees	$2,700

Financial Aid Available	Deadline (fall starts)	Awarded to Full-Time
Gift Aid	April 15	Yes
Federal College Work-Study	March	Yes
Federal Perkins Loans	Rolling	Yes
Federal Stafford Loans	Rolling	Yes
School-Based Loans	NA	
Outside and Private Loans	NA	
Graduate Assistantships	Rolling	Yes

Percentage of Students Receiving Aid	Full-Time
All students	97%
Minority students	97%
Women students	51%

CLARK UNIVERSITY
Graduate School of Management

950 Main Street
Worcester, Massachusetts 01610
Telephone: 508-793-7406

Total Enrollment (1993-94)	Full-Time	Part-Time
	100	280

Cost of Attendance (1993-94)

	Full-Time	Part-Time
Academic Year		
Standard Course Load per Semester/Term		
(credit hours/units)	12	6
Semesters/Terms per Academic Year	2	2
Tuition and Fees	$12,200	$6,100
Living Expenses	$ 7,000	NA
Summer Term		
(R = Required, O = Optional, N = None)	O	O
Standard Course Load	6	3
Tuition and Fees	$ 3,050	$1,525

Financial Aid Available

	Deadline (fall starts)	Awarded to Full-Time	Awarded to Part-Time
Gift Aid	None	Yes	Yes
Federal College Work-Study	NA	No	No
Federal Perkins Loans	None	Yes	Yes
Federal Stafford Loans	None	Yes	Yes
School-Based Loans	NA	No	No
Outside and Private Loans	None	Yes	Yes
Graduate Assistantships	None	Yes	No

Percentage of Students Receiving Aid	Full-Time	Part-Time
All students	60%	20%
Minority students	80%	
Women students	70%	
International students	30%	

CLARKSON UNIVERSITY
School of Management

145A Clarkson Hall
Potsdam, New York 13699-5770
Telephone: 315-268-6613

Total Enrollment (1993-94)	Full-Time	Part-Time
	81	23

Cost of Attendance (1993-94)

	Full-Time	Part-Time
Academic Year		
Standard Course Load per Semester/Term		
(credit hours/units)	16	3
Semesters/Terms per Academic Year	2	2
Tuition and Fees	$16,604	$1,004
Living Expenses	$ 6,950	NA
Summer Term		
(R = Required, O = Optional, N = None)	N	N
Standard Course Load		
Tuition and Fees		
Resident		
Nonresident		

Financial Aid Available

	Deadline (fall starts)	Awarded to Full-Time	Awarded to Part-Time
Gift Aid	None	Yes	No
Federal College Work-Study	NA		No
Federal Perkins Loans	None	Yes	No
Federal Stafford Loans	None	Yes	No
School-Based Loans	NA		No
Outside and Private Loans	None	Yes	No
Graduate Assistantships			

Percentage of Students Receiving Aid	Full-Time	Part-Time
All students	50%	
Minority students	100%	

CLEMSON UNIVERSITY
College of Commerce and Industry

124 Sirrine Hall
Box 341315
Clemson, South Carolina 29634-1315
Telephone: 803-656-3975

Total Enrollment (1993-94)	Full-Time	Part-Time
	250	240

Cost of Attendance (1993-94)

Academic Year		
Standard Course Load per Semester/Term		
(credit hours/units)	12	6
Semesters/Terms per Academic Year	3	3
Tuition and Fees		
Resident	$1,382	$ 930
Nonresident	$2,764	$1,860
Living Expenses	$7,000	$ 500
Summer Term		
(R = Required, O = Optional, N = None)	R	O
Standard Course Load	12	6
Tuition and Fees		
Resident	$1,344	$ 930
Nonresident	$2,688	$1,860

Financial Aid Available

	Deadline (fall starts)	Awarded to Full-Time	Part-Time
Gift Aid	April 1	Yes	No
Federal College Work-Study	NA	No	No
Federal Perkins Loans	NA	No	No
Federal Stafford Loans	April 1	Yes	Yes
School-Based Loans	NA	No	No
Outside and Private Loans	NA	No	No
Graduate Assistantships	June 1	Yes	No

Percentage of Students Receiving Aid	Full-Time	Part-Time
All students	30%	5%
Minority students	10%	10%
Women students	8%	8%
International students	17%	17%

CLEVELAND STATE UNIVERSITY
James J. Nance College of Business

2121 Euclid Avenue
University Center Room 460
Cleveland, Ohio 44115
Telephone: 216-687-3730

Total Enrollment (1993-94)	Full-Time	Part-Time
	240	675

Cost of Attendance (1993-94)

Academic Year		
Standard Course Load per Semester/Term		
(credit hours/units)	12	4
Semesters/Terms per Academic Year	4	4
Tuition and Fees		
Resident	$3,777	$1,284
Nonresident	$8,292	$2,556
Living Expenses	$5,000	$1,500
Summer Term		
(R = Required, O = Optional, N = None)	O	O
Standard Course Load	12	4
Tuition and Fees		
Resident	Same as above	
Nonresident		

Financial Aid Available

	Deadline (fall starts)	Awarded to Full-Time	Part-Time
Gift Aid	April 15	Yes	Yes
Federal College Work-Study	April 15	Yes	No
Federal Perkins Loans		No	No
Federal Stafford Loans	April 15	Yes	Yes
School-Based Loans	April 15	Yes	Yes
Outside and Private Loans	April 15	Yes	Yes
Graduate Assistantships	April 15	Yes	No

Percentage of Students Receiving Aid	Full-Time	Part-Time
All students	15%	3%
Minority students	15%	3%
Women students	15%	3%
International students	10%	3%

THE COLLEGE OF INSURANCE

101 Murray Street
New York, NY 10007
Telephone: 212-962-4111

Total Enrollment (1993-94)	Full-Time	Part-Time
	191	

Cost of Attendance (1993-94)

	Full-Time	Part-Time
Academic Year		
Standard Course Load per Semester/Term		
(credit hours/units)	9-12	3-6
Semesters/Terms per Academic Year	2	2
Tuition and Fees	$7,047	$4,608
Living Expenses		
Summer Term		
(R = Required, O = Optional, N = None)	O	O
Standard Course Load	9-12	3-6
Tuition and Fees	$3,591	$2,394

Financial Aid Available

	Deadline (fall starts)	Awarded to Full-Time	Awarded to Part-Time
Gift Aid	July 1	Yes	Yes
Federal College Work-Study	July 1	Yes	No
Federal Perkins Loans	July 1	Yes	No
Federal Stafford Loans	July 1	Yes	Yes
School-Based Loans	July 1	Yes	No
Outside and Private Loans	July 1	Yes	No
Graduate Assistantships	July 1	Yes	Yes

Percentage of Students Receiving Aid	Full-Time	Part-Time
All students	85%	40%
Minority students	80%	60%
Women students	80%	60%
International students	30%	20%

COLLEGE OF NOTRE DAME

1500 Ralston Avenue
Belmont, California 94002
Telephone: 415-508-3542

Total Enrollment (1993-94)	Full-Time	Part-Time
	55	120

Cost of Attendance (1993-94)

	Full-Time	Part-Time
Academic Year		
Standard Course Load per Semester/Term		
(credit hours/units)	9	3
Semesters/Terms per Academic Year	4	4
Tuition and Fees	$3,140	$1,065
Living Expenses	$7,400	NA
Summer Term		
(R = Required, O = Optional, N = None)	O	O
Standard Course Load	3	3
Tuition and Fees	$1,065	$1,065

Financial Aid Available

	Deadline (fall starts)	Awarded to Full-Time	Awarded to Part-Time
Gift Aid	August 1	Yes	No
Federal College Work-Study	NA		
Federal Perkins Loans	NA		
Federal Stafford Loans	August 1	Yes	Yes
School-Based Loans	NA		
Outside and Private Loans	NA	Yes	Yes
Graduate Assistantships	NA	Yes	Yes

THE COLLEGE OF SAINT ROSE
Graduate School of Business

432 Western Avenue
Albany, New York 12203
Telephone: 518-454-5136

Total Enrollment (1993-94)	Full-Time	Part-Time
	4	141

Cost of Attendance (1993-94)		
Academic Year		
Standard Course Load per Semester/Term		
(credit hours/units)	12	6
Semesters/Terms per Academic Year	2	2
Tuition and Fees	$3,432	$1,716
Living Expenses	$6,888	$6,888
Summer Term		
(R = Required, O = Optional, N = None)	O	O
Standard Course Load	12	6
Tuition and Fees	$3,432	$1,716

Financial Aid Available	Deadline (fall starts)	Awarded to Full-Time	Part-Time
Gift Aid	March 1	Yes	No
Federal College Work-Study	March 1	Yes	Yes
Federal Perkins Loans	March 1	Yes	Yes
Federal Stafford Loans	July 1	Yes	Yes
School-Based Loans	July 1	Yes	Yes
Outside and Private Loans	July 1	Yes	Yes
Graduate Assistantships	March 1	Yes	Yes

Percentage of Students Receiving Aid	Full-Time	Part-Time
All students	85%	85%
Minority students	90%	90%
Women students	85%	85%
International students	70%	70%

THE COLLEGE OF SANTA FE
Graduate and External Programs

1600 St. Michael's Drive
Santa Fe, New Mexico 87501
Telephone: 505-473-6177

Total Enrollment (1993-94)	Full-Time	Part-Time
	100	50

Cost of Attendance (1993-94)		
Academic Year		
Standard Course Load per Semester/Term		
(credit hours/units)	9	3-6
Semesters/Terms per Academic Year	5	5
Tuition and Fees	$4,011	$2,865
Living Expenses	$ 700	$300-$500
Summer Term		
(R = Required, O = Optional, N = None)	O	O
Standard Course Load	9	3-6
Tuition and Fees	$4,011	$2,865

Financial Aid Available	Deadline (fall starts)	Awarded to Full-Time	Part-Time
Gift Aid	March 31	Yes	Yes
Federal College Work-Study		No	No
Federal Perkins Loans		No	No
Federal Stafford Loans	March 31	Yes	Yes
School-Based Loans		No	No
Outside and Private Loans	March 31	Yes	Yes
Graduate Assistantships	March 31	Yes	Yes

COLLEGE OF WILLIAM AND MARY
Graduate School of Business

Blow Hall, Room 255
Williamsburg, Virginia 23185
Telephone: 804-221-2900

Total Enrollment (1993-94)	Full-Time	Part-Time
	180	

Cost of Attendance (1993-94)		
Academic Year		
Standard Course Load per Semester/Term		
(credit hours/units)	18	9
Semesters/Terms per Academic Year	2	2
Tuition and Fees		
Resident	$ 4,714	$2,160
Nonresident	$12,904	$5,400
Living Expenses		
Summer Term		
(R = Required, O = Optional, N = None)	N	O
Standard Course Load		3 hrs.
Tuition and Fees		$300/sem.hr.

Financial Aid Available	Deadline (fall starts)	Awarded to Full-Time	Part-Time
Gift Aid	March 1	Yes	No
Federal College Work-Study	March 1	No	No
Federal Perkins Loans	March 1	Yes	No
Federal Stafford Loans	April 1	Yes	Yes
School-Based Loans	April 1	Yes	Yes
Outside and Private Loans	April 1	Yes	Yes
Graduate Assistantships	March	Yes	No

Percentage of Students Receiving Aid	Full-Time
All students	75%
Minority students	100%
Women students	75%
International students	0%

COLORADO STATE UNIVERSITY
College of Business

B219 Clark Building
Colorado State University
Fort Collins, Colorado 80523
Telephone: 303-491-6471

Total Enrollment (1993-94)	Full-Time	Part-Time
	392 combined	

Cost of Attendance (1993-94)		
Academic Year		
Standard Course Load per Semester/Term		
(credit hours/units)	9-12	3-6
Semesters/Terms per Academic Year	3	3
Tuition and Fees		
Resident	$2,874	$121/cr.
Nonresident	$8,522	$357/cr.
Living Expenses	$8,000	$8,000
Summer Term		
(R = Required, O = Optional, N = None)	O	O
Standard Course Load	9	3-6
Tuition and Fees		
Resident	Same as above	
Nonresident		

Financial Aid Available	Deadline (fall starts)	Awarded to Full-Time	Part-Time
Gift Aid	April 1	Yes	Yes
Federal College Work-Study	April 1	Yes	Yes
Federal Perkins Loans			
Federal Stafford Loans	April 1	Yes	Yes
School-Based Loans			
Outside and Private Loans			
Graduate Assistantships	April 1	Yes	No

Percentage of Students Receiving Aid	Full-Time	Part-Time
All students		
Minority students	58%	58%
Women students	28%	28%
International students	28%	28%

COLUMBIA UNIVERSITY
Columbia Business School

Office of Financial Aid
218 Uris Hall
New York, New York 10027
Telephone: 212-854-4057

Total Enrollment (1993-94)	Full-Time
	1,400

Cost of Attendance (1993-94)	
Academic Year	
Standard Course Load per Semester/Term	
(credit hours/units)	15 points
Semesters/Terms per Academic Year	2
Tuition and Fees	$20,940
Living Expenses	$14,464
Summer Term	
(R = Required, O = Optional, N = None)	O
Standard Course Load	15 points
Tuition and Fees	$10,419

Financial Aid Available	Deadline (fall starts)	Awarded to Full-Time
Gift Aid	February 1	Yes
Federal College Work-Study	Upon request	Yes
Federal Perkins Loans	February 1	Yes
Federal Stafford Loans	No deadline	Yes
School-Based Loans	February 1	Yes
Outside and Private Loans	No deadline	Yes
Graduate Assistantships	NA	No

Percentage of Students Receiving Aid	Full-Time
All students	60%

CORNELL UNIVERSITY
Johnson Graduate School of Management

Malott Hall
Ithaca, New York 14853
Telephone: 607-255-2327

Total Enrollment (1993-94)	Full-Time
	500

Cost of Attendance (1993-94)	
Academic Year	
Standard Course Load per Semester/Term	
(credit hours/units)	15
Semesters/Terms per Academic Year	2
Tuition and Fees	$19,500
Living Expenses	$11,100
Summer Term	
(R = Required, O = Optional, N = None)	N
Standard Course Load	
Tuition and Fees	
Resident	
Nonresident	

Financial Aid Available	Deadline (fall starts)	Awarded to Full-Time
Gift Aid	No deadline	Yes
Federal College Work-Study	No deadline	Yes
Federal Perkins Loans	No deadline	Yes
Federal Stafford Loans	No deadline	Yes
School-Based Loans	No deadline	Yes
Outside and Private Loans	No deadline	Yes
Graduate Assistantships		No

Percentage of Students Receiving Aid	Full-Time
All students	50%
Minority students	100%
Women students	55%
International students	8%

DARTMOUTH COLLEGE
The Amos Tuck School of Business Administration

100 Tuck Hall
Hanover, New Hampshire 03755
Telephone: 603-646-3504

Total Enrollment (1993-94)	Full-Time
	360

Cost of Attendance (1993-94)

Academic Year	
Standard Course Load per Semester/Term (credit hours/units)	12
Semesters/Terms per Academic Year	3
Tuition and Fees	$19,950
Living Expenses	$13,550
Summer Term	
(R = Required, O = Optional, N = None)	N
Standard Course Load	
Tuition and Fees	
Resident	
Nonresident	

Financial Aid Available

	Deadline (fall starts)	Awarded to Full-Time
Gift Aid	April 1	Yes
Federal College Work-Study	August 1	Yes
Federal Perkins Loans	April 1	Yes
Federal Stafford Loans	August 1	Yes
School-Based Loans	August 1	Yes
Outside and Private Loans	NA	No
Graduate Assistantships	NA	No

Percentage of Students Receiving Aid	Full-Time
All students	60%
Minority students	78%
Women students	64%
International students	12%

DOWLING COLLEGE

Idle Hour Boulevard
Oakdale, New York 11769
Telephone: 516-244-3030

Total Enrollment (1993-94)	Full-Time	Part-Time
	750	

Cost of Attendance (1993-94)

Academic Year		
Standard Course Load per Semester/Term (credit hours/units)	12	6
Semesters/Terms per Academic Year	4	4
Tuition and Fees	$ 8,964	$ 4,582
Living Expenses	$17,334	$12,952
Summer Term		
(R = Required, O = Optional, N = None)	O	O
Standard Course Load	6	6
Tuition and Fees	$ 351	$ 351

Financial Aid Available

	Deadline (fall starts)	Awarded to Full-Time	Part-Time
Gift Aid	Rolling	Yes	Yes
Federal College Work-Study		No	No
Federal Perkins Loans		No	No
Federal Stafford Loans	Rolling	Yes	Yes
School-Based Loans	NA		
Outside and Private Loans	Rolling	Yes	Yes
Graduate Assistantships		Yes	Yes

Percentage of Students Receiving Aid	Full-Time	Part-Time
All students	80%	80%

DREXEL UNIVERSITY
College of Business and Administration

32nd & Chestnut Street
Philadelphia, Pennsylvania 19104
Telephone: 215-895-6700

Total Enrollment (1993-94)	Full-Time	Part-Time
	900	2,000

Cost of Attendance (1993-94)		
Academic Year		
Standard Course Load per Semester/Term		
(credit hours/units)	9	6
Semesters/Terms per Academic Year	3	3
Tuition and Fees	$10,845	$ 7,194
Living Expenses	$11,112	$10,812
Summer Term		
(R = Required, O = Optional, N = None)	O	O
Standard Course Load	9	6
Tuition and Fees	$ 3,615	$ 2,398

Financial Aid Available	Deadline (fall starts)	Awarded to Full-Time	Part-Time
Gift Aid	February 1	Yes	No
Federal College Work-Study		Yes	Yes
Federal Perkins Loans		Yes	Yes
Federal Stafford Loans		Yes	Yes
School-Based Loans		Yes	Yes
Outside and Private Loans		Yes	Yes
Graduate Assistantships	February 1	Yes	No

DRURY COLLEGE
Breech School of Business Administration

900 North Benton
Springfield, Missouri 65802
Telephone: 417 873-7240

Total Enrollment (1993-94)	Full-Time	Part-Time
	1	48

Cost of Attendance (1993-94)		
Academic Year		
Standard Course Load per Semester/Term		
(credit hours/units)	12	6
Semesters/Terms per Academic Year	2	2
Tuition and Fees	$4,800	$2,400
Living Expenses	NA	NA
Summer Term		
(R = Required, O = Optional, N = None)	R	R
Standard Course Load	6	6
Tuition and Fees	$1,200	$ 600

Financial Aid Available	Deadline (fall starts)	Awarded to Full-Time	Part-Time
Gift Aid		No	No
Federal College Work-Study		No	No
Federal Perkins Loans		No	No
Federal Stafford Loans		Yes	Yes
School-Based Loans		No	No
Outside and Private Loans		No	No
Graduate Assistantships		No	No

Percentage of Students Receiving Aid	Full-Time	Part-Time
All students	10%	5%

DUKE UNIVERSITY
Fuqua School of Business

Towerview Drive
Box 90104
Durham, North Carolina 27708
Telephone: 919-660-7705

Total Enrollment (1993-94)	Full-Time	Evening	Weekend
	677	108	41

Cost of Attendance (1993-94)			
Academic Year			
Standard Course Load per			
Semester/Term			
(credit hours/units)	9-12	6-9	6-9
Semesters/Terms per			
Academic Year	4	3	3
Tuition and Fees	$20,275	$6,600	$9,400
Living Expenses	$10,550	$2,500	$2,500
Summer Term			
(R = Required, O = Optional,			
N = None)	N	R	R
Standard Course Load		6-9	6-9
Tuition and Fees		$6,600	$9,400

Financial Aid Available

	Deadline (fall starts)	Awarded to Full-Time	Part-Time
Gift Aid	February 1	Yes	No
Federal College Work-Study	February 1	Yes	No
Federal Perkins Loans	February 1	Yes	No
Federal Stafford Loans	May 1	Yes	Yes
School-Based Loans	May 1	Yes	
Outside and Private Loans	Open	Yes	Yes
Graduate Assistantships		No	No

Percentage of Students Receiving Aid	Full-Time	Evening	Weekend
All students	63%	10%	1%
Minority students	93%	1%	
Women students	70%	1%	

DUQUESNE UNIVERSITY
Graduate School of Business and Administration

Rockwell Hall
Pittsburgh, Pennsylvania 15282
Telephone: 412-396-6269

Total Enrollment (1993-94)	Full-Time	Part-Time
	182	641

Cost of Attendance (1993-94)		
Academic Year		
Standard Course Load per Semester/Term		
(credit hours/units)	9	3-6
Semesters/Terms per Academic Year	3	3
Tuition and Fees	$7,146	$1,176-$2,352
Living Expenses	$6,000	NA
Summer Term		
(R = Required, O = Optional, N = None)	O	O
Standard Course Load	9	3-6
Tuition and Fees	$7,146	$1,176-$2,352

Financial Aid Available

	Deadline (fall starts)	Awarded to Full-Time	Part-Time
Gift Aid		No	No
Federal College Work-Study		No	No
Federal Perkins Loans	May 1	Yes	Yes
Federal Stafford Loans	May 1	Yes	Yes
School-Based Loans	May 1	Yes	Yes
Outside and Private Loans	May 1	Yes	Yes
Graduate Assistantships	June 1	Yes	

EAST CAROLINA UNIVERSITY
School of Business

Greenville, North Carolina 27858-4353
Telephone: 919-757-6970

Total Enrollment (1993-94)	Full-Time	Part-Time
	156	115

Cost of Attendance (1993-94)		
Academic Year		
Standard Course Load per Semester/Term		
(credit hours/units)	12-15	6
Semesters/Terms per Academic Year	2	2
Tuition and Fees		
Resident	$1,344	$ 874
Nonresident	$7,414	$5,412
Living Expenses	$5,000	$5,000
Summer Term		
(R = Required, O = Optional, N = None)	O	O
Standard Course Load	6	3
Tuition and Fees		
Resident	$ 382	$ 289
Nonresident	$2,656	$1,806

Financial Aid Available	Deadline (fall starts)	Awarded to Full-Time	Part-Time
Gift Aid	April 15	Yes	No
Federal College Work-Study	April 15	Yes	Yes
Federal Perkins Loans	April 15	Yes	Yes
Federal Stafford Loans	April 15	Yes	Yes
School-Based Loans	NA		
Outside and Private Loans	NA		
Graduate Assistantships	August 15	Yes	No

Percentage of Students Receiving Aid	Full-Time
All students	55%

EAST TENNESSEE STATE UNIVERSITY
College of Business

Box 70,699
Johnson City, Tennessee 37614
Telephone: 615-929-5314

Total Enrollment (1993-94)	Full-Time	Part-Time
	170	51

Cost of Attendance (1993-94)		
Academic Year		
Standard Course Load per Semester/Term		
(credit hours/units)	9	6
Semesters/Terms per Academic Year	2	2
Tuition and Fees		
Resident	$2,012	$1,212
Nonresident	$5,614	$3,096
Living Expenses	$3,500	NA
Summer Term		
(R = Required, O = Optional, N = None)	O	O
Standard Course Load	6	3
Tuition and Fees		
Resident	$ 606	$ 303
Nonresident	$1,548	$ 774

Financial Aid Available	Deadline (fall starts)	Awarded to Full-Time	Part-Time
Gift Aid		Yes	Yes
Federal College Work-Study		No	No
Federal Perkins Loans	NA		
Federal Stafford Loans	NA		
School-Based Loans		No	No
Outside and Private Loans		Yes	Yes
Graduate Assistantships	June 1	Yes	No

Percentage of Students Receiving Aid	Full-Time
All students	10%
Minority students	50%
Women sudents	20%
International students	20%

EAST TEXAS STATE UNIVERSITY AT TEXARKANA
Division of Business Administration

P.O. Box 5518
2600 North Robison Road
Texarkana, Texas 75505
Telephone: 903-838-6514

Total Enrollment (1993-94)	Full-Time	Part-Time
	10	200

Cost of Attendance (1993-94)		
Academic Year		
Standard Course Load per Semester/Term		
(credit hours/units)	9	3
Semesters/Terms per Academic Year	2	2
Tuition and Fees		
Resident	$ 518	$ 195
Nonresident	$1,742	$ 581
Living Expenses	$7,480	$7,080
Summer Term		
(R = Required, O = Optional, N = None)	O	O
Standard Course Load	6-9	3-6
Tuition and Fees		
Resident	$ 173	$ 195
Nonresident	$ 581	$ 581

Financial Aid Available	Deadline (fall starts)	Awarded to Full-Time	Part-Time
Gift Aid	May 1	Yes	Yes
Federal College Work-Study	May 1	Yes	Yes
Federal Perkins Loans	NA		
Federal Stafford Loans	May 1	Yes	Yes
School-Based Loans	As available	Yes	Yes
Outside and Private Loans	NA		
Graduate Assistantships	NA		

EASTERN COLLEGE
Graduate Programs

10 Fairview Drive
St. David's, Pennsylvania 19087
Telephone: 215-341-5972

Total Enrollment (1993-94)	Full-Time	Part-Time
	92	160

Cost of Attendance (1993-94)		
Academic Year		
Standard Course Load per Semester/Term		
(credit hours/units)	9-12	3-6
Semesters/Terms per Academic Year	2	2
Tuition and Fees	$ 315	$ 315
Living Expenses	$7,225	NA
Summer Term		
(R = Required, O = Optional, N = None)	O	O
Standard Course Load	3-6	3-6
Tuition and Fees		
Resident	Same as above	
Nonresident		

Financial Aid Available	Deadline (fall starts)	Awarded to Full-Time	Part-Time
Gift Aid	None	Yes	No
Federal College Work-Study	None	Yes	No
Federal Perkins Loans	None	No	No
Federal Stafford Loans	None	Yes	Yes
School-Based Loans	None	No	No
Outside and Private Loans	None	Yes	Yes
Graduate Assistantships	None	Yes	No

Percentage of Students Receiving Aid	Full-Time
All students	78%
Minority students	10%
Women students	29%
International students	64%

EASTERN KENTUCKY UNIVERSITY
College of Business

MBA Program
Bert Combs Building, Room 317
Richmond, Kentucky 40475-3111
Telephone: 606-622-1775

Total Enrollment (1993-94)	Full-Time	Part-Time
	111	20

Cost of Attendance (1993-94)		
Academic Year		
Standard Course Load per Semester/Term		
(credit hours/units)	9	6
Semesters/Terms per Academic Year	3	3
Tuition and Fees		
Resident	$ 930	$ 640
Nonresident	$2,590	$1,728
Living Expenses	NA	NA
Summer Term		
(R = Required, O = Optional, N = None)	O	O
Standard Course Load	6	3
Tuition and Fees		
Resident	$ 640	$ 640
Nonresident	$1,728	$1,728

Financial Aid Available	Deadline (fall starts)	Awarded to Full-Time	Part-Time
Gift Aid	NA	No	No
Federal College Work-Study	None	Yes	Yes
Federal Perkins Loans	April 15	Yes	Yes
Federal Stafford Loans	April 15	Yes	Yes
School-Based Loans	NA	No	No
Outside and Private Loans	NA	No	No
Graduate Assistantships	July 1	Yes	No

Percentage of Students Receiving Aid	Full-Time	Part-Time
All students		70%

EASTERN MICHIGAN UNIVERSITY
College of Business

401 Owen Building
Ypsilanti, Michigan 48197
Telephone: 313-487-4444

Total Enrollment (1993-94)	Full-Time	Part-Time
	188	534

Cost of Attendance (1993-94)		
Academic Year		
Standard Course Load per Semester/Term		
(credit hours/units)	12	6
Semesters/Terms per Academic Year	2	2
Tuition and Fees		
Resident	$2,980	$1,540
Nonresident	$6,340	$3,220
Living Expenses	$6,000	NA
Summer Term		
(R = Required, O = Optional, N = None)	O	O
Standard Course Load	9	6
Tuition and Fees		
Resident	$1,160	$ 800
Nonresident	$2,420	$1,640

Financial Aid Available	Deadline (fall starts)	Awarded to Full-Time	Part-Time
Gift Aid	March 15	Yes	No
Federal College Work-Study	March 15	Yes	Yes
Federal Perkins Loans	March 15	Yes	Yes
Federal Stafford Loans	September	Yes	Yes
School-Based Loans	NA		
Outside and Private Loans	NA		
Graduate Assistantships	March 15	Yes	No

Percentage of Students Receiving Aid	Full-Time	Part-Time
All students	24%	5%
Minority students	50%	50%
Women students	25%	5%
International students	30%	0%

EASTERN NEW MEXICO UNIVERSITY
College of Business

Station #49
Portales, New Mexico 88130
Telephone: 505-562-2744

Total Enrollment (1993-94)	Full-Time	Part-Time
	20	35

Cost of Attendance (1993-94)		
Academic Year		
Standard Course Load per Semester/Term		
(credit hours/units)	12	6
Semesters/Terms per Academic Year	2	2
Tuition and Fees		
Resident	$1,608	$67/cr. hr.
Nonresident	$5,448	$67/cr. hr.
Living Expenses	$7,500	$7,500
Summer Term		
(R = Required, O = Optional, N = None)	O	O
Standard Course Load	6	0-6
Tuition and Fees	$ 402	$67/cr. hr.

Financial Aid Available	Deadline (fall starts)	Awarded to Full-Time	Awarded to Part-Time
Gift Aid	March 1	Yes	Yes
Federal College Work-Study	March 1	Yes	Yes
Federal Perkins Loans	March 1	Yes	Yes
Federal Stafford Loans	March 1	Yes	Yes
School-Based Loans	March 1	Yes	Yes
Outside and Private Loans	March 1	Yes	Yes
Graduate Assistantships	April 15	Yes	Yes

Percentage of Students Receiving Aid	Full-Time	Part-Time
All students	80%	50%

EASTERN WASHINGTON UNIVERSITY
College of Business Administration

West 705 First Avenue
Spokane, Washington 99204
Telephone: 509-359-6413

Total Enrollment (1993-94)	Full-Time	Part-Time
	23	74

Cost of Attendance (1993-94)		
Academic Year		
Standard Course Load per Semester/Term		
(credit hours/units)	10	less than 10
Semesters/Terms per Academic Year	3	3
Tuition and Fees		
Resident	$1,046	$105/cr. hr.
Nonresident	$3,179	$308/cr. hr.
Living Expenses	$5,610	$5,610
Summer Term		
(R = Required, O = Optional, N = None)	O	O
Standard Course Load	10	less than 10
Tuition and Fees	NA	NA

Financial Aid Available	Deadline (fall starts)	Awarded to Full-Time	Awarded to Part-Time
Gift Aid	February 15	Yes	No
Federal College Work-Study	February 15	Yes	No
Federal Perkins Loans	NA		
Federal Stafford Loans	Open	Yes	Yes
School-Based Loans	NA		
Outside and Private Loans	NA		
Graduate Assistantships		Yes	No

Percentage of Students Receiving Aid	Full-Time	Part-Time
All students	8%	5%
Minority students	1%	0%
Women students	2%	2%
International students	0%	0%

ELON COLLEGE
The Martha and Spencer Love School of Business

2700 Campus Box
Elon College, North Carolina 27244
Telephone: 910-584-2370
800-334-8448

Total Enrollment (1993-94)	Full-Time	Part-Time
	11	100

Cost of Attendance (1993-94)

Academic Year
Standard Course Load per Semester/Term

(credit hours/units)	9-12	3-6
Semesters/Terms per Academic Year	2-4	1-4
Tuition and Fees	$185/cr. hr.	$185/cr. hr.
Living Expenses	$6,500	$5,800

Summer Term
(R = Required, O = Optional, N = None)

	O	O
Standard Course Load	3 hours per session	
Tuition and Fees	$185/cr. hr.	$185/ cr. hr.
$10 enrollment fee per session		

Financial Aid Available

	Deadline (fall starts)	Awarded to Full-Time	Part-Time
Gift Aid	NA	Yes	Yes
Federal College Work-Study	NA	Yes	Yes
Federal Perkins Loans	NA	No	No
Federal Stafford Loans	None	Yes	Yes
School-Based Loans	NA	No	No
Outside and Private Loans	NA	Yes	Yes
Graduate Assistantships	NA	No	No

Percentage of Students Receiving Aid	Full-Time	Part-Time
All students	36%	8%
Minority students	0%	0%
Women students	0%	4%
International students	11%	0%

EMBRY-RIDDLE AERONAUTICAL UNIVERSITY

Office of Graduate Programs
600 South Clyde Morris Boulevard
Daytona Beach, Florida 32114
Telephone: 904-226-6715

Total Enrollment (1993-94)	Full-Time	Part-Time
	88	91

Cost of Attendance (1993-94)

Academic Year
Standard Course Load per Semester/Term

(credit hours/units)	9	6
Semesters/Terms per Academic Year	3	3
Tuition and Fees	$5,490	$3,660
Living Expenses	$7,400	$7,400

Summer Term
(R = Required, O = Optional, N = None)

	O	O
Standard Course Load	6	3
Tuition and Fees	$1,830	$ 915

Financial Aid Available

	Deadline (fall starts)	Awarded to Full-Time	Part-Time
Gift Aid	April 15	Yes	Yes
Federal College Work-Study	December 24	No	No
Federal Perkins Loans	April 15	No	No
Federal Stafford Loans	April 15	Yes	Yes
School-Based Loans	April 15	No	No
Outside and Private Loans	April 15	Yes	Yes
Graduate Assistantships	August 30	Yes	Yes

Percentage of Students Receiving Aid	Full-Time	Part-Time
All students	26%	15%
Minority students	3%	3%
Women students	3%	2%
International students	3%	1%

EMORY UNIVERSITY
Goizueta Business School

1602 Mizell Drive
Atlanta, Georgia 30322-2710
Telephone: 404-727-6311

Total Enrollment (1993-94)	Full-Time	Part-Time
	255	96

Cost of Attendance (1993-94)		
Academic Year		
Standard Course Load per Semester/Term		
(credit hours/units)	15	6-7
Semesters/Terms per Academic Year	2	3
Tuition and Fees	$18,070	$12,117
Living Expenses	$10,810	
Summer Term		
(R = Required, O = Optional, N = None)	N	R
Standard Course Load		6-7
Tuition and Fees		$ 4,039

Financial Aid Available	Deadline (fall starts)	Awarded to Full-Time	Awarded to Part-Time
Gift Aid	March 1	Yes	No
Federal College Work-Study	April 1	Yes	No
Federal Perkins Loans	April 1	Yes	No
Federal Stafford Loans	None	Yes	Yes
School-Based Loans	None	Yes	Yes
Outside and Private Loans	None	Yes	Yes
Graduate Assistantships	September 1	Yes	No

Percentage of Students Receiving Aid	Full-Time	Part-Time
All students	71%	20%
Minority students	100%	2%
Women students	78%	6%
International students	3%	0%

FAIRFIELD UNIVERSITY
School of Business

Fairfield, Connecticut 06430
Telephone: 203-254-4000

Total Enrollment (1993-94)	Full-Time	Part-Time
	1	70

Cost of Attendance (1993-94)		
Academic Year		
Standard Course Load per Semester/Term		
(credit hours/units)	12	6
Semesters/Terms per Academic Year	2	2
Tuition and Fees	$3,960	$1,900
Living Expenses	NA	NA
Summer Term		
(R = Required, O = Optional, N = None)	O	O
Standard Course Load	6	6
Tuition and Fees	$1,900	$1,900

Financial Aid Available	Deadline (fall starts)	Awarded to Full-Time	Awarded to Part-Time
Gift Aid	February 1	Yes	Yes
Federal College Work-Study		No	No
Federal Perkins Loans	February 1	Yes	Yes
Federal Stafford Loans	February 1	Yes	Yes
School-Based Loans		No	No
Outside and Private Loans	February 1	Yes	Yes
Graduate Assistantships		No	No

FAIRLEIGH DICKINSON UNIVERSITY
Samuel J. Silberman College of Business Administration

1000 River Road
Teaneck, New Jersey 07666
Telephone: 201-692-2136

Total Enrollment (1993-94)	Full-Time	Part-Time
	392	2,094

Cost of Attendance (1993-94)		
Academic Year		
Standard Course Load per Semester/Term		
(credit hours/units)	9	6
Semesters/Terms per Academic Year	2	2
Tuition and Fees	$ 7,436	$ 4,903
Living Expenses	$11,722	$11,548
Summer Term		
(R = Required, O = Optional, N = None)	O	O
Standard Course Load	6	6
Tuition and Fees	$ 4,903	$ 4,903

Financial Aid Available	Deadline (fall starts)	Awarded to Full-Time	Part-Time
Gift Aid	August 1	Yes	Yes
Federal College Work-Study	NA	No	No
Federal Perkins Loans	NA	No	No
Federal Stafford Loans	August 1	Yes	Yes
School-Based Loans		No	No
Outside and Private Loans	August 1	Yes	Yes
Graduate Assistantships			

FLORIDA ATLANTIC UNIVERSITY
College of Business

500 NW 20th Street
Boca Raton, Florida 33431
Telephone: 407-367-3650

Total Enrollment (1993-94)	Full-Time	Part-Time
	147	477

Cost of Attendance (1993-94)		
Academic Year		
Standard Course Load per Semester/Term		
(credit hours/units)	9	3-6
Semesters/Terms per Academic Year	3	3
Tuition and Fees		
Resident	$2,010	$770-$1,340
Nonresident	$6,565	$2,190-$4,380
Living Expenses	$6,250	$6,000
Summer Term		
(R = Required, O = Optional, N = None)	O	O
Standard Course Load	9	3-6
Tuition and Fees		
Resident	$1,020	$350-$700
Nonresident	$3,300	$1,200-$2,400

Financial Aid Available	Deadline (fall starts)	Awarded to Full-Time	Part-Time
Gift Aid	July 1	Yes	Yes
Federal College Work-Study	April 1	Yes	Yes
Federal Perkins Loans	April 1	Yes	Yes
Federal Stafford Loans	April 1	Yes	Yes
School-Based Loans	April 1	Yes	Yes
Outside and Private Loans	April 1	Yes	Yes
Graduate Assistantships	Variable	Yes	Yes

Percentage of Students Receiving Aid	Full-Time	Part-Time
All students	13%	13%
Minority students	30%	30%
Women students	20%	20%
International students	30%	

FLORIDA INSTITUTE OF TECHNOLOGY
School of Business

150 West University Boulevard
Melbourne, Florida 32901
Telephone: 407-768-8000, extension 7345

Total Enrollment (1993-94)	Full-Time	Part-Time
	100	200

Cost of Attendance (1993-94)		
Academic Year		
Standard Course Load per Semester/Term		
(credit hours/units)	9	6
Semesters/Terms per Academic Year	3	3
Tuition and Fees	$8,208	$8,208
Living Expenses	$7,200	$7,200
Summer Term		
(R = Required, O = Optional, N = None)	O	O
Standard Course Load	6	6
Tuition and Fees	$8,208	$8,208

Financial Aid Available	Deadline (fall starts)	Awarded to Full-Time	Part-Time
Gift Aid		No	No
Federal College Work-Study		Yes	Yes
Federal Perkins Loans		Yes	Yes
Federal Stafford Loans		Yes	Yes
School-Based Loans		No	No
Outside and Private Loans		Yes	Yes
Graduate Assistantships		Yes	No

FLORIDA INTERNATIONAL UNIVERSITY
College of Business Administration

University Park BA-220
Miami, Florida 33199
Telephone: 305-348-3256

Total Enrollment (1993-94)	Full-Time	Part-Time
	96	224

Cost of Attendance (1993-94)		
Academic Year		
Standard Course Load per Semester/Term		
(credit hours/units)	9	6
Semesters/Terms per Academic Year	4	4
Tuition and Fees		
Resident	$108/cr.	$108/cr.
Nonresident	$361/cr.	$361/cr.
Living Expenses	$10,000	$10,000
Summer Term		
(R = Required, O = Optional, N = None)	O	O
Standard Course Load	6	6
Tuition and Fees		
Resident	$108/cr.	$108/cr.
Nonresident	$361/cr.	$361/cr.

Financial Aid Available	Deadline (fall starts)	Awarded to Full-Time	Part-Time
Gift Aid	June 1	Yes	No
Federal College Work-Study	April 1	Yes	No
Federal Perkins Loans	April 1	Yes	No
Federal Stafford Loans	April 1	Yes	No
School-Based Loans	April 1	Yes	No
Outside and Private Loans	June 1	Yes	Yes
Graduate Assistantships		No	No

Percentage of Students Receiving Aid	Full-Time	Part-Time
All students	15%	10%
Minority students	25%	20%
Women students	15%	15%
International students	5%	5%

FLORIDA STATE UNIVERSITY
College of Business

Tallahassee, Florida 32306
Telephone: 904-644-3090

Total Enrollment (1993-94)	Full-Time	Part-Time
	65	50

Cost of Attendance (1993-94)		
Academic Year		
Standard Course Load per Semester/Term		
(credit hours/units)	15	6
Semesters/Terms per Academic Year	3	3
Tuition and Fees		
Resident	$ 3,340	$1,335
Nonresident	$11,000	$4,370
Living Expenses	$ 8,200	$8,200
Summer Term		
(R = Required, O = Optional, N = None)	O*	O
Standard Course Load	12	3
Tuition and Fees		
Resident	$ 1,335	$ 335
Nonresident	$ 4,370	$1,100

*Required for one-year program

Financial Aid Available	Deadline (fall starts)	Awarded to Full-Time	Part-Time
Gift Aid	None	Yes	No
Federal College Work-Study	March 2	Yes	No
Federal Perkins Loans	March 2	Yes	No
Federal Stafford Loans	March 2	Yes	No
School-Based Loans	March 2	Yes	No
Outside and Private Loans	March 2	Yes	No
Graduate Assistantships	None	Yes	No

Percentage of Students Receiving Aid	Full-Time
All students	60%
Minority students	60%
Women students	60%
International students	25%

FORDHAM UNIVERSITY
Graduate School of Business Administration

113 West 60th Street
New York, New York 10023
Telephone: 212-636-6100

Total Enrollment (1993-94)	Full-Time	Part-Time
	400	1,500

Cost of Attendance (1993-94)		
Academic Year		
Standard Course Load per Semester/Term		
(credit hours/units)	12	6
Semesters/Terms per Academic Year	3	3
Tuition and Fees	$15,909	$ 7,989
Living Expenses	$12,600	$12,600
Summer Term		
(R = Required, O = Optional, N = None)		
Standard Course Load	12	6
Tuition and Fees	$ 5,303	$ 2,663

Financial Aid Available	Deadline (fall starts)	Awarded to Full-Time	Part-Time
Gift Aid	September 15	Yes	No
Federal College Work-Study	NA	No	No
Federal Perkins Loans	NA	No	No
Federal Stafford Loans	June 15	Yes	Yes
School-Based Loans	NA	Yes	Yes
Outside and Private Loans	None	Yes	Yes
Graduate Assistantships	June 30	Yes	No

Percentage of Students Receiving Aid	Full-Time	Part-Time
All students	70%	45%

FORT HAYS STATE UNIVERSITY

600 Park Street
Hays, Kansas 67601
Telephone: 913-628-4201

Total Enrollment (1993-94)	Full-Time	Part-Time
	40	20

Cost of Attendance (1993-94)		
Academic Year		
Standard Course Load per Semester/Term		
(credit hours/units)	9	3
Semesters/Terms per Academic Year	2	2
Tuition and Fees		
Resident	$ 69/cr.	$ 69/cr.
Nonresident	$172/cr.	$172/cr.
Living Expenses	$3,500	$3,500
Summer Term		
(R = Required, O = Optional, N = None)	O	O
Standard Course Load	6	3
Tuition and Fees		
Resident	$ 69/cr.	$ 69/cr.
Nonresident	$172/cr.	$172/cr.

Financial Aid Available	Deadline (fall starts)	Awarded to Full-Time	Part-Time
Gift Aid	March 1	Yes	Yes
Federal College Work-Study	Rolling	Yes	No
Federal Perkins Loans	Rolling	Yes	Yes
Federal Stafford Loans	May 1	Yes	Yes
School-Based Loans	NA		
Outside and Private Loans	May 1	Yes	Yes
Graduate Assistantships	March 1	Yes	No

Percentage of Students Receiving Aid	Full-Time	Part-Time
All students	80%	5%
Minority students		
Women students	80%	5%
International students	10%	

FRANCIS MARION UNIVERSITY
School of Business

P.O. Box 100547
Florence, South Carolina 29501-0547
Telephone: 803-661-1419

Total Enrollment (1993-94)	Part-Time
	60

Cost of Attendance (1993-94)	
Academic Year	
Standard Course Load per Semester/Term	
(credit hours/units)	6
Semesters/Terms per Academic Year	2
Tuition and Fees	
Resident	$ 900
Nonresident	$1,800
Living Expenses	$6,630
Summer Term	
(R = Required, O = Optional, N = None)	R
Standard Course Load	3
Tuition and Fees	
Resident	$ 450
Nonresident	$ 900

Financial Aid Available	Deadline (fall starts)	Awarded to Part-Time
Gift Aid	March 1	Yes
Federal College Work-Study		No
Federal Perkins Loans		No
Federal Stafford Loans	March 1	Yes
School-Based Loans		No
Outside and Private Loans	March 1	Yes
Graduate Assistantships	August 1	Yes

Percentage of Students Receiving Aid	Part-Time
All students	5%
Minority students	50%
Women students	5%
International students	50%

FRIENDS UNIVERSITY

2100 University
Wichita, Kansas 67213
Telephone: 316-292-5591

Total Enrollment (1993-94)	Full-Time
	46

Cost of Attendance (1993-94)	
Academic Year	
Standard Course Load per Semester/Term	
(credit hours/units)	9
Semesters/Terms per Academic Year	2
Tuition and Fees	$6,480
Living Expenses	$ 576
Summer Term	
(R = Required, O = Optional, N = Nonc)	R
Standard Course Load	9
Tuition and Fees	$ 360

Financial Aid Available	Deadline (fall starts)	Awarded to Full-Time
Gift Aid		No
Federal College Work-Study		No
Federal Perkins Loans		No
Federal Stafford Loans	May 1	Yes
School-Based Loans		No
Outside and Private Loans		No
Graduate Assistantships		No

Percentage of Students Receiving Aid	Full-Time
All students	33%
Minority students	4%
Women students	8%
International students	0%

GANNON UNIVERSITY
Dahlkemper School of Business

University Square
Erie, Pennsylvania 16541
Telephone: 814-871-7567

Total Enrollment (1993-94)	Full-Time	Part-Time
	16	203

Cost of Attendance (1993-94)		
Academic Year		
Standard Course Load per Semester/Term		
(credit hours/units)	9	3
Semesters/Terms per Academic Year	2	2
Tuition and Fees	$5,940	$1,980
Living Expenses	$8,200	$8,200
Summer Term		
(R = Required, O = Optional, N = None)	O	O
Standard Course Load	6	6
Tuition and Fees	$1,980	$1,980

Financial Aid Available	Deadline (fall starts)	Awarded to Full-Time	Part-Time
Gift Aid		No	No
Federal College Work-Study	February 15	Yes	No
Federal Perkins Loans		No	No
Federal Stafford Loans		No	No
School-Based Loans	July 1	Yes	Yes
Outside and Private Loans	May 1	Yes	No
Graduate Assistantships	February 15	Yes	No

Percentage of Students Receiving Aid	Full-Time
All students	40%
Minority students	100%
Women students	65%

GEORGE MASON UNIVERSITY
School of Business Administration

4400 University Drive
Robinson B # 406
Fairfax, Virginia 22030
Telephone: 703-993-2136

Total Enrollment (1993-94)	Full-Time	Part-Time
	170	400

Cost of Attendance (1993-94)		
Academic Year		
Standard Course Load per Semester/Term		
(credit hours/units)	4-5	2
Semesters/Terms per Academic Year	2	2
Tuition and Fees		
Resident	$ 3,888	$162/cr.
Nonresident	$10,056	$419/cr.
Living Expenses	$6,000	NA
Summer Term		
(R = Required, O = Optional, N = None)	O	O
Standard Course Load	2-3	1
Tuition and Fees		
Resident	NA	$162/cr.
Nonresident	NA	$419/cr.

Financial Aid Available	Deadline (fall starts)	Awarded to Full-Time	Awarded to Part-Time
Gift Aid	April 1	Yes	No
Federal College Work-Study		No	No
Federal Perkins Loans		No	No
Federal Stafford Loans	April 1	Yes	Yes
School-Based Loans		No	No
Outside and Private Loans	NA	Yes	Yes
Graduate Assistantships	April 1	Yes	No

Percentage of Students Receiving Aid	Full-Time	Part-Time
All students	13%	11%
Minority students	14%	2%
Women students	9%	2%

THE GEORGE WASHINGTON UNIVERSITY
School of Business and Public Management

710 21st Street, N.W.
Washington, DC 20052
Telephone: 202-994-6584

Total Enrollment (1993-94)	Full-Time	Part-Time
	645	854

Cost of Attendance (1993-94)		
Academic Year		
Standard Course Load per Semester/Term		
(credit hours/units)	12	6
Semesters/Terms per Academic Year	2	2
Tuition and Fees	$13,790	$6,954
Living Expenses	$ 9,600	
Summer Term		
(R = Required, O = Optional, N = None)	O	O
Standard Course Load	6	6
Tuition and Fees	$ 550	$ 550

Financial Aid Available	Deadline (fall starts)	Awarded to Full-Time	Awarded to Part-Time
Gift Aid	Varies	Yes	No
Federal College Work-Study	April 1	Yes	No
Federal Perkins Loans	April 1	Yes	Yes
Federal Stafford Loans	April 1	Yes	Yes
School-Based Loans	Varies	Yes	No
Outside and Private Loans	Varies	Yes	No
Graduate Assistantships	March 1	Yes	No

GEORGETOWN UNIVERSITY
School of Business

105 Old North
37th and O Streets, N.W.
Washington, DC 20057-1008
Telephone: 202-687-4200

Total Enrollment (1993-94)	Full-Time
	353

Cost of Attendance (1993-94)	
Academic Year	
Standard Course Load per Semester/Term	
(credit hours/units)	15
Semesters/Terms per Academic Year	2
Tuition and Fees	$18,650
Living Expenses	$10,000 (approx.)
Summer Term	
(R = Required, O = Optional, N = None)	N
Standard Course Load	
Tuition and Fees	
Resident	
Nonresident	

Financial Aid Available	Deadline (fall starts)	Awarded to Full-Time
Gift Aid	May 1	Yes
Federal College Work-Study	April 1	Yes
Federal Perkins Loans	April 1	Yes
Federal Stafford Loans	July 1	Yes
School-Based Loans	NA	No
Outside and Private Loans	July 1	Yes
Graduate Assistantships	Rolling	Yes

Percentage of Students Receiving Aid	Full-Time
All students	50%
Minority students	52%
Women students	56%
International students	31%

GEORGIA COLLEGE
The J. Whitney Bunting School of Business

Campus Box 19
Milledgeville, Georgia 31061
Telephone: 912-453-5115

Total Enrollment (1993-94)	Full-Time	Part-Time
	85	185

Cost of Attendance (1993-94)		
Academic Year		
Standard Course Load per Semester/Term		
(credit hours/units)	10 hrs.	5 hrs.
Semesters/Terms per Academic Year	3 qtrs.	3 qtrs.
Tuition and Fees		
Resident	$1,467	$ 593
Nonresident	$3,777	$1,748
Living Expenses	$2,678	
Summer Term		
(R = Required, O = Optional, N = None)	O	O
Standard Course Load	10	5
Tuition and Fees		
Resident	$ 437	$ 195
Nonresident	$1,207	$ 580

Financial Aid Available	Deadline (fall starts)	Awarded to Full-Time	Part-Time
Gift Aid	First Fri. in Feb.	Yes	Yes
Federal College Work-Study	April 15	Yes	Yes
Federal Perkins Loans	April 15	Yes	Yes
Federal Stafford Loans	August 1	Yes	Yes
School-Based Loans	NA		
Outside and Private Loans	NA		
Graduate Assistantships	September 30	Yes	Yes

GEORGIA INSTITUTE OF TECHNOLOGY
School of Management

212 School of Management
Atlanta, Georgia 30332-0520
Telephone: 404-894-2604

Total Enrollment (1993-94)	Full-Time
	225

Cost of Attendance (1993-94)

Academic Year
Standard Course Load per Semester/Term
(credit hours/units) — 12 quarter hrs.
Semesters/Terms per Academic Year — 3 qtrs.
Tuition and Fees
Resident — $2,277
Nonresident — $6,732
Living Expenses — $10,000 (in-state)
$15,000 (out-of-state)
Summer Term
(R = Required, O = Optional, N = None) — N
Standard Course Load
Tuition and Fees
Resident
Nonresident

Financial Aid Available

	Deadline (fall starts)	Awarded to Full-Time
Gift Aid	March 1	Yes
Federal College Work-Study	March 1	Yes
Federal Perkins Loans	March 1	Yes
Federal Stafford Loans	March 1	Yes
School-Based Loans	March 1	Yes
Outside and Private Loans	March 1	Yes
Graduate Assistantships	April 1	Yes

Percentage of Students Receiving Aid	Full-Time
All students	40%
Minority students	36%
Women students	30%
International students	3%

GEORGIA SOUTHERN UNIVERSITY
College of Business Administration

Graduate Studies Office
Landrum Box 8002
Statesboro, Georgia 30460-8002
Telephone: 912-681-5767

Total Enrollment (1993-94)	Full-Time	Part-Time
	74	86

Cost of Attendance (1993-94)

Academic Year		
Standard Course Load per Semester/Term		
(credit hours/units)	12	4
Semesters/Terms per Academic Year	4	4
Tuition and Fees		
Resident	$ 603	$179
Nonresident	$1,533	$487
Summer Term		
(R = Required, O = Optional, N = None)	O	O
Standard Course Load	8	4
Tuition and Fees		
Resident	$ 450	$179
Nonresident	$1,066	$487

Financial Aid Available

	Deadline (fall starts)	Awarded to Full-Time	Part-Time
Gift Aid	March 1	Yes	Yes
Federal College Work-Study	April 15	Yes	Yes
Federal Perkins Loans	April 15	Yes	Yes
Federal Stafford Loans	April 15	Yes	Yes
School-Based Loans	NA		
Outside and Private Loans	NA		
Graduate Assistantships	July 1	Yes	No

GEORGIA STATE UNIVERSITY
College of Business Administration

University Plaza
Atlanta, Georgia 30303
Telephone: 404-651-1913

Total Enrollment (1993-94)	Full-Time	Part-Time
Total combined (full-time and part-time) 1,900		

Cost of Attendance (1993-94)

Academic Year		
Standard Course Load per Semester/Term		
(credit hours/units)	10	5
Semesters/Terms per Academic Year	3	3
Tuition and Fees		
Resident	$1,404	$ 789
Nonresident	$4,359	$2,267
Living Expenses	$7,700	$7,500
Summer Term		
(R = Required, O = Optional, N = None)	O	O
Standard Course Load	10	5
Tuition and Fees		
Resident	$ 468	$ 263
Nonresident	$1,453	$ 756

Financial Aid Available

	Deadline (fall starts)	Awarded to Full-Time	Awarded to Part-Time
Gift Aid	May 1	Yes	Yes
Federal College Work-Study	May 1	Yes	Yes
Federal Perkins Loans	May 1	Yes	Yes
Federal Stafford Loans	May 1	Yes	Yes
School-Based Loans	May 1	Yes	Yes
Outside and Private Loans	May 1	Yes	Yes
Graduate Assistantships	September 1	Yes	No

Percentage of Students Receiving Aid	Full-Time	Part-Time
All students	15%	
Minority students	19%	
Women students	13%	
International students	10%	

GOLDEY-BEACOM COLLEGE

4701 Limestone Road
Wilmington, Delaware 19808
Telephone: 302-998-8814

Total Enrollment (1993-94)	Full-Time	Part-Time
		112

Cost of Attendance (1993-94)

Academic Year		
Standard Course Load per Semester/Term		
(credit hours/units)	9	6
Semesters/Terms per Academic Year	2	2
Tuition and Fees	$5,310	$3,540
Living Expenses	$5,000	
Summer Term		
(R = Required, O = Optional, N = None)	O	O
Standard Course Load	9	6
Tuition and Fees	$2,655	$1,770

Financial Aid Available

	Deadline (fall starts)	Awarded to Full-Time	Awarded to Part-Time
Gift Aid	March 30	Yes	Yes
Federal College Work-Study	April 1	Yes	Yes
Federal Perkins Loans	April 1	Yes	Yes
Federal Stafford Loans	April 1	Yes	Yes
School-Based Loans			
Outside and Private Loans			
Graduate Assistantships	June 15	Yes	Yes

Percentage of Students Receiving Aid	Part-Time
All students	12%
Minority students	2%
Women students	4%
International students	4%

GONZAGA UNIVERSITY

East 502 Boone
Spokane, Washington 99258-0001
Telephone: 509-328-4220

Total Enrollment (1993-94)	Full-Time	Part-Time
	68	33

Cost of Attendance (1993-94)		
Academic Year		
Standard Course Load per Semester/Term		
(credit hours/units)	9	6
Semesters/Terms per Academic Year	2	2
Tuition and Fees	$5,760	$3,840
Living Expenses	$6,700	$6,500
Summer Term		
(R = Required, O = Optional, N = None)	O	O
Standard Course Load	12	6
Tuition and Fees	$2,760	$1,380

Financial Aid Available	Deadline (fall starts)	Awarded to Full-Time	Part-Time
Gift Aid		No	No
Federal College Work-Study		No	No
Federal Perkins Loans		No	No
Federal Stafford Loans	None	Yes	Yes
School-Based Loans	None	Yes	Yes
Outside and Private Loans		No	No
Graduate Assistantships	None	Yes	No

Percentage of Students Receiving Aid	Full-Time
All students	33%

GOVERNORS STATE UNIVERSITY
College of Business and Public Administration

Academic Advising
University Park, Illinois 60466
Telephone: 708-534-4390

Total Enrollment (1993-94)	Full-Time	Part-Time
		252

Cost of Attendance (1993-94)		
Academic Year		
Standard Course Load per Semester/Term		
(credit hours/units)	12	6
Semesters/Terms per Academic Year	2	2
Tuition and Fees		
Resident	$2,094	$1,122
Nonresident	$5,982	$3,066
Living Expenses	$5,250	$4,225
Summer Term		
(R = Required, O = Optional, N = None)	O	O
Standard Course Load	12	6
Tuition and Fees		
Resident	$1,047	$ 561
Nonresident	$2,991	$1,533

Financial Aid Available	Deadline (fall starts)	Awarded to Full-Time	Part-Time
Gift Aid	September 1	Yes	Yes
Federal College Work-Study	October 1	Yes	Yes
Federal Perkins Loans	October 1	Yes	Yes
Federal Stafford Loans	October 1	Yes	Yes
School-Based Loans	NA		
Outside and Private Loans	October 1	Yes	Yes
Graduate Assistantships	August 1	Yes	Yes

Percentage of Students Receiving Aid	Full-Time	Part-Time
All students	15%	5%
Minority students		
Women students		
International students	0%	0%

GRAND CANYON UNIVERSITY
College of Business

3300 West Camelback Road
Phoenix, Arizona 85017
Telephone: 602-589-2867

Total Enrollment (1993-94)	Part-Time
	60

Cost of Attendance (1993-94)	
Academic Year	
Standard Course Load per Semester/Term	
(credit hours/units)	6
Semesters/Terms per Academic Year	3
Tuition and Fees	$212/cr. hr.
Living Expenses	Information not available
Summer Term	
(R = Required, O = Optional, N = None)	-
Standard Course Load	6
Tuition and Fees	$212/cr. hr.

Financial Aid Available	Deadline (fall starts)	Awarded to Part-Time
Gift Aid	July	Yes
Federal College Work-Study		No
Federal Perkins Loans		No
Federal Stafford Loans	July	Yes
School-Based Loans	July	Yes
Outside and Private Loans	July	Yes
Graduate Assistantships		No

Percentage of Students Receiving Aid	Part-Time
All students	10%

GRAND VALLEY STATE UNIVERSITY
F. E. Seidman School of Business

Eberhard Center
301 West Fulton
Grand Rapids, Michigan 49504
Telephone: 616-771-6677

Total Enrollment (1993-94)	Full-Time	Part-Time
	22	333

Cost of Attendance (1993-94)		
Academic Year		
Standard Course Load per Semester/Term		
(credit hours/units)	12	6
Semesters/Terms per Academic Year	2	2
Tuition and Fees		
Resident	$3,224	$1,652
Nonresident	$6,800	$3,440
Living Expenses	$6,500	$6,200
Summer Term		
(R = Required, O = Optional, N = None)	O	O
Standard Course Load	12	6
Tuition and Fees		
Resident	$1,612	$ 826
Nonresident	$3,400	$1,720

Financial Aid Available	Deadline (fall starts)	Awarded to Full-Time	Part-Time
Gift Aid			
Federal College Work-Study	Rolling	Yes	Yes
Federal Perkins Loans	Rolling	Yes	Yes
Federal Stafford Loans	Rolling	Yes	Yes
School-Based Loans		No	No
Outside and Private Loans			
Graduate Assistantships			

Percentage of Students Receiving Aid	Full-Time	Part-Time
All students	2%	4%
Minority students	0%	0%
Women students	.1%	4%
International students	25%	0%

HAMPTON UNIVERSITY
School of Business

Hampton, Virginia 23668
Telephone: 804-727-5762

Total Enrollment (1993-94)	Full-Time	Part-Time
	8	55

Cost of Attendance (1993-94)		
Academic Year		
Standard Course Load per Semester/Term		
(credit hours/units)	12	9
Semesters/Terms per Academic Year	2	2
Tuition and Fees	$3,100	$170/cr.
Living Expenses	$ 600	$600
Summer Term		
(R = Required, O = Optional, N = None)	O	O
Standard Course Load	6	6
Tuition and Fees	$170/cr.	$170/cr.

Financial Aid Available	Deadline (fall starts)	Awarded to Full-Time	Awarded to Part-Time
Gift Aid	No deadline	Yes	No
Federal College Work-Study		No	No
Federal Perkins Loans	No deadline	Yes	No
Federal Stafford Loans	No deadline	Yes	No
School-Based Loans		No	No
Outside and Private Loans	No deadline	Yes	Yes
Graduate Assistantships	June 30	Yes	No

Percentage of Students Receiving Aid	Part-Time
All students	11%

HOFSTRA UNIVERSITY
MBA Program

134 Hofstra University
Hempstead, New York 11550
Telephone: 516-463-5683

Total Enrollment (1993-94)	Full-Time	Part-Time
	190	682

Cost of Attendance (1993-94)		
Academic Year		
Standard Course Load per Semester/Term		
(credit hours/units)	12-15	6
Semesters/Terms per Academic Year	2	2
Tuition and Fees	$ 9,450	$ 4,132
Living Expenses	$10,000	$10,000
Summer Term		
(R = Required, O = Optional, N = None)	O	O
Standard Course Load	3-6	3-6
Tuition and Fees	$ 1,750	$ 1,750

Financial Aid Available	Deadline (fall starts)	Awarded to Full-Time	Awarded to Part-Time
Gift Aid	April 1	Yes	No
Federal College Work-Study	April 1	Yes	No
Federal Perkins Loans	April 1	Yes	No
Federal Stafford Loans	June 1	Yes	Yes
School-Based Loans			
Outside and Private Loans	June 1	Yes	Yes
Graduate Assistantships	April 1	Yes	No

Percentage of Students Receiving Aid	Full-Time	Part-Time
All students	65%	48%
Minority students	89%	57%
Women students	67%	55%
International students	1%	0%

HOLY NAMES COLLEGE

3500 Mountain Boulevard
Oakland, California 94619
Telephone: 510-436-1195

Total Enrollment (1993-94)	Full-Time	Part-Time
	4	24

Cost of Attendance (1993-94)		
Academic Year		
Standard Course Load per Semester/Term		
(credit hours/units)	9	6
Semesters/Terms per Academic Year	3	3
Tuition and Fees	$ 375	$ 375
Living Expenses	$18,558	$15,039
Summer Term		
(R = Required, O = Optional, N = None)	O	O
Standard Course Load	3	3
Tuition and Fees		
Resident	$ 375	$ 375
Nonresident	$ 375	$ 375

Financial Aid Available	Deadline (fall starts)	Awarded to Full-Time	Awarded to Part-Time
Gift Aid	March 2	Yes	Yes
Federal College Work-Study	March 2	Yes	Yes
Federal Perkins Loans	March 2	Yes	Yes
Federal Stafford Loans	March 2	Yes	Yes
School-Based Loans		No	No
Outside and Private Loans		No	No
Graduate Assistantships		No	No

HOWARD UNIVERSITY
School of Business

2600 6th Street, N.W.
Washington, DC 20059
Telephone: 202-806-1509

Total Enrollment (1993-94)	Full-Time	Part-Time
	132	88

Cost of Attendance (1993-94)		
Academic Year		
Standard Course Load per Semester/Term		
(credit hours/units)	12	3 or 6
Semesters/Terms per Academic Year	2	2
Tuition and Fees	$ 8,300	$461/hr.
Living Expenses	$12,451	$692/hr.
Summer Term		
(R = Required, O = Optional, N = None)	O	O
Standard Course Load	6	3
Tuition and Fees		
Resident	$481/hr.	$481/hr.
Nonresident	$722/hr.	$722/hr.

Financial Aid Available	Deadline (fall starts)	Awarded to Full-Time	Awarded to Part-Time
Gift Aid	April 1	Yes	No
Federal College Work-Study	April 1	Yes	No
Federal Perkins Loans	April 1	Yes	Yes
Federal Stafford Loans	April 1	Yes	Yes
School-Based Loans	April 1	Yes	Yes
Outside and Private Loans	NA		
Graduate Assistantships	April 1	Yes	No

Percentage of Students Receiving Aid	Full-Time	Part-Time
All students	76%	39%
Minority students	64%	33%
Women students	67%	29%
International students	54%	73%

HUMBOLDT STATE UNIVERSITY
School of Business and Economics

Arcata, California 95521
Telephone: 707-826-3224

Total Enrollment (1993-94)	Full-Time	Part-Time
	20	45

Cost of Attendance (1993-94)		
Academic Year		
Standard Course Load per Semester/Term		
(credit hours/units)	9	3
Semesters/Terms per Academic Year	2	NA
Tuition and Fees		
Resident	$1,190	$ 737
Nonresident	$ 246	$ 246
Living Expenses	$3,883	$3,883
Summer Term		
(R = Required, O = Optional, N = None)	N	N
Standard Course Load		
Tuition and Fees		
Resident		
Nonresident		

Financial Aid Available	Deadline (fall starts)	Awarded to Full-Time	Part-Time
Gift Aid	NA	Yes	No
Federal College Work-Study	NA	Yes	No
Federal Perkins Loans	NA	Yes	No
Federal Stafford Loans	NA	Yes	Yes
School-Based Loans	NA	Yes	No
Outside and Private Loans	NA	Yes	No
Graduate Assistantships	NA	Yes	No

IDAHO STATE UNIVERSITY
College of Business

Box 8020
Pocatel, Idaho 83209
Telephone: 208-236-2504

Total Enrollment (1993-94)	Full-Time	Part-Time
	43	92

Cost of Attendance (1993-94)		
Academic Year		
Standard Course Load per Semester/Term		
(credit hours/units)	12	6
Semesters/Terms per Academic Year	2	2
Tuition and Fees		
Resident	$2,030	$ 92/cr.
Nonresident	$5,644	$167/cr.
Living Expenses	$3,700	NA
Summer Term		
(R = Required, O = Optional, N = None)	R	O
Standard Course Load	6	3
Tuition and Fees		
Resident	$92/cr.	$ 92/cr.
Nonresident	$92/cr.	$ 92/cr.

Financial Aid Available	Deadline (fall starts)	Awarded to Full-Time	Part-Time
Gift Aid	March 1		Yes
Federal College Work-Study		Yes	Yes
Federal Perkins Loans	March 1	Yes	Yes
Federal Stafford Loans		Yes	Yes
School-Based Loans	NA		
Outside and Private Loans	NA		
Graduate Assistantships	April 1	Yes	

Percentage of Students Receiving Aid	Full-Time	Part-Time
All students	30%	10%

ILLINOIS BENEDICTINE COLLEGE

5700 College Road
Lisle, Illinois 60532
Telephone: 708-960-1500

Total Enrollment (1993-94)	Full-Time	Part-Time
	7	379

Cost of Attendance (1993-94)		
Academic Year		
Standard Course Load per Semester/Term		
(credit hours/units)	12	<12
Semesters/Terms per Academic Year	5	5
Tuition and Fees	$235/qtr.hr.	$235/qtr.hr.
Living Expenses	$800	$500
Summer Term		
(R = Required, O = Optional, N = None)	O	O
Standard Course Load	4	4
Tuition and Fees		
Resident	Same as above	
Nonresident		

Financial Aid Available	Deadline (fall starts)	Awarded to Full-Time	Part-Time
Gift Aid	NA		
Federal College Work-Study	NA		
Federal Perkins Loans	NA		
Federal Stafford Loans	No deadline	Yes	Yes
School-Based Loans	NA		
Outside and Private Loans	No deadline	Yes	Yes
Graduate Assistantships	September 15	Yes	Yes

ILLINOIS INSTITUTE OF TECHNOLOGY
Stuart School of Business

567 West Adams
Chicago, Illinois 60661
Telephone: 312-906-6501

Total Enrollment (1993-94)	Full-Time	Part-Time
	72	340

Cost of Attendance (1993-94)		
Academic Year		
Standard Course Load per Semester/Term		
(credit hours/units)	4	2
Semesters/Terms per Academic Year	4	4
Tuition and Fees	$4,850/qtr.	$1,170/course
Living Expenses	$7,000-$9,000	$400-$500
Summer Term		
(R = Required, O = Optional, N = None)	O	O
Standard Course Load	4	2
Tuition and Fees	$4,850/qtr.	$1,170/course

Financial Aid Available	Deadline (fall starts)	Awarded to Full-Time	Part-Time
Gift Aid	May 31	Yes	Yes
Federal College Work-Study	May 31	Yes	No
Federal Perkins Loans	May 31	Yes	Yes
Federal Stafford Loans	May 31	Yes	Yes
School-Based Loans			
Outside and Private Loans			
Graduate Assistantships	May 31	Yes	No

ILLINOIS STATE UNIVERSITY
College of Business

Graduate Programs and Research
5500/Illinois State University
Normal, Illinois 61790-5500
Telephone: 309-438-8388

Total Enrollment (1993-94)	Full-Time	Part-Time
	63	139

Cost of Attendance (1993-94)		
Academic Year		
Standard Course Load per Semester/Term		
(credit hours/units)	9	3-6
Semesters/Terms per Academic Year	2	2
Tuition and Fees		
Resident	$1,028	$320-$639
Nonresident	$2,532	$820-$1,641
Living Expenses	$7,000	
Summer Term		
(R = Required, O = Optional, N = None)	O	O
Standard Course Load	6	3
Tuition and Fees		
Resident	$639	$320
Nonresident	$1,641	$820

Financial Aid Available	Deadline (fall starts)	Awarded to Full-Time	Awarded to Part-Time
Gift Aid	March 15	Yes	Yes
Federal College Work-Study	March 1	Yes	Yes
Federal Perkins Loans	March 1	Yes	Yes
Federal Stafford Loans	March 1	Yes	Yes
School-Based Loans	NA		
Outside and Private Loans	NA		
Graduate Assistantships	March 15	Yes	No

Percentage of Students Receiving Aid	Full-Time	Part-Time
All students	77%	17%
Minority students	67%	11%
Women students	86%	24%
International students	59%	NA

INDIANA STATE UNIVERSITY
School of Business

9th and Sycamore Streets
Terre Haute, Indiana 47809
Telephone: 812-237-2000

Total Enrollment (1993-94)	Full-Time	Part-Time
	42	54

Cost of Attendance (1993-94)		
Academic Year		
Standard Course Load per Semester/Term		
(credit hours/units)	12	6
Semesters/Terms per Academic Year	2	2
Tuition and Fees		
Resident	$2,688	$1,344
Nonresident	$6,048	$3,024
Living Expenses	$8,218	$8,218
Summer Term		
(R = Required, O = Optional, N = None)	O	O
Standard Course Load	3	3
Tuition and Fees		
Resident	$336	$336
Nonresident	$756	$756

Financial Aid Available	Deadline (fall starts)	Awarded to Full-Time	Awarded to Part-Time
Gift Aid	March 1	Yes	No
Federal College Work-Study	March 1	Yes	Yes
Federal Perkins Loans	March 1	Yes	Yes
Federal Stafford Loans	None	Yes	Yes
School-Based Loans	NA		
Outside and Private Loans	None	Yes	Yes
Graduate Assistantships	March 1	Yes	No

Percentage of Students Receiving Aid	Full-Time	Part-Time
All students	36%	18%
Minority students	32%	58%
Women students	50%	14%
International students	32%	64%

INDIANA UNIVERSITY
Graduate School of Business

School of Business 254
10th and Fee Lane
Bloomington, Indiana 47405
Telephone: 812-855-8006

Total Enrollment (1993-94)	Full-Time
	516

Cost of Attendance (1993-94)

Academic Year	
Standard Course Load per Semester/Term	
(credit hours/units)	15
Semesters/Terms per Academic Year	2
Tuition and Fees	
Resident	$ 6,823
Nonresident	$13,303
Living Expenses	$13,290
Summer Term	
(R = Required, O = Optional, N = None)	N
Standard Course Load	
Tuition and Fees	
Resident	
Nonresident	

Financial Aid Available

	Deadline (fall starts)	Awarded to Full-Time
Gift Aid	March 1	Yes
Federal College Work-Study	NA	
Federal Perkins Loans	March 1	Yes
Federal Stafford Loans	March 1	Yes
School-Based Loans	NA	No
Outside and Private Loans	March 1	No
Graduate Assistantships	March 1	Yes

Percentage of Students Receiving Aid	Full-Time
All students	70%
Minority students	100%
Women students	70%
International students	1%

INDIANA UNIVERSITY NORTHWEST
Division of Business and Economics

3400 Broadway
Gary, Indiana 46408
Telephone: 219-980-6635

Total Enrollment (1993-94)	Full-Time	Part-Time
	5	255

Cost of Attendance (1993-94)

Academic Year		
Standard Course Load per Semester/Term		
(credit hours/units)	12	6
Semesters/Terms per Academic Year	3	3
Tuition and Fees		
Resident	$1,302	$ 651
Nonresident	$2,942	$1,471
Living Expenses	NA	NA
Summer Term		
(R = Required, O = Optional, N = None)	O	O
Standard Course Load	12	6
Tuition and Fees		
Resident	$1,302	$ 651
Nonresident	$2,942	$1,471

Financial Aid Available

	Deadline (fall starts)	Awarded to Full-Time	Part-Time
Gift Aid	NA	No	No
Federal College Work-Study	March 1	Yes	Yes
Federal Perkins Loans	March 1	Yes	Yes
Federal Stafford Loans	March 1	Yes	Yes
School-Based Loans	NA	No	No
Outside and Private Loans	NA	No	No
Graduate Assistantships	August 1	Yes	No

INDIANA UNIVERSITY - PURDUE UNIVERSITY FORT WAYNE

2101 Coliseum Boulevard East
Fort Wayne, Indiana 46805-1499
Telephone: 219-481-6498

Total Enrollment (1993-94)	Full-Time	Part-Time
	6	163

Cost of Attendance (1993-94)		
Academic Year		
Standard Course Load per Semester/Term		
(credit hours/units)	9	5
Semesters/Terms per Academic Year	2	2
Tuition and Fees		
Resident	$1,753	$ 487
Nonresident	$3,926	$ 974
Living Expenses	$5,990	$5,990
Summer Term		
(R = Required, O = Optional, N = None)	O	O
Standard Course Load	6	3
Tuition and Fees		
Resident	$ 584	$ 292
Nonresident	$1,308	$ 654

Financial Aid Available	Deadline (fall starts)	Awarded to Full-Time	Part-Time
Gift Aid	March 1	Yes	Yes
Federal College Work-Study	March 1	Yes	Yes
Federal Perkins Loans	March 1	Yes	Yes
Federal Stafford Loans	July 15	Yes	Yes
School-Based Loans	NA		
Outside and Private Loans	July 15	Yes	Yes
Graduate Assistantships		Yes	No

Percentage of Students Receiving Aid	Full-Time	Part-Time
All students	18%	24%

INDIANA UNIVERSITY SOUTH BEND
MBA Program

1700 Mishawaka Avenue
P.O. Box 7111
South Bend, Indiana 46634
Telephone: 219-237-4138

Total Enrollment (1993-94)	Full-Time	Part-Time
	42	265

Cost of Attendance (1993-94)		
Academic Year		
Standard Course Load per Semester/Term		
(credit hours/units)	9	6
Semesters/Terms per Academic Year	2	2
Tuition and Fees		
Resident	$ 986	$ 657
Nonresident	$2,730	$1,580
Living Expenses	NA	NA
Summer Term		
(R = Required, O = Optional, N = None)	O	O
Standard Course Load		
Tuition and Fees		
Resident	$ 657	$ 329
Nonresident	$1,580	$ 790

Financial Aid Available	Deadline (fall starts)	Awarded to Full-Time	Part-Time
Gift Aid		No	No
Federal College Work-Study	March 1	Yes	Yes
Federal Perkins Loans	March 1	Yes	Yes
Federal Stafford Loans	June 1	Yes	Yes
School-Based Loans		No	No
Outside and Private Loans		No	No
Graduate Assistantships		No	No

INDIANA UNIVERSITY OF PENNSYLVANIA
College of Business Graduate Programs

102 Uhler Hall
Indiana, Pennsylvania 15705
Telephone: 412-357-2522

Total Enrollment (1993-94)	Full-Time	Part-Time
	80	80

Cost of Attendance (1993-94)

	Full-Time	Part-Time
Academic Year		
Standard Course Load per Semester/Term		
(credit hours/units)	12	3-6
Semesters/Terms per Academic Year	3	3
Tuition and Fees		
Resident	$3,305/yr.	$164/cr.
Nonresident	$5,547/yr.	$289/cr.
Living Expenses	$3,650/yr.	
Summer Term		
(R = Required, O = Optional, N = None)	O	O
Standard Course Load	9-12	3-6
Tuition and Fees		
Resident	$1,477/sem.	$164/cr.
Nonresident	$2,598/sem.	$289/cr.

Financial Aid Available

	Deadline (fall starts)	Awarded to Full-Time	Part-Time
Gift Aid	April 15	Yes	
Federal College Work-Study	May 1	Yes	
Federal Perkins Loans	May 1	Yes	
Federal Stafford Loans	May 1	Yes	
School-Based Loans			
Outside and Private Loans			
Graduate Assistantships	April 15	Yes	

Percentage of Students Receiving Aid	Full-Time
All students	50%
Minority students	95%
Women students	50%
International students	30%

IONA COLLEGE
Hagan School of Business

715 North Avenue
New Rochelle, New York 10801
Telephone: 914-633-2288

Total Enrollment (1993-94)	Full-Time	Part-Time
	38	467

Cost of Attendance (1993-94)

	Full-Time	Part-Time
Academic Year		
Standard Course Load per Semester/Term		
(credit hours/units)	24	6
Semesters/Terms per Academic Year	3 trimesters/ 3 summer	3 trimesters/ 3 summer
Tuition and Fees	$8,760	$ 365/cr.
Living Expenses	$9,200	$7,830/cr.
Summer Term		
(R = Required, O = Optional, N = None)	O	O
Standard Course Load	6	2-6
Tuition and Fees	$365/cr.	$ 365/cr.

Financial Aid Available

	Deadline (fall starts)	Awarded to Full-Time	Part-Time
Gift Aid	NA	No	No
Federal College Work-Study	NA	No	No
Federal Perkins Loans	NA	No	No
Federal Stafford Loans		Yes	Yes
School-Based Loans	NA	No	No
Outside and Private Loans		Yes	Yes
Graduate Assistantships	October, 1994, February 1995, and May 1995	Yes	Yes

IOWA STATE UNIVERSITY
College of Business

396 Carver Hall
Ames, Iowa 50011
Telephone: 515-294-8118

Total Enrollment (1993-94)	Full-Time	Part-Time
	100	123

Cost of Attendance (1993-94)		
Academic Year		
Standard Course Load per Semester/Term		
(credit hours/units)	12	6
Semesters/Terms per Academic Year	2	2
Tuition and Fees		
Resident	$2,764	$2,180
Nonresident	$7,694	$5,468
Living Expenses	$5,400	$5,400
Summer Term		
(R = Required, O = Optional, N = None)	O	R
Standard Course Load	3	3
Tuition and Fees	$ 445	$ 535
Resident		
Nonresident		

Financial Aid Available	Deadline (fall starts)	Awarded to Full-Time	Awarded to Part-Time
Gift Aid	March 1	Yes	No
Federal College Work-Study	March 1	Yes	No
Federal Perkins Loans	NA		
Federal Stafford Loans	March 1	Yes	Yes
School-Based Loans	NA		
Outside and Private Loans	NA		
Graduate Assistantships	March 1	Yes	No

JACKSONVILLE UNIVERSITY

2800 University Boulevard North
Jacksonville, Florida 32211
Telephone: 904-745-7437

Total Enrollment (1993-94)	Full-Time	Part-Time
	54	122

Cost of Attendance (1993-94)		
Academic Year		
Standard Course Load per Semester/Term		
(credit hours/units)	13	6
Semesters/Terms per Academic Year	3	3
Tuition and Fees		
Resident	NA	NA
Nonresident	$14,175	$5,025
Living Expenses	NA	NA
Summer Term		
(R = Required, O = Optional, N = None)	O	O
Standard Course Load	13	3
Tuition and Fees		
Resident	NA	NA
Nonresident	$ 4,725	$ 885

Financial Aid Available	Deadline (fall starts)	Awarded to Full-Time	Awarded to Part-Time
Gift Aid			
Federal College Work-Study			
Federal Perkins Loans			
Federal Stafford Loans			
School-Based Loans			
Outside and Private Loans		Yes	Yes
Graduate Assistantships		No	No

Percentage of Students Receiving Aid	Full-Time	Part-Time
All students	20%	30%

JOHN CARROLL UNIVERSITY
School of Business

University Heights, Ohio 44118
Telephone: 216-397-4391

Total Enrollment (1993-94)

	Part-Time
	254

Cost of Attendance (1993-94)

Academic Year	
Standard Course Load per Semester/Term	
(credit hours/units)	6
Semesters/Terms per Academic Year	2
Tuition and Fees	$900
Living Expenses	NA
Summer Term	
(R = Required, O = Optional, N = None)	O
Standard Course Load	6
Tuition and Fees	$900

Financial Aid Available

	Deadline (fall starts)	Awarded to Part-Time
Gift Aid		No
Federal College Work-Study		No
Federal Perkins Loans		No
Federal Stafford Loans	March 1	Yes
School-Based Loans		No
Outside and Private Loans		No
Graduate Assistantships	None	Yes

Percentage of Students Receiving Aid

	Part-Time
All students	10%

KANSAS STATE UNIVERSITY
College of Business Administration

Calvin Hall - 110
Manhattan, Kansas 66506
Telephone: 913-532-7190

Total Enrollment (1993-94)

	Full-Time	Part-Time
	82	38

Cost of Attendance (1993-94)

Academic Year		
Standard Course Load per Semester/Term		
(credit hours/units)	12	6
Semesters/Terms per Academic Year	2	2
Tuition and Fees		
Resident	$ 1,191	$ 66/hr.*
Nonresident	$ 3,470	$218/hr.*
Living Expenses	$10,500	$10,500
Summer Term		
(R = Required, O = Optional, N = None)	O	O
Standard Course Load	3-6	3-6
Tuition and Fees		
Resident	$ 66/hr.*	$ 66/hr.*
Nonresident	$218/hr.*	$ 66/hr.*

*plus $85 one-time fee

Financial Aid Available

	Deadline (fall starts)	Awarded to Full-Time	Part-Time
Gift Aid	March 15	Yes	Yes
Federal College Work-Study	March 15	Yes	Yes
Federal Perkins Loans	March 15	Yes	Yes
Federal Stafford Loans	March 15	Yes	Yes
School-Based Loans	March 15	Yes	Yes
Outside and Private Loans	March 15	Yes	Yes
Graduate Assistantships	March 15	Yes	

Percentage of Students Receiving Aid

	Full-Time	Part-Time
All students	60%	20%
Minority students	100%	NA
Women students	75%	20%
International students	10%	0%

KENT STATE UNIVERSITY
Graduate School of Management

Rm. 306 BSA
P.O. Box 5190
Kent, Ohio 44242-0001
Telephone: 216-672-2282, extension 235

Total Enrollment (1993-94)	Full-Time	Part-Time
	179	265

Cost of Attendance (1993-94)

	Full-Time	Part-Time
Academic Year		
Standard Course Load per Semester/Term		
(credit hours/units)	12	6
Semesters/Terms per Academic Year	2	2
Tuition and Fees		
Resident	$3,983	$ 543
Nonresident	$7,723	$1,053
Living Expenses	$8,500	$ 650
Summer Term		
(R = Required, O = Optional, N = None)	R	O
Standard Course Load	12	6
Tuition and Fees		
Resident	$1,991	$543
Nonresident	$3,861	$1,053

Financial Aid Available

	Deadline (fall starts)	Awarded to Full-Time	Awarded to Part-Time
Gift Aid	April 1	Yes	No
Federal College Work-Study	February 15	Yes	No
Federal Perkins Loans	February 15	Yes	No
Federal Stafford Loans	February 15	Yes	No
School-Based Loans	NA		
Outside and Private Loans	NA	Yes	Yes
Graduate Assistantships	April 1	Yes	No

Percentage of Students Receiving Aid	Full-Time	Part-Time
All students	30%	NA
Minority students	50%	NA
Women students	30%	NA
International students	5%	

KUTZTOWN UNIVERSITY
College of Business

225 Beekey Building
Kutztown, Pennsylvania 19530
Telephone: 610-683-4200

Total Enrollment (1993-94)	Full-Time	Part-Time
	10	175

Cost of Attendance (1993-94)

	Full-Time	Part-Time
Academic Year		
Standard Course Load per Semester/Term		
(credit hours/units)	9	3
Semesters/Terms per Academic Year	3	3
Tuition and Fees		
Resident	$3,428	$1,121
Nonresident	$5,838	$1,927
Living Expenses		
Summer Term		
(R = Required, O = Optional, N = None)	O	O
Standard Course Load	6	6
Tuition and Fees		
Resident	$1,121	$1,121
Nonresident	$1,927	$1,927

Financial Aid Available

	Deadline (fall starts)	Awarded to Full-Time	Awarded to Part-Time
Gift Aid		No	No
Federal College Work-Study		Yes	Yes
Federal Perkins Loans		No	No
Federal Stafford Loans		Yes	Yes
School-Based Loans	NA	No	No
Outside and Private Loans		No	No
Graduate Assistantships		Yes	No

Percentage of Students Receiving Aid	Full-Time
All students	9%
Minority students	
Women students	4%
International students	3%

LA SALLE UNIVERSITY

20th and Olney Avenue
Philadelphia, Pennsylvania 19141
Telephone: 215-951-1057

Total Enrollment (1993-94)	Full-Time	Part-Time
	70	920

Cost of Attendance (1993-94)		
Academic Year		
Standard Course Load per Semester/Term		
(credit hours/units)	9	3-6
Semesters/Terms per Academic Year	3	3
Tuition and Fees	$383/cr.	$383/cr.
Living Expenses	$5,000	$5,000
Summer Term		
(R = Required, O = Optional, N = None)	O	O
Standard Course Load	9	3-6
Tuition and Fees	$383/cr.	$383/cr.

Financial Aid Available	Deadline (fall starts)	Awarded to Full-Time	Awarded to Part-Time
Gift Aid	June 15	Yes	No
Federal College Work-Study	NA	NA	NA
Federal Perkins Loans	June 15	Yes	No
Federal Stafford Loans	June 15	Yes	No
School-Based Loans	NA	NA	NA
Outside and Private Loans	June 15	Yes	No
Graduate Assistantships	August 1	Yes	No

Percentage of Students Receiving Aid	Full-Time	Part-Time
All students	20%	82%
Minority students		
Women students		
International students		

LA SIERRA UNIVERSITY
School of Business and Management

4700 Pierce Street
Riverside, California 92515
Telephone: 909-785-2064

Total Enrollment (1993-94)	Full-Time	Part-Time
	26	11

Cost of Attendance (1993-94)		
Academic Year		
Standard Course Load per Semester/Term		
(credit hours/units)	12	4
Semesters/Terms per Academic Year	3	3
Tuition and Fees	$12,501	$4,287
Living Expenses	$ 9,362	$9,362
Summer Term		
(R = Required, O = Optional, N = None)	R	O
Standard Course Load	12	4
Tuition and Fees	$ 4,197	$1,429

Financial Aid Available	Deadline (fall starts)	Awarded to Full-Time	Awarded to Part-Time
Gift Aid	Varies	Yes	Yes
Federal College Work-Study	NA	No	No
Federal Perkins Loans	May 1	No	No
Federal Stafford Loans	May 1	Yes	Yes
School-Based Loans	NA	No	No
Outside and Private Loans	NA	No	No
Graduate Assistantships	Varies	Yes	Yes

Percentage of Students Receiving Aid	Full-Time	Part-Time
All students	35%	5%
Minority students	35%	5%
Women students	35%	5%
International students		

LAKE FOREST GRADUATE SCHOOL OF MANAGEMENT

280 North Sheridan Road
Lake Forest, Illinois 60045
Telephone: 708-234-5080

Total Enrollment (1993-94)	Full-Time	Part-Time
		641

Cost of Attendance (1993-94)

Academic Year
  Standard Course Load per Semester/Term
    (credit hours/units)   2 courses/term   1 course/term
  Semesters/Terms per Academic Year   4
  Tuition and Fees $1,325/course
  Living Expenses   NA
Summer Term
  (R = Required, O = Optional, N = None)   O
  Standard Course Load   1 course
  Tuition and Fees $1,325/course
    Resident
    Nonresident

Financial Aid Available

	Deadline (fall starts)	Awarded to Full-Time	Part-Time
Gift Aid			No
Federal College Work-Study			No
Federal Perkins Loans			No
Federal Stafford Loans	NA	Yes	Yes
School-Based Loans			No
Outside and Private Loans			No
Graduate Assistantships			No

Percentage of Students Receiving Aid	Part-Time
All students	8%
Minority students	
Women students	2%
International students	

LAKE SUPERIOR STATE UNIVERSITY
MBA Program

1000 College Drive
Sault Ste. Marie, Michigan 49783
Telephone: 906-635-2688

Total Enrollment (1993-94)	Full-Time	Part-Time
	25	275

Cost of Attendance (1993-94)

Academic Year
  Standard Course Load per Semester/Term
    (credit hours/units)   12   3
  Semesters/Terms per Academic Year   2   2
    (trimesters—3 including summer semester)
  Tuition and Fees $3,512 $ 974
  Living Expenses $5,000 $4,500
Summer Term
  (R = Required, O = Optional, N = None)   O   O
  Standard Course Load   12   3
  Tuition and Fees $1,756 $ 487

Financial Aid Available

	Deadline (fall starts)	Awarded to Full-Time	Part-Time
Gift Aid		No	No
Federal College Work-Study		No	No
Federal Perkins Loans		No	No
Federal Stafford Loans	April 1	Yes	Yes
School-Based Loans		No	No
Outside and Private Loans		No	No
Graduate Assistantships		No	No

LAMAR UNIVERSITY

P.O. Box 10059
Beaumont, Texas 77710
Telephone: 409-880-8604

Total Enrollment (1993-94)	Full-Time	Part-Time
	38	79

Cost of Attendance (1993-94)		
Academic Year		
Standard Course Load per Semester/Term		
(credit hours/units)	12	6
Semesters/Terms per Academic Year	2	2
Tuition and Fees		
Resident	$ 553	$316
Nonresident	$1,801	$940
Living Expenses	$3,000	
Summer Term		
(R = Required, O = Optional, N = None)	O	O
Standard Course Load	6	3
Tuition and Fees		
Resident	$ 316	$178
Nonresident	$ 940	$490

Financial Aid Available	Deadline (fall starts)	Awarded to Full-Time	Part-Time
Gift Aid	March 1	Yes	No
Federal College Work-Study	March 1	Yes	No
Federal Perkins Loans	March 1	Yes	No
Federal Stafford Loans	March 1	Yes	No
School-Based Loans	NA	No	No
Outside and Private Loans	March 1	Yes	Yes
Graduate Assistantships	March 1	Yes	No

Percentage of Students Receiving Aid	Full-Time	Part-Time
All students	25%	10%
Minority students	NA	NA
Women students	NA	NA
International students	30%	

LAWRENCE TECHNOLOGICAL UNIVERSITY

21000 West 10 Mile Road
Southfield, Michigan 48075-1058
Telephone: 313-356-0200

Total Enrollment (1993-94)	Full-Time	Part-Time
	24	278

Cost of Attendance (1993-94)		
Academic Year		
Standard Course Load per Semester/Term		
(credit hours/units)	8	4
Semesters/Terms per Academic Year	3	3
Tuition and Fees	$7,440	$3,855
Living Expenses	$8,000	$8,000
Summer Term		
(R = Required, O = Optional, N = None)	O	O
Standard Course Load	8	4
Tuition and Fees	$1,650	$ 870

Financial Aid Available	Deadline (fall starts)	Awarded to Full-Time	Part-Time
Gift Aid	June 1	Yes	Yes
Federal College Work-Study	June 1	Yes	Yes
Federal Perkins Loans	June 1	Yes	Yes
Federal Stafford Loans	June 1	Yes	Yes
School-Based Loans	June 1	Yes	Yes
Outside and Private Loans	June 1	Yes	Yes
Graduate Assistantships		No	No

Percentage of Students Receiving Aid	Full-Time	Part-Time
All students	30%	20%
Minority students	75%	75%
Women students	40%	40%
International students	0%	0%

LEHIGH UNIVERSITY
College of Business and Economics

Rauch Business Center #37
621 Taylor Street
Bethlehem, Pennsylvania 18015
Telephone: 215-758-4450

Total Enrollment (1993-94)	Full-Time	Part-Time
	71	255

Cost of Attendance (1993-94)		
Academic Year		
Standard Course Load per Semester/Term		
(credit hours/units)	12	3-6
Semesters/Terms per Academic Year	2	2
Tuition and Fees	$670/cr.hr.	$670/cr.hr.
Living Expenses	NA	NA
Summer Term		
(R = Required, O = Optional, N = None)	O	O
Standard Course Load	3	3
Tuition and Fees	$670/cr.hr.	$670/cr.hr.

Financial Aid Available

	Deadline (fall starts)	Awarded to Full-Time	Awarded to Part-Time
Gift Aid	February 1	Yes	Yes
Federal College Work-Study	NA	No	No
Federal Perkins Loans	None	Yes	Yes
Federal Stafford Loans	None	Yes	Yes
School-Based Loans	NA	No	No
Outside and Private Loans	None	Yes	Yes
Graduate Assistantships	February 1	Yes	No

Percentage of Students Receiving Aid	Full-Time	Part-Time
All students	62%	92%
Minority students		
Women students	87%	
International students	15%	

LEWIS UNIVERSITY
Graduate School of Management

Route 53
Romeoville, Illinois 60441
Telephone: 815-838-0500, extension 348

Total Enrollment (1993-94)	Full-Time	Part-Time
	15	445

Cost of Attendance (1993-94)		
Academic Year		
Standard Course Load per Semester/Term		
(credit hours/units)	9	4
Semesters/Terms per Academic Year	3	3
Tuition and Fees	$2,997	$1,364
Living Expenses	$1,500	$1,000
Summer Term		
(R = Required, O = Optional, N = None)	O	O
Standard Course Load		4
Tuition and Fees		$1,364

Financial Aid Available

	Deadline (fall starts)	Awarded to Full-Time	Awarded to Part-Time
Gift Aid	NA		
Federal College Work-Study	August 15	Yes	Yes
Federal Perkins Loans	August 15	Yes	Yes
Federal Stafford Loans	August 15	Yes	Yes
School-Based Loans	NA		
Outside and Private Loans	NA		
Graduate Assistantships	NA		

LOUISIANA TECH UNIVERSITY
College of Administration and Business

P.O. Box 10318
Ruston, Louisiana 71272
Telephone: 318-257-4528

Total Enrollment (1993-94)	Full-Time	Part-Time
	63	22

Cost of Attendance (1993-94)		
Academic Year		
Standard Course Load per Semester/Term		
(credit hours/units)	6-9 hrs.	3 hrs.
Semesters/Terms per Academic Year	3	3
Tuition and Fees		
Resident	$2,289	$ 765
Nonresident	$3,744	$ 765
Living Expenses	$5,862	$5,862
Summer Term		
(R = Required, O = Optional, N = None)	O	O
Standard Course Load	6-9 hrs.	3 hrs.
Tuition and Fees		
Resident	$ 763	$ 255
Nonresident	$1,248	$ 255

Financial Aid Available	Deadline (fall starts)	Awarded to Full-Time	Awarded to Part-Time
Gift Aid		No	No
Federal College Work-Study	April 1	Yes	Yes
Federal Perkins Loans	April 1	Yes	Yes
Federal Stafford Loans	April 1	Yes	Yes
School-Based Loans		No	No
Outside and Private Loans		No	No
Graduate Assistantships	Varies	Yes	No

Percentage of Students Receiving Aid	Full-Time	Part-Time
All students	80%	50%
Minority students	NA	NA
Women students	NA	NA
International students	NA	NA

LOYOLA COLLEGE IN MARYLAND
Joseph A. Sellinger, S.J. School of Business and Management

4501 North Charles Street
Baltimore, Maryland 21210
Telephone: 410-617-5067

Total Enrollment (1993-94)	Full-Time	Part-Time
	65	880

Cost of Attendance (1993-94)		
Academic Year		
Standard Course Load per Semester/Term		
(credit hours/units)	12	6
Semesters/Terms per Academic Year	2 + 2	2 + 2
Tuition and Fees	$7,660	$3,830
Living Expenses	$5,000	$4,000
Summer Term		
(R = Required, O = Optional, N = None)	O	O
Standard Course Load	6	3
Tuition and Fees	$1,915	$ 970

Financial Aid Available	Deadline (fall starts)	Awarded to Full-Time	Awarded to Part-Time
Gift Aid			
Federal College Work-Study			
Federal Perkins Loans			
Federal Stafford Loans	6-8 weeks prior to term	Yes	Yes
School-Based Loans			
Outside and Private Loans			
Graduate Assistantships	1 month prior to term	Yes	Yes

Percentage of Students Receiving Aid	Full-Time	Part-Time
All students	80%	10%
Minority students	80%	10%
Women students	80%	10%
International students	40%	

LOYOLA MARYMOUNT UNIVERSITY

Loyola Boulevard at West 80th Street
Los Angeles, California 90045
Telephone: 310-338-2848

Total Enrollment (1993-94)	Full-Time	Part-Time
		365

Cost of Attendance (1993-94)		
Academic Year		
Standard Course Load per Semester/Term		
(credit hours/units)	3-4 classes	1-2 classes
Semesters/Terms per Academic Year	2	2
Tuition and Fees	$470/unit	$470/unit
Living Expenses		
Summer Term		
(R = Required, O = Optional, N = None)		O
Standard Course Load	4	2
Tuition and Fees		$470/unit

Financial Aid Available	Deadline (fall starts)	Awarded to Full-Time	Awarded to Part-Time
Gift Aid	March 2	Yes	Yes
Federal College Work-Study	NA	No	No
Federal Perkins Loans	NA	No	No
Federal Stafford Loans	March 2	Yes	Yes
School-Based Loans	NA	No	No
Outside and Private Loans	March 2	Yes	Yes
Graduate Assistantships	June 1	Yes	Yes

Percentage of Students Receiving Aid	Part-Time
All students	15%
Minority students	2%
Women students	2%
International students	0%

LOYOLA UNIVERSITY
Joseph A. Butt, S.J. College of Business Administration

Campus Box 15
6363 St. Charles Avenue
New Orleans, Louisiana 70118
Telephone: 504-865-3544

Total Enrollment (1993-94)	Full-Time	Part-Time
	49	180

Cost of Attendance (1993-94)		
Academic Year		
Standard Course Load per Semester/Term		
(credit hours/units)	12	6
Semesters/Terms per Academic Year	2	2
Tuition and Fees	$4,879	$2,447
Living Expenses	NA	NA
Summer Term		
(R = Required, O = Optional, N = None)	O	O
Standard Course Load	12	6
Tuition and Fees	$4,804	$2,422

Financial Aid Available	Deadline (fall starts)	Awarded to Full-Time	Awarded to Part-Time
Gift Aid	NA	No	No
Federal College Work-Study	May 30	Yes	Yes
Federal Perkins Loans	NA	No	No
Federal Stafford Loans	Varies	Yes	Yes
School-Based Loans	NA	No	No
Outside and Private Loans	Varies	Yes	Yes
Graduate Assistantships	May 30	Yes	

Percentage of Students Receiving Aid	Full-Time	Part-Time
All students	60%	32%
Minority students	30%	14%
Women students	25%	15%
International students	0%	0%

LYNCHBURG COLLEGE IN VIRGINIA

Lakeside Drive
Lynchburg, Virginia 24501
Telephone: 804-522-8255

Total Enrollment (1993-94)	Full-Time	Part-Time
	10	200

Cost of Attendance (1993-94)

	Full-Time	Part-Time
Academic Year		
Standard Course Load per Semester/Term		
(credit hours/units)	9	6
Semesters/Terms per Academic Year	2	2
Tuition and Fees	$200/cr.	$200/cr.
Living Expenses	NA	NA
Summer Term		
(R = Required, O = Optional, N = None)	O	O
Standard Course Load	3	3
Tuition and Fees	$200	$200

Financial Aid Available	Deadline (fall starts)	Awarded to Full-Time	Part-Time
Gift Aid	NA	No	No
Federal College Work-Study	NA	No	No
Federal Perkins Loans	NA	No	No
Federal Stafford Loans	NA	No	No
School-Based Loans	NA	No	No
Outside and Private Loans	NA	No	No
Graduate Assistantships	NA	No	No

MADONNA UNIVERSITY

36600 Schoolcraft Road
Livonia, Michigan 48150-1173
Telephone: 313-591-5154

Total Enrollment (1993-94)	Full-Time	Part-Time
	25	234

Cost of Attendance (1993-94)

	Full-Time	Part-Time
Academic Year		
Standard Course Load per Semester/Term		
(credit hours/units)	9	4-8
Semesters/Terms per Academic Year	3	3
Tuition and Fees	$1,872	$832 - $1,664
Living Expenses	NA	NA
Summer Term		
(R = Required, O = Optional, N = None)	O	O
Standard Course Load	9	4-8
Tuition and Fees	$1,872	$832 - $1,664

MAHARISHI INTERNATIONAL UNIVERSITY
School of Management

1000 North Fourth Street PB 1126
Fairfield, Iowa 52557-1126
Telephone: 515-472-1191

Total Enrollment (1993-94)	Full-Time	Part-Time
	15	37

Cost of Attendance (1993-94)		
Academic Year		
Standard Course Load per Semester/Term		
(credit hours/units)	20	10
Semesters/Terms per Academic Year	2	2
Tuition and Fees	$11,688	$5,860
Living Expenses	$ 5,180	$4,930
Summer Term		
(R = Required, O = Optional, N = None)	N	N
Standard Course Load		
Tuition and Fees		
Resident		
Nonresident		

Financial Aid Available	Deadline (fall starts)	Awarded to Full-Time	Part-Time
Gift Aid	June 1	Yes	Yes
Federal College Work-Study	June 1	Yes	Yes
Federal Perkins Loans	June 1	Yes	Yes
Federal Stafford Loans	June 1	Yes	Yes
School-Based Loans	June 1	No	No
Outside and Private Loans	June 1	No	No
Graduate Assistantships	June 1	No	No

Percentage of Students Receiving Aid	Full-Time	Part-Time
All students	85%	95%

MANHATTAN COLLEGE
School of Business

Manhattan College Parkway
Riverdale, New York 10704
Telephone: 718-920-0290

Total Enrollment (1993-94)	Part-Time
	155

Cost of Attendance (1993-94)	
Academic Year	
Standard Course Load per Semester/Term	
(credit hours/units)	6
Semesters/Terms per Academic Year	3
Tuition and Fees	$ 390/cr.
Living Expenses	$9,000
Summer Term	
(R = Required, O = Optional, N = None)	O
Standard Course Load	6
Tuition and Fees	$390/cr. + $50 reg. fee

Financial Aid Available	Deadline (fall starts)	Awarded to Full-Time	Part-Time
Gift Aid		No	No
Federal College Work-Study		No	No
Federal Perkins Loans		No	No
Federal Stafford Loans	April 15	Yes	Yes
School-Based Loans		No	No
Outside and Private Loans		No	No
Graduate Assistantships		No	No

MARIST COLLEGE
Graduate Program in Business

North Road
Poughkeepsie, New York 12601-1387
Telephone: 914-575-3530

Total Enrollment (1993-94)	Full-Time	Part-Time
	12	154

Cost of Attendance (1993-94)		
Academic Year		
Standard Course Load per Semester/Term		
(credit hours/units)	12	6
Semesters/Terms per Academic Year	2	2
Tuition and Fees	$8,042	$4,046
Living Expenses	$6,600	$6,150
Summer Term		
(R = Required, O = Optional, N = None)	O	O
Standard Course Load	3	3
Tuition and Fees	$1,024	$1,024

Financial Aid Available	Deadline (fall starts)	Awarded to Full-Time	Part-Time
Gift Aid	August 15	Yes	Yes
Federal College Work-Study	August 15	Yes	No
Federal Perkins Loans		No	No
Federal Stafford Loans	August 15	Yes	Yes
School-Based Loans		No	No
Outside and Private Loans		No	No
Graduate Assistantships	Varies	Yes	No

Percentage of Students Receiving Aid	Full-Time	Part-Time
All students	67%	4%
Minority students		
Women students	100%	10%
International students		

MARQUETTE UNIVERSITY
College of Business Administration

David A. Straz Jr. Hall
Milwaukee, Wisconsin 53233
Telephone: 414-288-7145

Total Enrollment (1993-94)	Full-Time	Part-Time
	59	481

Cost of Attendance (1993-94)		
Academic Year		
Standard Course Load per Semester/Term		
(credit hours/units)	12	6
Semesters/Terms per Academic Year	2	2
Tuition and Fees	$9,600	$4,800
Living Expenses	NA	NA
Summer Term		
(R = Required, O = Optional, N = None)	O	O
Standard Course Load	2	1
Tuition and Fees	$2,400	$1,200

Financial Aid Available	Deadline (fall starts)	Awarded to Full-Time	Part-Time
Gift Aid	February 15	Yes	Yes
Federal College Work-Study	March 1	Yes	No
Federal Perkins Loans	March 1	Yes	No
Federal Stafford Loans	March 1	Yes	Yes
School-Based Loans	NA	No	No
Outside and Private Loans	March 1	No	Yes
Graduate Assistantships	February 15	Yes	No

Percentage of Students Receiving Aid	Full-Time	Part-Time
All students	67%	NA
Minority students	NA	NA
Women students	NA	NA
International students	NA	NA

MARSHALL UNIVERSITY
College of Business

Corbly Hall
Huntington, West Virginia 25755
Telephone: 304-696-2613

Total Enrollment (1993-94)	Full-Time	Part-Time
	31	55

Cost of Attendance (1993-94)		
Academic Year		
Standard Course Load per Semester/Term		
(credit hours/units)	9	6
Semesters/Terms per Academic Year	2	2
Tuition and Fees		
Resident	$1,010	$ 338
Nonresident	$2,801	$ 935
Living Expenses	$4,400	$4,400
Summer Term		
(R = Required, O = Optional, N = None)	O	O
Standard Course Load	9	6
Tuition and Fees		
Resident	Same as above	
Nonresident		

Financial Aid Available	Deadline (fall starts)	Awarded to Full-Time	Part-Time
Gift Aid	August	Yes	No
Federal College Work-Study	NA	Yes	Yes
Federal Perkins Loans	NA	Yes	Yes
Federal Stafford Loans	NA	Yes	Yes
School-Based Loans		Yes	Yes
Outside and Private Loans			
Graduate Assistantships	None	Yes	No

Percentage of Students Receiving Aid	Full-Time
All students	50%

MARYMOUNT UNIVERSITY

2807 North Glebe Road
Arlington, Virginia 22207
Telephone: 703-284-5901

Total Enrollment (1993-94)	Full-Time	Part-Time
	100	600

Cost of Attendance (1993-94)		
Academic Year		
Standard Course Load per Semester/Term		
(credit hours/units)	9-12	3-6
Semesters/Terms per Academic Year	3	3
Tuition and Fees	$3,060	$2,040
Living Expenses	$3,800	$3,800
Summer Term		
(R = Required, O = Optional, N = None)	O	O
Standard Course Load	3	6
Tuition and Fees	$1,020	$2,040

Financial Aid Available	Deadline (fall starts)	Awarded to Full-Time	Part-Time
Gift Aid	March 1	Yes	No
Federal College Work-Study		No	No
Federal Perkins Loans		No	No
Federal Stafford Loans	March 1	Yes	No
School-Based Loans		No	No
Outside and Private Loans		No	No
Graduate Assistantships	March 1	No	No

Percentage of Students Receiving Aid	Full-Time	Part-Time
All students	50%	20%
Minority students		29%
Women students		57%

MARYWOOD COLLEGE
Business and Managerial Science

2300 Adams Avenue
Scranton, Pennsylvania 18509
Telephone: 717-348-6274

Total Enrollment (1993-94)	Full-Time	Part-Time
	6	78

Cost of Attendance (1993-94)		
Academic Year		
Standard Course Load per Semester/Term		
(credit hours/units)	9	6
Semesters/Terms per Academic Year	2	2
Tuition and Fees	$5,970	$4,020
Living Expenses	$5,200	NA
Summer Term		
(R = Required, O = Optional, N = None)	O	O
Standard Course Load	6	3
Tuition and Fees	$2,010	

Financial Aid Available	Deadline (fall starts)	Awarded to Full-Time	Awarded to Part-Time
Gift Aid	March 15	Yes	Yes
Federal College Work-Study		No	No
Federal Perkins Loans		No	No
Federal Stafford Loans	Contact FA	Yes	Yes
School-Based Loans		No	No
Outside and Private Loans	FA Application	Yes	Yes
Graduate Assistantships	March 10	Yes	No

Percentage of Students Receiving Aid	Full-Time	Part-Time
All students	0%	5%
Minority students	0%	0%
Women students	0%	0%
International students	0%	0%

MASSACHUSETTS INSTITUTE OF TECHNOLOGY
Sloan School of Business

50 Memorial Drive (E52-112)
Cambridge, Massachusetts 02142
Telephone: 617-253-3730

Total Enrollment (1993-94)	Full-Time
	480

Cost of Attendance (1993-94)	
Academic Year	
Standard Course Load per Semester/Term	
(credit hours/units)	5/course
Semesters/Terms per Academic Year	2
Tuition and Fees	$20,500
Living Expenses	$13,800
Summer Term	
(R = Required, O = Optional, N = None)	N
Standard Course Load	
Tuition and Fees	
Resident	
Nonresident	

Financial Aid Available	Deadline (fall starts)	Awarded to Full-Time
Gift Aid	Same as Admission	Yes
Federal College Work-Study	NA	
Federal Perkins Loans	NA	
Federal Stafford Loans	Same as Admission	Yes
School-Based Loans	Same as Admission	Yes
Outside and Private Loans	Same as Admission	Yes
Graduate Assistantships	Available to second-year students only	Yes

Percentage of Students Receiving Aid	Full-Time
All students	50%
Minority students	90-100%
Women students	85%
International students	50-80%

MERCY COLLEGE
Graduate Program in Human Resource Management

555 Broadway
Dobbs Ferry, New York 10522
Telephone: 914-674-7302

Total Enrollment (1993-94)	Full-Time	Part-Time
	8	158

Cost of Attendance (1993-94)		
Academic Year		
Standard Course Load per Semester/Term		
(credit hours/units)	9	3-6
Semesters/Terms per Academic Year	4	4
Tuition and Fees	$11,700	$975-$1,950
Living Expenses	$ 3,860	$3,365
Summer Term		
(R = Required, O = Optional, N = None)	O	O
Standard Course Load	9	3-6
Tuition and Fees	$11,700	$975-$1,950

Financial Aid Available	Deadline (fall starts)	Awarded to Full-Time	Part-Time
Gift Aid	NA		
Federal College Work-Study	Rolling	Yes	Yes
Federal Perkins Loans	Rolling	Yes	Yes
Federal Stafford Loans	Rolling	Yes	Yes
School-Based Loans ·	NA		
Outside and Private Loans	NA		
Graduate Assistantships	Rolling	Yes	Yes

Percentage of Students Receiving Aid	Full-Time	Part-Time
All students	87%	8%
Minority students	NA	NA
Women students	NA	NA
International students	NA	NA

MIAMI UNIVERSITY
The Richard T. Farmer School of Business Administration

107 Laws Hall
Oxford, Ohio 45056
Telephone: 513-529-6643

Total Enrollment (1993-94)	Full-Time	Part-Time
	75	40

Cost of Attendance (1993-94)		
Academic Year		
Standard Course Load per Semester/Term		
(credit hours/units)	16	6
Semesters/Terms per Academic Year	2	2
Tuition and Fees		
Resident	$4,512	$2,255
Nonresident	$9,384	$4,692
Living Expenses	$6,000	$ 250
Summer Term		
(R = Required, O = Optional, N = None)	R (first yr.)	R
Standard Course Load	12	3
Tuition and Fees		
Resident	$2,256	$2,256
Nonresident	$4,692	$4,692

Financial Aid Available	Deadline (fall starts)	Awarded to Full-Time	Part-Time
Gift Aid	March 1	Yes	No
Federal College Work-Study	NA	No	No
Federal Perkins Loans	NA	No	No
Federal Stafford Loans	Mid-May	Yes	Yes
School-Based Loans	NA	No	No
Outside and Private Loans	March 1	Yes	No
Graduate Assistantships	March 1	Yes	No

Percentage of Students Receiving Aid	Full-Time
All students	0%
Minority students	0%
Women students	0%
International students	0%

MICHIGAN STATE UNIVERSITY
The Eli Broad Graduate School of Management

215 Eppley Center
East Lansing, Michigan 48824-1121
Telephone: 517-355-7604
         800-467-8622

Total Enrollment (1993-94)	Full-Time
	280

Cost of Attendance (1993-94)

Academic Year	
Standard Course Load per Semester/Term	
(credit hours/units)	15
Semesters/Terms per Academic Year	2
Tuition and Fees	
Resident	$ 7,058
Nonresident	$13,755
Living Expenses	$ 8,004
Summer Term	
(R = Required, O = Optional, N = None)	N
Standard Course Load	
Tuition and Fees	
Resident	
Nonresident	

Financial Aid Available

	Deadline (fall starts)	Awarded to Full-Time
Gift Aid	February 15	Yes
Federal College Work-Study	February 15	Yes
Federal Perkins Loans	February 15	Yes
Federal Stafford Loans	February 15	Yes
School-Based Loans	Only short-term emergency loans	No
Outside and Private Loans	February 15	Yes
Graduate Assistantships	February 1	Yes

Percentage of Students Receiving Aid	Full-Time
All students	50%
Minority students	100%
Women students	60%
International students	10%

MICHIGAN TECHNOLOGICAL UNIVERSITY
School of Business and Engineering Administration

1400 Townsend Drive
Houghton, Michigan 49931-1295
Telephone: 906-487-2767 (SBEA)
         906-487-2327 (Graduate School)

Total Enrollment (1993-94)	Full-Time
	30

Cost of Attendance (1993-94)

Academic Year	
Standard Course Load per Semester/Term	
(credit hours/units)	14
Semesters/Terms per Academic Year	3
Tuition and Fees	
Resident	$4,341
Nonresident	$8,685
Living Expenses	$4,068
Summer Term	
(R = Required, O = Optional, N = None)	N
Standard Course Load	
Tuition and Fees	
Resident	
Nonresident	

Financial Aid Available

	Deadline (fall starts)	Awarded to Full-Time
Gift Aid		
Federal College Work-Study		
Federal Perkins Loans		
Federal Stafford Loans		
School-Based Loans		
Outside and Private Loans		
Graduate Assistantships	Spring	Yes

Percentage of Students Receiving Aid	Full-Time
All students	30%

MILLSAPS COLLEGE
Else School of Management

1701 North State Street
Jackson, Mississippi 39210
Telephone: 601-974-1253

Total Enrollment (1993-94)	Full-Time	Part-Time
	35	63

Cost of Attendance (1993-94)		
Academic Year		
Standard Course Load per Semester/Term		
(credit hours/units)	9-12	3-6
Semesters/Terms per Academic Year	3	3
Tuition and Fees	$10,826	$5,413
Living Expenses	$ 6,900	$6,900
Summer Term		
(R = Required, O = Optional, N = None)	O	O
Standard Course Load		
Tuition and Fees	$1,422/ course	$1,422/ course

Financial Aid Available	Deadline (fall starts)	Awarded to Full-Time	Part-Time
Gift Aid	April 30	Yes	
Federal College Work-Study	NA	No	No
Federal Perkins Loans	NA	No	No
Federal Stafford Loans	None	Yes	Yes
School-Based Loans	NA	No	No
Outside and Private Loans	None	Yes	Yes
Graduate Assistantships	None	Yes	No

Percentage of Students Receiving Aid	Full-Time	Part-Time
All students	79%	26%
Minority students	75%	
Women students	75%	
International students	50%	

MONTCLAIR STATE UNIVERSITY

Valley Road and Normal Avenue
Upper Montclair, New Jersey 07043-1624
Telephone: 201-655-4306

Total Enrollment (1993-94)	Full-Time	Part-Time
	26	208

Cost of Attendance (1993-94)		
Academic Year		
Standard Course Load per Semester/Term		
(credit hours/units)	9	6
Semesters/Terms per Academic Year	2	2
Tuition and Fees		
Resident	$2,795	$1,863
Nonresident	$3,465	$2,310
Living Expenses	$9,090	$9,090
Summer Term		
(R = Required, O = Optional, N = None)	O	O
Standard Course Load		
Tuition and Fees		
Resident	$2,795	$1,863
Nonresident	$3,465	$2,310

Financial Aid Available	Deadline (fall starts)	Awarded to Full-Time	Part-Time
Gift Aid	NA		
Federal College Work-Study	March 1	No	No
Federal Perkins Loans		No	No
Federal Stafford Loans	March 1	Yes	Yes
School-Based Loans	NA	No	No
Outside and Private Loans	NA		
Graduate Assistantships	March 31	Yes	No

MONTEREY INSTITUTE OF INTERNATIONAL STUDIES
International Management Division

425 Van Buren Street
Monterey, California 93940
Telephone: 408-647-4123

Total Enrollment (1993-94)	Full-Time	Part-Time
	213	0

Cost of Attendance (1993-94)

Academic Year
Standard Course Load per Semester/Term
(credit hours/units)	12-16
Semesters/Terms per Academic Year	2
Tuition and Fees	$13,200 + $45
Living Expenses	$7,400

Summer Term
(R = Required, O = Optional, N = None)	R (Advanced Entry)
	O (2-yr. program)
Standard Course Load	3-12 units
Tuition and Fees	$560/unit

Financial Aid Available

	Deadline (fall starts)	Awarded to Full-Time	Part-Time
Gift Aid	Feb. 25	Yes	No
Federal College Work-Study	NA	Yes	Yes
Federal Perkins Loans	NA	Yes	Yes
Federal Stafford Loans	NA	Yes	Yes
School-Based Loans	NA		
Outside and Private Loans	NA		
Graduate Assistantships	Varies by Department		

Percentage of Students Receiving Aid	Full-Time	Part-Time
All students	80%	50%
International students	20%	

MOREHEAD STATE UNIVERSITY

Combs Building
Morehead State University
Morehead, Kentucky 40351
Telephone: 606-783-2795

Total Enrollment (1993-94)	Full-Time	Part-Time
	32	40

Cost of Attendance (1993-94)

Academic Year
Standard Course Load per Semester/Term
(credit hours/units)	12	6
Semesters/Terms per Academic Year	2	
Tuition and Fees		
Resident	$1,850	$103/cr.
Nonresident	$5,170	$287/cr.
Living Expenses		

Summer Term
(R = Required, O = Optional, N = None)	O	O
Standard Course Load	6	
Tuition and Fees		
Resident	$103/cr.	
Nonresident	$287/cr.	

Financial Aid Available

	Deadline (fall starts)	Awarded to Full-Time	Part-Time
Gift Aid	April 1	Yes	Yes
Federal College Work-Study			
Federal Perkins Loans	April 1	Yes	Yes
Federal Stafford Loans	Anytime	Yes	Yes
School-Based Loans			
Outside and Private Loans			
Graduate Assistantships	Anytime	Yes	Yes

Percentage of Students Receiving Aid	Full-Time
All students	62%
Minority students	90%
Women students	62%
International students	10%

MOUNT SAINT MARY'S COLLEGE

Emmitsburg, Maryland 21727
Telephone: 301-447-5326

Total Enrollment (1993-94)	Full-Time	Part-Time
	90	134

Cost of Attendance (1993-94)		
Academic Year		
Standard Course Load per Semester/Term		
(credit hours/units)	9	6
Semesters/Terms per Academic Year	3	3
Tuition and Fees	$4,995	$3,300
Living Expenses	$7,000	$7,000
Summer Term		
(R = Required, O = Optional, N = None)	O	O
Standard Course Load	9	6
Tuition and Fee	$4,995	$3,300

Financial Aid Available	Deadline (fall starts)	Awarded to Full-Time	Awarded to Part-Time
Gift Aid		No	No
Federal College Work-Study		No	No
Federal Perkins Loans		No	No
Federal Stafford Loans		Yes	Yes
School-Based Loans	NA		
Outside and Private Loans			
Graduate Assistantships	April 1		No

Percentage of Students Receiving Aid	Full-Time	Part-Time
All students	20%	0%
Minority students	20%	0%
Women students	20%	0%
International students	75%	0%

MURRAY STATE UNIVERSITY
College of Business & Public Affairs

1 Murray Street
Murray, Kentucky 42071
Telephone: 502-762-6970

Total Enrollment (1993-94)	Full-Time	Part-Time
	70	121

Cost of Attendance (1993-94)		
Academic Year		
Standard Course Load per Semester/Term		
(credit hours/units)	9	6
Semesters/Terms per Academic Year	2	
Tuition and Fees		
Resident	$ 970/sem.	$ 99/cr. hr.
Nonresident	$2,630/sem.	$282/cr. hr.
Living Expenses		
Summer Term		
(R = Required, O = Optional, N = None)	O	O
Standard Course Load	6	3
Tuition and Fees		
Resident	$ 93/cr. hr.	$ 93/cr. hr.
Nonresident	$269/cr. hr.	$269/cr. hr.

Financial Aid Available	Deadline (fall starts)	Awarded to Full-Time	Awarded to Part-Time
Gift Aid		No	No
Federal College Work-Study	Rolling	Yes	Yes
Federal Perkins Loans	April 1	Yes	Yes
Federal Stafford Loans	April 1	Yes	Yes
School-Based Loans	None	Yes	Yes
Outside and Private Loans	NA		
Graduate Assistantships	August 1	Yes	

NEW MEXICO STATE UNIVERSITY
College of Business Administration and Economics

Graduate Studies Programs/MBA Program
P.O. Box 30001/Dept 3GSP
Las Cruces, New Mexico 88003
Telephone: 505-646-8003

Total Enrollment (1993-94)	Full-Time	Part-Time
	89	69

Cost of Attendance (1993-94)		
Academic Year		
Standard Course Load per Semester/Term		
(credit hours/units)	9-15	3-8
Semesters/Terms per Academic Year	2	2
Tuition and Fees		
Resident	$ 975	$ 81/cr.
Nonresident	$3,072	$256/cr.
Living Expenses	$3,000	$2,500
Summer Term		
(R = Required, O = Optional, N = None)	O	O
Standard Course Load	6	6
Tuition and Fees	$81/cr.	$81/cr.

Financial Aid Available	Deadline (fall starts)	Awarded to Full-Time	Awarded to Part-Time
Gift Aid	NA	Yes	Yes
Federal College Work-Study	March 1	Yes	Yes
Federal Perkins Loans	NA	No	No
Federal Stafford Loans	March 1	Yes	Yes
School-Based Loans	NA	No	No
Outside and Private Loans	NA		
Graduate Assistantships	Fall-April 15	Yes	
	Spring-November 15		

Percentage of Students Receiving Aid	Full-Time
All students	10%
Minority students	2%
Women students	5%
International students	3%

NEW YORK UNIVERSITY
Stern School of Business

44 West 4th Street MEC 10-150
New York, New York 10012
Telephone: 212-998-0794

Total Enrollment (1993-94)	Full-Time	Part-Time
	935	2,505

Cost of Attendance (1993-94)		
Academic Year		
Standard Course Load per Semester/Term		
(credit hours/units)	15	6
Semesters/Terms per Academic Year	2	2
Tuition and Fees	$19,116	$ 9,190
Living Expenses	$13,400	$13,400
Summer Term		
(R = Required, O = Optional, N = None)	O	O
Standard Course Load		6
Tuition and Fees		$ 4,595

Financial Aid Available	Deadline (fall starts)	Awarded to Full-Time	Awarded to Part-Time
Gift Aid	January 31	Yes	No
Federal College Work-Study	January 31	Yes	No
Federal Perkins Loans	January 31	Yes	No
Federal Stafford Loans	12 wks. prior to sem. start	Yes	Yes
School-Based Loans	NA		
Outside and Private Loans	12 wks. prior to sem. start	Yes	Yes
Graduate Assistantships	January 31	Yes	No

Percentage of Students Receiving Aid	Full-Time	Part-Time
All students	60%	20%
Minority students	90%	20%
Women students	60%	20%
International students	6%	0%

NICHOLLS STATE UNIVERSITY
College of Business Administration

P.O. Box 2015
Thibodaux, Louisiana 70310
Telephone: 504-448-4240

Total Enrollment (1993-94)	Full-Time	Part-Time
	73	74

Cost of Attendance (1993-94)		
Academic Year		
Standard Course Load per Semester/Term		
(credit hours/units)	9	6
Semesters/Terms per Academic Year	2	2
Tuition and Fees		
Resident	$1,980	$ 782
Nonresident	$4,572	$2,215
Living Expenses	$1,275	$1,275
Summer Term		
(R = Required, O = Optional, N = None)	O	O
Standard Course Load	6	3
Tuition and Fees		
Resident	$ 440	$ 218
Nonresident	$ 890	$ 218

Financial Aid Available	Deadline (fall starts)	Awarded to Full-Time	Awarded to Part-Time
Gift Aid	NA	No	No
Federal College Work-Study	NA	No	No
Federal Perkins Loans	None	No	No
Federal Stafford Loans	None	No	No
School-Based Loans	None	No	No
Outside and Private Loans	None	No	No
Graduate Assistantships	July 13	Yes	Yes

Percentage of Students Receiving Aid	Full-Time	Part-Time
All students	100%	
Minority students	16%	
Women students	44%	
International students	61%	

NORTH CENTRAL COLLEGE

Office of Graduate Programs
P.O. Box 3063
30 North Brainard
Naperville, Illinois 60566-7063
Telephone: 708-420-3313

Total Enrollment (1993-94)	Full-Time	Part-Time
	50	200

Cost of Attendance (1993-94)		
Academic Year		
Standard Course Load per Semester/Term		
(credit hours/units)	2 courses	1 course
Semesters/Terms per Academic Year	3	3
Tuition and Fees	$6,900	$3,450
Living Expenses	NA	NA
Summer Term		
(R = Required, O = Optional, N = None)	O	O
Standard Course Load	2	1
Tuition and Fees	$2,300	$1,150

Financial Aid Available	Deadline (fall starts)	Awarded to Full-Time	Awarded to Part-Time
Gift Aid	2 wks. before term start	Yes	Yes
Federal College Work-Study	NA	No	No
Federal Perkins Loans		Yes	Yes
Federal Stafford Loans		Yes	Yes
School-Based Loans	NA	No	No
Outside and Private Loans	NA	No	No
Graduate Assistantships	NA	No	No

Percentage of Students Receiving Aid	Full-Time	Part-Time
All students	8%	8%

NORTH PARK COLLEGE

3225 West Foster Avenue
Chicago, Illinois 60625
Telephone: 312-509-5860

Total Enrollment (1993-94)	Full-Time	Part-Time
	79	52

Cost of Attendance (1993-94)		
Academic Year		
Standard Course Load per Semester/Term		
(credit hours/units)	8	4
Semesters/Terms per Academic Year	4	4
Tuition and Fees	$8,480	$4,240
Living Expenses	$ 750	$ 450
Summer Term		
(R = Required, O = Optional, N = None)	O	O
Standard Course Load	8	4
Tuition and Fees	$2,120	$1,060

Financial Aid Available	Deadline (fall starts)	Awarded to Full-Time	Part-Time
Gift Aid	April 1	Yes	Yes
Federal College Work-Study	NA	No	No
Federal Perkins Loans	NA	No	No
Federal Stafford Loans	April 15	Yes	No
School-Based Loans	NA	No	No
Outside and Private Loans	NA	No	No
Graduate Assistantships	NA	No	No

Percentage of Students Receiving Aid	Full-Time	Part-Time
All students	65%	48%
Minority students	16%	29%
Women students	30%	25%
International students	71%	0%

NORTHEAST LOUISIANA UNIVERSITY
College of Business Administration

700 University Avenue
Monroe, Louisiana 71209-0100
Telephone: 318-342-1100

Total Enrollment (1993-94)	Full-Time	Part-Time
	74	21

Cost of Attendance (1993-94)		
Academic Year		
Standard Course Load per Semester/Term		
(credit hours/units)	9	6
Semesters/Terms per		
Academic Year	2 semesters + 2 summer terms	
Tuition and Fees		
Resident	$1,830	$1,233
Nonresident	$3,592	$2,409
Living Expenses	$1,980	
Summer Term		
(R = Required, O = Optional, N = None)	O	O
Standard Course Load	6	3
Tuition and Fees		
Resident	$1,200/term	$612/term
Nonresident	$2,495/term	$612/term

Financial Aid Available	Deadline (fall starts)	Awarded to Full-Time	Part-Time
Gift Aid	NA	No	No
Federal College Work-Study	NA	No	No
Federal Perkins Loans	NA	No	No
Federal Stafford Loans	NA	No	No
School-Based Loans	NA	No	No
Outside and Private Loans	June 1	Yes	Yes
Graduate Assistantships	None	Yes	No

Percentage of Students Receiving Aid	Full-Time	Part-Time
All students	60%	0%
Minority students	100%	0%
Women students	75%	0%
International students	95%	0%

NORTHEAST MISSOURI STATE UNIVERSITY
Division of Business and Accountancy

Kirksville, Missouri 63501
Telephone: 816-785-4346

Total Enrollment (1993-94)	Full-Time	Part-Time
	18	2

Cost of Attendance (1993-94)		
Academic Year		
Standard Course Load per Semester/Term		
(credit hours/units)	9-12	< 9
Semesters/Terms per Academic Year	2	2
Tuition and Fees		
Resident	$109/hr.	$109/hr.
Nonresident	$193/hr.	$193/hr.
Living Expenses	$4,500	
Summer Term		
(R = Required, O = Optional, N = None)	O	O
Standard Course Load	6	< 6
Tuition and Fees		
Resident	$109/hr.	$109/hr.
Nonresident	$193/hr.	$193/hr.

Financial Aid Available	Deadline (fall starts)	Awarded to Full-Time	Awarded to Part-Time
Gift Aid	NA		
Federal College Work-Study	None	Yes	No
Federal Perkins Loans	None	Yes	No
Federal Stafford Loans	May 1	Yes	
School-Based Loans	NA		
Outside and Private Loans	NA		
Graduate Assistantships	April 15	Yes	No

Percentage of Students Receiving Aid	Full-Time	Part-Time
All students	75%	0%
Minority students	100%	0%
Women students	86%	0%
International students	33%	

NORTHEASTERN ILLINOIS UNIVERSITY
College of Business and Management

5500 North St. Louis Avenue
Chicago, Illinois 60625
Telephone: 312-794-2655

Total Enrollment (1993-94)	Full-Time	Part-Time
	5	57

Cost of Attendance (1993-94)		
Academic Year		
Standard Course Load per Semester/Term		
(credit hours/units)	12	6
Semesters/Terms per Academic Year	3	3
Tuition and Fees		
Resident	$1,060	$ 544
Nonresident	$3,003	$1,516
Living Expenses	NA	NA
Summer Term		
(R = Required, O = Optional, N = None)	O	O
Standard Course Load	6	3
Tuition and Fees		
Resident	$ 544	$ 301
Nonresident	$1,516	$ 787

Financial Aid Available	Deadline (fall starts)	Awarded to Full-Time	Awarded to Part-Time
Gift Aid		Yes	No
Federal College Work-Study		Yes	Yes
Federal Perkins Loans		Yes	Yes
Federal Stafford Loans		Yes	Yes
School-Based Loans		No	No
Outside and Private Loans		No	No
Graduate Assistantships		Yes	Yes

Percentage of Students Receiving Aid	Full-Time	Part-Time
All students	90%	25%
Minority students	NA	NA
Women students	NA	NA
International students	100%	NA

NORTHEASTERN UNIVERSITY
Graduate School of Business Administration

350 Dodge Hall
Boston, Massachusetts 02115
Telephone: 617-373-2714

Total Enrollment (1993-94)	Full-Time	Part-Time
	300	800

Cost of Attendance (1993-94)

Academic Year
  Standard Course Load per Semester/Term

(credit hours/units)	4-6	2
Semesters/Terms per Academic Year	4	4
Tuition and Fees	$16,306*	$9,000
Living Expenses	$ 7,763	

*Please note: Full tuition and fees for Co-op Program of $32,612
  offset by Co-op earnings averaging $15,000

Summer Term
(R = Required, O = Optional, N = None)

	O	O
Standard Course Load	4-6	2
Tuition and Fees		
Resident	Same as above	
Nonresident		

Financial Aid Available

	Deadline (fall starts)	Awarded to Full-Time	Part-Time
Gift Aid	Varies	Yes	No
Federal College Work-Study	March 1	Yes	No
Federal Perkins Loans	March 1	Yes	No
Federal Stafford Loans	Ongoing	Yes	Yes
School-Based Loans	NA		
Outside and Private Loans	Ongoing	Yes	Yes
Graduate Assistantships	April 15	Yes	Yes

Percentage of Students Receiving Aid	Full-Time	Part-Time
All students	78%	NA
Minority students	90%	NA
Women students	72%	NA
International students	25%	NA

NORTHEASTERN UNIVERSITY
Graduate School of Professional Accounting

412 Dodge Hall
Boston, Massachusetts 02115
Telephone: 617-373-3244

Total Enrollment (1993-94)	Full-Time
	70

Cost of Attendance (1993-94)

Academic Year
  Standard Course Load per Semester/Term

(credit hours/units)	24
Semesters/Terms per Academic Year	4
Tuition and Fees	$16,905
Living Expenses	$ 9,000

Summer Term
(R = Required, O = Optional, N = None)

	R
Standard Course Load	24
Tuition and Fees	$ 5,635

Financial Aid Available

	Deadline (fall starts)	Awarded to Full-Time
Gift Aid	No Deadline	Yes
Federal College Work-Study	No Deadline	Yes
Federal Perkins Loans	No Deadline	Yes
Federal Stafford Loans	No Deadline	Yes
School-Based Loans	No Deadline	Yes
Outside and Private Loans	No Deadline	Yes
Graduate Assistantships	No Deadline	Yes

Percentage of Students Receiving Aid	Full-Time
All students	93%
Minority students	100%
Women students	90%
International students	100%

NORTHERN ARIZONA UNIVERSITY
College of Business Administration

Box 15066
Flagstaff, Arizona 86011-5066
Telephone: 602-523-7339

Total Enrollment (1993-94)	Full-Time	Part-Time
	95	19

Cost of Attendance (1993-94)		
Academic Year		
Standard Course Load per Semester/Term		
(credit hours/units)	12	6
Semesters/Terms per Academic Year	2	2
Tuition and Fees		
Resident	$3,295	$1,451
Nonresident	$8,025	$3,599
Living Expenses	$6,294	$5,854
Summer Term		
(R = Required, O = Optional, N = None)	R	R
Standard Course Load	9	3
Tuition and Fees		
Resident	$ 881	$ 295
Nonresident	$2,482	$ 832

Financial Aid Available	Deadline (fall starts)	Awarded to Full-Time	Awarded to Part-Time
Gift Aid	March 1	Yes	No
Federal College Work-Study	April 15	Yes	No
Federal Perkins Loans	April 15	Yes	No
Federal Stafford Loans	April 15	Yes	Yes
School-Based Loans	NA	No	No
Outside and Private Loans	April 15	Yes	Yes
Graduate Assistantships	March 1	Yes	No

Percentage of Students Receiving Aid	Full-Time	Part-Time
All students	40% of students combined	
Minority students		
Women students		
International students		

NORTHERN ILLINOIS UNIVERSITY
College of Business

Wirtz Hall 323
DeKalb, Illinois 60115-2897
Telephone: 815-753-1245
　　　　　 800-323-8714 (in Illinois)

Total Enrollment (1993-94)	Full-Time	Part-Time
	118	635

Cost of Attendance (1993-94)		
Academic Year		
Standard Course Load per Semester/Term		
(credit hours/units)	9	3
Semesters/Terms per Academic Year	3	3
Tuition and Fees		
Resident	$1,306	$327/course ($662 off campus)
Nonresident	$3,310	$828
Living Expenses		
Summer Term		
(R = Required, O = Optional, N = None)	O	O
Standard Course Load	12	3
Tuition and Fees		
Resident	$1,266	$317 ($662 off campus)
Nonresident	$3,270	$818

Financial Aid Available	Deadline (fall starts)	Awarded to Full-Time	Awarded to Part-Time
Gift Aid	None	Yes	No
Federal College Work-Study	None	Yes	No
Federal Perkins Loans	None	Yes	No
Federal Stafford Loans	None	Yes	No
School-Based Loans	None	Yes	No
Outside and Private Loans	None	No	No
Graduate Assistantships	None	Yes	No

Percentage of Students Receiving Aid	Full-Time
All students	67%
Minority students	
Women students	
International students	

NORTHERN KENTUCKY UNIVERSITY

Highland Heights, Kentucky 41099-6008
Telephone: 606-572-5165

Total Enrollment (1993-94)	Full-Time	Part-Time
	6	114

Cost of Attendance (1993-94)		
Academic Year		
Standard Course Load per Semester/Term		
(credit hours/units)	9	< 9
Semesters/Terms per Academic Year	3	3
Tuition and Fees		
Resident	$1,880	$103/sem.hr.
Nonresident	$5,200	$284/sem.hr.
Living Expenses	$8,492	$8,492
Summer Term		
(R = Required, O = Optional, N = None)	O	O
Standard Course Load	6	< 6
Tuition and Fees		
Resident	$103/sem.hr.	$103/sem.hr.
Nonresident	$287/sem.hr.	$287/sem.hr.

Financial Aid Available	Deadline (fall starts)	Awarded to Full-Time	Part-Time
Gift Aid	NA	No	No
Federal College Work-Study	April 1	Yes	Yes
Federal Perkins Loans	April 1	Yes	Yes
Federal Stafford Loans	April 1	Yes	Yes
School-Based Loans	April 1	Yes	Yes
Outside and Private Loans	April 1	Yes	Yes
Graduate Assistantships	None	Yes	No

NORTHWEST MISSOURI STATE UNIVERSITY
College of Business, Government, and Computer Science

800 University Drive - CH 220
Maryville, Missouri 64468-6001
Telephone: 816-562-1277

Total Enrollment (1993-94)	Full-Time	Part-Time
	29	50

Cost of Attendance (1993-94)		
Academic Year		
Standard Course Load per Semester/Term		
(credit hours/units)	9	3-8
Semesters/Terms per Academic Year	3	3
Tuition and Fees		
Resident	$ 82	$ 82
Nonresident	$147	$147
Living Expenses	NA	
Summer Term		
(R = Required, O = Optional, N = None)	O	O
Standard Course Load	12	3-11
Tuition and Fees		
Resident	$ 82	$ 82
Nonresident	$147	$147

Financial Aid Available	Deadline (fall starts)	Awarded to Full-Time	Part-Time
Gift Aid	April 1	Yes	Yes
Federal College Work-Study	April 1	Yes	Yes
Federal Perkins Loans	April 1	Yes	
Federal Stafford Loans	April 1	Yes	
School-Based Loans	NA	No	No
Outside and Private Loans	NA	No	No
Graduate Assistantships	April 1	Yes	No

Percentage of Students Receiving Aid	Full-Time	Part-Time
All students	60%	5%
Minority students	85%	5%
Women students	60%	5%
International students	10%	0%

NORTHWESTERN UNIVERSITY
J.L. Kellogg School of Business

Leverone Hall
2001 Sheridan Road
Evanston, Illinois 60208
Telephone: 708-491-3308

Total Enrollment (1993-94)	Full-Time	Part-Time
	1,051	1,300

Cost of Attendance (1993-94)		
Academic Year		
Standard Course Load per Semester/Term		
(credit hours/units)	4	1-2
Semesters/Terms per Academic Year	3	4
Tuition and Fees	$19,698	$1,642/course
Living Expenses	$13,492	NA
Summer Term		
(R = Required, O = Optional, N = None)	N	O
Standard Course Load		
Tuition and Fees		$1,642/course

Financial Aid Available	Deadline (fall starts)	Awarded to Full-Time	Part-Time
Gift Aid	May 1	Yes	No
Federal College Work-Study		No	No
Federal Perkins Loans	Rolling	Yes	No
Federal Stafford Loans	Rolling	Yes	Yes
School-Based Loans	May 1	Yes	No
Outside and Private Loans	Rolling	Yes	Yes
Graduate Assistantships		No	No

Percentage of Students Receiving Aid	Full-Time
All students	70%
Minority students	87%
Women students	61%
International students	1%

OAKLAND UNIVERSITY
MBA Program

416 Varner Hall
Rochester, Michigan 48309-4401
Telephone: 313-370-3370

Total Enrollment (1993-94)	Full-Time	Part-Time
	15	285

Cost of Attendance (1993-94)		
Academic Year		
Standard Course Load per Semester/Term		
(credit hours/units)	9	6
Semesters/Terms per Academic Year	2	2
Tuition and Fees		
Resident	$1,657	$1,140
Nonresident	$3,457	$2,339
Living Expenses	$6,304	$6,304
Summer Term		
(R = Required, O = Optional, N = None)	O	O
Standard Course Load	6	3
Tuition and Fees		
Resident	$1,140	$ 623
Nonresident	$2,339	$1,223

Financial Aid Available	Deadline (fall starts)	Awarded to Full-Time	Part-Time
Gift Aid	April 1	Yes	Yes
Federal College Work-Study	March 15	Yes	Yes
Federal Perkins Loans	March 15	Yes	Yes
Federal Stafford Loans	NA	Yes	Yes
School-Based Loans	NA	Yes	Yes
Outside and Private Loans		No	No
Graduate Assistantships	April 1	Yes	No

Percentage of Students Receiving Aid	Full-Time	Part-Time
All students	NA	NA
Minority students	NA	NA
Women students	NA	NA
International students	NA	NA

THE OHIO STATE UNIVERSITY
College of Business

Hagerty Hall
1775 College Road
Columbus, Ohio 43210
Telephone: 614-292-8511

Total Enrollment (1993-94)	Full-Time	Part-Time
	255	160

Cost of Attendance (1993-94)		
Academic Year		
Standard Course Load per Semester/Term		
(credit hours/units)	17	8
Semesters/Terms per Academic Year	3	3
Tuition and Fees		
Resident	$ 4,266	$1,138
Nonresident	$11,082	$2,956
Living Expenses	$ 5,668	NA
Summer Term		
(R – Required, O = Optional, N = None)	N	R
Standard Course Load		10
Tuition and Fees		
Resident		$1,422
Nonresident		$3,694

Financial Aid Available	Deadline (fall starts)	Awarded to Full-Time	Awarded to Part-Time
Gift Aid	March 1	Yes	No
Federal College Work-Study	March 1	Yes	Yes
Federal Perkins Loans	March 1	Yes	Yes
Federal Stafford Loans	Rolling	Yes	Yes
School-Based Loans	July 15	Yes	Yes
Outside and Private Loans	NA	Yes	Yes
Graduate Assistantships			No

Percentage of Students Receiving Aid	Full-Time	Part-Time
All students	24%	0%
Minority students	62%	0%
Women students	43%	0%
International students	8%	0%

OHIO UNIVERSITY
MBA Program

100 Haning Hall
Athens, Ohio 45701
Telephone: 614-593-2007

Total Enrollment (1993-94)	Full-Time	Part-Time
	38	30

Cost of Attendance (1993-94)	
Academic Year	
Standard Course Load per Semester/Term	
(credit hours/units)	13-month program
Semesters/Terms per Academic Year	
Tuition and Fees	
Resident	$ 5,320
Nonresident	$10,496
Living Expenses	$ 5,668
Summer Term	
(R = Required, O = Optional, N = None)	
Standard Course Load	
Tuition and Fees	
Resident	
Nonresident	

Financial Aid Available	Deadline (fall starts)	Awarded to Full-Time	Awarded to Part-Time
Gift Aid	None	Yes	No
Federal College Work-Study	April 1	Yes	No
Federal Perkins Loans	April 1	Yes	Yes
Federal Stafford Loans	April 1	Yes	Yes
School-Based Loans	April 1	Yes	Yes
Outside and Private Loans	April 1	Yes	Yes
Graduate Assistantships	March 15	Yes	No

Percentage of Students Receiving Aid	Full-Time	Part-Time
All students	80%	0%
Minority students		
Women students		
International students		

OKLAHOMA STATE UNIVERSITY
College of Business Administration

104A College of Business Administration
Stillwater, Oklahoma 74078-0555
Telephone: 405-744-2951

Total Enrollment (1993-94)	Full-Time	Part-Time
	190	275

Cost of Attendance (1993-94)		
Academic Year		
Standard Course Load per Semester/Term		
(credit hours/units)	12	6
Semesters/Terms per Academic Year	2	2
Tuition and Fees		
Resident	$ 1,876	$ 938
Nonresident	$ 5,459	$ 2,730
Living Expenses	$10,123	$10,123
Summer Term		
(R = Required, O = Optional, N = None)	N	O
Standard Course Load		3
Tuition and Fees		
Resident		$ 234
Nonresident		$ 682

Financial Aid Available	Deadline (fall starts)	Awarded to Full-Time	Part-Time
Gift Aid	March 1	Yes	Yes
Federal College Work-Study	March 1	Yes	Yes
Federal Perkins Loans	March 1	Yes	Yes
Federal Stafford Loans	March 1	Yes	Yes
School-Based Loans	March 1	Yes	No
Outside and Private Loans	Varies	Yes	Yes
Graduate Assistantships	June 1	Yes	No

Percentage of Students Receiving Aid	Full-Time	Part-Time
All students	50%	80%*
Minority students	75%	100%*
Women students	75%	75%*
International students	60%	NA

*Includes employer reimbursement of tuition/books

OLD DOMINION UNIVERSITY
Graduate School of Business and Public Administration

Hughes Hall #2087
Norfolk, Virginia 23529
Telephone: 804-683-5138

Total Enrollment (1993-94)	Full-Time	Part-Time
	113	289

Cost of Attendance (1993-94)		
Academic Year		
Standard Course Load per Semester/Term		
(credit hours/units)	12	6
Semesters/Terms per Academic Year	3	3
Tuition and Fees		
Resident	$1,969	$ 966
Nonresident	$4,957	$2,460
Living Expenses		
Summer Term		
(R = Required, O = Optional, N = None)	R	O
Standard Course Load	6	3
Tuition and Fees		
Resident	$ 966	$ 483
Nonresident	$2,460	$1,230

Financial Aid Available	Deadline (fall starts)	Awarded to Full-Time	Part-Time
Gift Aid	May	Yes	No
Federal College Work-Study	May	Yes	Yes
Federal Perkins Loans	May	Yes	Yes
Federal Stafford Loans	May	Yes	Yes
School-Based Loans	NA		
Outside and Private Loans	May	Yes	Yes
Graduate Assistantships	May	Yes	No

Percentage of Students Receiving Aid	Full-Time	Part-Time
All students	20%	0%
Minority students	80%	75%
Women students		
International students	50%	0%

ORAL ROBERTS UNIVERSITY
School of Business

7777 South Lewis
Tulsa, Oklahoma 74171
Telephone: 918-495-6117

Total Enrollment (1993-94)	Full-Time	Part-Time
	38	36

Cost of Attendance (1993-94)		
Academic Year		
Standard Course Load per Semester/Term		
(credit hours/units)	9.5	3-6
Semesters/Terms per Academic Year	2	2
Tuition and Fees	$215/hr.	$215/hr.
Living Expenses	$11,000	
Summer Term		
(R = Required, O = Optional, N = None)	O	O
Standard Course Load	3	3
Tuition and Fees	$215/hr.	$215/hr.

Financial Aid Available	Deadline (fall starts)	Awarded to Full-Time	Awarded to Part-Time
Gift Aid	August 1	Yes	No
Federal College Work-Study	NA	No	No
Federal Perkins Loans	Rolling	Yes	Yes
Federal Stafford Loans	Rolling	Yes	Yes
School-Based Loans	NA	No	No
Outside and Private Loans	NA	No	No
Graduate Assistantships	Rolling	Yes	No

Percentage of Students Receiving Aid	Full-Time	Part-Time
All students	80%	80%
Minority students	80%	80%
Women students	80%	80%
International students	80%	80%

OREGON STATE UNIVERSITY
College of Business

200 Bexell Hall
Corvallis, Oregon 97331-2603
Telephone: 503-737-3716

Total Enrollment (1993-94)	Full-Time	Part-Time
	100	25

Cost of Attendance (1993-94)	
Academic Year	
Standard Course Load per Semester/Term	
(credit hours/units)	9
Semesters/Terms per Academic Year	3
Tuition and Fees	
Resident	$1,391
Nonresident	$2,211
Living Expenses	$8,000
Summer Term	
(R = Required, O = Optional, N = None)	O
Standard Course Load	9
Tuition and Fees	NA

Financial Aid Available	Deadline (fall starts)	Awarded to Full-Time	Part-Time
Gift Aid	NA	Yes	
Federal College Work-Study		Yes	
Federal Perkins Loans		Yes	
Federal Stafford Loans		Yes	
School-Based Loans		Yes	
Outside and Private Loans			
Graduate Assistantships	May 15	Yes	

PACE UNIVERSITY
Lubin School of Business

New York City campus: Pace Plaza, New York, New York 10038
Telephone: 212-346-1531
White Plains campus: 1 Martine Avenue, White Plains, New York 10606
Telephone: 914-422-4283

Total Enrollment (1993-94)	Full-Time	Part-Time
	233	1,454

Cost of Attendance (1993-94)		
Academic Year		
Standard Course Load per Semester/Term		
(credit hours/units)	12	6
Semesters/Terms per Academic Year	2	2
Tuition and Fees	$ 9,900	$ 4,890
Living Expenses	$15,800	$15,800
Summer Term		
(R = Required, O = Optional, N = None)	O	O
Standard Course Load	3	3
Tuition and Fees	$ 1,200	$ 1,200

Financial Aid Available	Deadline (fall starts)	Awarded to Full-Time	Awarded to Part-Time
Gift Aid	June 15	Yes	Yes
Federal College Work-Study	June 15	Yes	Yes
Federal Perkins Loans	June 15	Yes	Yes
Federal Stafford Loans	June 15	Yes	Yes
School-Based Loans	NA	No	No
Outside and Private Loans	June 15	Yes	Yes
Graduate Assistantships	May 15	Yes	Yes

Percentage of Students Receiving Aid	Full-Time	Part-Time
All students	45%	15%
Minority students	43%	20%
Women students	45%	18%
International students	11%	13%

PENN STATE
The Smeal College of Business Administration

106 Business Administration Building
University Park, Pennsylvania 16802-3000
Telephone: 814-863-0474

Total Enrollment (1993-94)	Full-Time
	260

Cost of Attendance (1993-94)	
Academic Year	
Standard Course Load per Semester/Term	
(credit hours/units)	12
Semesters/Terms per Academic Year	2
Tuition and Fees	
Resident	$2,658
Nonresident	$5,368
Living Expenses	$8,300
Summer Term	
(R = Required, O = Optional, N = None)	O
Standard Course Load	6
Tuition and Fees	
Resident	$1,140
Nonresident	$1,710

Financial Aid Available	Deadline (fall starts)	Awarded to Full-Time
Gift Aid	Feb. 1	Yes
Federal College Work-Study	Feb. 15	Yes
Federal Perkins Loans	Feb. 15	Yes
Federal Stafford Loans	None	Yes
School-Based Loans	NA	No
Outside and Private Loans	NA	No
Graduate Assistantships	2nd-yr. students	Yes

Percentage of Students Receiving Aid	Full-Time
All students	80%
Minority students	100%
Women students	83%
International students	60%

PENN STATE ERIE
The Behrend College School of Business

Station Road
Erie, Pennsylvania 16563
Telephone: 814-898-6319

Total Enrollment (1993-94)	Full-Time	Part-Time
	8	122

Cost of Attendance (1993-94)		
Academic Year		
Standard Course Load per Semester/Term		
(credit hours/units)	9	6
Semesters/Terms per Academic Year	2	2
Tuition and Fees		
Resident	$4,678	$3,142
Nonresident	$8,134	$5,446
Living Expenses	$7,954	$7,954
Summer Term		
(R = Required, O = Optional, N = None)	O	O
Standard Course Load	6	3
Tuition and Fees		
Resident	$1,561	$ 780
Nonresident	$2,713	$1,356

Financial Aid Available	Deadline (fall starts)	Awarded to Full-Time	Awarded to Part-Time
Gift Aid	Feb. 15	Yes	Yes
Federal College Work-Study	Feb. 15	Yes	Yes
Federal Perkins Loans	Feb. 15	Yes	Yes
Federal Stafford Loans	Feb. 15	Yes	Yes
School-Based Loans	NA		
Outside and Private Loans	NA		
Graduate Assistantships	NA		

Percentage of Students Receiving Aid	Full-Time	Part-Time
All students	6%	94%*
Minority students	NA	33%*
Women students	100%	10%*
International students	NA	NA

*75% of part-time students receive employer reimbursement

THE PENNSYLVANIA STATE UNIVERSITY AT HARRISBURG
School of Business Administration

777 West Harrisburg Pike
Middletown, Pennsylvania 17057
Telephone: 717-948-6200

Total Enrollment (1993-94)	Full-Time	Part-Time
	12	203

Cost of Attendance (1993-94)		
Academic Year		
Standard Course Load per Semester/Term		
(credit hours/units)	12	6
Semesters/Terms per Academic Year	2	2
Tuition and Fees		
Resident	$ 6,144	$3,072
Nonresident	$11,712	$5,856
Living Expenses		
Summer Term		
(R = Required, O = Optional, N = None)	O	O
Standard Course Load	12	6
Tuition and Fees		
Resident	$ 3,072	$1,536
Nonresident	$ 5,856	$2,928

Financial Aid Available	Deadline (fall starts)	Awarded to Full-Time	Awarded to Part-Time
Gift Aid	Feb. 15	Yes	Yes
Federal College Work-Study	Feb. 15	Yes	Yes
Federal Perkins Loans	Feb. 15	Yes	Yes
Federal Stafford Loans	30 days prior to end of current semester	Yes	Yes
School-Based Loans			
Outside and Private Loans			
Graduate Assistantships	Rolling	Yes	

PEPPERDINE UNIVERSITY
School of Business and Management

24255 Pacific Coast Highway
Malibu, California 90263-4100
Telephone: 310-456-4858

Total Enrollment (1993-94)	Full-Time
	175

Cost of Attendance (1993-94)

Academic Year

Standard Course Load per Semester/Term (credit hours/units)	16
Semesters/Terms per Academic Year	2
Tuition and Fees	$17,230
Living Expenses	$10,530

Summer Term

(R = Required, O = Optional, N = None)	R*
Standard Course Load	16 (1-yr. MBA)
	8 (MIB)
Tuition and Fees	$4,300 per half term

* Summer term required for one-year MBA and MIB students only

Financial Aid Available	Deadline (fall starts)	Awarded to Full-Time
Gift Aid	June 1	Yes
Federal College Work-Study		
Federal Perkins Loans		
Federal Stafford Loans	June 15	Yes
School-Based Loans		
Outside and Private Loans	June 15	Yes
Graduate Assistantships	June 1	Yes

Percentage of Students Receiving Aid	Full-Time
All students	80%
Minority students	
Women students	
International students	

PHILADELPHIA COLLEGE OF TEXTILES AND SCIENCE
Graduate School of Business Administration

School House Lane and Henry Avenue
Philadelphia, Pennsylvania 19144
Telephone: 215-951-2943

Total Enrollment (1993-94)	Full-Time	Part-Time
	42	243

Cost of Attendance (1993-94)

Academic Year

Standard Course Load per Semester/Term (credit hours/units)	12	6
Semesters/Terms per Academic Year	2	2
Tuition and Fees	$8,208	$4,104
Living Expenses	$7,000	$7,000

Summer Term

(R = Required, O = Optional, N = None)	O	O
Standard Course Load	6	3
Tuition and Fees	$2,052	$1,026

Financial Aid Available	Deadline (fall starts)	Awarded to Full-Time	Part-Time
Gift Aid	Rolling	Yes	Yes
Federal College Work-Study	Rolling	Yes	Yes
Federal Perkins Loans	Rolling	Yes	Yes
Federal Stafford Loans	Rolling	Yes	Yes
School-Based Loans	NA		
Outside and Private Loans	NA		
Graduate Assistantships	Rolling	Yes	No

Percentage of Students Receiving Aid	Full-Time	Part-Time
All students	25%	15%
Minority students		
Women students		
International students		

PITTSBURG STATE UNIVERSITY
Kelce School of Business

101 Kelce Center
Pittsburg, Kansas 66762
Telephone: 316-235-4598

Total Enrollment (1993-94)	Full-Time	Part-Time
	100	38

Cost of Attendance (1993-94)		
Academic Year		
Standard Course Load per Semester/Term		
(credit hours/units)	12	3
Semesters/Terms per Academic Year	2	2
Tuition and Fees		
Resident	$ 995	$198
Nonresident	$2,547	$510
Living Expenses	$7,049	
Summer Term		
(R = Required, O = Optional, N = None)	O	O
Standard Course Load	6	3
Tuition and Fees		
Resident	$ 360	$180
Nonresident	$ 948	$474

Financial Aid Available	Deadline (fall starts)	Awarded to Full-Time	Awarded to Part-Time
Gift Aid	February 28	Yes	No
Federal College Work-Study	March 15	Yes	No
Federal Perkins Loans	March 15	Yes	No
Federal Stafford Loans	March 15	Yes	No
School-Based Loans	NA	No	No
Outside and Private Loans	NA	No	No
Graduate Assistantships	April 1	Yes	Yes

PLYMOUTH STATE COLLEGE

Office of Graduate Studies
Speare Building Room 215
Plymouth, New Hampshire 03264
Telephone: 603-535-2735
800-367-4723

Total Enrollment (1993-94)	Full-Time	Part-Time
	39	196

Cost of Attendance (1993-94)		
Academic Year		
Standard Course Load per Semester/Term		
(credit hours/units)	6-12 cr.	3 cr.
Semesters/Terms per Academic Year	4	4
Tuition and Fees		
Resident	$565/course	$565/course
Nonresident	$625/course	$625/course
Living Expenses	$9,000	NA
Summer Term		
(R = Required, O = Optional, N = None)	O	O
Standard Course Load	6 cr.	3 cr.
Tuition and Fees		
Resident	$565/course	$565/course
Nonresident	$625/course	$625/course

Financial Aid Available	Deadline (fall starts)	Awarded to Full-Time	Awarded to Part-Time
Gift Aid		No	No
Federal College Work-Study	March 1	Yes	Yes
Federal Perkins Loans		No	No
Federal Stafford Loans	March 1	Yes	Yes
School-Based Loans	NA		
Outside and Private Loans	March 1	Yes	Yes
Graduate Assistantships	March 15	Yes	No

Percentage of Students Receiving Aid	Full-Time	Part-Time
All students	2%	2%
Minority students	2%	2%
Women students	2%	2%
International students	2%	2%

POINT PARK COLLEGE
Master of Business Administration (International)

201 Wood Street
Pittsburgh, Pennsylvania 15222
Telephone: 412-392-3498

Total Enrollment (1993-94)	Full-Time	Part-Time
	16	36

Cost of Attendance (1993-94)		
Academic Year		
Standard Course Load per Semester/Term		
(credit hours/units)	9	9
Semesters/Terms per Academic Year	3	3
Tuition and Fees	$290/cr.	$290/cr.
Living Expenses	$5,000	$5,000
Summer Term		
(R = Required, O = Optional, N = None)	O	O
Standard Course Load	9	3
Tuition and Fees	$290/cr.	$290/cr.

Financial Aid Available	Deadline (fall starts)	Awarded to Full-Time	Part-Time
Gift Aid	April 1	Yes	Yes
Federal College Work-Study	NA	No	No
Federal Perkins Loans	NA	No	No
Federal Stafford Loans	None	Yes	Yes
School-Based Loans	NA	No	No
Outside and Private Loans	NA	No	No
Graduate Assistantships	April 1	Yes	No

Percentage of Students Receiving Aid	Full-Time	Part-Time
All students	19%	65%
Minority students	27%	80%
Women students	25%	67%
International students	19%	NA

PORTLAND STATE UNIVERSITY
School of Business Administration

631 South West Harrison Street
P.O. Box 751
Portland, Oregon 97207
Telephone: 503-725-3712

Total Enrollment (1993-94)	Full-Time	Part-Time
	178	341

Cost of Attendance (1993-94)		
Academic Year		
Standard Course Load per Semester/Term		
(credit hours/units)	12	8
Semesters/Terms per Academic Year	3	3
Tuition and Fees		
Resident	$4,122	$3,654
Nonresident	$6,612	$5,910
Living Expenses	$8,000	$8,000
Summer Term		
(R = Required, O = Optional, N = None)	O	O
Standard Course Load		
Tuition and Fees	$539/4 cr. hrs.	

Financial Aid Available	Deadline (fall starts)	Awarded to Full-Time	Part-Time
Gift Aid	June 15	Yes	Yes
Federal College Work-Study	January 31	Yes	No
Federal Perkins Loans	January 31	Yes	No
Federal Stafford Loans	June 15	Yes	Yes
School-Based Loans	January 31	Yes	No
Outside and Private Loans	June 15	Yes	Yes
Graduate Assistantships	None	Yes	No

PURDUE UNIVERSITY
Krannert Graduate School of Management

1310 Krannert Center Room 104
West Lafayette, Indiana 47907-1310
Telephone: 317-494-4365

Total Enrollment (1993-94)	Full-Time
	255

Cost of Attendance (1993-94)

Academic Year	
Standard Course Load per Semester/Term	
(credit hours/units)	15
Semesters/Terms per Academic Year	2
Tuition and Fees	
Resident	$2,696
Nonresident	$8,848
Living Expenses	$7,600
Summer Term	
(R = Required, O = Optional, N = None)	O
Standard Course Load	11
Tuition and Fees	
Resident	$ 866
Nonresident	$2,794

Financial Aid Available

	Deadline (fall starts)	Awarded to Full-Time
Gift Aid	March 1	Yes
Federal College Work-Study	NA	No
Federal Perkins Loans	NA	No
Federal Stafford Loans	March 1	Yes
School-Based Loans	NA	No
Outside and Private Loans	Rolling	Yes
Graduate Assistantships	Rolling	Yes

Percentage of Students Receiving Aid	Full-Time
All students	50%
Minority students	100%
Women students	55%
International students	10%

QUINNIPIAC COLLEGE
School of Graduate and Continuing Education

Mt. Carmel Avenue
Hamden, Connecticut 06518
Telephone: 203-281-8672

Total Enrollment (1993-94)	Full-Time	Part-Time
	112	419

Cost of Attendance (1993-94)

Academic Year		
Standard Course Load per Semester/Term		
(credit hours/units)	≥ 9	< 9
Semesters/Terms per Academic Year	3	3
Tuition and Fees	$310/hr.	$310/hr.
Living Expenses	NA	NA
Summer Term		
(R = Required, O = Optional, N = None)	O	O
Standard Course Load		
Tuition and Fees	$310/hr.	$310/hr.

Financial Aid Available

	Deadline (fall starts)	Awarded to Full-Time	Awarded to Part-Time
Gift Aid		No	No
Federal College Work-Study		No	No
Federal Perkins Loans		No	No
Federal Stafford Loans		Yes	Yes
School-Based Loans		No	No
Outside and Private Loans		Yes	Yes
Graduate Assistantships	Rolling	Yes	Yes

RADFORD UNIVERSITY
College of Business and Economics

P.O. Box 6956
Radford, Virginia 24142
Telephone: 703-831-5258

Total Enrollment (1993-94)	Full-Time	Part-Time
	25	35

Cost of Attendance (1993-94)

	Full-Time	Part-Time
Academic Year		
Standard Course Load per Semester/Term		
(credit hours/units)	9	3-6
Semesters/Terms per Academic Year	3	3
Tuition and Fees		
Resident	$3,070	$128/sem. hr.
Nonresident	$5,632	$128/sem. hr.
Living Expenses	$8,000	
Summer Term		
(R = Required, O = Optional, N = None)	O	O
Standard Course Load	3-6	3
Tuition and Fees		
Resident	$128/sem. hr.	$128/sem. hr.
Nonresident	$235/sem. hr.	$235/sem. hr.

Financial Aid Available

	Deadline (fall starts)	Awarded to Full-Time	Awarded to Part-Time
Gift Aid		Yes	No
Federal College Work-Study	March 1	Yes	Yes
Federal Perkins Loans	March 1	Yes	Yes
Federal Stafford Loans	March 1	Yes	Yes
School-Based Loans	March 1	No	No
Outside and Private Loans	March 1	Yes	Yes
Graduate Assistantships	Continuous	Yes	No

Percentage of Students Receiving Aid	Full-Time	Part-Time
All students	45%	0%
Minority students		
Women students		
International students		

REGENT UNIVERSITY
College of Administration and Management

1000 Centerville Turnpike
Virginia Beach, Virginia 23464-5091
Telephone: 804-523-7421

Total Enrollment (1993-94)	Full-Time	Part-Time
	134	102

Cost of Attendance (1993-94)

	Full-Time	Part-Time
Academic Year		
Standard Course Load per Semester/Term		
(credit hours/units)	8-12	4
Semesters/Terms per Academic Year	3	3
Tuition and Fees	$4,560-$6,840	$2,280
Living Expenses		
Summer Term		
(R = Required, O = Optional, N = None)	O	O
Standard Course Load	8	4
Tuition and Fees	$1,520	$760

Financial Aid Available

	Deadline (fall starts)	Awarded to Full-Time	Awarded to Part-Time
Gift Aid	July 15	Yes	No
Federal College Work-Study	NA		
Federal Perkins Loans	NA		
Federal Stafford Loans	NA		
School-Based Loans	NA		
Outside and Private Loans	Varies	Yes	
Graduate Assistantships	NA		

Percentage of Students Receiving Aid	On-Campus	Distance Education
All students	59%	38%
Minority students		
Women students		
International students		

RENSSELAER POLYTECHNIC INSTITUTE
School of Management

MBA Enrollment Office
Lally Management Center, Room 204
Troy, New York 12180-3590
Telephone: 518-276-8785

Total Enrollment (1993-94)	Full-Time	Part-Time
	175	70

Cost of Attendance (1993-94)		
Academic Year		
Standard Course Load per Semester/Term		
(credit hours/units)	15	6
Semesters/Terms per Academic Year	2	2
Tuition and Fees	$15,150	$505/cr.hr.
Living Expenses	$ 9,500	$9,500
Summer Term		
(R = Required, O = Optional, N = None)	O	O
Standard Course Load	6-12	6-12
Tuition and Fees	$505/cr.hr.	$505/cr.hr.

Financial Aid Available	Deadline (fall starts)	Awarded to Full-Time	Awarded to Part-Time
Gift Aid	Feb. 15	Yes	No
Federal College Work-Study	NA	No	No
Federal Perkins Loans	None	Yes	No
Federal Stafford Loans	None	Yes	No
School-Based Loans	After admission	Yes	No
Outside and Private Loans	After admission	Yes	No
Graduate Assistantships	March 15	Yes	No

Percentage of Students Receiving Aid	Full-Time	Part-Time
All students	80%	0%
Minority students	100%	0%
Women students	100%	0%
International students	10%	0%

RICE UNIVERSITY
Jesse H. Jones Graduate School of Administration

P.O. Box 1892
Houston, Texas 77251-1892
Telephone: 713-527 4918

Total Enrollment (1993-94)	Full-Time
	217

Cost of Attendance (1993-94)	
Academic Year	
Standard Course Load per Semester/Term	
(credit hours/units)	16
Semesters/Terms per Academic Year	2
Tuition and Fees	$10,300
Living Expenses	$ 7,450
Summer Term	
(R = Required, O = Optional, N = None)	N
Standard Course Load	
Tuition and Fees	
Resident	
Nonresident	

Financial Aid Available	Deadline (fall starts)	Awarded to Full-Time
Gift Aid	June 1	Yes
Federal College Work-Study	June 1	Yes
Federal Perkins Loans	NA	No
Federal Stafford Loans	June 1	Yes
School-Based Loans	June 1	Yes
Outside and Private Loans	June 1	Yes
Graduate Assistantships	NA	No

Percentage of Students Receiving Aid	Full-Time
All students	85%
Minority students	85%
Women students	85%
International students	0%

RIDER UNIVERSITY
School of Business Administration

2083 Lawrenceville Road
Lawrenceville, New Jersey 08648-3099
Telephone: 609-896-5127

Total Enrollment (1993-94)	Full-Time	Part-Time
	32	

Cost of Attendance (1993-94)		
Academic Year		
Standard Course Load per Semester/Term		
(credit hours/units)	9	3 or 6
Semesters/Terms per Academic Year	2	2
Tuition and Fees	$3,015	$1,005 or $2,010
Living Expenses	NA	NA
Summer Term		
(R = Required, O = Optional, N = None)	O	O
Standard Course Load	1	1
Tuition and Fees	$1,005	$1,005

Financial Aid Available	Deadline (fall starts)	Awarded to Full-Time	Awarded to Part-Time
Gift Aid	NA	No	
Federal College Work-Study	NA	No	
Federal Perkins Loans	NA	No	
Federal Stafford Loans	Rolling	Yes	
School-Based Loans	NA		
Outside and Private Loans	NA		
Graduate Assistantships	Must be in program for 1 semester	Yes	Yes

Percentage of Students Receiving Aid	Full-Time
All students	2%
Minority students	
Women students	
International students	

ROCHESTER INSTITUTE OF TECHNOLOGY
College of Business

104 Lomb Memorial Drive
Rochester, New York 14623-5608
Telephone: 716-475-2256

Total Enrollment (1993-94)	Full-Time	Part-Time
	100 MBA; 23 EMBA	400 (+ students in Czechoslovakia)

Cost of Attendance (1993-94)		
Academic Year		
Standard Course Load per Semester/Term		
(credit hours/units)	12-18	11 or fewer
Semesters/Terms per Academic Year	4	4
Tuition and Fees	$14,475	$1,624-$3,248
Living Expenses	$ 6,500	$300-$450 (books)
Summer Term		
(R = Required, O = Optional, N = None)	O	O
Standard Course Load	12-18	11 or fewer
Tuition and Fees	$ 4,825	$1,624-$3,248

Financial Aid Available	Deadline (fall starts)	Awarded to Full-Time	Awarded to Part-Time
Gift Aid	None	Yes	Yes
Federal College Work-Study	None	Yes	Yes
Federal Perkins Loans	NA	No	No
Federal Stafford Loans	None	Yes	Yes
School-Based Loans	NA	Yes	Yes
Outside and Private Loans	None	Yes	Yes
Graduate Assistantships	None	Yes	Yes

Percentage of Students Receiving Aid	Full-Time
All students	26%
Minority students	
Women students	
International students	

ROCKFORD COLLEGE

505 East State Street
Rockford, Illinois 61108
Telephone: 815-226-4040

Total Enrollment (1993-94)	Full-Time	Part-Time
	9	181

Cost of Attendance (1993-94)		
Academic Year		
Standard Course Load per Semester/Term		
(credit hours/units)	9-12	3-6
Semesters/Terms per Academic Year	2	2
Tuition and Fees	$11,540	$295/cr.hr.
Living Expenses	$ 6,000	
Summer Term		
(R = Required, O = Optional, N = None)	O	O
Standard Course Load	3-6	3-6
Tuition and Fees	$295/cr.hr.	$295/cr.hr.

Financial Aid Available	Deadline (fall starts)	Awarded to Full-Time	Part-Time
Gift Aid	NA	No	No
Federal College Work-Study	NA	No	No
Federal Perkins Loans	NA	No	No
Federal Stafford Loans	May 2	Yes	Yes
School-Based Loans	NA	No	No
Outside and Private Loans	NA	No	No
Graduate Assistantships	NA	No	No

ROLLINS COLLEGE
Crummer Graduate School of Business

1000 Holt Avenue - 2722
Winter Park, Florida 32789-4499
Telephone: 407-646-2405

Total Enrollment (1993-94)	Full-Time	Part-Time
	183	163

Cost of Attendance (1993-94)		
Academic Year		
Standard Course Load per Semester/Term		
(credit hours/units)	12	6
Semesters/Terms per Academic Year	2	3
Tuition and Fees	$15,400	$9,400
Living Expenses		
Summer Term		
(R = Required, O = Optional, N = None)	N	R
Standard Course Load		6
Tuition and Fees		$2,700

Financial Aid Available	Deadline (fall starts)	Awarded to Full-Time	Part-Time
Gift Aid	April 1	Yes	No
Federal College Work-Study	NA	No	No
Federal Perkins Loans	NA	No	No
Federal Stafford Loans	August 1	Yes	Yes
School-Based Loans		No	No
Outside and Private Loans	August 1	Yes	Yes
Graduate Assistantships	April 1	Yes	Yes

Percentage of Students Receiving Aid	Full-Time	Part-Time
All students	46%	0%
Minority students	2%	0%
Women students	12%	0%
International students	9%	0%

ROOSEVELT UNIVERSITY
Walter E. Heller College of Business Administration

430 South Michigan Avenue
Chicago, Illinois 60605
Telephone: 312-341-3820

Total Enrollment (1993-94)	Full-Time	Part-Time
	164	110

Cost of Attendance (1993-94)		
Academic Year		
Standard Course Load per Semester/Term		
(credit hours/units)`	9-15 hrs.	3-6 hrs.
Semesters/Terms per Academic Year	3	3
Tuition and Fees	$332/cr.hr.	$332/cr.hr.
Living Expenses	$14,898	
Summer Term		
(R = Required, O = Optional, N = None)	O	O
Standard Course Load	9-15 hrs.	3-6 hrs.
Tuition and Fees	$332/cr.hr.	$332/cr.hr.

Financial Aid Available	Deadline (fall starts)	Awarded to Full-Time	Awarded to Part-Time
Gift Aid	May 1	Yes	Yes
Federal College Work-Study	May 1	Yes	Yes
Federal Perkins Loans	May 1	Yes	Yes
Federal Stafford Loans	May 1	Yes	Yes
School-Based Loans	NA		
Outside and Private Loans	May 1	Yes	Yes
Graduate Assistantships	May 1	Yes	No

Percentage of Students Receiving Aid	Full-Time	Part-Time
All students	15%	85%
Minority students	18%	82%
Women students	9%	91%
International students	85%	15%

ROSARY COLLEGE
Graduate School of Business

7900 West Division
River Forest, Illinois 60305
Telephone: 708-524-6810

Total Enrollment (1993-94)	Full-Time	Part-Time
	50	400

Cost of Attendance (1993-94)		
Academic Year		
Standard Course Load per Semester/Term		
(credit hours/units)	3	1-2
Semesters/Terms per Academic Year	3	3
Tuition and Fees	$9,450	$3,150-$6,450
Living Expenses	$5,000	
Summer Term		
(R = Required, O = Optional, N = None)		
Standard Course Load	O	O
Tuition and Fees	$9,450	$3,150-$6,450

Financial Aid Available	Deadline (fall starts)	Awarded to Full-Time	Awarded to Part-Time
Gift Aid	July 1	Yes	No
Federal College Work-Study		No	No
Federal Perkins Loans		No	No
Federal Stafford Loans	Rolling	Yes	Yes
School-Based Loans		No	No
Outside and Private Loans		No	No
Graduate Assistantships	August 1	Yes	Yes

Percentage of Students Receiving Aid	Full-Time	Part-Time
All students	20%	10%
Minority students		
Women students		
International students	5%	

ROWAN COLLEGE OF NEW JERSEY
School of Business Administration

Bunce Hall
201 Mullica Hill Road
Glassboro, New Jersey 08028-1701
Telephone: 609-863-5161

Total Enrollment (1993-94)	Full-Time	Part-Time
	5	89

Cost of Attendance (1993-94)		
Academic Year		
Standard Course Load per Semester/Term		
(credit hours/units)	9	< 9
Semesters/Terms per Academic Year	2	2
Tuition and Fees		
Resident	$1,966	$164/sem.hr.
Nonresident	$2,986	$248/sem.hr.
Summer Term		
(R = Required, O = Optional, N = None)	O	O
Standard Course Load		
Tuition and Fees		
Resident	$164/sem.hr.	
Nonresident	$248/sem.hr.	

Financial Aid Available	Deadline (fall starts)	Awarded to Full-Time	Awarded to Part-Time
Gift Aid	NA	No	No
Federal College Work-Study	None	Yes	Yes
Federal Perkins Loans	March 15	Yes	Yes
Federal Stafford Loans	None	Yes	Yes
School-Based Loans	NA	No	No
Outside and Private Loans	NA	No	No
Graduate Assistantships	Rolling	Yes	No

RUTGERS, THE STATE UNIVERSITY OF NEW JERSEY
Graduate School of Management

92 New Street
Newark, New Jersey 07102
Telephone: 201-648-1234

Total Enrollment (1993-94)	Full-Time	Part-Time
	507	1,066

Cost of Attendance (1993-94)		
Academic Year		
Standard Course Load per Semester/Term		
(credit hours/units)	15	6
Semesters/Terms per Academic Year	3	3
Tuition and Fees		
Resident	$ 7,118	$3,596
Nonresident	$10,798	$5,258
Living Expenses	$10,000	$2,000
Summer Term		
(R = Required, O = Optional, N = None)	O	O
Standard Course Load	15	6
Tuition and Fees		
Resident	$ 3,559	$1,798
Nonresident	$ 5,399	$2,629

Financial Aid Available	Deadline (fall starts)	Awarded to Full-Time	Awarded to Part-Time
Gift Aid	March 15	Yes	No
Federal College Work-Study	May 15	Yes	No
Federal Perkins Loans	May 15	Yes	No
Federal Stafford Loans	None	Yes	Yes
School-Based Loans	None	Yes	No
Outside and Private Loans	None	Yes	No
Graduate Assistantships	March 15	Yes	No

Percentage of Students Receiving Aid	Full-Time	Part-Time
All students	66%	10%
Minority students	63%	10%
Women students	75%	10%
International students	1%	0%

SAGE COLLEGE
MBA Program

Sage Graduate School
140 New Scotland Avenue
Albany, New York 12208
Telephone: 518-445-1763

Total Enrollment (1993-94)	Full-Time	Part-Time
	30	150

Cost of Attendance (1993-94)

Academic Year
Standard Course Load per Semester/Term

	Full-Time	Part-Time
(credit hours/units)	9	6
Semesters/Terms per Academic Year	4	4
Tuition and Fees (includes summer tuition)	$7,020	$4,680
Living Expenses	$9,000	

Summer Term
(R = Required, O = Optional, N = None)

	Full-Time	Part-Time
	O	O
Standard Course Load	12	6
Tuition and Fees		

Financial Aid Available

	Deadline (fall starts)	Awarded to Full-Time	Part-Time
Gift Aid	April 1	Yes	Yes
Federal College Work-Study			
Federal Perkins Loans	60 days before the beginning of term	Yes	
Federal Stafford Loans	60 days before the beginning of term	Yes	
School-Based Loans	NA		
Outside and Private Loans	Varies	Yes	
Graduate Assistantships	August 1	Yes	

Percentage of Students Receiving Aid

	Full-Time	Part-Time
All students		
Minority students	20%	
Women students		
International students		

ST. AMBROSE UNIVERSITY
H.L. McLaughlin MBA Program

518 West Locust Street
Davenport, Iowa 52803
Telephone: 319-383-8760

Total Enrollment (1993-94)	Full-Time	Part-Time
		681

Cost of Attendance (1993-94)

Academic Year
Standard Course Load per Semester/Term

	Full-Time	Part-Time
(credit hours/units)	9	4.5
Semesters/Terms per Academic Year	2	2
Tuition and Fees	$307/sem.hr.	$307/sem.hr.
Living Expenses	$9,030	$4,515

Summer Term
(R = Required, O = Optional, N = None)

	Full-Time	Part-Time
	O	
Standard Course Load		
Tuition and Fees	$307/sem.hr.	$307/sem.hr.

Financial Aid Available

	Deadline (fall starts)	Awarded to Full-Time	Part-Time
Gift Aid	Rolling	Yes	Yes
Federal College Work-Study		No	No
Federal Perkins Loans	Rolling	Yes	Yes
Federal Stafford Loans	Rolling	Yes	Yes
School-Based Loans		No	No
Outside and Private Loans		No	No
Graduate Assistantships	3-4 weeks prior to semester	Yes	Yes

Percentage of Students Receiving Aid

	Full-Time	Part-Time
All students	30% estimate (combined)	
Minority students		
Women students		
International students		

ST. BONAVENTURE UNIVERSITY
School of Business

P.O. Box 108
Mecom Center
St. Bonaventure, New York 14778
Telephone: 716-375-2277

Total Enrollment (1993-94)	Full-Time	Part-Time
	30	200

Cost of Attendance (1993-94)

Academic Year		
Standard Course Load per Semester/Term		
(credit hours/units)	15	3-9
Semesters/Terms per Academic Year	2 + summer	2 + summer
Tuition and Fees	$305/cr.	$305/cr.
Living Expenses	$5,500	$5,500
Summer Term		
(R = Required, O = Optional, N = None)	R	O
Standard Course Load	0-15	6
Tuition and Fees	$305/cr.	$305/cr.

Financial Aid Available

	Deadline (fall starts)	Awarded to Full-Time	Awarded to Part-Time
Gift Aid		No	No
Federal College Work-Study	July 1	Yes	Yes
Federal Perkins Loans	July 1	Yes	Yes
Federal Stafford Loans	July 1	Yes	Yes
School-Based Loans	NA	No	No
Outside and Private Loans	NA	No	No
Graduate Assistantships	May 1	Yes	NA

Percentage of Students Receiving Aid	Full-Time	Part-Time
All students	30%	15%
Minority students		
Women students		
International students		

ST. CLOUD STATE UNIVERSITY
College of Business

720 4th Avenue South
St. Cloud, Minnesota 56301-4498
Telephone: 612-255-3212

Total Enrollment (1993-94)	Full-Time	Part-Time
	70	55

Cost of Attendance (1993-94)

Academic Year		
Standard Course Load per Semester/Term		
(credit hours/units)	8	4
Semesters/Terms per Academic Year	3	3
Tuition and Fees		
Resident	$585	$293
Nonresident	$855	$428
Living Expenses		
Summer Term		
(R = Required, O = Optional, N = None)	O	O
Standard Course Load		
Tuition and Fees		
Resident	$585	$293
Nonresident	$855	$428

Financial Aid Available

	Deadline (fall starts)	Awarded to Full-Time	Awarded to Part-Time
Gift Aid		No	No
Federal College Work-Study	Rolling	Yes	Yes
Federal Perkins Loans	Rolling	Yes	Yes
Federal Stafford Loans	Rolling	Yes	Yes
School-Based Loans	Rolling	Yes	Yes
Outside and Private Loans	Rolling	Yes	Yes
Graduate Assistantships	Rolling	Yes	Yes

SAINT FRANCIS COLLEGE

2701 Spring Street
Fort Wayne, Indiana 46808
Telephone: 219-434-3270

Total Enrollment (1993-94)	Full-Time	Part-Time
		106

Cost of Attendance (1993-94)		
Academic Year		
Standard Course Load per Semester/Term		
(credit hours/units)	9	3
Semesters/Terms per Academic Year	2	2
Tuition and Fees	$269	$269
Living Expenses		
Summer Term		
(R = Required, O = Optional, N = None)		
Standard Course Load		
Tuition and Fees	Same as above	

Financial Aid Available	Deadline (fall starts)	Awarded to Full-Time	Awarded to Part-Time
Gift Aid	May 1	Yes	Yes
Federal College Work-Study		No	No
Federal Perkins Loans			
Federal Stafford Loans	Rolling	Yes	Yes
School-Based Loans		No	No
Outside and Private Loans			
Graduate Assistantships	May 1	Yes	Yes

ST. JOHN'S UNIVERSITY
Graduate School of Business

8000 Utopia Parkway
Jamaica, New York 11439
Telephone: 718-990-6418

Total Enrollment (1993-94)	Full-Time	Part-Time
	204	1,284

Cost of Attendance (1993-94)		
Academic Year		
Standard Course Load per Semester/Term		
(credit hours/units)	12	6
Semesters/Terms per Academic Year	2	2
Tuition and Fees	$9,534	$4,842
Living Expenses	$8,500	$8,200
Summer Term		
(R = Required, O = Optional, N = None)	O	O
Standard Course Load	6	3
Tuition and Fees	$2,366	$1,193

Financial Aid Available	Deadline (fall starts)	Awarded to Full-Time	Awarded to Part-Time
Gift Aid	April 1	Yes	Yes
Federal College Work-Study	April 1	Yes	No
Federal Perkins Loans	April 1	Yes	Yes
Federal Stafford Loans	April 1	Yes	Yes
School-Based Loans		No	No
Outside and Private Loans	April 1	Yes	Yes
Graduate Assistantships	April 1	Yes	No

Percentage of Students Receiving Aid	Full-Time	Part-Time
All students	92%	18%
Minority students	74%	35%
Women students	96%	19%
International students	56%	28%

SAINT JOSEPH'S UNIVERSITY
MBA Program

5600 City Avenue
Philadelphia, Pennsylvania 19131-1395
Telephone: 610-660-1690

Total Enrollment (1993-94)	Full-Time	Part-Time
	115	1,445

Cost of Attendance (1993-94)

	Full-Time	Part-Time
Academic Year		
Standard Course Load per Semester/Term		
(credit hours/units)	9	3-6
Semesters/Terms per Academic Year	2 + summer	2 + summer
Tuition and Fees	$1,095/class	$1,095/class
Living Expenses	$5,000	$5,000
Summer Term		
(R = Required, O = Optional, N = None)	O	O
Standard Course Load	2 classes	1 class
Tuition and Fees	$2,190	$1,095

Financial Aid Available

	Deadline (fall starts)	Awarded to Full-Time	Awarded to Part-Time
Gift Aid	NA		
Federal College Work-Study	May 1	Yes	Yes
Federal Perkins Loans	May 1	Yes	Yes
Federal Stafford Loans	6 wks. before semester	Yes	Yes
School-Based Loans	NA	No	No
Outside and Private Loans	None	Yes	Yes
Graduate Assistantships	June 1	Yes	No

Percentage of Students Receiving Aid	Full-Time	Part-Time
All students	36%	58%
Minority students		
Women students		
International students		

SAINT LEO COLLEGE
Graduate Business Studies

SR 52, P.O. Box 2067
Saint Leo, Florida 33574
Telephone: 904-588-8311

Total Enrollment (1993-94)	Part-Time
	41

Cost of Attendance (1993-94)

	Part-Time
Academic Year	
Standard Course Load per Semester/Term	
(credit hours/units)	6
Semesters/Terms per Academic Year	12
Tuition and Fees	$2,000
Living Expenses	
Summer Term	
(R = Required, O = Optional, N = None)	R
Standard Course Load	6
Tuition and Fees	$1,000

Financial Aid Available

	Deadline (fall starts)	Awarded to Part-Time
Gift Aid	NA	No
Federal College Work-Study	NA	No
Federal Perkins Loans	NA	No
Federal Stafford Loans	April 1	Yes
School-Based Loans	NA	No
Outside and Private Loans	NA	No
Graduate Assistantships	NA	No

Percentage of Students Receiving Aid	Part-Time
All students	15-20%
Minority students	
Women students	
International students	

SAINT LOUIS UNIVERSITY
School of Business and Administration

3674 Lindell Boulevard
St. Louis, Missouri 63108
Telephone: 314-658-3801

Total Enrollment (1993-94)	Full-Time	Part-Time
	293	509

Cost of Attendance (1993-94)		
Academic Year		
Standard Course Load per Semester/Term		
(credit hours/units)	9	3-6
Semesters/Terms per Academic Year	2 + summer	2 + summer
Tuition and Fees	$ 3,875	$ 1,290-
		$ 2,580
Living Expenses	$14,000	$14,000
Summer Term		
(R = Required, O = Optional, N = None)	O	O
Standard Course Load	6	3
Tuition and Fees	$ 2,580	$ 1,290

Financial Aid Available	Deadline (fall starts)	Awarded to Full-Time	Awarded to Part-Time
Gift Aid	None	Yes	Yes
Federal College Work-Study	None	Yes	Yes
Federal Perkins Loans	None	Yes	Yes
Federal Stafford Loans	None	Yes	Yes
School-Based Loans	NA	No	No
Outside and Private Loans	None	Yes	Yes
Graduate Assistantships	None	Yes	Yes

SAINT MARTIN'S COLLEGE
Graduate Studies in Business Administration

5300 Pacific Avenue Southeast
Lacey, Washington 98503
Telephone: 206-438-4512

Total Enrollment (1993-94)	Full-Time
	125

Cost of Attendance (1993-94)	
Academic Year	
Standard Course Load per Semester/Term	
(credit hours/units)	3 hrs./term
Semesters/Terms per Academic Year	5 terms
Tuition and Fees	$358/credit
Living Expenses	Varies
Summer Term	
(R = Required, O = Optional, N = None)	O
Standard Course Load	
Tuition and Fees	$358/credit

Financial Aid Available	Deadline (fall starts)	Awarded to Full-Time	Awarded to Part-Time
Gift Aid	March 1	Yes	Yes
Federal College Work-Study	March 1	Yes	Yes
Federal Perkins Loans	March 1	Yes	Yes
Federal Stafford Loans	March 1	Yes	Yes
School-Based Loans	NA	No	No
Outside and Private Loans	March 1	Yes	Yes
Graduate Assistantships	NA	No	No

Percentage of Students Receiving Aid	Full-Time
All students	75%
Minority students	
Women students	
International students	

SAINT XAVIER UNIVERSITY
Graham School of Management

3700 West 103rd Street
Chicago, Illinois 60655
Telephone: 312-298-3050

Total Enrollment (1993-94)	Full-Time	Part-Time
	13	266

Cost of Attendance (1993-94)		
Academic Year		
Standard Course Load per Semester/Term		
(credit hours/units)	9	3
Semesters/Terms per Academic Year	3	3
Tuition and Fees	$10,017	$1,121
Living Expenses		
Summer Term		
(R = Required, O = Optional, N = None)	O	O
Standard Course Load	9	3
Tuition and Fees	$10,017	$1,121

Financial Aid Available	Deadline (fall starts)	Awarded to Full-Time	Awarded to Part-Time
Gift Aid	Rolling	Yes	Yes
Federal College Work-Study	Rolling	Yes	Yes
Federal Perkins Loans	NA	No	No
Federal Stafford Loans	Rolling	Yes	Yes
School-Based Loans	NA	No	No
Outside and Private Loans	NA	No	No
Graduate Assistantships	Rolling	Yes	Yes

Percentage of Students Receiving Aid	Full-Time	Part-Time
All students	17%	8%
Minority students	8%	1%
Women students	8%	5%
International students	8%	0%

SALEM STATE COLLEGE
MBA Program

352 Lafayette Street
Salem, Massachusetts 01920
Telephone: 508-741-6320

Total Enrollment (1993-94)	Full-Time	Part-Time
	200 combined	

Cost of Attendance (1993-94)		
Academic Year		
Standard Course Load per Semester/Term		
(credit hours/units)	9	6
Semesters/Terms per Academic Year	2	2
Tuition and Fees		
Resident	$2,880	$1,920
Nonresident	$4,500	$3,000
Living Expenses		
Summer Term		
(R = Required, O = Optional, N = None)	R/O	R/O
Standard Course Load	9	6
Tuition and Fees		
Resident	$1,440	$ 960
Nonresident	$2,250	$1,500

Financial Aid Available	Deadline (fall starts)	Awarded to Full-Time	Awarded to Part-Time
Gift Aid	April 15	Yes	Yes
Federal College Work-Study	April 15	Yes	Yes
Federal Perkins Loans		No	No
Federal Stafford Loans	Rolling	Yes	Yes
School-Based Loans		No	No
Outside and Private Loans	Rolling	Yes	Yes
Graduate Assistantships	May 2	Yes	Yes

SALISBURY STATE UNIVERSITY
The Franklin P. Perdue School of Business

Holloway Hall
1101 Camden Avenue
Salisbury, Maryland 21801
Telephone: 410-543-6317

Total Enrollment (1993-94)	Full-Time	Part-Time
	115	25

Cost of Attendance (1993-94)		
Academic Year		
Standard Course Load per Semester/Term		
(credit hours/units)	9	3-6
Semesters/Terms per Academic Year	2	2
Tuition and Fees		
Resident	$114/cr.	$114/cr.
Nonresident	$127/cr.	$127/cr.
Living Expenses		
Summer Term		
(R = Required, O = Optional, N = None)	O	O
Standard Course Load	6	3
Tuition and Fees		
Resident	$114/cr.	$114/cr.
Nonresident	$127/cr.	$127/cr.

Financial Aid Available	Deadline (fall starts)	Awarded to Full-Time	Part-Time
Gift Aid	July 1	Yes	Yes
Federal College Work-Study	NA		
Federal Perkins Loans	NA		
Federal Stafford Loans	July 1	Yes	Yes
School-Based Loans	NA		
Outside and Private Loans	NA		
Graduate Assistantships	July 1	Yes	

Percentage of Students Receiving Aid	Full-Time	Part-Time
All students	5%	5%
Minority students	1%	1%
Women students	1%	1%
International students		

SAM HOUSTON STATE UNIVERSITY
College of Business

P.O Box 2056
Huntsville, Texas 77341
Telephone: 409-294-1246

Total Enrollment (1993-94)	Full-Time	Part-Time
	40	75

Cost of Attendance (1993-94)		
Academic Year		
Standard Course Load per Semester/Term		
(credit hours/units)	9	< 9
Semesters/Terms per Academic Year	3	
Tuition and Fees		
Resident	$ 4,725	
Nonresident	$ 6,999	
Living Expenses	$12,000	
Summer Term		
(R = Required, O = Optional, N = None)	O	O
Standard Course Load		
Tuition and Fees		
Resident	$ 1,500	
Nonresident	$ 2,500	

Financial Aid Available	Deadline (fall starts)	Awarded to Full-Time	Part-Time
Gift Aid		No	No
Federal College Work-Study		No	No
Federal Perkins Loans		No	No
Federal Stafford Loans		No	No
School-Based Loans		No	No
Outside and Private Loans		No	No
Graduate Assistantships	March	Yes	Yes

Percentage of Students Receiving Aid	Full-Time	Part-Time
All students	15%	15%
Minority students	15%	15%
Women students	15%	15%
International students	3%	3%

SAN FRANCISCO STATE UNIVERSITY

1600 Holloway Avenue
San Francisco, California 94132
Telephone: 415-338-1935

Total Enrollment (1993-94)	Full-Time	Part-Time
	400	500

Cost of Attendance (1993-94)		
Academic Year		
Standard Course Load per Semester/Term		
(credit hours/units)	12-15	3-6
Semesters/Terms per Academic Year	2	2
Tuition and Fees		
Resident	$ 1,792	$ 1,186
Nonresident	$ 1,792	$ 1,186
Living Expenses	$13,000	$13,000
Summer Term		
(R = Required, O = Optional, N = None)	O	O
Standard Course Load	3-6	3-6
Tuition and Fees		
Resident	$130/unit	$130/unit
Nonresident	$130/unit	$130/unit

Financial Aid Available	Deadline (fall starts)	Awarded to Full-Time	Part-Time
Gift Aid	May 1	Yes	Yes
Federal College Work-Study	May 1	Yes	Yes
Federal Perkins Loans	May 1	Yes	Yes
Federal Stafford Loans	May 1	Yes	Yes
School-Based Loans	NA	No	No
Outside and Private Loans	May 1	Yes	Yes
Graduate Assistantships	Beginning of semester	Yes	Yes

SANTA CLARA UNIVERSITY
Leavey School of Business

500 El Camino Real
Santa Clara, California 95050-9980
Telephone: 408-554-4500

Total Enrollment (1993-94)	Full-Time	Part-Time
	143	911

Cost of Attendance (1993-94)		
Academic Year		
Standard Course Load per Semester/Term		
(credit hours/units)	9	6
Semesters/Terms per Academic Year	3	3
Tuition and Fees	$9,099	$6,066
Living Expenses	$8,370	$5,580
Summer Term		
(R = Required, O = Optional, N = None)	O	O
Standard Course Load	9	6
Tuition and Fees	$9,099	$6,066
Resident		
Nonresident		

Financial Aid Available	Deadline (fall starts)	Awarded to Full-Time	Part-Time
Gift Aid	February 1	Yes	Yes
Federal College Work-Study	February 1	Yes	Yes
Federal Perkins Loans	February 1	Yes	No
Federal Stafford Loans	February 1	Yes	Yes
School-Based Loans	NA	No	No
Outside and Private Loans	February 1	Yes	Yes
Graduate Assistantships	July 1	Yes	Yes

SEATTLE UNIVERSITY
Albers School of Business and Economics

Broadway and Madison
Seattle, Washington 98122-4460
Telephone: 206-296-5700

Total Enrollment (1993-94)	Full-Time	Part-Time
	37	103

Cost of Attendance (1993-94)		
Academic Year		
Standard Course Load per Semester/Term		
(credit hours/units)	12	6
Semesters/Terms per Academic Year	4	4
Tuition and Fees	$16,800	$8,400
Living Expenses		
Summer Term		
(R = Required, O = Optional, N = None)	O	O
Standard Course Load	6	3
Tuition and Fees	$ 2,100	$1,050

Financial Aid Available	Deadline (fall starts)	Awarded to Full-Time	Part-Time
Gift Aid—Albers School	November 8 and May 1		
—Financial Aid	November 1 and May 1	Yes	Yes
Federal College Work-Study	February 15	Yes	Yes
Federal Perkins Loans	February 15	Yes	Yes
Federal Stafford Loans	None	Yes	Yes
School-Based Loans	None	No	No
Outside and Private Loans	None	Yes	Yes
Graduate Assistantships	None	Yes	Yes

SETON HALL UNIVERSITY
W. Paul Stillman School of Business

400 South Orange Avenue
South Orange, New Jersey 07079
Telephone: 201-761-9222

Total Enrollment (1993-94)	Full-Time	Part-Time
	97	842

Cost of Attendance (1993-94)		
Academic Year		
Standard Course Load per Semester/Term		
(credit hours/units)	12	6
Semesters/Terms per Academic Year	2	2
Tuition and Fees	$10,055	$ 5,090
Living Expenses	$10,746	$10,746
Summer Term		
(R = Required, O = Optional, N = None)		
Standard Course Load	6	3
Tuition and Fees	$ 2,505	$ 1,275
Resident		
Nonresident		

Financial Aid Available	Deadline (fall starts)	Awarded to Full-Time	Part-Time
Gift Aid	NA	No	No
Federal College Work-Study	NA	No	No
Federal Perkins Loans	NA	No	No
Federal Stafford Loans	April 1	Yes	No
School-Based Loans	NA	No	No
Outside and Private Loans	NA	No	No
Graduate Assistantships	April 1	Yes	No

SHENANDOAH UNIVERSITY
Byrd School of Business

1460 University Drive
Winchester, Virginia 22601
Telephone: 703-665-4572

Total Enrollment (1993-94)	Full-Time	Part-Time
	20	109

Cost of Attendance (1993-94)		
Academic Year		
Standard Course Load per Semester/Term		
(credit hours/units)	9 hrs.	6 hrs.
Semesters/Terms per Academic Year	3	3
Tuition and Fees	$6,300	$4,200
Living Expenses	$4,200	$4,200
Summer Term		
(R = Required, O = Optional, N = None)	R	R
Standard Course Load	9 hrs.	6 hrs.
Tuition and Fees	$3,150	$2,100

Financial Aid Available	Deadline (fall starts)	Awarded to Full-Time	Part-Time
Gift Aid	February 1	Yes	No
Federal College Work-Study	NA	No	No
Federal Perkins Loans	NA	No	No
Federal Stafford Loans	None	Yes	Yes
School-Based Loans	NA	No	No
Outside and Private Loans	NA	No	No
Graduate Assistantships	February 1	Yes	No

Percentage of Students Receiving Aid	Full-Time	Part-Time
All students	6%	1%
Minority students	0%	0%
Women students	2%	1%
International students	0%	0%

SIMMONS COLLEGE
Graduate School of Management

409 Commonwealth Avenue
Boston, Massachusetts 02215
Telephone: 617-521-3840

Total Enrollment (1993-94)	1-year	2-year	3-year
	34	230 (combined)	

Cost of Attendance (1993-94)			
Academic Year			
Standard Course Load per Semester/Term			
(credit hours/units)	15	8	5
Semesters/Terms per Academic Year	3	3	3
Tuition and Fees	$24,030	$12,816	$ 8,010
Living Expenses	$ 9,000-	$ 9,000-	$ 9,000-
	$20,000	$20,000	$20,000
Summer Term			
(R = Required, O = Optional, N = None)	Included as third semester		
Standard Course Load			
Tuition and Fees			
Resident			
Nonresident			

Financial Aid Available	Deadline (fall starts)	Awarded to Full-Time	Part-Time
Gift Aid	March 1	Yes	Yes
Federal College Work-Study	March 1	Yes	No
Federal Perkins Loans	March 1	Yes	No
Federal Stafford Loans	March 1	Yes	Yes
School-Based Loans	March 1	Yes	No
Outside and Private Loans	March 1	Yes	Yes
Graduate Assistantships	March 1	Yes	Yes

Percentage of Students Receiving Aid	Full-Time	Part-Time
All students	85%	21%
Minority students	100%	32%
Women students	100%	100%
International students	12%	38%

SOUTHEASTERN LOUISIANA UNIVERSITY
College of Business

SLU 735
Hammond, Louisiana 70402
Telephone: 504-549-2146

Total Enrollment (1993-94)	Full-Time	Part-Time
	69	67

Cost of Attendance (1993-94)		
Academic Year		
Standard Course Load per Semester/Term		
(credit hours/units)	9	6
Semesters/Terms per Academic Year	3	3
Tuition and Fees		
Resident	$1,900	$1,055
Nonresident	$3,844	$2,027
Living Expenses	$2,460	$2,460
Summer Term		
(R = Required, O = Optional, N = None)	O	O
Standard Course Load	6	3
Tuition and Fees		
Resident	$ 527	$ 267
Nonresident	$1,013	$ 267

Financial Aid Available	Deadline (fall starts)	Awarded to Full-Time	Awarded to Part-Time
Gift Aid	Early spring	Yes	Yes
Federal College Work-Study	Before registration	Yes	Yes
Federal Perkins Loans	NA	No	No
Federal Stafford Loans	Before registration	Yes	Yes
School-Based Loans	Before registration	Yes	No
Outside and Private Loans	NA	Yes	Yes
Graduate Assistantships	Early spring	Yes	No

SOUTHERN COLLEGE OF TECHNOLOGY
School of Management

1100 South Marietta Parkway
Marietta, Georgia 30060
Telephone: 404-528-7440

Total Enrollment (1993-94)	Full-Time	Part-Time
	38	84

Cost of Attendance (1993-94)		
Academic Year		
Standard Course Load per Semester/Term		
(credit hours/units)	10	5
Semesters/Terms per Academic Year	3	3
Tuition and Fees		
Resident	$1,422	$ 578
Nonresident	$3,732	$1,733
Living Expenses	$6,500	$6,500
Summer Term		
(R = Required, O = Optional, N = None)	O	O
Standard Course Load	10	5
Tuition and Fees		
Resident	$ 474	$ 193
Nonresident	$1,244	$ 578

Financial Aid Available	Deadline (fall starts)	Awarded to Full-Time	Awarded to Part-Time
Gift Aid	March 15	Yes	No
Federal College Work-Study	March 15	Yes	Yes
Federal Perkins Loans	March 15	Yes	Yes
Federal Stafford Loans	March 15	Yes	Yes
School-Based Loans		No	No
Outside and Private Loans	March 15	Yes	Yes
Graduate Assistantships	March 15	Yes	No

Percentage of Students Receiving Aid	Full-Time	Part-Time
All students	35%	35%
Minority students	35%	35%
Women students	35%	35%
International students	20%	

SOUTHERN ILLINOIS UNIVERSITY AT CARBONDALE
College of Business and Administration

Rehn Hall 133
Carbondale, Illinois 62901-4620
Telephone: 618-343-3030

Total Enrollment (1993-94)	Full-Time	Part-Time
	127	7

Cost of Attendance (1993-94)

Academic Year		
Standard Course Load per Semester/Term		
(credit hours/units)	12	
Semesters/Terms per Academic Year	3	
Tuition and Fees		
Resident	$1,299	$ 743/sem.
Nonresident	$3,099	$1,643/sem.
Living Expenses	$6,225	
Summer Term		
(R = Required, O = Optional, N = None)	O	
Standard Course Load	6	
Tuition and Fees		
Resident	$ 743	
Nonresident	$1,643	

Financial Aid Available

	Deadline (fall starts)	Awarded to Full-Time	Part-Time
Gift Aid	November 15	Yes	No
Federal College Work-Study	Rolling	Yes	
Federal Perkins Loans	Rolling	Yes	
Federal Stafford Loans	Rolling	Yes	
School-Based Loans	Rolling	Yes	
Outside and Private Loans	Rolling		
Graduate Assistantships	March 15	Yes	

Percentage of Students Receiving Aid	Full-Time	Part-Time
All students	75%	
Minority students		
Women students		
International students		

SOUTHERN ILLINOIS UNIVERSITY AT EDWARDSVILLE
School of Business

Box 1051
Edwardsville, Illinois 62026-1051
Telephone: 618-692-3840

Total Enrollment (1993-94)	Full-Time	Part-Time
	150	469

Cost of Attendance (1993-94)

Academic Year		
Standard Course Load per Semester/Term		
(credit hours/units)	9	8
Semesters/Terms per Academic Year	3	3
Tuition and Fees		
Resident	$ 834	$ 77/hour
Nonresident	$2,200	$230/hour
Living Expenses	$4,000	$4,000
Summer Term		
(R = Required, O = Optional, N = None)	O	O
Standard Course Load	9	8 or less
Tuition and Fees		
Resident	$ 834	$ 77/hour
Nonresident	$2,200	$230/hour

Financial Aid Available

	Deadline (fall starts)	Awarded to Full-Time	Part-Time
Gift Aid	April 1	Yes	Yes
Federal College Work-Study	April 1	Yes	Yes
Federal Perkins Loans	April 1	Yes	Yes
Federal Stafford Loans	April 1	Yes	Yes
School-Based Loans	April 1	Yes	Yes
Outside and Private Loans	April 1	Yes	Yes
Graduate Assistantships	April 1	Yes	Yes

Percentage of Students Receiving Aid	Full-Time	Part-Time
All students	60%	60%
Minority students		
Women students		
International students		

SOUTHERN METHODIST UNIVERSITY
Edwin L. Cox School of Business

282 Crow Building
Dallas, Texas 75275-0333
Telephone: 214-768-2630

Total Enrollment (1993-94)	Full-Time	Part-Time
	220	376

Cost of Attendance (1993-94)		
Academic Year		
Standard Course Load per Semester/Term		
(credit hours/units)	15	6
Semesters/Terms per Academic Year	2	3
Tuition and Fees	$17,012	$10,440
Living Expenses	$ 9,550	$ 600
Summer Term		
(R = Required, O = Optional, N = None)	O	R
Standard Course Load	Varies	6 hrs.
Tuition and Fees	$567/cr.	$ 3,480

Financial Aid Available	Deadline (fall starts)	Awarded to Full-Time	Part-Time
Gift Aid	Rolling	Yes	No
Federal College Work-Study	May 1	Yes	No
Federal Perkins Loans	NA	No	No
Federal Stafford Loans	May 1	Yes	Yes
School-Based Loans	NA	No	No
Outside and Private Loans	May 1	Yes	Yes
Graduate Assistantships	Rolling	Yes	No

Percentage of Students Receiving Aid	Full-Time	Part-Time
All students	60%	43%
Minority students		
Women students		
International students		

SOUTHERN OREGON STATE COLLEGE

1250 Siskiyou Boulevard
Ashland, Oregon 97520
Telephone: 503-552-6724

Total Enrollment (1993-94)	Full-Time	Part-Time
	20	18

Cost of Attendance (1993-94)		
Academic Year		
Standard Course Load per Semester/Term		
(credit hours/units)	12-15	6
Semesters/Terms per Academic Year	3	3
Tuition and Fees		
Resident	$1,302	$808
Nonresident	$2,093	$808
Living Expenses	$4,950	NA
Summer Term		
(R = Required, O = Optional, N = None)	O	O
Standard Course Load	12	6
Tuition and Fees	$1,256-$1,544	$649

Financial Aid Available	Deadline (fall starts)	Awarded to Full-Time	Part-Time
Gift Aid	March 1	Yes	No
Federal College Work-Study	March 1	Yes	Yes
Federal Perkins Loans	March 1	Yes	Yes
Federal Stafford Loans	Open	Yes	Yes
School-Based Loans	Open	Yes	No
Outside and Private Loans	Open	Yes	Yes
Graduate Assistantships	May 1	Yes	No

Percentage of Students Receiving Aid	Full-Time	Part-Time
All students	60%	15%
Minority students		
Women students		
International students		

SOUTHWEST TEXAS STATE UNIVERSITY
Graduate School of Business

105 Derrick Hall
San Marcos, Texas 78666
Telephone: 512-245-3591

Total Enrollment (1993-94)	Full-Time	Part-Time
	60	240

Cost of Attendance (1993-94)		
Academic Year		
Standard Course Load per Semester/Term		
(credit hours/units)	12	6
Semesters/Terms per Academic Year	3	3
Tuition and Fees		
Resident	$ 689	$ 403
Nonresident	$2,321	$1,219
Living Expenses	$3,000	$3,000
Summer Term		
(R = Required, O = Optional, N = None)	O	O
Standard Course Load	12	6
Tuition and Fees		
Resident	$ 689	$ 403
Nonresident	$2,321	$1,219

Financial Aid Available	Deadline (fall starts)	Awarded to Full-Time	Awarded to Part-Time
Gift Aid	April 1	Yes	Yes
Federal College Work-Study	April 1	Yes	Yes
Federal Perkins Loans	April 1	Yes	Yes
Federal Stafford Loans	April 1	Yes	Yes
School-Based Loans	NA		
Outside and Private Loans	NA		
Graduate Assistantships	NA		

Percentage of Students Receiving Aid	Full-Time	Part-Time
All students	35%	35%
Minority students	50%	50%
Women students	NA	NA
International students	15%	15%

STANFORD UNIVERSITY
Graduate School of Business

350 Memorial Way
Stanford, California 94305-5015
Telephone: 415-723-3282

Total Enrollment (1993-94)	Full-Time
	712

Cost of Attendance (1993-94)	
Academic Year	
Standard Course Load per Semester/Term	
(credit hours/units)	16
Semesters/Terms per Academic Year	3
Tuition and Fees	$20,196
Living Expenses	$12,728 (off campus)
Summer Term	
(R = Required, O = Optional, N = None)	N
Standard Course Load	
Tuition and Fees	
Resident	
Nonresident	

Financial Aid Available	Deadline (fall starts)	Awarded to Full-Time
Gift Aid	3 weeks after admission	Yes
Federal College Work-Study	NA	No
Federal Perkins Loans	3 weeks after admission	Yes
Federal Stafford Loans	None	Yes
School-Based Loans	None	Yes
Outside and Private Loans	None	Yes
Graduate Assistantships	NA	No

Percentage of Students Receiving Aid	Full-Time
All students	68%
Minority students	95%
Women students	67%
International students	35%

STATE UNIVERSITY OF NEW YORK AT BINGHAMTON
School of Management

Binghamton University
Binghamton, New York 13902-6000
Telephone: 607-777-2314

Total Enrollment (1993-94)	Full-Time	Part-Time
	132	89

Cost of Attendance (1993-94)		
Academic Year		
Standard Course Load per Semester/Term		
(credit hours/units)	16	8
Semesters/Terms per Academic Year	2	2
Tuition and Fees		
Resident	$4,224	$2,748
Nonresident	$7,540	$4,988
Living Expenses	$9,800	
Summer Term		
(R = Required, O = Optional, N = None)	O	O
Standard Course Load	8	4
Tuition and Fees		
Resident	$1,374	$ 672
Nonresident	$2,494	$1,232

Financial Aid Available	Deadline (fall starts)	Awarded to Full-Time	Awarded to Part-Time
Gift Aid	April 15	Yes	No
Federal College Work-Study	April 15	Yes	No
Federal Perkins Loans	April 15	No	No
Federal Stafford Loans	April 15	Yes	Yes
School-Based Loans	April 15		
Outside and Private Loans	April 15	No	No
Graduate Assistantships	April 15	Yes	No

STATE UNIVERSITY OF NEW YORK AT OSWEGO
School of Business

1 Swetman Hall
Oswego, New York 13126
Telephone: 315-341-2272

Total Enrollment (1993-94)	Full-Time	Part-Time
	25	120

Cost of Attendance (1993-94)		
Academic Year		
Standard Course Load per Semester/Term		
(credit hours/units)	12-15	3-11
Semesters/Terms per Academic Year	2	2
Tuition and Fees		
Resident	$4,025	$173/cr.
Nonresident	$7,341	$308/cr.
Living Expenses	$6,455	$6,455
Summer Term		
(R = Required, O = Optional, N = None)	O	O
Standard Course Load	12	3-11
Tuition and Fees		
Resident	$2,012	$173/cr.
Nonresident	$3,670	$308/cr.

Financial Aid Available	Deadline (fall starts)	Awarded to Full-Time	Awarded to Part-Time
Gift Aid	January 31	Yes	
Federal College Work-Study	April 1	Yes	Yes
Federal Perkins Loans	April 1	Yes	Yes
Federal Stafford Loans	April 1		
School-Based Loans	NA		
Outside and Private Loans	NA		
Graduate Assistantships	April 1	Yes	

STEPHEN F. AUSTIN STATE UNIVERSITY

P.O. Box 13004 - SFA Station
Nacogdoches, Texas 75962
Telephone: 409-568-3101

Total Enrollment (1993-94)	Full-Time	Part-Time

Cost of Attendance (1993-94)		
Academic Year		
Standard Course Load per Semester/Term		
(credit hours/units)	9	6
Semesters/Terms per Academic Year	4	4
Tuition and Fees		
Resident	$ 464	$ 311
Nonresident	$1,688	$1,127
Living Expenses	$6,000	$5,400
Summer Term		
(R = Required, O = Optional, N = None)	O	O
Standard Course Load	6	3-6
Tuition and Fees		
Resident	$308.50	$ 77.50-$308.50
Nonresident	$1,124	$ 563-$ 1,124

Financial Aid Available	Deadline (fall starts)	Awarded to Full-Time	Part-Time
Gift Aid	August 1	Yes	
Federal College Work-Study	September 15	Yes	
Federal Perkins Loans	August 1	Yes	
Federal Stafford Loans			
School-Based Loans	September 1	Yes	
Outside and Private Loans		Yes	Yes
Graduate Assistantships	September 1	Yes	

STETSON UNIVERSITY
School of Business

Graduate Programs Office
DeLand, Florida 32720
Telephone: 904-822-7410

Total Enrollment (1993-94)	Full-Time	Part-Time
	20	50

Cost of Attendance (1993-94)		
Academic Year		
Standard Course Load per Semester/Term		
(credit hours/units)	12-15	3-6
Semesters/Terms per Academic Year	3	3
Tuition and Fees	$255/cr.	$255/cr.
Living Expenses	$9,800	
Summer Term		
(R = Required, O = Optional, N = None)	O	O
Standard Course Load	6	2-3
Tuition and Fees	$255/cr.	$255/cr.

Financial Aid Available	Deadline (fall starts)	Awarded to Full-Time	Part-Time
Gift Aid	60 days prior to enrollment	No	No
Federal College Work-Study	60 days prior to enrollment	No	No
Federal Perkins Loans	none	Yes	Yes
Federal Stafford Loans	none	Yes	Yes
School-Based Loans	none	No	No
Outside and Private Loans	none	Yes	Yes
Graduate Assistantships	none	Yes	Yes

Percentage of Students Receiving Aid	Full-Time	Part-Time
All students	25%	75%
Minority students	2%	2%
Women students	50%	50%
International students	10%	10%

SUFFOLK UNIVERSITY
School of Management

8 Ashburton Place
Boston, Massachusetts 02108
Telephone: 617-573-8302

Total Enrollment (1993-94)	Full-Time	Part-Time
	120	838

Cost of Attendance (1993-94)

	Full-Time	Part-Time
Academic Year		
Standard Course Load per Semester/Term		
(credit hours/units)	4-5 courses	1-3 courses
Semesters/Terms per Academic Year	2	2
Tuition and Fees	$13,500	$1,350/course
Living Expenses	$23,100	
Summer Term		
(R = Required, O = Optional, N = None)	O	O
Standard Course Load	2 courses	1 course
Tuition and Fees	$13,500	$1,350/course

Financial Aid Available

	Deadline (fall starts)	Awarded to Full-Time	Part-Time
Gift Aid	April 1	Yes	Yes
Federal College Work-Study	April 1	Yes	Yes
Federal Perkins Loans	April 1	Yes	Yes
Federal Stafford Loans	April 1	Yes	Yes
School-Based Loans	April 1	Yes	Yes
Outside and Private Loans	April 1	Yes	Yes
Graduate Assistantships	April 1	Yes	Yes

Percentage of Students Receiving Aid	Full-Time	Part-Time
All students	8%	17%
Minority students	25%	19%
Women students	17%	17%
International students	18%	10%

SYRACUSE UNIVERSITY
School of Management

Suite 222 CHM
Syracuse, New York 13244
Telephone: 315-443-9214

Total Enrollment (1993-94)	Full-Time	Part-Time
	235	490

Cost of Attendance (1993-94)

	Full-Time	Part-Time
Academic Year		
Standard Course Load per Semester/Term		
(credit hours/units)	15	6
Semesters/Terms per Academic Year	2	2
Tuition and Fees	$12,960	$2,592
Living Expenses		
Summer Term		
(R = Required, O = Optional, N = None)	O	O
Standard Course Load	6	6
Tuition and Fees	$ 2,592	$2,592

Financial Aid Available

	Deadline (fall starts)	Awarded to Full-Time	Part-Time
Gift Aid—Fellowship	January 10	Yes	No
—Scholarship	March 1		
Federal College Work-Study	April 20	Yes	No
Federal Perkins Loans	April 20	Yes	No
Federal Stafford Loans	April 20	Yes	No
School-Based Loans			
Outside and Private Loans			
Graduate Assistantships	March 1	Yes	No

Percentage of Students Receiving Aid	Full-Time
All students	90%
Minority students	95%
Women students	90%
International students	10%

TEMPLE UNIVERSITY

Speakman Hall
Philadelphia, Pennsylvania 19122
Telephone: 215-204-7678

Total Enrollment (1993-94)	Full-Time	Part-Time
	275	836

Cost of Attendance (1993-94)		
Academic Year		
Standard Course Load per Semester/Term		
(credit hours/units)	≤ 9	1-8
Semesters/Terms per Academic Year	2	2
Tuition and Fees		
Resident	$247/cr.	$247/cr.
Nonresident	$333/cr.	$333/cr.
Living Expenses	$9,040	
Summer Term		
(R = Required, O = Optional, N = None)		O - 2 summer sessions
Standard Course Load		2-course max./term
Tuition and Fees		
Resident	$247/cr.	$247/cr.
Nonresident	$333/cr.	$333/cr.

Financial Aid Available	Deadline (fall starts)	Awarded to Full-Time	Awarded to Part-Time
Gift Aid	NA	No	No
Federal College Work-Study	May 1	Yes	Yes
Federal Perkins Loans	May 1	Yes	Yes
Federal Stafford Loans	May 1	Yes	Yes
School-Based Loans	NA	No	No
Outside and Private Loans	NA	No	No
Graduate Assistantships	March 15	Yes	No

TENNESSEE STATE UNIVERSITY

330 10th Avenue North
Nashville, Tennessee 37203
Telephone: 615-251-1505

Total Enrollment (1993-94)	Full-Time	Part-Time
	15	85

Cost of Attendance (1993-94)		
Academic Year		
Standard Course Load per Semester/Term		
(credit hours/units)	12	6
Semesters/Terms per Academic Year	2	2
Tuition and Fees		
Resident	$1,098	$ 637
Nonresident	$2,989	$1,627
Living Expenses	$3,400	
Summer Term		
(R = Required, O = Optional, N = None)	O	O
Standard Course Load	6	3
Tuition and Fees		
Resident	$ 637	$ 319
Nonresident	$1,627	$ 814

Financial Aid Available	Deadline (fall starts)	Awarded to Full-Time	Awarded to Part-Time
Gift Aid		No	No
Federal College Work-Study		No	No
Federal Perkins Loans		No	No
Federal Stafford Loans		No	No
School-Based Loans		No	No
Outside and Private Loans		No	No
Graduate Assistantships	None	Yes	No

Percentage of Students Receiving Aid	Full-Time	Part-Time
All students	50%	0%
Minority students		
Women students		
International students		

TENNESSEE TECHNOLOGICAL UNIVERSITY
College of Business Administration, Division of MBA Studies

Box 5023
Cookeville, Tennessee 38505
Telephone: 615-372-3600

Total Enrollment (1993-94)	Full-Time	Part-Time
	77	49

Cost of Attendance (1993-94)		
Academic Year		
Standard Course Load per Semester/Term		
(credit hours/units)	10	6
Semesters/Terms per Academic Year	2	2
Tuition and Fees		
Resident	$2,200	$1,320
Nonresident	$5,982	$3,300
Living Expenses	$4,380	$4,780
Summer Term		
(R = Required, O = Optional, N = None)	O	O
Standard Course Load	6	3
Tuition and Fees		
Resident	$ 660	$ 330
Nonresident	$1,650	$ 825

Financial Aid Available	Deadline (fall starts)	Awarded to Full-Time	Part-Time
Gift Aid	March 15	Yes	No
Federal College Work-Study	NA	No	No
Federal Perkins Loans	NA	No	No
Federal Stafford Loans	April 15	Yes	No
School-Based Loans	October 1	Yes	No
Outside and Private Loans	NA	No	No
Graduate Assistantships	March 15	Yes	No

Percentage of Students Receiving Aid	Full-Time	Part-Time
All students	45%	0%
Minority students	100%	0%
Women students	23%	0%
International students	38%	0%

TEXAS A&M UNIVERSITY
College of Business Administration

Graduate School of Business
331 Blocker Building
College Station, Texas 77843-4117
Telephone: 409-845-4714

Total Enrollment (1993-94)	Full-Time
	505

Cost of Attendance (1993-94)	
Academic Year	
Standard Course Load per Semester/Term	
(credit hours/units)	13
Semesters/Terms per Academic Year	2
Tuition and Fees	
Resident	$1,800
Nonresident	$5,600
Living Expenses	$5,100
Summer Term	
(R = Required, O = Optional, N = None)	O
Standard Course Load	3
Tuition and Fees	
Resident	$ 180
Nonresident	$ 600

Financial Aid Available	Deadline (fall starts)	Awarded to Full-Time
Gift Aid	February 1	Yes
Federal College Work-Study	April 15	Yes
Federal Perkins Loans	April 15	Yes
Federal Stafford Loans	April 15	Yes
School-Based Loans	April 15	Yes
Outside and Private Loans	NA	
Graduate Assistantships	February 1	Yes

TEXAS A&M UNIVERSITY - CORPUS CHRISTI
College of Business Administration

6300 Ocean Drive
Corpus Christi, Texas 78412
Telephone: 512-994-2653

Total Enrollment (1993-94)	Full-Time	Part-Time
	49	196

Cost of Attendance (1993-94)		
Academic Year		
Standard Course Load per Semester/Term		
(credit hours/units)	9	6
Semesters/Terms per Academic Year	2	2
Tuition and Fees		
Resident	$ 446	$ 299
Nonresident	$1,670	$1,115
Living Expenses	$7,568	$7,568
Summer Term		
(R = Required, O = Optional, N = None)	O	O
Standard Course Load	6	3
Tuition and Fees		
Resident	$ 297	$ 150
Nonresident	$1,113	$ 558

Financial Aid Available	Deadline (fall starts)	Awarded to Full-Time	Part-Time
Gift Aid	March 15	Yes	Yes
Federal College Work-Study	March 15	Yes	Yes
Federal Perkins Loans	March 15	Yes	Yes
Federal Stafford Loans	March 15	Yes	Yes
School-Based Loans	September 15	Yes	Yes
Outside and Private Loans	NA		
Graduate Assistantships	August 1	Yes	No

Percentage of Students Receiving Aid	Full-Time	Part-Time
All students	37%	12%
Minority students	43%	10%
Women students	35%	10%
International students		

TEXAS CHRISTIAN UNIVERSITY
M.J. Neeley School of Business

P.O. Box 32868
Fort Worth, Texas 76129
Telephone: 817-921-7531

Total Enrollment (1993-94)	Full-Time	Part-Time
	141	98

Cost of Attendance (1993-94)		
Academic Year		
Standard Course Load per Semester/Term		
(credit hours/units)	12	6
Semesters/Terms per Academic Year	2	2
Tuition and Fees	$7,500	$3,500
Living Expenses	$4,500	$4,500
Summer Term		
(R = Required, O = Optional, N = None)	N	R
Standard Course Load		3-6
Tuition and Fees		$819-$1,638

Financial Aid Available	Deadline (fall starts)	Awarded to Full-Time	Part-Time
Gift Aid	May 1	Yes	No
Federal College Work-Study	May 1	Yes	Yes
Federal Perkins Loans	May 1	Yes	Yes
Federal Stafford Loans	May 1	Yes	Yes
School-Based Loans	Open	Yes	Yes
Outside and Private Loans	Open	Yes	Yes
Graduate Assistantships	April 30	Yes	No

Percentage of Students Receiving Aid	Full-Time	Part-Time
All students	58%	19%
Minority students	50%	17%
Women students	57%	33%
International students	29%	NA

TEXAS SOUTHERN UNIVERSITY
Graduate Programs in Business

3100 Cleburne Avenue
Houston, Texas 77004
Telephone: 713-527-7734

Total Enrollment (1993-94)	Full-Time	Part-Time
	52	68

Cost of Attendance (1993-94)		
Academic Year		
Standard Course Load per Semester/Term		
(credit hours/units)	12	6
Semesters/Terms per Academic Year	2	2
Tuition and Fees		
Resident	$1,274	$ 689
Nonresident	$4,442	$2,273
Living Expenses	$8,400	$8,400
Summer Term		
(R = Required, O = Optional, N = None)	O	O
Standard Course Load	6	3
Tuition and Fees		
Resident	$ 303	$151
Nonresident	$1,107	$553

Financial Aid Available	Deadline (fall starts)	Awarded to	
		Full-Time	Part-Time
Gift Aid	After enrollment	Yes	Yes
Federal College Work-Study	After enrollment	Yes	No
Federal Perkins Loans	None	Yes	
Federal Stafford Loans	None	Yes	Yes
School-Based Loans	Varies	Yes	Yes
Outside and Private Loans			
Graduate Assistantships	After enrollment	Yes	

Percentage of Students Receiving Aid	Full-Time
All students	5%
Minority students	5%
Women students	5%
International students	2%

TEXAS TECH UNIVERSITY
College of Business Administration

P.O. Box 42101
Lubbock, Texas 79409-2101
Telephone: 806-742-3184

Total Enrollment (1993-94)	Full-Time	Part-Time
382 combined (full- and part-time)		

Cost of Attendance (1993-94)		
Academic Year		
Standard Course Load per Semester/Term		
(credit hours/units)	12	6
Semesters/Terms per Academic Year	3	3
Tuition and Fees		
Resident	$1,700	$1,000
Nonresident	$6,000	$3,000
Living Expenses	$8,380	$8,000
Summer Term		
(R = Required, O = Optional, N = None)	O	O
Standard Course Load	6	3
Tuition and Fees		
Resident	$1,700	$1,000
Nonresident	$6,000	$3,000

Financial Aid Available	Deadline (fall starts)	Awarded to	
		Full-Time	Part-Time
Gift Aid	August 1	Yes	Yes
Federal College Work-Study	August 1	Yes	No
Federal Perkins Loans	August 1	Yes	No
Federal Stafford Loans	August 1	Yes	Yes
School-Based Loans	August 1	Yes	No
Outside and Private Loans	None	No	No
Graduate Assistantships	April 1	Yes	No

Percentage of Students Receiving Aid	Full-Time
All students	49%
Minority students	60%
Women students	56%
International students	55%

THOMAS COLLEGE
Graduate and Continuing Education

180 West River Road
Waterville, Maine 04901
Telephone: 207-877-0102

Total Enrollment (1993-94)	Part-Time
	160

Cost of Attendance (1993-94)	
Academic Year	
Standard Course Load per Semester/Term	
(credit hours/units)	1-3
Semesters/Terms per Academic Year	3
Tuition and Fees	$410/course
Living Expenses	NA
Summer Term	
(R = Required, O = Optional, N = None)	N
Standard Course Load	
Tuition and Fees	
Resident	
Nonresident	

Financial Aid Available	Deadline (fall starts)	Awarded to Full-Time	Part-Time
Gift Aid		No	No
Federal College Work-Study		No	No
Federal Perkins Loans		No	No
Federal Stafford Loans	Rolling	Yes	No
School-Based Loans		No	No
Outside and Private Loans	Rolling	Yes	No
Graduate Assistantships		No	No

Percentage of Students Receiving Aid	Part-Time
All students	1%
Minority sudents	
Women students	
International students	

TIFFIN UNIVERSITY

Office of Graduate Studies
155 Miami Street
Tiffin, Ohio 44883
Telephone: 800-968-6446

Total Enrollment (1993-94)	Full-Time	Part-Time
	35	45

Cost of Attendance (1993-94)		
Academic Year		
Standard Course Load per Semester/Term		
(credit hours/units)	6	3
Semesters/Terms per Academic Year	3	3
Tuition and Fees	$6,000	$3,000
Living Expenses	$9,850	$7,650
Summer Term		
(R = Required, O = Optional, N = None)	R	R
Standard Course Load	6	3
Tuition and Fees	$1,000	$1,000

Financial Aid Available	Deadline (fall starts)	Awarded to Full-Time	Part-Time
Gift Aid	NA	No	No
Federal College Work-Study	NA	No	No
Federal Perkins Loans	None	Yes	Yes
Federal Stafford Loans	None	Yes	Yes
School-Based Loans	NA	No	No
Outside and Private Loans			
Graduate Assistantships	NA	No	No

TROY STATE UNIVERSITY
Sorrell College of Business

Bibb Graves Room 149
Troy, Alabama 36082
Telephone: 205-670-3509

Total Enrollment (1993-94)	Full-Time	Part-Time
	29	4

Cost of Attendance (1993-94)		
Academic Year		
Standard Course Load per Semester/Term		
(credit hours/units)	10	5
Semesters/Terms per Academic Year	3	3
Tuition and Fees		
Resident	$1,913	$ 833
Nonresident	$3,199	$1,384
Living Expenses	$3,993	$3,893
Summer Term		
(R = Required, O = Optional, N = None)	O	O
Standard Course Load	15	5
Tuition and Fees		
Resident	$ 813	$ 263
Nonresident	$1,339	$ 446

Financial Aid Available	Deadline (fall starts)	Awarded to Full-Time
Gift Aid		
Federal College Work-Study		
Federal Perkins Loans		
Federal Stafford Loans		
School-Based Loans		
Outside and Private Loans		
Graduate Assistantships	June 15	Yes

Percentage of Students Receiving Aid	Full-Time
All students	21%
Minority students	
Women students	6%
International students	3%

TULANE UNIVERSITY
A.B. Freeman School of Business

Office of Admissions
Goldring/Woldenberg Hall, Suite 400
New Orleans, Louisiana 70118
Telephone: 504-865-5410
　　　　　800-223-5402

Total Enrollment (1993-94)	Full-Time	Part-Time
	235	127

Cost of Attendance (1993-94)		
Academic Year		
Standard Course Load per Semester/Term		
(credit hours/units)	15	6
Semesters/Terms per Academic Year	2	3
Tuition and Fees	$18,760	$11,000
Living Expenses	$ 9,810	$ 9,810
Summer Term		
(R = Required, O = Optional, N = None)	O	O
Standard Course Load	3-6	3-6
Tuition and Fees (based on 6 hours)	$ 3,668	$ 3,668

Financial Aid Available	Deadline (fall starts)	Awarded to Full-Time	Part-Time
Gift Aid	April 1	Yes	No
Federal College Work-Study	April 15	Yes	No
Federal Perkins Loans	April 15	Yes	No
Federal Stafford Loans	April 15	Yes	Yes
School-Based Loans	NA	No	No
Outside and Private Loans	NA	No	No
Graduate Assistantships	NA	No	No

Percentage of Students Receiving Aid	Full-Time	Part-Time
All students	69%	12%
Minority students	95%	19%
Women sstudents	65%	18%
International students	58%	0%

UNION COLLEGE
Graduate Management Institute

Bailey Hall
Schenectady, New York 12308
Telephone: 518-388-6237

Total Enrollment (1993-94)	Full-Time	Part-Time
	80	300

Cost of Attendance (1993-94)

Academic Year		
Standard Course Load per Semester/Term		
(credit hours/units)		
Semesters/Terms per Academic Year	3 + summer	3 + summer
Tuition and Fees	$10,035	$3,345
Living Expenses	$5,000-6,000	
Summer Term		
(R = Required, O = Optional, N = None)	O	O
Standard Course Load	9/yr.	1/term
Tuition and Fees	$1,115/ course	$1,115/ course

Financial Aid Available

	Deadline (fall starts)	Awarded to Full-Time	Part-Time
Gift Aid	March 1	Yes	No
Federal College Work-Study	NA		
Federal Perkins Loans		Yes	
Federal Stafford Loans		Yes	
School-Based Loans		No	
Outside and Private Loans		Yes	
Graduate Assistantships	March 1	Yes	

Percentage of Students Receiving Aid	Full-Time
All students	30%
Minority students	50%
Women students	40%
International students	80%

UNION UNIVERSITY
School of Business Administration

2447 Hwy. 45 Bypass
Jackson, Tennessee 38305
Telephone: 901-661-5360

Total Enrollment (1993-94)	Full-Time	Part-Time
	Program begins fall 1994	

Cost of Attendance (1993-94)

Academic Year		
Standard Course Load per Semester/Term		
(credit hours/units)	9	3
Semesters/Terms per Academic Year	3	3
Tuition and Fees	$5,250	$2,250
Living Expenses	$4,200	$4,200
Summer Term		
(R = Required, O = Optional, N = None)	O	O
Standard Course Load	6	3
Tuition and Fees	$1,500	$ 750

Financial Aid Available

	Deadline (fall starts)	Awarded to Full-Time	Part-Time
Gift Aid	April 15	Yes	Yes
Federal College Work-Study		No	No
Federal Perkins Loans		No	No
Federal Stafford Loans	April 15	Yes	Yes
School-Based Loans		No	No
Outside and Private Loans	April 15	Yes	Yes
Graduate Assistantships	April 15	Yes	Yes

UNITED STATES INTERNATIONAL UNIVERSITY
College of Business Administration

10455 Pomerado Road
San Diego, California 92131
Telephone: 619-693-4695

Total Enrollment (1993-94)	Full-Time	Part-Time
	106	26

Cost of Attendance (1993-94)		
Academic Year		
Standard Course Load per Semester/Term		
(credit hours/units)	10	5
Semesters/Terms per Academic Year	3	3
Tuition and Fees	$7,740	$3,960
Living Expenses	$9,054	$9,054
Summer Term		
(R = Required, O = Optional, N = None)	O	O
Standard Course Load	10	5
Tuition and Fees	$2,580	$1,320

Financial Aid Available	Deadline (fall starts)	Awarded to Full-Time	Part-Time
Gift Aid	NA	Yes	Yes
Federal College Work-Study	April 15	Yes	Yes
Federal Perkins Loans	April 15	Yes	Yes
Federal Stafford Loans	NA	Yes	Yes
School-Based Loans	NA		
Outside and Private Loans	NA	Yes	
Graduate Assistantships	April 15	Yes	Yes

THE UNIVERSITY OF AKRON
College of Business Administration

Graduate Programs in Business
Akron, Ohio 44325-4805
Telephone: 216-972-7043

Total Enrollment (1993-94)	Full-Time	Part-Time
	475	110

Cost of Attendance (1993-94)		
Academic Year		
Standard Course Load per Semester/Term		
(credit hours/units)	9	3
Semesters/Terms per Academic Year	4	4
Tuition and Fees		
Resident	$1,191	$ 397
Nonresident	$2,234	$ 772
Living Expenses	$9,700	$9,350
Summer Term		
(R = Required, O = Optional, N = None)	O	O
Standard Course Load	3	3
Tuition and Fees		
Resident	$ 397	$ 397
Nonresident	$ 772	$ 772

Financial Aid Available	Deadline (fall starts)	Awarded to Full-Time	Part-Time
Gift Aid	March 1	Yes	No
Federal College Work-Study	NA	No	No
Federal Perkins Loans	NA	No	No
Federal Stafford Loans	April 1	Yes	Yes
School-Based Loans	NA	No	No
Outside and Private Loans	None	Yes	Yes
Graduate Assistantships	March 1	Yes	No

Percentage of Students Receiving Aid	Full-Time	Part-Time
All students	55%	0%
Minority students	100%	0%
Women students		
International students	70%	0%

UNIVERSITY OF ALABAMA
The Manderson Graduate School of Business

Room 306 Carmichael Hall, Box 870223
Tuscaloosa, Alabama 35487-0223
Telephone: 205-348-6517
        800-365-8583

Total Enrollment (1993-94)	Full-Time
	191 EMBA and MBA combined

Cost of Attendance (1993-94)	
Academic Year	
Standard Course Load per Semester/Term	
(credit hours/units)	12
Semesters/Terms per Academic Year	2
Tuition and Fees	
Resident	$2,000
Nonresident	$5,000
Living Expenses	NA
Summer Term	
(R = Required, O = Optional, N = None)	O
Standard Course Load	Varies
Tuition and Fees	
Resident	
Nonresident	

Financial Aid Available	Deadline (fall starts)	Awarded to Full-Time
Gift Aid	March 1	Yes
Federal College Work-Study	March 1	Yes
Federal Perkins Loans	March 1	Yes
Federal Stafford Loans	March 1	Yes
School-Based Loans	March 1	Yes
Outside and Private Loans	March 1	Yes
Graduate Assistantships	April 15	Yes

Percentage of Students Receiving Aid	Full-Time
All students	50%
Minority students	50%
Women students	50%
International students	50%

UNIVERSITY OF ALASKA ANCHORAGE
School of Business

3211 Providence Drive
Anchorage, Alaska 99508
Telephone: 907-786-4129

Total Enrollment (1993-94)	Full-Time	Part-Time
	15	85

Cost of Attendance (1993-94)		
Academic Year		
Standard Course Load per Semester/Term		
(credit hours/units)	9	6
Semesters/Terms per Academic Year	2	2
Tuition and Fees		
Resident	$2,458	$1,690
Nonresident	$4,762	$3,226
Living Expenses		
Summer Term		
(R = Required, O = Optional, N = None)	O	O
Standard Course Load	6	3
Tuition and Fees		
Resident	$ 788	$ 404
Nonresident	$1,556	$ 404

Financial Aid Available	Deadline (fall starts)	Awarded to Full-Time	Part-Time
Gift Aid	April 1	Yes	No
Federal College Work-Study	April 1	Yes	No
Federal Perkins Loans	April 1	Yes	No
Federal Stafford Loans	April 1	Yes	No
School-Based Loans	April 1	Yes	No
Outside and Private Loans	April 1	Yes	No
Graduate Assistantships	Rolling	Yes	No

UNIVERSITY OF ALASKA FAIRBANKS
School of Management

Admissions and Records
Signers' Hall
Fairbanks, Alaska 99775-0060
Telephone: 907-474-7521

Total Enrollment (1993-94)	Full-Time	Part-Time
	40	20

Cost of Attendance (1993-94)		
Academic Year		
Standard Course Load per Semester/Term		
(credit hours/units)	9	< 9
Semesters/Terms per Academic Year	2	2
Tuition and Fees		
Resident	$2,864	$128/cr.hr.
Nonresident	$5,168	$256/cr.hr.
Living Expenses	$6,154	$6,154
Summer Term		
(R = Required, O = Optional, N = None)	O	O
Standard Course Load	6	< 6
Tuition and Fees		
Resident	$128/cr.	$128/cr.
Nonresident	$256/cr.	$256/cr.

Financial Aid Available	Deadline (fall starts)	Awarded to Full-Time	Part-Time
Gift Aid	May 15	Yes	No
Federal College Work-Study	May 15	Yes	
Federal Perkins Loans		No	No
Federal Stafford Loans	May 15	Yes	Yes
School-Based Loans		No	No
Outside and Private Loans	May 15	Yes	Yes
Graduate Assistantships	May 15	Yes	No

Percentage of Students Receiving Aid	Full-Time	Part-Time
All students	70%	NA
Minority students	NA	NA
Women students	NA	NA
International students	NA	NA

UNIVERSITY AT ALBANY - STATE UNIVERSITY OF NEW YORK
School of Business

BA 361A
1400 Washington Avenue
Albany, New York 12222
Telephone: 518-442-4961

Total Enrollment (1993-94)	Full-Time	Part-Time
	225	235

Cost of Attendance (1993-94)		
Academic Year		
Standard Course Load per Semester/Term		
(credit hours/units)	15	6
Semesters/Terms per Academic Year	2	2
Tuition and Fees		
Resident	$4,000	$2,016
Nonresident	$7,316	$3,696
Living Expenses	$4,000	
Summer Term		
(R = Required, O = Optional, N = None)	N	O
Standard Course Load		3
Tuition and Fees		
Resident		$ 504
Nonresident		$ 924

Financial Aid Available	Deadline (fall starts)	Awarded to Full-Time	Part-Time
Gift Aid	April 1	Yes	No
Federal College Work-Study	Rolling	Yes	Yes
Federal Perkins Loans	Rolling	Yes	Yes
Federal Stafford Loans	Rolling	Yes	Yes
School-Based Loans	NA	No	No
Outside and Private Loans	None	Yes	Yes
Graduate Assistantships	None	Yes	No

Percentage of Students Receiving Aid	Full-Time	Part-Time
All students	80%	25%
Minority students	100%	NA
Women students	80%	NA
International students	2%	0%

UNIVERSITY OF ARIZONA
Karl Eller Graduate School of Management

McClelland Hall, Room 210
Tucson, Arizona 85721
Telephone: 602-621-2169

Total Enrollment (1993-94)	Full-Time	Part-Time
	146	74

Cost of Attendance (1993-94)		
Academic Year		
Standard Course Load per Semester/Term		
(credit hours/units)	17	6
Semesters/Terms per Academic Year	2	2
Tuition and Fees		
Resident	$ 1,844	$ 1,146
Nonresident	$ 7,350	$ 3,706
Living Expenses	$10,830	$10,830
Summer Term		
(R = Required, O = Optional, N = Nonc)	O	R
Standard Course Load		3
Tuition and Fees		
Resident		$ 304
Nonresident		$ 927

Financial Aid Available	Deadline (fall starts)	Awarded to Full-Time	Awarded to Part-Time
Gift Aid	March 1	Yes	No
Federal College Work-Study	March 1	Yes	No
Federal Perkins Loans	March 1	Yes	No
Federal Stafford Loans	March 1	Yes	Yes
School-Based Loans	September 1	Yes	No
Outside and Private Loans	NA	No	No
Graduate Assistantships	March 1	Yes	No

Percentage of Students Receiving Aid	Full-Time	Part-Time
All students	90%	40%
Minority students	100%	
Women students	70%	
International students	50%	

UNIVERSITY OF ARKANSAS
College of Business Administration

CBA 334
Fayetteville, Arkansas 72701
Telephone: 501-575 2851

Total Enrollment (1993-94)	Full-Time	Part-Time
	105	84

Cost of Attendance (1993-94)		
Academic Year		
Standard Course Load per Semester/Term		
(credit hours/units)	12 hrs.	6 hrs.
Semesters/Terms per Academic Year	3	3
Tuition and Fees		
Resident	$2,500	$125/hr.
Nonresident	$5,720	$286/hr.
Living Expenses	$6,200	
Summer Term		
(R = Required, O = Optional, N = None)	R	O
Standard Course Load	6-9 hrs.	3 hrs.
Tuition and Fees		
Resident	$125/hr.	$125/hr.
Nonresident	$286/hr.	$286/hr.

Financial Aid Available	Deadline (fall starts)	Awarded to Full-Time	Awarded to Part-Time
Gift Aid	April 1	Yes	No
Federal College Work-Study	NA	No	No
Federal Perkins Loans	April 1	Yes	No
Federal Stafford Loans	April 1	Yes	No
School-Based Loans	NA	No	No
Outside and Private Loans	Open	Yes	Yes
Graduate Assistantships	April 1	Yes	No

Percentage of Students Receiving Aid	Full-Time	Part-Time
All students	40%	0%
Minority students	40%	0%
Women students	40%	0%
International students	25%	0%

UNIVERSITY OF ARKANSAS AT LITTLE ROCK
College of Business Administration

2801 South University Avenue
Little Rock, Arkansas 72204-1099
Telephone: 501-569-8891

Total Enrollment (1993-94)	Full-Time	Part-Time
	140	30

Cost of Attendance (1993-94)		
Academic Year		
Standard Course Load per Semester/Term		
(credit hours/units)	12	6
Semesters/Terms per Academic Year	4	4
Tuition and Fees		
Resident	$1,285	$ 720
Nonresident	$2,773	$1,530
Living Expenses		
Summer Term		
(R = Required, O = Optional, N = None)	O	O
Standard Course Load	3	3
Tuition and Fees		
Resident	$ 360	$ 360
Nonresident	$ 765	$ 765

Financial Aid Available	Deadline (fall starts)	Awarded to Full-Time	Part-Time
Gift Aid	June 1	Yes	Yes
Federal College Work-Study	June 1	Yes	No
Federal Perkins Loans	June 1	Yes	Yes
Federal Stafford Loans	June 1	Yes	Yes
School-Based Loans	June 1	Yes	Yes
Outside and Private Loans	June 1	Yes	Yes
Graduate Assistantships	June 1	Yes	No

Percentage of Students Receiving Aid	Full-Time	Part-Time
All students	20%	70%
Minority students		
Women students		
International students		

UNIVERSITY OF BALTIMORE
Robert G. Merrick School of Business

1420 North Charles Street
Baltimore, Maryland 21201
Telephone: 410-837-4777

Total Enrollment (1993-94)	Full-Time	Part-Time
		929

Cost of Attendance (1993-94)		
Academic Year		
Standard Course Load per Semester/Term		
(credit hours/units)	9	3
Semesters/Terms per Academic Year	2	2
Tuition and Fees		
Resident	$1,690	$ 591
Nonresident	$1,690	$ 591
Living Expenses	$3,000	$3,000
Summer Term		
(R = Required, O = Optional, N = None)	O	O
Standard Course Load		3
Tuition and Fees		
Resident	$ 591	$ 591
Nonresident	$ 591	$ 591

Financial Aid Available	Deadline (fall starts)	Awarded to Full-Time	Part-Time
Gift Aid	April 1	Yes	Yes
Federal College Work-Study	April 1	Yes	Yes
Federal Perkins Loans	April 1	Yes	Yes
Federal Stafford Loans	April 1	Yes	Yes
School-Based Loans	April 1	Yes	Yes
Outside and Private Loans	April 1	Yes	Yes
Graduate Assistantships	April 1	Yes	Yes

Percentage of Students Receiving Aid	Part-Time
All students	60%
Minority students	12%
Women students	unknown
International students	unknown

UNIVERSITY OF BRIDGEPORT
College of Business

230 Park Avenue
Bridgeport, Connecticut 06601
Telephone: 203-576-4363

Total Enrollment (1993-94)	Full-Time	Part-Time
	34	72

Cost of Attendance (1993-94)		
Academic Year		
Standard Course Load per Semester/Term		
(credit hours/units)	9	6
Semesters/Terms per Academic Year	3	3
Tuition and Fees	$5,825	$3,675
Living Expenses	$7,900	$7,690
Summer Term		
(R = Required, O = Optional, N = None)	O	O
Standard Course Load	9	6
Tuition and Fees	$2,725	$1,825

Financial Aid Available	Deadline (fall starts)	Awarded to Full-Time	Part-Time
Gift Aid	NA	No	No
Federal College Work-Study	None	Yes	Yes
Federal Perkins Loans	None	Yes	No
Federal Stafford Loans	None	Yes	Yes
School-Based Loans	NA	No	No
Outside and Private Loans	NA	No	No
Graduate Assistantships	None	Yes	No

Percentage of Students Receiving Aid	Full-Time	Part-Time
All students	23%	0%
Minority students	0%	25%
Women students	NA	NA
International students	49%	0%

UNIVERSITY AT BUFFALO, STATE UNIVERSITY OF NEW YORK
School of Management

Jacobs Management Center
Box 604000
Buffalo, New York 14260-4000
Telephone: 716-645-3204

Total Enrollment (1993-94)	Full-Time	Part-Time
	340	416

Cost of Attendance (1993-94)		
Academic Year		
Standard Course Load per Semester/Term		
(credit hours/units)	15	6
Semesters/Terms per Academic Year	2	2
Tuition and Fees		
Resident	$4,300	$2,184
Nonresident	$7,616	$3,864
Living Expenses	$10,000-$11,000	
Summer Term		
(R = Required, O = Optional, N = None)	O	O
Standard Course Load	6	3
Tuition and Fees		
Resident	$1,014	$ 507
Nonresident	$1,854	$ 927

Financial Aid Available	Deadline (fall starts)	Awarded to Full-Time	Part-Time
Gift Aid	April 15	Yes	No
Federal College Work-Study	April 15	Yes	Yes
Federal Perkins Loans	April 15	Yes	Yes
Federal Stafford Loans	April 15	Yes	Yes
School-Based Loans	April 15	Yes	No
Outside and Private Loans	NA	No	No
Graduate Assistantships	Feb. 1	Yes	No

Percentage of Students Receiving Aid	Full-Time	Part-Time
All students	50%	20%
Minority students	50%	20%
Women students	50%	20%
International students	50%	20%

UNIVERSITY OF CALIFORNIA AT BERKELEY
Haas School of Business

MBA Program
350 Barrows Hall
Berkeley, California 94720
Telephone: 510-642-1405

Total Enrollment (1993-94)	Full-Time	Part-Time
	450	250

Cost of Attendance (1993-94)		
Academic Year		
Standard Course Load per Semester/Term		
(credit hours/units)	12	6
Semesters/Terms per Academic Year	2	2
Tuition and Fees		
Resident	$ 4,006	$ 8,312
Nonresident	$11,706	$12,162
Living Expenses	$ 9,965	NA
Summer Term		
(R = Required, O = Optional, N = None)	O	O
Standard Course Load	3	3
Tuition and Fees	$ 465	$ 465

Financial Aid Available	Deadline (fall starts)	Awarded to Full-Time	Part-Time
Gift Aid	March 21	Yes	No
Federal College Work-Study	March 21	Yes	No
Federal Perkins Loans	March 21	Yes	Yes
Federal Stafford Loans		Yes	Yes
School-based loans		No	No
Outside and private loans		No	No
Graduate Assistantships		Yes	No

UNIVERSITY OF CALIFORNIA AT DAVIS
Graduate School of Management

Room 106 AOB IV
Davis, California 95616-8609
Telephone: 916-752-7362

Total Enrollment (1993-94)	Full-Time	Part-Time
	141	8

Cost of Attendance (1993-94)		
Academic Year		
Standard Course Load per Semester/Term		
(credit hours/units)	12	6
Semesters/Terms per Academic Year	3	3
Tuition and Fees		
Resident	$ 1,400	$ 900
Nonresident	$12,006	NA
Living Expenses	$10,600	$10,600
Summer Term		
(R = Required, O = Optional, N = None)	N	N
Standard Course Load		
Tuition and Fees		
Resident		
Nonresident		

Financial Aid Available	Deadline (fall starts)	Awarded to Full-Time	Part-Time
Gift Aid	January 15	Yes	No
Federal College Work-Study	March 1	Yes	No
Federal Perkins Loans	March 1	Yes	Yes
Federal Stafford Loans	NA	Yes	Yes
School-Based Loans	March 1	Yes	No
Outside and Private Loans	NA	Yes	Yes
Graduate Assistantships	NA	Yes	No

Percentage of Students Receiving Aid	Full-Time	Part-Time
All students	50%	NA
Minority students	85%	
Women students	52%	
International students	0%	

UNIVERSITY OF CALIFORNIA, IRVINE
Graduate School of Management

Irvine, California 92717
Telephone: 714-856-5232

Total Enrollment (1993-94)	Full-Time
	221

Cost of Attendance (1993-94)

Academic Year
Standard Course Load per Semester/Term

(credit hours/units)	16
Semesters/Terms per Academic Year	3

Tuition and Fees

Resident	$4,388
Nonresident	$12,086
Living Expenses	$15,000

Summer Term

(R = Required, O = Optional, N = None)	O
Standard Course Load	8
Tuition and Fees	$500/course

Financial Aid Available

	Deadline (fall starts)	Awarded to Full-Time
Gift Aid	May 2	Yes
Federal College Work-Study	May 2	Yes
Federal Perkins Loans	May 2	Yes
Federal Stafford Loans	No deadline	Yes
School-Based Loans	No	
Outside and Private Loans	No deadline	Yes
Graduate Assistantships	Varies	Yes

Percentage of Students Receiving Aid	Full-Time
All students	80%
Minority students	90%
Women students	85%
International students	0%

UNIVERSITY OF CALIFORNIA, LOS ANGELES
Anderson School

405 Hilgard Avenue 3371 AGSM
Los Angeles, California 90024-1448
Telephone: 310-825 6944

Total Enrollment (1993-94)	Full-Time	Part-Time
	650	249

Cost of Attendance (1993-94)

Academic Year
Standard Course Load per Semester/Term

(credit hours/units)	16	8
Semesters/Terms per Academic Year	3	3

Tuition and Fees

Resident	$ 4,177	$15,500
Nonresident	$11,876	$21,500
Living Expenses	$13,560	

Summer Term

(R = Required, O = Optional, N = None)	O	O
Standard Course Load	4-8	
Tuition and Fees	$ 525	

Financial Aid Available

	Deadline (fall starts)	Awarded to Full-Time	Part-Time
Gift Aid	September 1	Yes	No
Federal College Work-Study	September 1	Yes	No
Federal Perkins Loans	September 1	Yes	No
Federal Stafford Loans	September 1	Yes	Yes
School-Based Loans	NA	No	No
Outside and Private Loans	NA	Yes	Yes
Graduate Assistantships	NA	Yes	No

Percentage of Students Receiving Aid	Full-Time	Part-Time
All students	70%	65%
Minority students	100%	50%
Women students		40%
International students	1%	2%

UNIVERSITY OF CALIFORNIA, RIVERSIDE
Graduate School of Management

Riverside, California 92521
Telephone: 909-787-4551

Total Enrollment (1993-94)	Full-Time	Part-Time
	98	22

Cost of Attendance (1993-94)		
Academic Year		
Standard Course Load per Semester/Term		
(credit hours/units)	16	8
Semesters/Terms per Academic Year	3	3
Tuition and Fees		
Resident	$ 4,365	$ 4,365
Nonresident	$12,064	$12,064
Living Expenses		
Summer Term		
(R = Required, O = Optional, N = None)	O	O
Standard Course Load	8	4
Tuition and Fees	$ 640	$ 320

Financial Aid Available	Deadline (fall starts)	Awarded to Full-Time	Part-Time
Gift Aid	March 1	Yes	No
Federal College Work-Study	NA	No	No
Federal Perkins Loans	NA	No	No
Federal Stafford Loans	May 1	Yes	Yes
School-Based Loans	NA	No	No
Outside and Private Loans	NA	Yes	Yes
Graduate Assistantships	May 1	Yes	No

Percentage of Students Receiving Aid	Full-Time	Part-Time
All students	40%	10%
Minority students		
Women students		
International students		

UNIVERSITY OF CENTRAL ARKANSAS
College of Business Administration

Conway, Arkansas 72032
Telephone: 501-450-3411

Total Enrollment (1993-94)	Full-Time	Part-Time
	31	51

Cost of Attendance (1993-94)		
Academic Year		
Standard Course Load per Semester/Term		
(credit hours/units)	9	3
Semesters/Terms per Academic Year	2	2
Tuition and Fees		
Resident	$7.50	
Nonresident	$1,707	$188/hr. + $7.50
Living Expenses	$3,250	$3,250
Summer Term		
(R = Required, O = Optional, N = None)	O	O
Standard Course Load	6	3
Tuition and Fees	Same as above	

Financial Aid Available	Deadline (fall starts)	Awarded to Full-Time	Part-Time
Gift Aid	February 15	Yes	Yes
Federal College Work-Study	February 15	Yes	No
Federal Perkins Loans	February 15	Yes	Yes
Federal Stafford Loans	February 15	Yes	Yes
School-Based Loans	February 15	Yes	Yes
Outside and Private Loans	February 15	Yes	Yes
Graduate Assistantships	February 15	Yes	No

UNIVERSITY OF CENTRAL FLORIDA
College of Business Administration

P.O. Box 16140
BA 241
Orlando, Florida 32816
Telephone: 407-823-2184

Total Enrollment (1993-94)	Full-Time	Part-Time
	345	366

Cost of Attendance (1993-94)		
Academic Year		
Standard Course Load per Semester/Term		
(credit hours/units)	9	3
Semesters/Terms per Academic Year	3	3
Tuition and Fees		
Resident	$ 966	$ 322
Nonresident	$3,243	$1,081
Living Expenses	$3,800	$3,800
Summer Term		
(R = Required, O = Optional, N = None)	O	O
Standard Course Load	6	3
Tuition and Fees		
Resident	$ 644	$ 322
Nonresident	$2,162	$1,081

Financial Aid Available	Deadline (fall starts)	Awarded to Full-Time	Part-Time
Gift Aid	Varies	Yes	No
Federal College Work-Study	March 1	Yes	No
Federal Perkins Loans	March 1	Yes	Yes
Federal Stafford Loans	March 1	Yes	Yes
School-Based Loans	NA	No	No
Outside and Private Loans	Varies	Yes	Yes
Graduate Assistantships	None	Yes	No

Percentage of Students Receiving Aid	Full-Time	Part-Time
All students	20%	0%
Minority students	18%	0%
Women students	11%	0%
International students	4%	0%

UNIVERSITY OF CENTRAL OKLAHOMA

100 North University Drive
Edmond, Oklahoma 73034-0108
Telephone: 405-341-2980, extension 2423

Total Enrollment (1993-94)	Full-Time	Part-Time
	336	335

Cost of Attendance (1993-94)		
Academic Year		
Standard Course Load per Semester/Term		
(credit hours/units)	9	6
Semesters/Terms per Academic Year	3	3
Tuition and Fees		
Resident	$ 572	$ 381
Nonresident	$1,369	$ 912
Living Expenses	$4,000	$4,000
Summer Term		
(R = Required, O = Optional, N = None)	O	O
Standard Course Load	6	3
Tuition and Fees		
Resident	$ 381	$ 191
Nonresident	$ 912	$ 456

Financial Aid Available	Deadline (fall starts)	Awarded to Full-Time	Part-Time
Gift Aid	March 1	Yes	Yes
Federal College Work-Study	May 17	Yes	Yes
Federal Perkins Loans	May 17	Yes	Yes
Federal Stafford Loans	May 17	Yes	Yes
School-Based Loans	May 17	Yes	Yes
Outside and Private Loans	March 1	Yes	Yes
Graduate Assistantships	March 1	Yes	No

Percentage of Students Receiving Aid	Full-Time	Part-Time
All students	8%	8%
Minority students		
Women students		
International students		

UNIVERSITY OF CHICAGO
Graduate School of Business

1101 East 58th Street
Chicago, Illinois 60637
Telephone: 312-702-7369

Total Enrollment (1993-94)	Full-Time	Part-Time
	1,200	1,530

Cost of Attendance (1993-94)		
Academic Year		
Standard Course Load per Semester/Term		
(credit hours/units)	3	2
Semesters/Terms per Academic Year	3	3
Tuition and Fees	$20,020	$4,040
Living Expenses	$11,868	
Summer Term		
(R = Required, O = Optional, N = None)	O	O
Standard Course Load	3	2
Tuition and Fees	$ 6,060	$ 4,040

Financial Aid Available	Deadline (fall starts)	Awarded to Full-Time	Part-Time
Gift Aid	March 1	Yes	No
Federal College Work-Study	April 1	Yes	No
Federal Perkins Loans	April 1	Yes	No
Federal Stafford Loans	April 1	Yes	Yes
School-Based Loans	NA	No	No
Outside and Private Loans	NA	Yes	Yes
Graduate Assistantships	NA	No	No

Percentage of Students Receiving Aid	Full-Time	Part-Time
All students	60%	10%
Minority students	NA	NA
Women students	NA	NA
International students	NA	NA

UNIVERSITY OF CINCINNATI
College of Business

Lindner Hall, Suite 103
Cincinnati, Ohio 45221
Telephone: 513-556-7020

Total Enrollment (1993-94)	Full-Time	Part-Time
	120	350

Cost of Attendance (1993-94)		
Academic Year		
Standard Course Load per Semester/Term		
(credit hours/units)	15-17	6
Semesters/Terms per Academic Year	4 qtrs.	4 qtrs.
Tuition and Fees		
Resident	$ 7,784	$ 3,792
Nonresident	$15,080	$ 7,440
Living Expenses	$12,150	$12,150
Summer Term		
(R = Required, O = Optional, N = None)	R	R
Standard Course Load	12	3-6
Tuition and Fees	$158/cr.hr.	$310/cr.hr.

Financial Aid Available	Deadline (fall starts)	Awarded to Full-Time	Part-Time
Gift Aid	February 15	Yes	No
Federal College Work-Study		No	No
Federal Perkins Loans	February 15	Yes	No
Federal Stafford Loans	February 15	Yes	No
School-Based Loans		No	No
Outside and Private Loans	February 15	Yes	Yes
Graduate Assistantships	February 15	Yes	No

Percentage of Students Receiving Aid	Full-Time	Part-Time
All students	70%	NA
Minority students	100%	NA
Women students	85%	NA
International students	30%	NA

UNIVERSITY OF COLORADO AT BOULDER

Campus Box 419
Boulder, Colorado 80309-0419
Telephone: 303-492-8771

Total Enrollment (1993-94)

	Full-Time
	214

Cost of Attendance (1993-94)

Academic Year
Standard Course Load per Semester/Term

(credit hours/units)	15
Semesters/Terms per Academic Year	2

Tuition and Fees

Resident	$ 3,552
Nonresident	$12,088

Living Expenses
Summer Term

(R = Required, O = Optional, N = None)	N

Standard Course Load
Tuition and Fees
Resident
Nonresident

Financial Aid Available

	Deadline (fall starts)	Awarded to Full-Time
Gift Aid	April 1	Yes
Federal College Work-Study	April 1	Yes
Federal Perkins Loans	April 1	Yes
Federal Stafford Loans	April 1	Yes
School-Based Loans	April 1	Yes
Outside and Private Loans	April 1	Yes
Graduate Assistantships	April 1	Yes

Percentage of Students Receiving Aid	Full-Time
All students	50%
Minority students	50%
Women students	50%
International students	50%

UNIVERSITY OF CONNECTICUT
School of Business Administration

368 Fairfield Road, U-41MBA
Storrs, Connecticut 06269 2041
Telephone: 203-486-2872

Total Enrollment (1993-94)

	Full-Time	Part-Time
	230	1,145

Cost of Attendance (1993-94)

Academic Year
Standard Course Load per Semester/Term

(credit hours/units)	15	6
Semesters/Terms per Academic Year	2	3

Tuition and Fees

Resident	$2,518	$4,575
Nonresident	$5,938	$4,575
Living Expenses	$3,173	NA

Summer Term

(R = Required, O = Optional, N = None)	O	O
Standard Course Load	3	6

Tuition and Fees

Resident	$ 714	$1,830
Nonresident	$1,854	$1,830

Financial Aid Available

	Deadline (fall starts)	Awarded to Full-Time	Awarded to Part-Time
Gift Aid	February 15	Yes	Yes
Federal College Work-Study	February 15	Yes	No
Federal Perkins Loans	February 15	Yes	No
Federal Stafford Loans	February 15	Yes	No
School-Based Loans	February 15	Yes	No
Outside and Private Loans	February 15	Yes	Yes
Graduate Assistantships	February 15	Yes	No

UNIVERSITY OF DALLAS
Graduate School of Management

1845 East Northgate Drive
Irving, Texas 75062-4799
Telephone: 214-721-5174

Total Enrollment (1993-94)	Full-Time	Part-Time
	305	1,221

Cost of Attendance (1993-94)		
Academic Year		
Standard Course Load per Semester/Term		
(credit hours/units)	9	6
Semesters/Terms per Academic Year	3	3
Tuition and Fees	$295/hr.	$295/hr.
Living Expenses		
Summer Term		
(R = Required, O = Optional, N = None)	O	O
Standard Course Load	9	6
Tuition and Fees	$295/hr.	$295/hr.

Financial Aid Available	Deadline (fall starts)	Awarded to Full-Time	Part-Time
Gift Aid		No	No
Federal College Work-Study		No	No
Federal Perkins Loans		No	No
Federal Stafford Loans	April 1	Yes	Yes
School-Based Loans		No	No
Outside and Private Loans	April 1	Yes	Yes
Graduate Assistantships		Yes	Yes

Percentage of Students Receiving Aid	Full-Time	Part-Time
All students	11%	2%
Minority students	1%	1%
Women students	4%	1%
International students	9%	<1%

UNIVERSITY OF DAYTON
School of Business Administration

300 College Park Avenue
Dayton, Ohio 45469-2226
Telephone: 513-229-3733

Total Enrollment (1993-94)	Full-Time	Part-Time
	41	628

Cost of Attendance (1993-94)		
Academic Year		
Standard Course Load per Semester/Term		
(credit hours/units)	9	6
Semesters/Terms per Academic Year	2	2
Tuition and Fees	$5,550	$3,700
Living Expenses	NA	NA
Summer Term		
(R = Required, O = Optional, N = None)	O	O
Standard Course Load	6	6
Tuition and Fees	$3,700	$3,700

Financial Aid Available	Deadline (fall starts)	Awarded to Full-Time	Part-Time
Gift Aid	August 1	Yes	Yes
Federal College Work-Study	NA	No	No
Federal Perkins Loans	NA	No	No
Federal Stafford Loans	July 1	Yes	Yes
School-Based Loans	NA	No	No
Outside and Private Loans	July 1	Yes	Yes
Graduate Assistantships	July 1	Yes	Yes

Percentage of Students Receiving Aid	Full-Time	Part-Time
All students	33%	5%
Minority students	30%	2%
Women students	30%	2%
International students	2%	0%

UNIVERSITY OF DELAWARE
College of Business and Economics

MBA Program
108 Purnell Hall
Newark, Delaware 19716
Telephone: 302-831-2221

Total Enrollment (1993-94)	Full-Time	Part-Time
	80	300

Cost of Attendance (1993-94)

Academic Year		
Standard Course Load per Semester/Term		
(credit hours/units)	12	6
Semesters/Terms per Academic Year	2	2
Tuition and Fees		
Resident	$4,466	$1,488
Nonresident	$9,650	$3,216
Living Expenses	$4,000-$10,000	NA
Summer Term		
(R = Required, O = Optional, N = None)	O	O
Standard Course Load	6	6
Tuition and Fees		
Resident	Same as above	
Nonresident		

Financial Aid Available

	Deadline (fall starts)	Awarded to Full-Time	Part-Time
Gift Aid	February 15	Yes	No
Federal College Work-Study	NA	No	No
Federal Perkins Loans	March 15	Yes	No
Federal Stafford Loans	March 15	Yes	No
School-Based Loans	March 15	Yes	No
Outside and Private Loans	NA	No	No
Graduate Assistantships	February 15	Yes	No

Percentage of Students Receiving Aid	Full-Time
All students	20%
Minority students	85%
Women students	5%
International students	50%

UNIVERSITY OF DENVER
Graduate School of Business

2020 South Race Street, BA 122
Denver, Colorado 80208
Telephone: 303-871-3416

Total Enrollment (1993-94)	Full-Time	Part-Time
	366	299

Cost of Attendance (1993-94)

Academic Year		
Standard Course Load per Semester/Term		
(credit hours/units)	12-16	8
Semesters/Terms per Academic Year	3	3
Tuition and Fees	$14,364	$9,576
Living Expenses	$ 9,228	$9,228
Summer Term		
(R = Required, O = Optional, N = None)	O	O
Standard Course Load	12-16	8
Tuition and Fees	$ 4,788	$3,192

Financial Aid Available

	Deadline (fall starts)	Awarded to Full-Time	Part-Time
Gift Aid	March 1	Yes	Yes
Federal College Work-Study	March 1	Yes	Yes
Federal Perkins Loans	March 1	Yes	Yes
Federal Stafford Loans	March 1	Yes	Yes
School-Based Loans	NA	No	No
Outside and Private Loans	NA	No	No
Graduate Assistantships	March 1	Yes	No

Percentage of Students Receiving Aid	Full-Time	Part-Time
All students	46%	30%
Minority students	55%	30%
Women students	50%	30%
International students	4%	0%

UNIVERSITY OF DETROIT MERCY
Graduate Business Programs

4001 West McNichols Road
P.O. Box 19900
Detroit, Michigan 48219-0900
Telephone: 313-993-1202

Total Enrollment (1993-94)	Full-Time	Part-Time
	100	550

Cost of Attendance (1993-94)		
Academic Year		
Standard Course Load per Semester/Term		
(credit hours/units)	9	6
Semesters/Terms per Academic Year	4	4
Tuition and Fees	$6,930	$4,620
Living Expenses	$6,000	$6,000
Summer Term		
(R = Required, O = Optional, N = None)	O	O
Standard Course Load	6	3
Tuition and Fees	$2,310	$1,155

Financial Aid Available	Deadline (fall starts)	Awarded to Full-Time	Awarded to Part-Time
Gift Aid		Yes	Yes
Federal College Work-Study		Yes	Yes
Federal Perkins Loans	April 1	Yes	Yes
Federal Stafford Loans	April 1	Yes	Yes
School-Based Loans	April 1	Yes	Yes
Outside and Private Loans		Yes	No
Graduate Assistantships		Yes	No

Percentage of Students Receiving Aid	Full-Time	Part-Time
All students	75-80%	75-80%
Minority students	75-80%	75-80%
Women students	75-80%	75-80%
International students		

UNIVERSITY OF FLORIDA
MBA Program

134 Bryan Hall
Gainesville, Florida 32611
Telephone: 904-392-7992, extension 200

Total Enrollment (1993-94)	Full-Time
	250

Cost of Attendance (1993-94)	
Academic Year	
Standard Course Load per Semester/Term	
(credit hours/units)	12
Semesters/Terms per Academic Year	2
Tuition and Fees	
Resident	$ 2,559
Nonresident	$ 8,703
Living Expenses	$10,000
Summer Term	
(R = Required, O = Optional, N = None)	N
Standard Course Load	
Tuition and Fees	
Resident	
Nonresident	

Financial Aid Available	Deadline (fall starts)	Awarded to Full-Time
Gift Aid	March 1	Yes
Federal College Work-Study	March 1	No
Federal Perkins Loans	March 1	Yes
Federal Stafford Loans	March 1	Yes
School-Based Loans	March 1	No
Outside and Private Loans	March 1	No
Graduate Assistantships	March 1	Yes

Percentage of Students Receiving Aid	Full-Time
All students	60%
Minority students	85%
Women students	50%
International students	5%

UNIVERSITY OF GEORGIA
Terry College of Business

350 Brooks Hall
Athens, Georgia 30602-6264
Telephone: 706-542-5671

Total Enrollment (1993-94)	Full-Time
	152

Cost of Attendance (1993-94)	
Academic Year	
Standard Course Load per Semester/Term	
(credit hours/units)	16
Semesters/Terms per Academic Year	3
Tuition and Fees	
Resident	$2,250
Nonresident	$5,940
Living Expenses	$6,000
Summer Term	
(R = Required, O = Optional, N = None)	O
Standard Course Load	16
Tuition and Fees	
Resident	$ 750
Nonresident	$1,980

Financial Aid Available	Deadline (fall starts)	Awarded to Full-Time
Gift Aid	Varies	Yes
Federal College Work-Study	March 1 (priority)	Yes
Federal Perkins Loans	August 1	Yes
Federal Stafford Loans	August 1	Yes
School-Based Loans	NA	No
Outside and Private Loans	NA	No
Graduate Assistantships	February 15	Yes

Percentage of Students Receiving Aid	Full-Time
All students	75%
Minority students	90%
Women students	75%
International students	65%

UNIVERSITY OF HAWAII AT MANOA
College of Business Administration

2404 Maile Way
Honolulu, Hawaii 96822
Telephone: 808-956-8266

Total Enrollment (1993-94)	Full-Time	Part-Time
	274	73

Cost of Attendance (1993-94)		
Academic Year		
Standard Course Load per Semester/Term		
(credit hours/units)	12	6
Semesters/Terms per Academic Year	2	2
Tuition and Fees		
Resident	$ 978	$ 510
Nonresident	$2,878	$1,458
Living Expenses	$8,931	$8,931
Summer Term		
(R = Required, O = Optional, N = None)	O	O
Standard Course Load	12	6
Tuition and Fees		
Resident	$ 911	$ 461
Nonresident	$1,571	$ 791

Financial Aid Available	Deadline (fall starts)	Awarded to Full-Time	Awarded to Part-Time
Gift Aid	May 10	Yes	No
Federal College Work-Study	March 1 (priority)	Yes	Yes
Federal Perkins Loans	March 1 (priority)	Yes	Yes
Federal Stafford Loans	March 1 (priority)	Yes	Yes
School-Based Loans	NA	Yes	Yes
Outside and Private Loans	NA	Yes	Yes
Graduate Assistantships	May 10	Yes	Yes

Percentage of Students Receiving Aid	Full-Time	Part-Time
All students	42%	4%
Minority students	NA	NA
Women students	NA	NA
International students	NA	NA

UNIVERSITY OF HOUSTON
College of Business Administration

Melcher Hall
Houston, Texas 77204-6283
Telephone: 713-743-4900

Total Enrollment (1993-94)	Full-Time	Part-Time
	342	1,119

Cost of Attendance (1993-94)		
Academic Year		
Standard Course Load per Semester/Term		
(credit hours/units)	12	9
Semesters/Terms per Academic Year	3	2
Tuition and Fees		
Resident	$ 891	$ 717
Nonresident	$ 2,259	$ 1,743
Living Expenses	$14,078	$14,078
Summer Term		
(R = Required, O = Optional, N = None)	O	O
Standard Course Load	12	9
Tuition and Fees		
Resident	$ 891	$ 717
Nonresident	$ 2,259	$ 1,717

Financial Aid Available	Deadline (fall starts)	Awarded to Full-Time	Part
Gift Aid	February 28	Yes	Yes
Federal College Work-Study	NA	No	No
Federal Perkins Loans	None	Yes	Yes
Federal Stafford Loans	April 1	Yes	Yes
School-Based Loans	NA	No	No
Outside and Private Loans	NA	No	No
Graduate Assistantships		Yes	No

Percentage of Students Receiving Aid	Full-Time	Part-Time
All students	3%	1%
Minority students	1%	
Women students	1%	
International students	1%	

UNIVERSITY OF ILLINOIS AT CHICAGO
College of Business Administration

703 South Morgan Street (M/C 077)
Chicago, Illinois 60607-7025
Telephone: 312-996-4573

Total Enrollment (1993-94)	Full-Time	Part-Time
	167	268

Cost of Attendance (1993-94)		
Academic Year		
Standard Course Load per Semester/Term		
(credit hours/units)	14	8
Semesters/Terms per Academic Year	2	2
Tuition and Fees		
Resident	$ 5,066	$1,415
Nonresident	$10,566	$3,259
Living Expenses	$ 9,727	$ 627
Summer Term		
(R = Required, O = Optional, N = None)	O	O
Standard Course Load	NA	4
Tuition and Fees		
Resident	NA	NA
Nonresident	NA	NA

Financial Aid Available	Deadline (fall starts)	Awarded to Full-Time	Part-Time
Gift Aid	January 15	Yes	No
Federal College Work-Study	May 1	Yes	Yes
Federal Perkins Loans	May 1	Yes	Yes
Federal Stafford Loans	May 1	Yes	Yes
School-Based Loans	NA	No	No
Outside and Private Loans	May 1	Yes	Yes
Graduate Assistantships	NA	No	No

Percentage of Students Receiving Aid	Full-Time	Part-Time
All students	79%	32%
Minority students	88%	20%
Women students	69%	30%
International students	29%	NA

UNIVERSITY OF ILLINOIS AT URBANA-CHAMPAIGN
MBA Program

15 Commerce West Building
1206 S. Sixth Street
Champaign, Illinois 61820
Telephone: 217-244-8019
          800-MBA-UIUC

Total Enrollment (1993-94)	Full-Time
	560

Cost of Attendance (1993-94)

Academic Year	
Standard Course Load per Semester/Term	
(credit hours/units)	5 units/first yr.
	4 units/second yr.
Semesters/Terms per Academic Year	2
Tuition and Fees	
Resident	$ 5,046
Nonresident	$10,578
Living Expenses	$ 7,642
Summer Term	
(R = Required, O = Optional, N = None)	O
Standard Course Load	2
Tuition and Fees	
Resident	$ 1,097
Nonresident	$ 2,480

Financial Aid Available

	Deadline (fall starts)	Awarded to Full-Time
Gift Aid	None	Yes
Federal College Work-Study		No
Federal Perkins Loans		No
Federal Stafford Loans	Rolling	Yes
School-Based Loans		No
Outside and Private Loans	Rolling	Yes
Graduate Assistantships	Early spring	Yes

Percentage of Students Receiving Aid	Full-Time
All students	50%
Minority students	
Women students	
International students	

THE UNIVERSITY OF IOWA
School of Management

121 Philips Hall
Iowa City, Iowa 52242
Telephone: 319-335-1039
          800-553-4692, extension 1039

Total Enrollment (1993-94)	Full-Time	Part-Time
	250	200

Cost of Attendance (1993-94)

Academic Year		
Standard Course Load per Semester/Term		
(credit hours/units)	15	6
Semesters/Terms per Academic Year	2	2
Tuition and Fees		
Resident	$3,396	$2,268
Nonresident	$8,708	$5,808
Living Expenses	$7,158	$6,792
Summer Term		
(R = Required, O = Optional, N = None)	O	O
Standard Course Load	6	3
Tuition and Fees		
Resident	$1,134	$ 567
Nonresident	$2,904	$ 567

Financial Aid Available

	Deadline (fall starts)	Awarded to Full-Time	Part-Time
Gift Aid	March 1	Yes	No
Federal College Work-Study	March 1	Yes	Yes
Federal Perkins Loans	March 1	Yes	Yes
Federal Stafford Loans	NA	Yes	Yes
School-Based Loans	NA	Yes	Yes
Outside and Private Loans	NA	Yes	Yes
Graduate Assistantships	March 1	Yes	No

Percentage of Students Receiving Aid	Full-Time	Part-Time
All students	60%	NA
Minority students	100%	NA
Women students	65%	NA
International students	30%	NA

UNIVERSITY OF KANSAS

206 Summerfield Hall
Lawrence, Kansas 66045
Telephone: 913-864-4254

Total Enrollment (1993-94)	Full-Time	Part-Time
	239	201

Cost of Attendance (1993-94)

	Full-Time	Part-Time
Academic Year		
Standard Course Load per Semester/Term		
(credit hours/units)	15	7
Semesters/Terms per Academic Year	2	2
Tuition and Fees		
Resident	$2,322	$1,470
Nonresident	$6,880	$1,470
Living Expenses	$6,000	$6,000
Summer Term		
(R = Required, O = Optional, N = None)	O	O
Standard Course Load	3	3
Tuition and Fees		
Resident	$ 239	$ 291
Nonresident	$ 662	$ 291

Financial Aid Available

	Deadline (fall starts)	Awarded to Full-Time	Awarded to Part-Time
Gift Aid	May 1	Yes	Yes
Federal College Work-Study	March 1	Yes	Yes
Federal Perkins Loans	NA	No	No
Federal Stafford Loans	March 1	Yes	Yes
School-Based Loans	NA	No	No
Outside and Private Loans	March 1	Yes	Yes
Graduate Assistantships	May 1	Yes	No

Percentage of Students Receiving Aid	Full-Time	Part-Time
All students	15%	0%
Minority students	100%	0%
Women students	20%	0%
International students	15%	0%

UNIVERSITY OF KENTUCKY
College of Business and Economics

145 Business and Economics Building
Lexington, Kentucky 40506-0034
Telephone: 606-257-3592

Total Enrollment (1993-94)	Full-Time	Part-Time
	166	129

Cost of Attendance (1993-94)

	Full-Time	Part-Time
Academic Year		
Standard Course Load per Semester/Term		
(credit hours/units)	9 cr. hr.	> 9 cr. hr.
Semesters/Terms per Academic Year	2	2
Tuition and Fees		
Resident	$1,239	$126/cr. hr.
Nonresident	$3,399	$366/cr. hr.
Living Expenses	$4,646	$4,646
Summer Term		
(R = Required, O = Optional, N = None)	O	O
Standard Course Load	6 cr. hr.	> 6 cr. hr.
Tuition and Fees		
Resident	$ 656	$126/cr. hr.
Nonresident	$1,836	$366/cr. hr.

Financial Aid Available

	Deadline (fall starts)	Awarded to Full-Time	Awarded to Part-Time
Gift Aid	July 1	Yes	No
Federal College Work-Study	April 1	Yes	Yes
Federal Perkins Loans	April 1	Yes	Yes
Federal Stafford Loans	None	Yes	Yes
School-Based Loans	NA	No	No
Outside and Private Loans	NA	No	No
Graduate Assistantships	April 1	Yes	No

Percentage of Students Receiving Aid	Full-Time	Part-Time
All students	16%	0%
Minority students	75%	0%
Women students	28%	0%
International students	6%	0%

UNIVERSITY OF LA VERNE
School of Business and Economics

1950 Third Street
La Verne, California 91750
Telephone: 909-593-3511, extension 4207

Total Enrollment (1993-94)	Full-Time	Part-Time
	125	250

Cost of Attendance (1993-94)		
Academic Year		
Standard Course Load per Semester/Term		
(credit hours/units)	9	6
Semesters/Terms per Academic Year	3	3
Tuition and Fees	$ 6,405	$ 4,575
Living Expenses	$21,400	$19,630
Summer Term		
(R = Required, O = Optional, N = None)	O	O
Standard Course Load	3	3
Tuition and Fees	$ 945	$ 945

Financial Aid Available	Deadline (fall starts)	Awarded to Full-Time	Part-Time
Gift Aid	NA	Yes	Yes
Federal College Work-Study	NA	No	No
Federal Perkins Loans	NA	No	No
Federal Stafford Loans	NA	Yes	Yes
School-Based Loans	NA	No	No
Outside and Private Loans	NA	Yes	Yes
Graduate Assistantships	NA	Yes	Yes

UNIVERSITY OF MAINE
College of Business Administration

209 Donald P. Corbett Hall
Orono, Maine 04469-5723
Telephone: 207-581-1973

Total Enrollment (1993-94)	Full-Time	Part-Time
	52	55

Cost of Attendance (1993-94)		
Academic Year		
Standard Course Load per Semester/Term		
(credit hours/units)	9	3
Semesters/Terms per Academic Year	2	2
Tuition and Fees		
Resident	$2,705	$ 879
Nonresident	$7,133	$2,355
Living Expenses	$7,000	$7,000
Summer Term		
(R = Required, O = Optional, N = None)	O	O
Standard Course Load	9	3
Tuition and Fees		
Resident	$1,275	$ 447
Nonresident	$3,489	$1,185

Financial Aid Available	Deadline (fall starts)	Awarded to Full-Time	Part-Time
Gift Aid	February 15	Yes	No
Federal College Work-Study	March 1	Yes	Yes
Federal Perkins Loans	March 1	Yes	Yes
Federal Stafford Loans	March 1	Yes	Yes
School-Based Loans	NA	No	No
Outside and Private Loans	NA	No	No
Graduate Assistantships	March 1	Yes	No

Percentage of Students Receiving Aid	Full-Time	Part-Time
All students	40%	5%
Minority students		
Women students		
International students		

UNIVERSITY OF MARY HARDIN-BAYLOR
School of Business

UMHB Station Box 8018
Belton, Texas 76513
Telephone: 817-939-4644

Total Enrollment (1993-94)	Full-Time	Part-Time
		30

Cost of Attendance (1993-94)	
Academic Year	
Standard Course Load per Semester/Term	
(credit hours/units)	7
Semesters/Terms per Academic Year	3
Tuition and Fees	$6,000
Living Expenses	NA
Summer Term	
(R = Required, O = Optional, N = None)	R
Standard Course Load	6
Tuition and Fees	$6,000

Financial Aid Available	Deadline (fall starts)	Awarded to Full-Time	Awarded to Part-Time
Gift Aid	NA	No	No
Federal College Work-Study	NA	No	No
Federal Perkins Loans	NA	No	No
Federal Stafford Loans	NA	No	Yes
School-Based Loans	NA	No	No
Outside and Private Loans	NA	No	No
Graduate Assistantships	NA	No	No

Percentage of Students Receiving Aid	Full-Time	Part-Time
All students		60%
Minority students		NA
Women students		60%
International students		NA

UNIVERSITY OF MARYLAND AT COLLEGE PARK
College of Business and Management

Van Munching Hall
College Park, Maryland 20742
Telephone: 301-405-2279

Total Enrollment (1993-94)	Full-Time	Part-Time
	280	600

Cost of Attendance (1993-94)		
Academic Year		
Standard Course Load per Semester/Term		
(credit hours/units)	280	497
Semesters/Terms per Academic Year	15/12	2
Tuition and Fees		
Resident	$3,212	$1,440
Nonresident	$6,600	
Living Expenses		
Summer Term		
(R = Required, O = Optional, N = None)	O	R
Standard Course Load	Varies	6
Tuition and Fees		
Resident	$ 189	$1,194
Nonresident	$ 324	$2,016

Financial Aid Available	Deadline (fall starts)	Awarded to Full-Time	Awarded to Part-Time
Gift Aid	March 1	Yes	No
Federal College Work-Study	February 1	Yes	No
Federal Perkins Loans	February 1	Yes	No
Federal Stafford Loans	February 1	Yes	No
School-Based Loans	February 1	Yes	No
Outside and Private Loans	February 1	Yes	No
Graduate Assistantships	March 1	Yes	No

Percentage of Students Receiving Aid	Full-Time	Part-Time
All students	50%	0%
Minority students	90%	0%
Women students	40%	0%
International students	25%	0%

UNIVERSITY OF MASSACHUSETTS, AMHERST
School of Management

209 School of Management Building
Amherst, Massachusetts 01003
Telephone: 413-545-5608

Total Enrollment (1993-94)	Full-Time	Part-Time
	80	180

Cost of Attendance (1993-94)		
Academic Year		
Standard Course Load per Semester/Term		
(credit hours/units)	15	6
Semesters/Terms per Academic Year	2	2
Tuition and Fees		
Resident	$ 5,510	$3,280
Nonresident	$11,300	$3,280
Living Expenses	NA	NA
Summer Term		
(R = Required, O = Optional, N = None)	N	O
Standard Course Load		6
Tuition and Fees		$1,640

Financial Aid Available	Deadline (fall starts)	Awarded to Full-Time	Part-Time
Gift Aid	March 1	Yes	No
Federal College Work-Study	August 1	Yes	No
Federal Perkins Loans	August 1	Yes	Yes
Federal Stafford Loans	August 1	Yes	Yes
School-Based Loans	NA	No	No
Outside and Private Loans	NA	No	No
Graduate Assistantships	March 1	Yes	No

Percentage of Students Receiving Aid	Full-Time
All students	80%
Minority students	100%
Women students	80%
International students	80%

UNIVERSITY OF MASSACHUSETTS BOSTON
College of Management

100 Morrissey Boulevard
Boston, Massachusetts 02125-3393
Telephone: 617-287-7720

Total Enrollment (1993-94)	Full-Time	Part-Time
	82	247

Cost of Attendance (1993-94)		
Academic Year		
Standard Course Load per Semester/Term		
(credit hours/units)	4	2
Semesters/Terms per Academic Year	2	2
Tuition and Fees		
Resident	$ 4,818	$2,110
Nonresident	$10,606	$5,002
Living Expenses	$ 9,350	$9,350
Summer Term		
(R = Required, O = Optional, N = None)	O	O
Standard Course Load	2	1
Tuition and Fees	$ 720	$ 360

Financial Aid Available	Deadline (fall starts)	Awarded to Full-Time	Part-Time
Gift Aid	NA	No	No
Federal College Work-Study	March 1	Yes	Yes
Federal Perkins Loans	March 1	Yes	Yes
Federal Stafford Loans	March 1	Yes	Yes
School-Based Loans	NA	No	No
Outside and Private Loans	Varies	Yes	Yes
Graduate Assistantships	September 1	Yes	Yes

UNIVERSITY OF MASSACHUSETTS DARTMOUTH
College of Business and Industry

MBA Program
Old Westport Road
North Dartmouth, Massachusetts 02747
Telephone: 508-999-8026

Total Enrollment (1993-94)	Full-Time	Part-Time
	21	76

Cost of Attendance (1993-94)		
Academic Year		
Standard Course Load per Semester/Term		
(credit hours/units)	9	3
Semesters/Terms per Academic Year	2	2
Tuition and Fees		
Resident	$3,268	$ 821
Nonresident	$7,085	$2,046
Living Expenses	$6,000	$6,000
Summer Term		
(R = Required, O = Optional, N = None)	N	N
Standard Course Load		
Tuition and Fees		
Resident		
Nonresident		

Financial Aid Available	Deadline (fall starts)	Awarded to Full-Time	Awarded to Part-Time
Gift Aid	NA	No	No
Federal College Work-Study	March 15	Yes	Yes
Federal Perkins Loans	March 1	Yes	Yes
Federal Stafford Loans	March 1	Yes	Yes
School-Based Loans	NA	No	No
Outside and Private Loans	NA	No	No
Graduate Assistantships	June 1	Yes	Yes

Percentage of Students Receiving Aid	Full-Time	Part-Time
All students		
Minority students		
Women students		
International students		

Twenty-five percent of M.B.A. students receive some kind of financial aid

UNIVERSITY OF MIAMI
School of Business Administration

P.O. Box 248505
Coral Gables, Florida 33124-6524
Telephone: 305-284-4607

Total Enrollment (1993-94)	Full-Time	Part-Time
	168	72

Cost of Attendance (1993-94)		
Academic Year		
Standard Course Load per Semester/Term		
(credit hours/units)	12	6
Semesters/Terms per Academic Year	2	2
Tuition and Fees	$15,534	$3,927
Living Expenses	$ 8,834	NA
Summer Term		
(R = Required, O = Optional, N = None)	O	O
Standard Course Load	6	3
Tuition and Fees	$ 3,927	$2,007

Financial Aid Available	Deadline (fall starts)	Awarded to Full-Time	Awarded to Part-Time
Gift Aid	March 1	Yes	No
Federal College Work-Study	March 1	Yes	No
Federal Perkins Loans	March 1	Yes	No
Federal Stafford Loans	None	Yes	Yes
School-Based Loans	NA	No	No
Outside and Private Loans	NA	No	No
Graduate Assistantships	April 1	Yes	No

Percentage of Students Receiving Aid	Full-Time	Part-Time
All students	55%	38%
Minority students		
Women students		
International students		

UNIVERSITY OF MICHIGAN
Michigan Business School

701 Tappan Street
Ann Arbor, Michigan 48109-1234
Telephone: 313-764-5139

Total Enrollment (1993-94)	Full-Time	Part-Time
	850	1,000

Cost of Attendance (1993-94)		
Academic Year		
Standard Course Load per Semester/Term		
(credit hours/units)	15	6
Semesters/Terms per Academic Year	2	2
Tuition and Fees	$6,354	$6,354
Living Expenses	$7,000	$6,500
Summer Term		
(R = Required, O = Optional, N = None)	N	O
Standard Course Load		1-2 courses
Tuition and Fees		$490/cr. hr.

Financial Aid Available	Deadline (fall starts)	Awarded to Full-Time	Awarded to Part-Time
Gift Aid	March 1	Yes	No
Federal College Work-Study	September 30	Yes	No
Federal Perkins Loans	September 30	Yes	No
Federal Stafford Loans	September 30	Yes	Yes
School-Based Loans	NA	No	No
Outside and Private Loans	September 30	Yes	Yes
Graduate Assistantships	NA	No	No

Percentage of Students Receiving Aid	Full-Time	Part-Time
All students	65%	4%
Minority students	84%	1%
Women students	69%	1%
International students	0%	0%

UNIVERSITY OF MICHIGAN - DEARBORN
School of Management

4901 Evergreen Road
Dearborn, Michigan 48128-1491
Telephone: 313-593-5460

Total Enrollment (1993-94)	Full-Time	Part-Time
	18	295

Cost of Attendance (1993-94)		
Academic Year		
Standard Course Load per Semester/Term		
(credit hours/units)	12	6
Semesters/Terms per Academic Year	3	3
Tuition and Fees		
Resident	$ 4,930	$3,076
Nonresident	$15,324	$8,948
Living Expenses	$ 5,973	$5,735
Summer Term		
(R = Required, O = Optional, N = None)	O	O
Standard Course Load	6	3
Tuition and Fees		
Resident	$ 1,538	$ 809
Nonresident	$ 4,474	$2,302

Financial Aid Available	Deadline (fall starts)	Awarded to Full-Time	Awarded to Part-Time
Gift Aid	April 1	Yes	Yes
Federal College Work-Study	April 1	Yes	Yes
Federal Perkins Loans	Apirl 1	Yes	Yes
Federal Stafford Loans	April 1	Yes	Yes
School-Based Loans	Emergency basis	Yes	Yes
Outside and Private Loans	NA	No	No
Graduate Assistantships	NA	No	No

Percentage of Students Receiving Aid	Full-Time	Part-Time
All students	0%	0%
Minority students	0%	0%
Women students	0%	0%
International students	0%	0%

UNIVERSITY OF MINNESOTA
Curtis L. Carlson School of Management

295 Humphrey Center
271 19th Avenue South
Minneapolis, Minnesota 55455
Telephone: 612-624-0006

Total Enrollment (1993-94)	Full-Time	Part-Time
	260	1,200

Cost of Attendance (1993-94)		
Academic Year		
Standard Course Load per Semester/Term		
(credit hours/units)	16	4-8
Semesters/Terms per Academic Year	3	3
Tuition and Fees		
Resident	$ 8,268	$ 202
Nonresident	$12,617	$ 202
Living Expenses	$13,000	$13,000
Summer Term		
(R = Required, O = Optional, N = None)	O	O
Standard Course Load	16	4
Tuition and Fees		
Resident	$ 2,756	$ 202
Nonresident	$ 4,206	$ 202

Financial Aid Available	Deadline (fall starts)	Awarded to Full-Time	Awarded to Part-Time
Gift Aid	preferred Dec. 1	Yes	No
Federal College Work-Study	End of May	Yes	No
Federal Perkins Loans	End of May	Yes	Yes
Federal Stafford Loans	End of May	Yes	Yes
School-Based Loans	NA	No	No
Outside and Private Loans	Varies	Yes	No
Graduate Assistantships	April 1	Yes	No

Percentage of Students Receiving Aid	Full-Time	Part-Time
All students	23%	0%
Minority students	95%	0%
Women students	NA	0%
International students	NA	0%

UNIVERSITY OF MISSISSIPPI
School of Business Administration

218 Conner Hall
University, Mississippi 38677
Telephone: 601-232-5820

Total Enrollment (1993-94)	Full-Time	Part-Time
	120	20

Cost of Attendance (1993-94)		
Academic Year		
Standard Course Load per Semester/Term		
(credit hours/units)	9-12 hrs.	6 hrs.
Semesters/Terms per Academic Year	2	2
Tuition and Fees		
Resident	$2,456	$1,332
Nonresident	$4,920	$2,976
Living Expenses	$6,546	$6,546
Summer Term		
(R = Required, O = Optional, N = None)	O	O
Standard Course Load	12	6
Tuition and Fees	$1,332	$ 666

Financial Aid Available	Deadline (fall starts)	Awarded to Full-Time	Awarded to Part-Time
Gift Aid	May 1	Yes	No
Federal College Work-Study	May 1	Yes	No
Federal Perkins Loans	May 1	Yes	No
Federal Stafford Loans	May 1	Yes	Yes
School-Based Loans	May 1	Yes	No
Outside and Private Loans	May 1	Yes	Yes
Graduate Assistantships	May 1	Yes	No

Percentage of Students Receiving Aid	Full-Time	Part-Time
All students	66%	66%
Minority students	98%	98%
Women students	66%	66%
International students	80%	80%

UNIVERSITY OF MISSOURI - COLUMBIA

303-D Middlebush Hall
Columbia, Missouri 65211
Telephone: 314-882-3694

Total Enrollment (1993-94)	Full-Time	Part-Time
	98	37

Cost of Attendance (1993-94)		
Academic Year		
Standard Course Load per Semester/Term		
(credit hours/units)	9-12	3-6
Semesters/Terms per Academic Year	3	3
Tuition and Fees		
Resident	$127/cr.	$127/cr.
Nonresident	$341/cr.	$341/cr.
Living Expenses		
Summer Term		
(R = Required, O = Optional, N = None)	O	O
Standard Course Load	3-6	3
Tuition and Fees		
Resident	Same as above	
Nonresident		

Financial Aid Available	Deadline (fall starts)	Awarded to Full-Time	Awarded to Part-Time
Gift Aid	None	Yes	No
Federal College Work-Study	March 1	Yes	Yes
Federal Perkins Loans	March 1	Yes	Yes
Federal Stafford Loans	None	Yes	Yes
School-Based Loans	None	Yes	Yes
Outside and Private Loans	None	Yes	Yes
Graduate Assistantships	None	Yes	No

Percentage of Students Receiving Aid	Full-Time	Part-Time
All students	30%	0%
Minority students	100%	0%
Women students	30%	0%
International students	10%	0%

UNIVERSITY OF MISSOURI - KANSAS CITY
Henry W. Bloch School of Business and Public Administration

5110 Cherry
Kansas City, Missouri 64110
Telephone: 816-235-2215

Total Enrollment (1993-94)	Full-Time	Part-Time
	100	300

Cost of Attendance (1993-94)		
Academic Year		
Standard Course Load per Semester/Term		
(credit hours/units)	9	3-6
Semesters/Terms per Academic Year	2	2
Tuition and Fees		
Resident	$2,300	$ 806-$1,581
Nonresident	$6,166	$2,094-$4,158
Living Expenses	NA	NA
Summer Term		
(R = Required, O = Optional, N = None)	O	O
Standard Course Load	3	3
Tuition and Fees	$ 418	$418

Financial Aid Available	Deadline (fall starts)	Awarded to Full-Time	Awarded to Part-Time
Gift Aid	March 1	Yes	Yes
Federal College Work-Study	March 15	Yes	Yes
Federal Perkins Loans	March 15	Yes	Yes
Federal Stafford Loans	March 15	Yes	Yes
School-Based Loans	NA	No	No
Outside and Private Loans	Varies	Yes	Yes
Graduate Assistantships	Ongoing	Yes	No

UNIVERSITY OF MISSOURI - ST. LOUIS
Graduate Programs in Business

461 Social Sciences and Business Building
8001 Natural Bridge Road
St. Louis, Missouri 63121
Telephone: 314-553-5885

Total Enrollment (1993-94)	Full-Time	Part-Time
	158	293

Cost of Attendance (1993-94)		
Academic Year		
Standard Course Load per Semester/Term		
(credit hours/units)	12	6
Semesters/Terms per Academic Year	2	2
Tuition and Fees		
Resident	$3,158	$1,582
Nonresident	$8,314	$4,160
Living Expenses	NA	NA
Summer Term		
(R = Required, O = Optional, N = None)	O	O
Standard Course Load	6	3
Tuition and Fees		
Resident	$ 791	$ 397
Nonresident	$2,080	$1,041

Financial Aid Available	Deadline (fall starts)	Awarded to Full-Time	Part-Time
Gift Aid	April 1	Yes	Yes
Federal College Work Study			
Federal Perkins Loans			
Federal Stafford Loans	April 1	Yes	Yes
School-Based Loans	April 1	Yes	Yes
Outside and Private Loans	April 1	Yes	Yes
Graduate Assistantships	July 1	Yes	No

Percentage of Students Receiving Aid *	Full-Time	Part-Time
All students	90%	64%
Minority students	94%	82%
Women students	84%	76%
International students	2%	0%

*Percentages are for UM-St. Louis graduate students as a whole

---

UNIVERSITY OF MONTANA
School of Business

Missoula, Montana 59812
Telephone: 406-243-4983

Total Enrollment (1993-94)	Full-Time	Part-Time
	110	70

Cost of Attendance (1993-94)		
Academic Year		
Standard Course Load per Semester/Term		
(credit hours/units)	12	3-6
Semesters/Terms per Academic Year	2-3	2-3
Tuition and Fees		
Resident	$1,150	$600
Nonresident	$3,138	$600
Living Expenses	$1,850	NA
Summer Term		
(R = Required, O = Optional, N = None)	O	O
Standard Course Load	6	3
Tuition and Fees		
Resident	$ 700	$600
Nonresident	$1,200	$600

Financial Aid Available	Deadline (fall starts)	Awarded to Full-Time	Part-Time
Gift Aid	March 1	Yes	No
Federal College Work-Study		Yes	No
Federal Perkins Loans		Yes	No
Federal Stafford Loans		Yes	No
School-Based Loans	NA	No	No
Outside and Private Loans	NA	No	No
Graduate Assistantships	March 1	Yes	No

Percentage of Students Receiving Aid	Full-Time	Part-Time
All students	10%	0%
Minority students	20%	0%
Women students	10%	0%
International students	10%	0%

UNIVERSITY OF NEBRASKA AT KEARNEY
Master of Business Administration

West Center E-200
Kearney, Nebraska 68849-5180
Telephone: 308-234-8346

Total Enrollment (1993-94)	Full-Time	Part-Time
	30	96

Cost of Attendance (1993-94)		
Academic Year		
Standard Course Load per Semester/Term		
(credit hours/units)	12	3-6
Semesters/Terms per Academic Year	2-3	1-2
Tuition and Fees		
Resident	$57/hr.	$57/hr.
Nonresident	$98/hr.	$98/hr.
Living Expenses	$3,000	
Summer Term		
(R = Required, O = Optional, N = None)	O	O
Standard Course Load		
Tuition and Fees		
Resident	Same as above	
Nonresident		

Financial Aid Available	Deadline (fall starts)	Awarded to Full-Time	Part-Time
Gift Aid	March 1	Yes	No
Federal College Work-Study	March 1	Yes	No
Federal Perkins Loans	NA	No	No
Federal Stafford Loans	March 1	Yes	No
School-Based Loans	NA	No	No
Outside and Private Loans	March 1	Yes	No
Graduate Assistantships	May 1	Yes	Yes

Percentage of Students Receiving Aid	Full-Time
All students	37%
Minority students	44%
Women students	48%
International students	28%

UNIVERSITY OF NEBRASKA - LINCOLN
College of Business Administration

CBA 126
Lincoln, Nebraska 68359
Telephone: 402-472-2338

Total Enrollment (1993-94)	Full-Time	Part-Time
	139	146

Cost of Attendance (1993-94)		
Academic Year		
Standard Course Load per Semester/Term		
(credit hours/units)	12	6
Semesters/Terms per Academic Year	2	2
Tuition and Fees		
Resident	$2,400	$1,190
Nonresident	$5,418	$2,700
Living Expenses	$8,087	$8,087
Summer Term		
(R = Required, O = Optional, N = None)	O	O
Standard Course Load	12	6
Tuition and Fees		
Resident	$1,134	$ 574
Nonresident	$2,643	$1,328

Financial Aid Available	Deadline (fall starts)	Awarded to Full-Time	Part-Time
Gift Aid	February 15	Yes	Yes
Federal College Work-Study	None	Yes	Yes
Federal Perkins Loans	None	Yes	Yes
Federal Stafford Loans	None	Yes	Yes
School-Based Loans	None	Yes	Yes
Outside and Private Loans			
Graduate Assistantships	NA	No	No

UNIVERSITY OF NEBRASKA AT OMAHA
College of Business

Room 414
60th & Dodge Streets
Omaha, Nebraska 68182-0048
Telephone: 402-554-4836

Total Enrollment (1993-94)	Full-Time	Part-Time
	54	356

Cost of Attendance (1993-94)		
Academic Year		
Standard Course Load per Semester/Term		
(credit hours/units)	9	3-6
Semesters/Terms per Academic Year	2 + summer	2 + summer
Tuition and Fees		
Resident	$ 71/cr. hr.	$ 71/cr. hr.
Nonresident	$156/cr. hr.	$156/cr. hr.
Living Expenses	Information not available	
Summer Term		
(R = Required, O = Optional, N = None)	O	O
Standard Course Load	6	3
Tuition and Fees		
Resident	Same as above	
Nonresident		

Financial Aid Available	Deadline (fall starts)	Awarded to Full-Time	Awarded to Part-Time
Gift Aid	December 1	Yes	No
Federal College Work-Study	NA	No	Yes
Federal Perkins Loans	March 1	Yes	Yes
Federal Stafford Loans	Varies	Yes	Yes
School-Based Loans	NA	No	No
Outside and Private Loans	NA	No	No
Graduate Assistantships	July 1	Yes	No

Percentage of Students Receiving Aid	Full-Time	Part-Time
All students	50%	50%
Minority students	NA	NA
Women students	NA	NA
International students	NA	NA

UNIVERSITY OF NEVADA, LAS VEGAS
College of Business and Economics

4505 Maryland Parkway
Box 456031
Las Vegas, Nevada 89154-6031
Telephone: 702-895-3655

Total Enrollment (1993-94)	Full-Time	Part-Time
	75	225

Cost of Attendance (1993-94)		
Academic Year		
Standard Course Load per Semester/Term		
(credit hours/units)	12	6
Semesters/Terms per Academic Year	2	2
Tuition and Fees		
Resident	$ 930	$465
Nonresident	$4,300	
Living Expenses	$5,000	
Summer Term		
(R = Required, O = Optional, N = None)	O	O
Standard Course Load	6	6
Tuition and Fees	$ 480	$480

Financial Aid Available	Deadline (fall starts)	Awarded to Full-Time	Awarded to Part-Time
Gift Aid	February 2	Yes	Yes
Federal College Work-Study	February 15	Yes	Yes
Federal Perkins Loans	February 15	Yes	Yes
Federal Stafford Loans	February 15	Yes	Yes
School-Based Loans	As needed	Yes	No
Outside and Private Loans	Varies	Yes	No
Graduate Assistantships	March 1	Yes	No

Percentage of Students Receiving Aid	Full-Time	Part-Time
All students	40%	10%
Minority students	50%	10%
Women students	50%	10%
International students	40%	10%

UNIVERSITY OF NEW HAMPSHIRE
Whittemore School of Business and Economics

15 College Road, McConnell Hall
Durham, New Hampshire 03824-3593
Telephone: 603-862-1367

Total Enrollment (1993-94)	Full-Time
	117

Cost of Attendance (1993-94)

Academic Year	
Standard Course Load per Semester/Term	
(credit hours/units)	15
Semesters/Terms per Academic Year	2
Tuition and Fees	
Resident	$ 4,605
Nonresident	$12,235
Living Expenses	
Summer Term	
(R = Required, O = Optional, N = None)	O
Standard Course Load	3
Tuition and Fees	
Resident	$ 435
Nonresident	$ 480

Financial Aid Available

	Deadline (fall starts)	Awarded to Full-Time
Gift Aid	March 1	Yes
Federal College Work-Study	March 1	Yes
Federal Perkins Loans	March 1	Yes
Federal Stafford Loans	March 1	Yes
School-Based Loans		No
Outside and Private Loans		No
Graduate Assistantships	March 1	Yes

Percentage of Students Receiving Aid	Full-Time
All students	60%
Minority students	15%
Women students	30%
International students	20%

THE UNIVERSITY OF NORTH CAROLINA AT CHAPEL HILL
The Kenan-Flagler Business School

Campus Box 3490, Carroll Hall
Chapel Hill, North Carolina 27599-3490
Telephone: 919-962-3236

Total Enrollment (1993-94)	Full-Time	Part-Time
	384	128

Cost of Attendance (1993-94)

Academic Year		
Standard Course Load per Semester/Term		
(credit hours/units)	15	6
Semesters/Terms per Academic Year	2	4
Tuition and Fees		
Resident	$1,996	$8,250
Nonresident	$9,038	$8,250
Living Expenses	$7,200	
Summer Term		
(R = Required, O = Optional, N = None)	N	R
Standard Course Load		6
Tuition and Fees		
Resident		$2,750
Nonresident		$2,750

Financial Aid Available

	Deadline (fall starts)	Awarded to Full-Time	Part-Time
Gift Aid	March 1	Yes	Yes
Federal College Work-Study	NA	No	No
Federal Perkins Loans	NA	No	No
Federal Stafford Loans	March 1	Yes	Yes
School-Based Loans	NA	No	No
Outside and Private Loans	March 1	Yes	Yes
Graduate Assistantships	NA	No	No

Percentage of Students Receiving Aid	Full-Time	Part-Time
All students	62%	10%
Minority students	100%	2%
Women students	NA	5%
International students	0%	0%

THE UNIVERSITY OF NORTH CAROLINA AT CHARLOTTE
The Belk College of Business Administration

Charlotte, North Carolina 28223
Telephone: 704-547-2461

Total Enrollment (1993-94)	Full-Time	Part-Time
	50	325

Cost of Attendance (1993-94)		
Academic Year		
Standard Course Load per Semester/Term		
(credit hours/units)	9	3 or 6
Semesters/Terms per Academic Year	2	2
Tuition and Fees		
Resident	$1,253	$ 482
Nonresident	$7,389	$5,362
Living Expenses	$1,715	$ 500
Summer Term		
(R = Required, O = Optional, N = None)	O	O
Standard Course Load	1 course/sem.	1 course/sem.
Tuition and Fees		
Resident	$ 220	
Nonresident	$1,650	

Financial Aid Available	Deadline (fall starts)	Awarded to Full-Time
Gift Aid	April 1	Yes
Federal College Work-Study	April 1	Yes
Federal Perkins Loans	April 1	Yes
Federal Stafford Loans	April 1	Yes
School-Based Loans	April 1	Yes
Outside and Private Loans	April 1	Yes
Graduate Assistantships	April 1	Yes

Percentage of Students Receiving Aid	Full-Time
All students	5%
Minority students	5%
Women students	5%
International students	5%

THE UNIVERSITY OF NORTH CAROLINA AT GREENSBORO
Joseph M. Bryan School of Business and Economics

MBA Program
1000 Spring Garden Street
220 Bryan Building
Greensboro, North Carolina 27412-5001
Telephone: 919-334-5390

Total Enrollment (1993-94)	Full-Time	Part-Time
	41	207

Cost of Attendance (1993-94)		
Academic Year		
Standard Course Load per Semester/Term		
(credit hours/units)	12	6
Semesters/Terms per Academic Year	2	2
Tuition and Fees		
Resident	$1,717	$1,147
Nonresident	$8,759	$6,429
Living Expenses	$5,000	Varies
Summer Term		
(R = Required, O = Optional, N = None)	O	O
Standard Course Load	Varies	Varies
Tuition and Fees		
Resident	$ 251	$ 251
Nonresident	$1,041	$1,041

Financial Aid Available	Deadline (fall starts)	Awarded to Full-Time	Part-Time
Gift Aid	March 1	Yes	Yes
Federal College Work-Study	March 1	Yes	No
Federal Perkins Loans	March 1	Yes	Yes
Federal Stafford Loans	March 1	Yes	Yes
School-Based Loans	NA	No	No
Outside and Private Loans	March 1	Yes	Yes
Graduate Assistantships	NA	Yes	No

Percentage of Students Receiving Aid	Full-Time
All students	33%
Minority students	
Women students	
International students	

UNIVERSITY OF NORTH CAROLINA - WILMINGTON

Cameron Hall
601 South College Road
Wilmington, North Carolina 28403
Telephone: 910-395-3777

Total Enrollment (1993-94)	Part-Time
	103

Cost of Attendance (1993-94)	
Academic Year	
Standard Course Load per Semester/Term	
(credit hours/units)	6
Semesters/Terms per Academic Year	4
Tuition and Fees	
Resident	$ 651
Nonresident	$3,178
Living Expenses	
Summer Term	
(R = Required, O = Optional, N = None)	O
Standard Course Load	6
Tuition and Fees	
Resident	$ 651
Nonresident	$3,178

Financial Aid Available	Deadline (fall starts)	Awarded to Part-Time
Gift Aid	March 31	Yes
Federal College Work-Study	NA	
Federal Perkins Loans	NA	
Federal Stafford Loans	NA	
School-Based Loans	NA	
Outside and Private Loans	NA	
Graduate Assistantships	March 31	Yes

Percentage of Students Receiving Aid	Part-Time
All students	13%
Minority students	
Women students	7%
International students	

UNIVERSITY OF NORTH DAKOTA
College of Business and Public Administration

P.O. Box 8098
Grand Forks, North Dakota 58202-8098
Telephone: 701-777-2135

Total Enrollment (1993-94)	Full-Time	Part-Time
	22	81

Cost of Attendance (1993-94)		
Academic Year		
Standard Course Load per Semester/Term		
(credit hours/units)	12	6
Semesters/Terms per Academic Year	2	2
Tuition and Fees		
Resident	$2,508	$1,554
Nonresident	$6,174	$3,387
Living Expenses	$3,500	$3,250
Summer Term		
(R = Required, O = Optional, N = None)	O	O
Standard Course Load	6-8	3
Tuition and Fees		
Resident	$ 594	$ 297
Nonresident	$1,462	$ 731

Financial Aid Available	Deadline (fall starts)	Awarded to Full-Time	Awarded to Part-Time
Gift Aid	May 1	Yes	Yes
Federal College Work-Study	None	Yes	Yes
Federal Perkins Loans	March 1	Yes	Yes
Federal Stafford Loans	May 1	Yes	Yes
School-Based Loans	May 1	Yes	Yes
Outside and Private Loans	None	Yes	Yes
Graduate Assistantships	None	Yes	No

UNIVERSITY OF NORTHERN IOWA
College of Business Administration

Cedar Falls, Iowa 50614-0123
Telephone: 319-273-6243

Total Enrollment (1993-94)	Full-Time	Part-Time
	50	21

Cost of Attendance (1993-94)		
Academic Year		
Standard Course Load per Semester/Term		
(credit hours/units)	≥ 9	< 9
Semesters/Terms per Academic Year	2	2
Tuition and Fees		
Resident	$2,624	$351/hr. + $70/sem.
Nonresident	$6,468	$351/hr. + $70/sem.
Living Expenses	$2,785	$2,785
Summer Term		
(R = Required, O = Optional, N = None)	N	N
Standard Course Load		
Tuition and Fees		
Resident		
Nonresident		

Financial Aid Available	Deadline (fall starts)	Awarded to Full-Time	Awarded to Part-Time
Gift Aid	None	Yes	No
Federal College Work-Study	NA	No	No
Federal Perkins Loans	None	Yes	Yes
Federal Stafford Loans	None	Yes	Yes
School-Based Loans	NA	No	No
Outside and Private Loans	NA	No	No
Graduate Assistantships	None	Yes	No

UNIVERSITY OF NOTRE DAME
MBA Program

109 Hurley Building
Notre Dame, Indiana 46556
Telephone: 219-631-8488

Total Enrollment (1993-94)	Full-Time
	265

Cost of Attendance (1993-94)	
Academic Year	
Standard Course Load per Semester/Term	
(credit hours/units)	16
Semesters/Terms per Academic Year	2
Tuition and Fees	$17,050
Living Expenses	$ 6,900
Summer Term	
(R = Required, O = Optional, N = None)	R for 3-semester term; N for 2-year
Standard Course Load	14
Tuition and Fees	$ 6,560

Financial Aid Available	Deadline (fall starts)	Awarded to Full-Time
Gift Aid	February 25	Yes
Federal College Work-Study	None	Yes
Federal Perkins Loans	None	Yes
Federal Stafford Loans	None	Yes
School-Based Loans	None	Yes
Outside and Private Loans	NA	
Graduate Assistantships	None	Yes

Percentage of Students Receiving Aid	Full-Time
All students	70%
Minority students	100%
Women students	69%
International students	

UNIVERSITY OF OKLAHOMA
Graduate School of Business Administration

307 West Brooks, Room 203
Norman, Oklahoma 73019
Telephone: 405-325-4107

Total Enrollment (1993-94)	Full-Time	Part-Time
	158	96

Cost of Attendance (1993-94)

Academic Year		
Standard Course Load per Semester/Term		
(credit hours/units)	12	6
Semesters/Terms per Academic Year	3	3
Tuition and Fees		
Resident	$ 76	$ 76
Nonresident	$ 225	$ 225
Living Expenses	$12,400	$6,200
Summer Term		
(R = Required, O = Optional, N = None)	O	O
Standard Course Load	6	3
Tuition and Fees		
Resident	Same as above	
Nonresident		

Financial Aid Available

	Deadline (fall starts)	Awarded to Full-Time	Part-Time
Gift Aid	August 1	Yes	No
Federal College Work-Study	March 1	Yes	No
Federal Perkins Loans	March 1	Yes	Yes
Federal Stafford Loans	March 1	Yes	Yes
School-Based Loans	March 1	Yes	Yes
Outside and Private Loans	None	Yes	Yes
Graduate Assistantships	August	Yes	No

Percentage of Students Receiving Aid	Full-Time	Part-Time
All students	22%	0%
Minority students	7%	0%
Women students	61%	0%
International students	32%	0%

UNIVERSITY OF OREGON
Graduate School of Management

Eugene, Oregon 97403
Telephone: 503-346-3306

Total Enrollment (1993-94)	Full-Time	Part-Time
	156	15

Cost of Attendance (1993-94)

Academic Year		
Standard Course Load per Semester/Term		
(credit hours/units)	12	6
Semesters/Terms per Academic Year	3	3
Tuition and Fees		
Resident	$4,210	$2,955
Nonresident	$7,680	$5,277
Living Expenses	$6,625	$6,625
Summer Term		
(R = Required, O = Optional, N = None)	O	O
Standard Course Load	9	6
Tuition and Fees		
Resident	Not available at this time	
Nonresident		

Financial Aid Available

	Deadline (fall starts)	Awarded to Full-Time	Part-Time
Gift Aid	January 31	Yes	No
Federal College Work-Study	January 31	Yes	Yes
Federal Perkins Loans	January 31	Yes	Yes
Federal Stafford Loans	January 31	Yes	Yes
School-Based Loans	NA		
Outside and Private Loans	NA		
Graduate Assistantships	March 15	Yes	No

(Not available to first-year M.B.A.s)

Percentage of Students Receiving Aid	Full-Time	Part-Time
All students	19%	0%
Minority students	50%	0%
Women students	15%	0%
International students	11%	0%

UNIVERSITY OF THE PACIFIC
School of Business and Public Administration

3601 Pacific Avenue
Stockton, California 95211
Telephone: 209-946-2642

Total Enrollment (1993-94)

	Full-Time	Part-Time
	27	32

Cost of Attendance (1993-94)

	Full-Time	Part-Time
Academic Year		
Standard Course Load per Semester/Term		
(credit hours/units)	12	6
Semesters/Terms per Academic Year	2	2
Tuition and Fees	$11,640	$5,820
Living Expenses	$ 7,000	$7,000
Summer Term		
(R = Required, O = Optional, N = None)	O	O
Standard Course Load	6	3
Tuition and Fees	$ 2,910	$1,455

Financial Aid Available

	Deadline (fall starts)	Awarded to Full-Time	Awarded to Part-Time
Gift Aid	March 2	Yes	No
Federal College Work-Study	March 2	Yes	No
Federal Perkins Loans		No	No
Federal Stafford Loans	March 2	Yes	Yes
School-Based Loans		No	No
Outside and Private Loans		No	No
Graduate Assistantships	March 2	Yes	No

Percentage of Students Receiving Aid

	Full-Time	Part-Time
All students	80%	25%
Minority students	80%	50%
Women students	80%	25%
International students	66%	0%

UNIVERSITY OF PITTSBURGH
Katz Graduate School of Business

276 Mervis Hall
Pittsburgh, Pennsylvania 15260
Telephone: 412-648-1700

Total Enrollment (1993-94)

	Full-Time	Part-Time
	330	570

Cost of Attendance (1993-94)

	Full-Time	Part-Time
Academic Year		
Standard Course Load per Semester/Term		
(credit hours/units)	16-18	6
Semesters/Terms per Academic Year	3	3
Tuition and Fees		
Resident	$13,090	$ 6,768
Nonresident	$21,844	$12,420
Living Expenses	$10,400	NA
Summer Term		
(R = Required, O = Optional, N = None)	R	R
Standard Course Load	16-18	6
Tuition and Fees		
Resident	Same as above	
Nonresident		

Financial Aid Available

	Deadline (fall starts)	Awarded to Full-Time	Awarded to Part-Time
Gift Aid	None	Yes	No
Federal College Work-Study	NA	Yes	No
Federal Perkins Loans	NA	No	No
Federal Stafford Loans	June 1	Yes	Yes
School-Based Loans	None	Yes	No
Outside and Private Loans	Variable	Yes	Yes
Graduate Assistantships	NA	No	No

Percentage of Students Receiving Aid

	Full-Time	Part-Time
All students	80%	35%
Minority students	90%	70%
Women students	85%	65%
International students	0%	0%

UNIVERSITY OF PORTLAND

5000 North Willamette Boulevard
Portland, Oregon 97203
Telephone: 800-227-4568

Total Enrollment (1993-94)	Full-Time	Part-Time
	140	25

Cost of Attendance (1993-94)		
Academic Year		
Standard Course Load per Semester/Term		
(credit hours/units)	12	Variable
Semesters/Terms per Academic Year	2	2
Tuition and Fees	$375/cr.	$375/cr.
Living Expenses	$4,100	$4,100
Summer Term		
(R = Required, O = Optional, N = None)	O	O
Standard Course Load	6	Variable
Tuition and Fees	$ 260	$ 260

Financial Aid Available	Deadline (fall starts)	Awarded to Full-Time	Part-Time
Gift Aid		No	No
Federal College Work-Study	Rolling	Yes	Yes
Federal Perkins Loans	April 15	Yes	Yes
Federal Stafford Loans	Rolling	Yes	Yes
School-Based Loans		No	No
Outside and Private Loans	Rolling	Yes	Yes
Graduate Assistantships		No	No

Percentage of Students Receiving Aid	Full-Time	Part-Time
All students	23%	23%
Minority students	NA	NA
Women students	NA	NA
International students	0%	0%

UNIVERSITY OF PUERTO RICO
Graduate School of Business Administration

Box 23325, University Station
San Juan, Puerto Rico 00931-3325
Telephone: 809-764-0000, extension 2043

Total Enrollment (1993-94)	Full-Time	Part-Time
	90	282

Cost of Attendance (1993-94)		
Academic Year		
Standard Course Load per Semester/Term		
(credit hours/units)	8	2-3
Semesters/Terms per Academic Year	3	2
Tuition and Fees		
Resident (U.S.)	$300-$1,850	$300-$1,850
Nonresident (non-U.S.)	$3,500 or $279/cr.	$3,500 or $279/cr.
Living Expenses	Information not available	
Summer Term		
(R = Required, O = Optional, N = None)	O	O
Standard Course Load	6	3
Tuition and Fees		
Resident	$ 75/cr.	$ 75/cr.
Nonresident	$279/cr.	$279/cr.

Financial Aid Available	Deadline (fall starts)	Awarded to Full-Time	Part-Time
Gift Aid	April 30	Yes	No
Federal College Work-Study	April 30	Yes	No
Federal Perkins Loans	April 30	Yes	No
Federal Stafford Loans	April 30	Yes	No
School-Based Loans	NA	No	No
Outside and Private Loans	NA	No	No
Graduate Assistantships	Varies	Yes	No

Percentage of Students Receiving Aid	Full-Time	Part-Time
All students	24%	76%
Minority students		
Women students	34%	64%
International students		2%

UNIVERSITY OF PUERTO RICO, MAYAGUEZ CAMPUS
Graduate School of Business Administration

Box 5000
Mayaguez, Puerto Rico 00681-5000
Telephone: 809-265-3887
         809-265-3800

Total Enrollment (1993-94)	Full-Time	Part-Time
	25	42

Cost of Attendance (1993-94)		
Academic Year		
Standard Course Load per Semester/Term		
(credit hours/units)	12	6
Semesters/Terms per Academic Year	2	2
Tuition and Fees		
Resident	$ 905	$ 515
Nonresident	$1,750	
Living Expenses		
Summer Term		
(R = Required, O = Optional, N = None)	O	O
Standard Course Load	3	3
Tuition and Fees		
Resident	$ 230	$ 230
Nonresident		

Financial Aid Available	Deadline (fall starts)	Awarded to Full-Time	Part-Time
Gift Aid			
Federal College Work-Study			
Federal Perkins Loans			
Federal Stafford Loans			
School-Based Loans			
Outside and Private Loans			
Graduate Assistantships	April 15	Yes	

Percentage of Students Receiving Aid	Full-Time
All students	31%
Minority students	NA
Women students	32%
International students	100%

UNIVERSITY OF RHODE ISLAND
College of Business Administration

210 Ballentine Hall
Kingston, Rhode Island 02881
Telephone: 401-792-5000

Total Enrollment (1993-94)	Full-Time	Part-Time
	99	219

Cost of Attendance (1993-94)		
Academic Year		
Standard Course Load per Semester/Term		
(credit hours/units)	15	6
Semesters/Terms per Academic Year	2	2
Tuition and Fees		
Resident	$3,582	$1,048
Nonresident	$7,520	$2,338
Living Expenses	$8,885	$8,885
Summer Term		
(R = Required, O = Optional, N = None)	O	O
Standard Course Load	6	3
Tuition and Fees		
Resident	$170/cr.	$170/cr.
Nonresident	$385/cr.	$385/cr.

Financial Aid Available	Deadline (fall starts)	Awarded to Full-Time	Part-Time
Gift Aid	April 15	Yes	Yes
Federal College Work-Study	NA	Yes	No
Federal Perkins Loans	NA	Yes	No
Federal Stafford Loans	NA	Yes	Yes
School-Based Loans	NA	Yes	No
Outside and Private Loans	NA	Yes	No
Graduate Assistantships	April 15	Yes	No

UNIVERSITY OF RICHMOND
Richard S. Reynolds Graduate School, E. Claiborne Robins School of Business

Richmond, Virginia 23173
Telephone: 804-289-8553

Total Enrollment (1993-94)	Full-Time	Part-Time
	28	205

Cost of Attendance (1993-94)

Academic Year		
Standard Course Load per Semester/Term		
(credit hours/units)	12	6
Semesters/Terms per Academic Year	2	2
Tuition and Fees	$13,640	$8,160
Living Expenses	$ 6,450	$6,450
Summer Term		
(R = Required, O = Optional, N = None)	O	O
Standard Course Load	6	6
Tuition and Fees	$ 1,230	$1,230

Financial Aid Available

	Deadline (fall starts)	Awarded to Full-Time	Awarded to Part-Time
Gift Aid	NA	No	No
Federal College Work-Study	NA	No	No
Federal Perkins Loans	NA	No	No
Federal Stafford Loans	NA	Yes	Yes
School-Based Loans	NA	No	No
Outside and Private Loans	NA	No	No
Graduate Assistantships	July 1	Yes	No

Percentage of Students Receiving Aid	Full-Time	Part-Time
All students	50%	<1%
Minority students		
Women students		
International students		

UNIVERSITY OF ROCHESTER
William E. Simon Graduate School of Business Administration

Schlegel Hall
Rochester, New York 14627
Telephone: 716-275-3533

Total Enrollment (1993-94)	Full-Time	Part-Time
	400	400

Cost of Attendance (1993-94)

Academic Year		
Standard Course Load per Semester/Term		
(credit hours/units)	9	6
Semesters/Terms per Academic Year	3	3
Tuition and Fees	$18,000	$10,800
Living Expenses	$ 9,000	$ 9,000
Summer Term		
(R = Required, O = Optional, N = None)	O	O
Standard Course Load	9	6
Tuition and Fees	$ 5,400	$ 3,600

Financial Aid Available

	Deadline (fall starts)	Awarded to Full-Time	Awarded to Part-Time
Gift Aid	March 1	Yes	No
Federal College Work-Study	NA	No	No
Federal Perkins Loans	NA	No	No
Federal Stafford Loans	June 1	Yes	Yes
School-Based Loans	June 1	Yes	Yes
Outside and Private Loans	June 1	Yes	Yes
Graduate Assistantships	None	Yes	No

Percentage of Students Receiving Aid	Full-Time	Part-Time
All students	80%	5%
Minority students	100%	5%
Women students	80%	5%
International students	40%	NA

UNIVERSITY OF ST. THOMAS
Cameron School of Business

3800 Montrose Boulevard
Houston, Texas 77006
Telephone: 713-525-2100

Total Enrollment (1993-94)	Full-Time	Part-Time
	288	865

Cost of Attendance (1993-94)		
Academic Year		
Standard Course Load per Semester/Term		
(credit hours/units)	9	3
Semesters/Terms per Academic Year	3	3
Tuition and Fees	$295	$295
Living Expenses		
Summer Term		
(R = Required, O = Optional, N = None)	O	O
Standard Course Load	6	3
Tuition and Fees	$295	$295

Financial Aid Available	Deadline (fall starts)	Awarded to Full-Time	Part-Time
Gift Aid	None	No	No
Federal College Work-Study	None	Yes	Yes
Federal Perkins Loans	None	No	No
Federal Stafford Loans	None	Yes	Yes
School-Based Loans	NA	No	No
Outside and Private Loans	NA	No	No
Graduate Assistantships	None	Yes	Yes

Percentage of Students Receiving Aid	Full-Time	Part-Time
All students	5%	8%
Minority students	NA	NA
Women students	NA	NA
International students	NA	NA

UNIVERSITY OF SAN DIEGO
School of Business Administration

5998 Alcala Park
San Diego, California 92110-2492
Telephone: 619-260-4524
　　　　　800-248-4873

Total Enrollment (1993-94)	Full-Time	Part-Time
	135	315

Cost of Attendance (1993-94)		
Academic Year		
Standard Course Load per Semester/Term		
(credit hours/units)	9-12	3-6
Semesters/Terms per Academic Year	2	2
Tuition and Fees	$4,095-$5,460	$1,365-$2,730
Living Expenses	$4,700-$8,600	$4,700-$8,600
Summer Term		
(R = Required, O = Optional, N = None)	O	O
Standard Course Load	6	3
Tuition and Fees		
Resident	$2,730	$1,365
Nonresident	$2,730	$1,365

Financial Aid Available	Deadline (fall starts)	Awarded to Full-Time	Part-Time
Gift Aid	May 1	Yes	Yes
Federal College Work-Study	May 1	Yes	Yes
Federal Perkins Loans	May 1	Yes	Yes
Federal Stafford Loans	NA	Yes	Yes
School-Based Loans	NA	No	No
Outside and Private Loans	NA	Yes	Yes
Graduate Assistantships	NA	Yes	Yes

Percentage of Students Receiving Aid	Full-Time
All students	16-37% of all students
Minority students	
Women students	
International students	33%

UNIVERSITY OF SAN FRANCISCO
McLaren School of Business

MBA Program
Ignatian Heights
San Francisco, California 94117-1080
Telephone: 415-666-6314

Total Enrollment (1993-94)	Full-Time	Part-Time
	260	220

Cost of Attendance (1993-94)		
Academic Year		
Standard Course Load per Semester/Term		
(credit hours/units)	12	4-6
Semesters/Terms per Academic Year	3	3
Tuition and Fees	$ 492	$ 492
Living Expenses	$10,000	$10,000
Summer Term		
(R = Required, O = Optional, N = None)	O	O
Standard Course Load	6-12	6-12
Tuition and Fees	$ 492	$ 492

Financial Aid Available	Deadline (fall starts)	Awarded to Full-Time	Part-Time
Gift Aid	March 2	Yes	No
Federal College Work-Study	March 2	Yes	No
Federal Perkins Loans	March 2	Yes	No
Federal Stafford Loans	March 2	Yes	Yes
School-Based Loans	NA	No	No
Outside and Private Loans	March 2	Yes	Yes
Graduate Assistantships	None	Yes	No

Percentage of Students Receiving Aid	Full-Time	Part-Time
All students	8%	14%
Minority students	<1%	1%
Women students	6%	11%
International students	2%	5%

UNIVERSITY OF SCRANTON
The Graduate School

MBA Program
Scranton, Pennsylvania 18510-4631
Telephone: 717-941-7600
800-366-4723

Total Enrollment (1993-94)	Full-Time	Part-Time
	60	125

Cost of Attendance (1993-94)		
Academic Year		
Standard Course Load per Semester/Term		
(credit hours/units)	12	3-6
Semesters/Terms per Academic Year	2	2
Tuition and Fees	$8,400	$350/cr.
Living Expenses	$6,600	
Summer Term		
(R = Required, O = Optional, N = None)	O	O
Standard Course Load	6	3
Tuition and Fees	$2,100	$1,050

Financial Aid Available	Deadline (fall starts)	Awarded to Full-Time	Part-Time
Gift Aid	NA	No	No
Federal College Work-Study	April 15	Yes	Yes
Federal Perkins Loans	NA	No	No
Federal Stafford Loans	None	Yes	Yes
School-Based Loans	NA	No	No
Outside and Private Loans	NA	No	No
Graduate Assistantships	March 1	Yes	No

UNIVERSITY OF SOUTH CAROLINA
College of Business Administration

H. William Close Building
Columbia, South Carolina 29208
Telephone: 803-777-2306

Total Enrollment (1993-94)	Full-Time	Part-Time
	831	325

Cost of Attendance (1993-94)		
Academic Year		
Standard Course Load per Semester/Term		
(credit hours/units)	15	6
Semesters/Terms per Academic Year	2	3
Tuition and Fees		
Resident	$3,230	$2,772
Nonresident	$6,524	$5,634
Living Expenses	$9,000	$ 900
Summer Term		
(R = Required, O = Optional, N = None)	R	R
Standard Course Load	6	3
Tuition and Fees		
Resident	$ 924	$ 462
Nonresident	$1,878	$ 939

Financial Aid Available	Deadline (fall starts)	Awarded to Full-Time	Awarded to Part-Time
Gift Aid	February 1	Yes	No
Federal College Work-Study	April 15	Yes	No
Federal Perkins Loans	April 15	Yes	Yes
Federal Stafford Loans	April 15	Yes	Yes
School-Based Loans	April 15	Yes	Yes
Outside and Private Loans	NA	No	No
Graduate Assistantships	February 1	Yes	No

Percentage of Students Receiving Aid	Full-Time	Part-Time
All students	40%	0%
Minority students	40%	0%
Women students	40%	0%
International sudents	30%	0%

UNIVERSITY OF SOUTH DAKOTA
Graduate Business Programs

210 Patterson Hall
414 East Clark Street
Vermillion, South Dakota 57069
Telephone: 605-677-5232

Total Enrollment (1993-94)	Full-Time	Part-Time
	40	340

Cost of Attendance (1993-94)		
Academic Year		
Standard Course Load per Semester/Term		
(credit hours/units)	12	3-6
Semesters/Terms per Academic Year	2	2
Tuition and Fees		
Resident	$1,167	$ 292-$ 584
Nonresident	$2,002	$ 500-$1,001
Living Expenses	$7,000	NA
Summer Term		
(R = Required, O = Optional, N = None)	R	R
Standard Course Load	9	3-6
Tuition and Fees		
Resident	$ 876	$ 292-$ 584
Nonresident	$1,502	$ 501-$1,001

Financial Aid Available	Deadline (fall starts)	Awarded to Full-Time	Awarded to Part-Time
Gift Aid	NA	No	No
Federal College Work-Study	NA	No	No
Federal Perkins Loans	February 15	Yes	No
Federal Stafford Loans	None	Yes	No
School-Based Loans	None	Yes	Yes
Outside and Private Loans	None	Yes	Yes
Graduate Assistantships	May 1	Yes	No

Percentage of Students Receiving Aid	Full-Time	Part-Time
All students	35%	0%
Minority students	25%	0%
Women students	20%	0%
International students	20%	0%

UNIVERSITY OF SOUTH FLORIDA
College of Business Administration

4202 East Fowler Avenue
Tampa, Florida 33620
Telephone: 813-974-3335

Total Enrollment (1993-94)	Full-Time	Part-Time
	171	371

Cost of Attendance (1993-94)		
Academic Year		
Standard Course Load per Semester/Term		
(credit hours/units)	12	6
Semesters/Terms per Academic Year	3	3
Tuition and Fees		
Resident	$1,365	$ 683
Nonresident	$4,402	$2,201
Living Expenses	$5,000	$4,800
Summer Term		
(R = Required, O = Optional, N = None)	O	O
Standard Course Load	6	3
Tuition and Fees		
Resident	$ 623	$ 341
Nonresident	$2,201	$1,100

Financial Aid Available	Deadline (fall starts)	Awarded to Full-Time	Part-Time
Gift Aid	Varies	Yes	No
Federal College Work-Study	April 2	Yes	Yes
Federal Perkins Loans	April 2	Yes	Yes
Federal Stafford Loans	May 15	Yes	Yes
School-Based Loans	April 2	Yes	Yes
Outside and Private Loans	Open	No	No
Graduate Assistantships	Open	No	No

Percentage of Students Receiving Aid	Full-Time	Part-Time
All students	30%	NA
Minority students	70%	NA
Women students	14%	NA
International students	12%	NA

UNIVERSITY OF SOUTHERN CALIFORNIA
Graduate School of Business Administration

University Park - Bridge Hall Room 101
MC 1421
Los Angeles, California 90089-1421
Telephone: 213-740-7846

Total Enrollment (1993-94)	Full-Time	Part-Time
	400	700

Cost of Attendance (1993-94)		
Academic Year		
Standard Course Load per Semester/Term		
(credit hours/units)	18	6-9
Semesters/Terms per Academic Year	2	2
Tuition and Fee	$16,490	$12,070-$13,400
Living Expenses	$16,690	NA
Summer Term		
(R = Required, O = Optional, N = None)	O	O
Standard Course Load	6	6
Tuition and Fees	$ 3,330	$ 3,330
FAFSA required; FAF accepted		

Financial Aid Available	Deadline (fall starts)	Awarded to Full-Time	Part-Time
Gift Aid	April 1	Yes	No
Federal College Work-Study	March 2	Yes	No
Federal Perkins Loans	March 2	Yes	No
Federal Stafford Loans	March 2	Yes	Yes
School-Based Loans	NA	No	No
Outside and Private Loans	Varies	Yes	Yes
Graduate Assistantships	NA	No	No

Percentage of Students Receiving Aid	Full-Time	Part-Time
All students	90%	NA
Minority students	NA	NA
Women students	NA	NA
International students	0%	0%

UNIVERSITY OF SOUTHERN COLORADO
School of Business

2200 Bonforte Boulevard
Pueblo, Colorado 81001
Telephone: 719-549-2142

Total Enrollment (1993-94)	Full-Time	Part-Time
	23	81

Cost of Attendance (1993-94)		
Academic Year		
Standard Course Load per Semester/Term		
(credit hours/units)	9	6
Semesters/Terms per Academic Year	2	2
Tuition and Fees		
Resident	$1,703	$1,135
Nonresident	$6,095	$4,063
Living Expenses	$4,000	$4,000
Summer Term		
(R = Required, O = Optional, N = None)	O	O
Standard Course Load	6	3
Tuition and Fees		
Resident	$ 567	$ 284
Nonresident	$2,031	$1,016

Financial Aid Available	Deadline (fall starts)	Awarded to Full-Time	Awarded to Part-Time
Gift Aid	March 1	Yes	No
Federal College Work-Study	March 1	Yes	No
Federal Perkins Loans	March 1	Yes	No
Federal Stafford Loans	March 1	Yes	Yes
School-Based Loans	NA	No	No
Outside and Private Loans	NA	Yes	No
Graduate Assistantships	August 15	Yes	No

Percentage of Students Receiving Aid	Full-Time	Part-Time
All students	10%	0%
Minority students	5%	0%
Women students	2%	0%
International students	0%	0%

UNIVERSITY OF SOUTHERN INDIANA
Master of Business Administration

8600 University Boulevard
Evansville, Indiana 47712
Telephone: 812-464-1926

Total Enrollment (1993-94)	Full-Time	Part-Time
		235

Cost of Attendance (1993-94)		
Academic Year		
Standard Course Load per Semester/Term		
(credit hours/units)	9	3
Semesters/Terms per Academic Year	2	2
Tuition and Fees		
Resident	$2,451	$1,225
Nonresident	$4,869	$2,434
Living Expenses	$5,849	$5,599
Summer Term		
(R = Required, O = Optional, N = None)	O	O
Standard Course Load	3	NA
Tuition and Fees		
Resident	$ 301	
Nonresident	$ 601	

Financial Aid Available	Deadline (fall starts)	Awarded to Full-Time	Awarded to Part-Time
Gift Aid	NA		
Federal College Work-Study	March 1	Yes	Yes
Federal Perkins Loans	March 1	Yes	Yes
Federal Stafford Loans	March 1	Yes	Yes
School-Based Loans	NA		
Outside and Private Loans	May 1	Yes	Yes
Graduate Assistantships	NA		

Percentage of Students Receiving Aid	Part-Time
All students	6%
Minority students	25%
Women students	6%
International students	

UNIVERSITY OF SOUTHERN MAINE
MBA Program

96 Falmouth Street
113 Luther Bonney
Portland, Maine 04103
Telephone: 207-780-4184

Total Enrollment (1993-94)	Full-Time	Part-Time
	18	180

Cost of Attendance (1993-94)		
Academic Year		
Standard Course Load per Semester/Term		
(credit hours/units)	12	6
Semesters/Terms per Academic Year	3	3
Tuition and Fees		
Resident	$3,264	$1,632
Nonresident	$9,048	$4,524
Living Expenses	Information not available	
Summer Term		
(R = Required, O = Optional, N = None)	O	O
Standard Course Load	6	3
Tuition and Fees		
Resident	$ 816	$ 408
Nonresident	$2,262	$1,131

Financial Aid Available	Deadline (fall starts)	Awarded to Full-Time	Part-Time
Gift Aid	May 1	Yes	
Federal College Work-Study	March 31	Yes	Yes
Federal Perkins Loans	March 31	Yes	Yes
Federal Stafford Loans	March 31	Yes	Yes
School-Based Loans	March 31	Yes	Yes
Outside and Private Loans	NA		
Graduate Assistantships	March 15	Yes	Yes

THE UNIVERSITY OF SOUTHERN MISSISSIPPI
Graduate School of Management

Box 5096
Hattiesburg, Mississippi 39406-5096
Telephone: 601-266-4663

Total Enrollment (1993-94)	Full-Time	Part-Time
	34	31

Cost of Attendance (1993-94)		
Academic Year		
Standard Course Load per Semester/Term		
(credit hours/units)	13	6
Semesters/Terms per Academic Year	3	3
Tuition and Fees		
Resident	$3,228	$2,116
Nonresident	$5,118	$2,770
Living Expenses	$4,650	$4,650
Summer Term		
(R = Required, O = Optional, N = None)	R	O
Standard Course Load	9	6
Tuition and Fees		
Resident	$ 836	$ 684
Nonresident		

Financial Aid Available	Deadline (fall starts)	Awarded to Full-Time	Part-Time
Gift Aid			
Federal College Work-Study	March 15	Yes	No
Federal Perkins Loans	March 15	Yes	No
Federal Stafford Loans	March 15	Yes	Yes
School-Based Loans			
Outside and Private Loans	March 15	Yes	Yes
Graduate Assistantships	March 15	Yes	No

Percentage of Students Receiving Aid	Full-Time
All students	83%
Minority students	70%
Women students	79%
International students	71%

UNIVERSITY OF SOUTHWESTERN LOUISIANA
MBA Program

P.O. Box 44568
Lafayette, Louisiana 70504
Telephone: 318-231-6119

Total Enrollment (1993-94)	Full-Time	Part-Time
	159	118

Cost of Attendance (1993-94)

	Full-Time	Part-Time
Academic Year		
Standard Course Load per Semester/Term		
(credit hours/units)	12	3
Semesters/Terms per Academic Year	2	2
Tuition and Fees		
Resident	$ 942	$ 280
Nonresident	$2,228	$ 388
Living Expenses	$5,885	$5,599
Summer Term		
(R = Required, O = Optional, N = None)	O	O
Standard Course Load	6	3
Tuition and Fees		
Resident	$ 474	$ 258
Nonresident	$1,081	$ 329

Financial Aid Available

	Deadline (fall starts)	Awarded to Full-Time	Awarded to Part-Time
Gift Aid		No	No
Federal College Work-Study		No	No
Federal Perkins Loans	April 15	Yes	Yes
Federal Stafford Loans	April 15	Yes	No
School-Based Loans			
Outside and Private Loans			
Graduate Assistantships	April 15	Yes	No

THE UNIVERSITY OF TENNESSEE AT CHATTANOOGA
Graduate School of Business

615 McCallie Avenue
Chattanooga, Tennessee 37403-2598
Telephone: 615-755-4210
          800-532-3028

Total Enrollment (1993-94)	Full-Time	Part-Time
Total combined is 354		

Cost of Attendance (1993-94)

Academic Year	
Standard Course Load per Semester/Term	
(credit hours/units)	Information not available
Semesters/Terms per Academic Year	
Tuition and Fees	
Resident	
Nonresident	
Living Expenses	
Summer Term	
(R = Required, O = Optional, N = None)	
Standard Course Load	Information not available
Tuition and Fees	
Resident	
Nonresident	

Financial Aid Available

	Deadline (fall starts)	Awarded to Full-Time	Awarded to Part-Time
Gift Aid		Yes	Yes
Federal College Work-Study	April 1	Yes	Yes
Federal Perkins Loans			
Federal Stafford Loans	April 1	Yes	Yes
School-Based Loans			
Outside and Private Loans			
Graduate Assistantships		Yes	Yes

UNIVERSITY OF TENNESSEE, KNOXVILLE
College of Business Administration

527 Stokely Management Center
Knoxville, Tennessee 37996-0552
Telephone: 615-974-5033

Total Enrollment (1993-94)	Full-Time
	144

Cost of Attendance (1993-94)

Academic Year	
Standard Course Load per Semester/Term	
(credit hours/units)	15
Semesters/Terms per Academic Year	2
Tuition and Fees	
Resident	$2,412
Nonresident	$6,192
Living Expenses	$1,500
Summer Term	
(R = Required, O = Optional, N = None)	N
Standard Course Load	
Tuition and Fees	
Resident	
Nonresident	

Financial Aid Available

	Deadline (fall starts)	Awarded to Full-Time
Gift Aid	April 1	Yes
Federal College Work-Study	February 14	Yes
Federal Perkins Loans	February 14	Yes
Federal Stafford Loans	February 14	Yes
School-Based Loans	February 14	Yes
Outside and Private Loans	NA	No
Graduate Assistantships	April 1	Yes

Percentage of Students Receiving Aid	Full-Time
All students	60%
Minority students	75%
Women students	50%
International students	10%

UNIVERSITY OF TENNESSEE AT MARTIN
School of Business Administration

112 Business Administration Building
Martin, Tennessee 38238
Telephone: 901-587-7208

Total Enrollment (1993-94)	Full-Time	Part-Time
	11	40

Cost of Attendance (1993-94)

Academic Year		
Standard Course Load per Semester/Term		
(credit hours/units)	9	6
Semesters/Terms per Academic Year	3	3
Tuition and Fees		
Resident	$1,085	$117
Nonresident	$2,885	$317
Living Expenses		
Summer Term		
(R = Required, O = Optional, N = None)	O	
Standard Course Load	6	
Tuition and Fees		
Resident		
Nonresident		

Financial Aid Available

	Deadline (fall starts)	Awarded to Full-Time	Part-Time
Gift Aid	March 1	Yes	NA
Federal College Work-Study	March 1	Yes	NA
Federal Perkins Loans	March 1	Yes	NA
Federal Stafford Loans	None	Yes	NA
School-Based Loans			
Outside and Private Loans			
Graduate Assistantships	May 1	Yes	No

Percentage of Students Receiving Aid	Full-Time	Part-Time
All students	31%	69%
Minority students	1%	3%
Women students	8%	11%
International students	3%	5%

THE UNIVERSITY OF TEXAS AT ARLINGTON

UTA Box 19376
Arlington, Texas 76019
Telephone: 817-273-3004

Total Enrollment (1993-94)	Full-Time	Part-Time
	316	638

Cost of Attendance (1993-94)		
Academic Year		
Standard Course Load per Semester/Term		
(credit hours/units)	12	6
Semesters/Terms per Academic Year	2	2
Tuition and Fees		
Resident	$1,716	$ 858
Nonresident	$4,596	$2,298
Living Expenses	$7,430	$7,180
Summer Term		
(R = Required, O = Optional, N = None)	O	O
Standard Course Load	9	3
Tuition and Fees		
Resident	$ 644	$ 215
Nonresident	$1,724	$ 575

Financial Aid Available	Deadline (fall starts)	Awarded to Full-Time	Awarded to Part-Time
Gift Aid	June 1	Yes	No
Federal College Work-Study	June 1	Yes	No
Federal Perkins Loans	June 1	Yes	No
Federal Stafford Loans	June 1	Yes	Yes
School-Based Loans		No	No
Outside and Private Loans	June 1	Yes	Yes
Graduate Assistantships	June 1	Yes	No

Percentage of Students Receiving Aid	Full-Time	Part-Time
All students	27%	9%
Minority students	22%	13%
Women students	30%	8%
International students	17%	8%

THE UNIVERSITY OF TEXAS AT AUSTIN
Graduate School of Business

P.O. Box 7999
Austin, Texas 78713-7999
Telephone: 512-471-7612

Total Enrollment (1993-94)	Full-Time
	791

Cost of Attendance (1993-94)	
Academic Year	
Standard Course Load per Semester/Term	
(credit hours/units)	15
Semesters/Terms per Academic Year	2
Tuition and Fees	
Resident	$3,140
Nonresident	$7,340
Living Expenses	$5,700
Summer Term	
(R = Required, O = Optional, N = None)	O
Standard Course Load	
Tuition and Fees	
Resident	
Nonresident	

Financial Aid Available	Deadline (fall starts)	Awarded to Full-Time	Awarded to Part-Time
Gift Aid	April 1	Yes	Yes
Federal College Work-Study	April 1	Yes	Yes
Federal Perkins Loans	April 1	Yes	Yes
Federal Stafford Loans	April 1	Yes	Yes
School-Based Loans		No	No
Outside and Private Loans	April 1	Yes	Yes
Graduate Assistantships	None	Yes	Yes

Percentage of Students Receiving Aid	Full-Time
All students	83%
Minority students	
Women students	
International students	

THE UNIVERSITY OF TEXAS AT TYLER
School of Business Administration

3900 University Boulevard
Tyler, Texas 75799
Telephone: 903-566-7360

Total Enrollment (1993-94)	Part-Time
	110

Cost of Attendance (1993-94)	
Academic Year	
Standard Course Load per Semester/Term	
(credit hours/units)	6-9
Semesters/Terms per Academic Year	4
Tuition and Fees	
Resident	$ 500
Nonresident	$1,500
Living Expenses	$9,800
Summer Term	
(R = Required, O = Optional, N = None)	O
Standard Course Load	6
Tuition and Fees	
Resident	$ 350
Nonresident	$1,350

Financial Aid Available	Deadline (fall starts)	Awarded to Part-Time
Gift Aid	June 1	Yes
Federal College Work-Study	June 1	Yes
Federal Perkins Loans	June 1	Yes
Federal Stafford Loans	June 1	Yes
School-Based Loans	June 1	Yes
Outside and Private Loans	June 1	Yes
Graduate Assistantships	June 1	Yes

Percentage of Students Receiving Aid	Part-Time
All students	25%
Minority students	100%
Women students	25%
International students	100%

THE UNIVERSITY OF TULSA
College of Business Administration

600 South College, BAH 308
Tulsa, Oklahoma 74104
Telephone: 918-631-2680

Total Enrollment (1993-94)	Full-Time	Part-Time
	65	166

Cost of Attendance (1993-94)		
Academic Year		
Standard Course Load per Semester/Term		
(credit hours/units)	12	6
Semesters/Terms per Academic Year	2	2
Tuition and Fees	$4,920	$2,460
Living Expenses	$7,005	NA
Summer Term		
(R = Required, O = Optional, N = None)	O	O
Standard Course Load	6	3
Tuition and Fees	$2,460	$ 410

Financial Aid Available	Deadline (fall starts)	Awarded to Full-Time	Awarded to Part-Time
Gift Aid	April 15	Yes	No
Federal College Work-Study			
Federal Perkins Loans			
Federal Stafford Loans			
School-Based Loans			
Outside and Private Loans			
Graduate Assistantships	April 15	Yes	No

Percentage of Students Receiving Aid	Full-Time
All students	80%
Minority students	80%
Women students	75%
International students	100%

UNIVERSITY OF UTAH
David Eccles School of Business

403 BuC
Salt Lake City, Utah 84112
Telephone: 801-581-7785

Total Enrollment (1993-94)	Full-Time	Part-Time
	118	118

Cost of Attendance (1993-94)		
Academic Year		
Standard Course Load per Semester/Term		
(credit hours/units)	16	8
Semesters/Terms per Academic Year	3-4	3-4
Tuition and Fees		
Resident	$2,585	$1,608
Nonresident	$7,799	$4,661
Living Expenses	$4,309	$4,309
Summer Term		
(R = Required, O = Optional, N = None)	R	R
Standard Course Load	16	8
Tuition and Fees	$ 862	$ 536

Financial Aid Available	Deadline (fall starts)	Awarded to Full-Time	Awarded to Part-Time
Gift Aid	February 15	Yes	Yes
Federal College Work-Study	February 15	Yes	Yes
Federal Perkins Loans	February 15	Yes	No
Federal Stafford Loans	February 15	Yes	Yes
School-Based Loans	October 15	Yes	No
Outside and Private Loans	NA		
Graduate Assistantships	February 15	Yes	Yes

Percentage of Students Receiving Aid	Full-Time	Part-Time
All students	28%	5%
Minority students	100%	
Women students	46%	16%
International students	33%	

UNIVERSITY OF VIRGINIA
Darden Graduate School of Business Administration

P.O. Box 6550
Charlottesville, Virginia 22906
Telephone: 800-UVA-MBA-1

Total Enrollment (1993-94)	Full-Time
	480

Cost of Attendance (1993-94)	
Academic Year	
Standard Course Load per Semester/Term	
(credit hours/units)	22.5(First year)/16.5(Second year)
Semesters/Terms per Academic Year	2
Tuition and Fees	
Resident	$ 8,655
Nonresident	$16,055
Living Expenses	$ 9,260
Summer Term	
(R = Required, O = Optional, N = None)	N
Standard Course Load	
Tuition and Fees	
Resident	
Nonresident	

Financial Aid Available	Deadline (fall starts)	Awarded to Full-Time
Gift Aid	None	Yes
Federal College Work-Study	NA	No
Federal Perkins Loans	None	Yes
Federal Stafford Loans	None	Yes
School-Based Loans	None	Yes
Outside and Private Loans	None	Yes
Graduate Assistantships	NA	No

Percentage of Students Receiving Aid	Full-Time
All students	65%
Minority students	90%
Women students	75%
International students	

UNIVERSITY OF WASHINGTON

110 MacKenzie Hall, DJ-10
Seattle, Washington 98195
Telephone: 206-543-4660

Total Enrollment (1993-94)	Full-Time
	340

Cost of Attendance (1993-94)	
Academic Year	
Standard Course Load per Semester/Term	
(credit hours/units)	16
Semesters/Terms per Academic Year	3
Tuition and Fees	
Resident	$ 3,978
Nonresident	$ 9,963
Living Expenses	$10,053
Summer Term	
(R = Required, O = Optional, N = None)	O
Standard Course Load	12
Tuition and Fees	$ 1,015

Financial Aid Available	Deadline (fall starts)	Awarded to Full-Time
Gift Aid	March 1	Yes
Federal College Work-Study	March 1	Yes
Federal Perkins Loans	March 1	Yes
Federal Stafford Loans	March 1	Yes
School-Based Loans	NA	
Outside and Private Loans	NA	
Graduate Assistantships	March 1	Yes

Percentage of Students Receiving Aid	Full-Time
All students	25%
Minority students	35%
Women students	25%
International students	

UNIVERSITY OF WISCONSIN - EAU CLAIRE
School of Business

SSS117
Eau Claire, Wisconsin 54701
Telephone: 715-836-5473

Total Enrollment (1993-94)	Full-Time	Part-Time
New program beginning January 1995		

Cost of Attendance (1993-94)		
Academic Year		
Standard Course Load per Semester/Term		
(credit hours/units)	9	6
Semesters/Terms per Academic Year	2	
Tuition and Fees		
Resident	$1,303	$145/cr.
Nonresident	$3,948	$439/cr.
Living Expenses	$3,000	
Summer Term		
(R = Required, O = Optional, N = None)	O	O
Standard Course Load	2/3	2/3
Tuition and Fees		
Resident	$ 145	$145
Nonresident	$ 439	$439

Financial Aid Available	Deadline (fall starts)	Awarded to Full-Time Part-Time
Gift Aid		
Federal College Work-Study		
Federal Perkins Loans		Information not available
Federal Stafford Loans		New program begins January 1995
School-Based Loans		
Outside and Private Loans		
Graduate Assistantships		

UNIVERSITY OF WISCONSIN - MADISON

2266 Grainger Hall
975 University Avenue
Madison, Wisconsin 53706
Telephone: 608-262-1555

Total Enrollment (1993-94)	Full-Time	Part-Time
	482	150

Cost of Attendance (1993-94)		
Academic Year		
Standard Course Load per Semester/Term		
(credit hours/units)	15	6
Semesters/Terms per Academic Year	2	2
Tuition and Fees		
Resident	$2,165	$ 271
Nonresident	$5,733	$ 717
Living Expenses	$6,860	$6,860
Summer Term		
(R = Required, O = Optional, N = None)	O	O
Standard Course Load	6	3
Tuition and Fees		
Resident	$1,020	$ 765
Nonresident	$2,708	$2,031

Financial Aid Available	Deadline (fall starts)	Awarded to Full-Time	Part-Time
Gift Aid	January 1	Yes	No
Federal College Work-Study	None	Yes	
Federal Perkins Loans	None	No	No
Federal Stafford Loans	None	Yes	Yes
School-Based Loans	NA		
Outside and Private Loans	Varies	Yes	Yes
Graduate Assistantships	January 1	Yes	No

Percentage of Students Receiving Aid	Full-Time
All students	17%
Minority students	79%
Women students	22%
International students	1%

UNIVERSITY OF WISCONSIN - MILWAUKEE
School of Business Administration

P.O. Box 742
Milwaukee, Wisconsin 53201-0742
Telephone: 414-229-5271

Total Enrollment (1993-94)	Full-Time	Part-Time
	138	520

Cost of Attendance (1993-94)		
Academic Year		
Standard Course Load per Semester/Term		
(credit hours/units)		
Semesters/Terms per Academic Year		
Tuition and Fees		
Resident	$2,165	$5,699
Nonresident	$ 332	$ 774
Living Expenses		
Summer Term		
(R = Required, O = Optional, N = None)	O	O
Standard Course Load	6	3
Tuition and Fees		
Resident	$1,020	$ 765
Nonresident	$2,708	$2,031

Financial Aid Available	Deadline (fall starts)	Awarded to Full-Time	Part-Time
Gift Aid	January/February	Yes	No
Federal College Work-Study	March 1	Yes	Yes
Federal Perkins Loans	March 1	Yes	Yes
Federal Stafford Loans	March 1	Yes	Yes
School-Based Loans		No	No
Outside and Private Loans	March 1	Yes	Yes
Graduate Assistantships	January 1	Yes	No

UNIVERSITY OF WISCONSIN - OSHKOSH
College of Business Administration

MBA Program
Oshkosh, Wisconsin 54901
Telephone: 800-633-1430

Total Enrollment (1993-94)	Full-Time	Part-Time
	30	475

Cost of Attendance (1993-94)		
Academic Year		
Standard Course Load per Semester/Term		
(credit hours/units)	9-12	3
Semesters/Terms per Academic Year	3	3
Tuition and Fees		
Resident	$ 2,900	$ 960
Nonresident	$ 8,100	$1,700
Living Expenses	$14,500	NA
Summer Term		
(R = Required, O = Optional, N = Nonc)	O	O
Standard Course Load	6	3
Tuition and Fees		
Resident	$ 950	$ 480
Nonresident	$2,700	$1,350

Financial Aid Available	Deadline (fall starts)	Awarded to Full-Time	Part-Time
Gift Aid		No	No
Federal College Work-Study		Yes	No
Federal Perkins Loans		Yes	Yes
Federal Stafford Loans		Yes	Yes
School-Based Loans		Yes	Yes
Outside and Private Loans		No	No
Graduate Assistantships	May 1	Yes	No

Percentage of Students Receiving Aid	Full-Time	Part-Time
All students	50%	1%
Minority students		
Women students		
International students		

UNIVERSITY OF WISCONSIN - WHITEWATER
College of Business and Economics

800 West Main Street
Whitewater, Wisconsin 53190
Telephone: 414-472-1945

Total Enrollment (1993-94)	Full-Time	Part-Time
	138	243

Cost of Attendance (1993-94)		
Academic Year		
Standard Course Load per Semester/Term		
(credit hours/units)	12	3
Semesters/Terms per Academic Year	2	3
Tuition and Fees		
Resident	$2,962	$ 986
Nonresident	$8,252	$2,750
Living Expenses	$5,000	$5,000
Summer Term		
(R = Required, O = Optional, N = None)	O	O
Standard Course Load	6	3
Tuition and Fees		
Resident	$ 783	$ 470
Nonresident	$2,200	$1,310

Financial Aid Available	Deadline (fall starts)	Awarded to Full-Time	Part-Time
Gift Aid	June 1	Yes	Yes
Federal College Work-Study	June 1	Yes	Yes
Federal Perkins Loans	June 1	Yes	Yes
Federal Stafford Loans	June 1	Yes	Yes
School-Based Loans	June 1	Yes	Yes
Outside and Private Loans	June 1	Yes	Yes
Graduate Assistantships	June 1	Yes	Yes

Percentage of Students Receiving Aid	Full-Time
All students	15%
Minority students	80%
Women students	17%
International students	12%

UNIVERSITY OF WYOMING
College of Business

P.O. Box 3275
Laramie, Wyoming 82071-3275
Telephone: 307-766-2063

Total Enrollment (1993-94)	Full-Time	Part-Time
	50	6

Cost of Attendance (1993-94)		
Academic Year		
Standard Course Load per Semester/Term		
(credit hours/units)	12	6
Semesters/Terms per Academic Year	2	2
Tuition and Fees		
Resident	$1,994	$ 95/cr.
Nonresident	$5,528	$243/cr.
Living Expenses	$ 560	$560
Summer Term		
(R = Required, O = Optional, N = None)	O	O
Standard Course Load	6	
Tuition and Fees		
Resident	$ 522	
Nonresident	$1,272	

Financial Aid Available	Deadline (fall starts)	Awarded to Full-Time	Part-Time
Gift Aid	March 1		No
Federal College Work-Study	March 1	Yes	No
Federal Perkins Loans	March 1	Yes	Yes
Federal Stafford Loans	March 1	Yes	Yes
School-Based Loans	NA		
Outside and Private Loans	NA		
Graduate Assistantships	March 30	Yes	No

Percentage of Students Receiving Aid	Full-Time
All students	50%
Minority students	4%
Women students	36%
International students	24%

UTAH STATE UNIVERSITY
Business Graduate Studies

Logan, Utah 84322-3535
Telephone: 801-750-2360

Total Enrollment (1993-94)	Full-Time	Part-Time
	85	80

Cost of Attendance (1993-94)		
Academic Year		
Standard Course Load per Semester/Term		
(credit hours/units)	12	8
Semesters/Terms per Academic Year	4	4
Tuition and Fees		
Resident	$ 578	$720
Nonresident	$1,679	$720
Living Expenses		
Summer Term		
(R = Required, O = Optional, N = None)	O	R
Standard Course Load		
Tuition and Fees		
Resident	$ 578	$720
Nonresident	$ 578	$720

Financial Aid Available	Deadline (fall starts)	Awarded to Full-Time	Part-Time
Gift Aid	April 1	Yes	
Federal College Work-Study	March 15	Yes	Yes
Federal Perkins Loans	February 10	Yes	Yes
Federal Stafford Loans	March 15	Yes	Yes
School-Based Loans		No	No
Outside and Private Loans			
Graduate Assistantships	April 1	Yes	

Percentage of Students Receiving Aid	Full-Time
All students	10%
Minority students	
Women students	
International students	

VANDERBILT UNIVERSITY
Owen Graduate School of Management

401 21st Avenue South
Nashville, Tennessee 37203
Telephone: 615-322-6469

Total Enrollment (1993-94)	Full-Time
	197

Cost of Attendance (1993-94)

Academic Year
  Standard Course Load per Semester/Term
    (credit hours/units)   16.5
  Semesters/Terms per Academic Year   2
  Tuition and Fees $18,600
  Living Expenses $10,700
Summer Term
(R = Required, O = Optional, N = None)   N
  Standard Course Load
  Tuition and Fees

Financial Aid Available

	Deadline (fall starts)	Awarded to Full-Time
Gift Aid	March 31	Yes
Federal College Work-Study	March 31	Yes
Federal Perkins Loans	March 31	Yes
Federal Stafford Loans	May 31	Yes
School-Based Loans	March 31	Yes
Outside and Private Loans	May 31	Yes
Graduate Assistantships		No

Percentage of Students Receiving Aid	Full-Time
All students	67%
Minority students	79%
Women students	75%
International students	32%

VIRGINIA COMMONWEALTH UNIVERSITY

1015 Floyd Avenue
Box 4000
Richmond, Virginia 23284
Telephone: 804-367-1741

Total Enrollment (1993-94)	Full-Time	Part-Time
	77	224

Cost of Attendance (1993-94)

Academic Year
  Standard Course Load per Semester/Term

	Full-Time	Part-Time
(credit hours/units)	9	< 9
Semesters/Terms per Academic Year	2	2
Tuition and Fees		
Resident	$ 4,273	$223/cr.hr.
Nonresident	$10,291	$557/cr.hr.
Living Expenses	$ 8,000	$4,000
Summer Term		
(R = Required, O = Optional, N = None)	O	O
Standard Course Load	6	< 5
Tuition and Fees		
Resident	$223/cr.hr.	$223/cr.hr.
Nonresident	$557/cr.hr.	$556/cr.hr.

Financial Aid Available

	Deadline (fall starts)	Awarded to Full-Time	Part-Time
Gift Aid	April 1	Yes	No
Federal College Work-Study	April 1	Yes	No
Federal Perkins Loans			
Federal Stafford Loans	April 1	Yes	No
School-Based Loans			
Outside and Private Loans			
Graduate Assistantships	April 15	Yes	No

Percentage of Students Receiving Aid	Full-Time	Part-Time
All students	90%	10%
Minority students	80%	20%
Women students	90%	10%
International students	65%	35%

VIRGINIA POLYTECHNIC INSTITUTE AND STATE UNIVERSITY
R. B. Pamplin College of Business

1044 Pamplin Hall
Blacksburg, Virginia 24061-0209
Telephone: 703-231-6152

Total Enrollment (1993-94)	Full-Time	Part-Time
	202	18

Cost of Attendance (1993-94)		
Academic Year		
Standard Course Load per Semester/Term		
(credit hours/units)	12	3
Semesters/Terms per Academic Year	4	4
Tuition and Fees		
Resident	$4,400	$ 769/course
Nonresident	$6,254	$1,013/course
Living Expenses	$7,300	NA
Summer Term		
(R = Required, O = Optional, N = None)	O	O
Standard Course Load	6	3
Tuition and Fees		
Resident	$2,096	$1,160
Nonresident	$2,966	$1,682

Financial Aid Available

	Deadline (fall starts)	Awarded to Full-Time	Part-Time
Gift Aid	February 15	Yes	No
Federal College Work-Study	February 15	Yes	No
Federal Perkins Loans	February 15	Yes	No
Federal Stafford Loans	February 15	Yes	Yes
School-Based Loans	February 15	Yes	Yes
Outside and Private Loans			
Graduate Assistantships	April 15	Yes	No

Percentage of Students Receiving Aid	Full-Time
All students	40%
Minority students	100%
Women students	
International students	

WAKE FOREST UNIVERSITY
Babcock Graduate School of Management

Box 7659 Reynolda Station
Winston-Salem, North Carolina 27012
Telephone: 919-759-5422
800-722-1622

Total Enrollment (1993-94)	Full-Time	Part-Time
	216	330

Cost of Attendance (1993-94)	Full-Time	Part-Time	Evening
Academic Year			
Standard Course Load per Semester/Term			
(credit hours/units)		12	6
Semesters/Terms per Academic Year		2	2
Tuition and Fees			
Resident	$14,500	$16,000	$6,800
Nonresident	$11,500	NA	NA
Living Expenses			
Summer Term			
(R = Required, O = Optional, N = None)	N	R	O
Standard Course Load		3	2
Tuition and Fees			$3,400

Financial Aid Available

	Deadline (fall starts)	Awarded to Full-Time	Part-Time
Gift Aid	April 1	Yes	
Federal College Work-Study		No	
Federal Perkins Loans		Yes	
Federal Stafford Loans		Yes	
School-Based Loans		No	
Outside and Private Loans		Yes	
Graduate Assistantships		No	

Percentage of Students Receiving Aid	Full-Time	Part-Time	Evening
All students	60%	27%	10%
Minority sudents	100%	50%	50%
Women students	55%	25%	18%
International students	60%		

WASHINGTON STATE UNIVERSITY
Graduate Programs in Business

Todd 473
Pullman, Washington 99164-4744
Telephone: 509-335-7617

Total Enrollment (1993-94)	Full-Time
	200

Cost of Attendance (1993-94)

Academic Year	
Standard Course Load per Semester/Term	
(credit hours/units)	12
Semesters/Terms per Academic Year	2
Tuition and Fees	
Resident	$1,989
Nonresident	$4,982
Living Expenses	$9,000
Summer Term	
(R = Required, O = Optional, N = None)	O
Standard Course Load	NA
Tuition and Fees	$145/cr.

Financial Aid Available

	Deadline (fall starts)	Awarded to Full-Time
Gift Aid	April 15	Yes
Federal College Work-Study	March 1	Yes
Federal Perkins Loans	NA	Yes
Federal Stafford Loans	NA	Yes
School-Based Loans		No
Outside and Private Loans		No
Graduate Assistantships	March 15	Yes

Percentage of Students Receiving Aid	Full-Time
All students	40%
Minority students	80%
Women students	40%
International students	5%

WASHINGTON UNIVERSITY
John M. Olin School of Business

Campus Box 1133
One Brookings Drive
St. Louis, Missouri 63130-4899
Telephone: 314-935-7301

Total Enrollment (1993-94)	Full-Time	Part-Time
	289	352

Cost of Attendance (1993-94)

Academic Year		
Standard Course Load per Semester/Term		
(credit hours/units)	15	6
Semesters/Terms per Academic Year	2	2
Tuition and Fees	$17,600	$530/cr.
Living Expenses	$14,000	$14,000
Summer Term		
(R = Required, O = Optional, N = None)	O	O
Standard Course Load	NA	NA
Tuition and Fees	per credit	per credit

Financial Aid Available

	Deadline (fall starts)	Awarded to Full-Time	Part-Time
Gift Aid	No deadline	Yes	No
Federal College Work-Study	No deadline	Yes	No
Federal Perkins Loans	No deadline	Yes	No
Federal Stafford Loans	No deadline	Yes	Yes
School-Based Loans		No	No
Outside and Private Loans	No deadline	Yes	Yes
Graduate Assistantships	No deadline	Yes	

Percentage of Students Receiving Aid	Full-Time	Part-Time
All students	66%	15%
Minority students	98%	
Women students	80%	6%
International students	10%	

WAYNE STATE UNIVERSITY
School of Business Administration

103 Prentis Building
Office of Student Services
Detroit, Michigan 48202
Telephone: 313-577-4510

Total Enrollment (1993-94)	Full-Time	Part-Time
	180	1,844

Cost of Attendance (1993-94)		
Academic Year		
Standard Course Load per Semester/Term		
(credit hours/units)	9	6
Semesters/Terms per Academic Year	3	3
Tuition and Fees		
Resident	$2,570	$1,760
Nonresident	$5,396	$3,644
Living Expenses		
Summer Term		
(R = Required, O = Optional, N = None)	O	O
Standard Course Load	9	6
Tuition and Fees		
Resident	$1,285	$ 880
Nonresident	$2,698	$1,822

Financial Aid Available	Deadline (fall starts)	Awarded to Full-Time	Part-Time
Gift Aid	May 1	Yes	Yes
Federal College Work-Study	NA	Yes	Yes
Federal Perkins Loans		No	No
Federal Stafford Loans	September 1	Yes	Yes
School-Based Loans		No	No
Outside and Private Loans	February 28	Yes	Yes
Graduate Assistantships	NA	Yes	

Percentage of Students Receiving Aid	Full-Time	Part-Time
All students	NA	NA
Minority students	NA	NA
Women students	NA	NA
International students	NA	NA

WAYNESBURG COLLEGE
MBA Program

51 West College Street
Waynesburg, Pennsylvania 15370
Telephone: 412-852-3202

Total Enrollment (1993-94)	Full-Time	Part-Time
	4	42

Cost of Attendance (1993-94)		
Academic Year		
Standard Course Load per Semester/Term		
(credit hours/units)	9	3
Semesters/Terms per Academic Year	4	4
Tuition and Fees	$4,590	$1,530
Living Expenses (book expense only)	$ 400	$ 120
Summer Term		
(R = Required, O = Optional, N = None)	O	O
Standard Course Load	12	6
Tuition and Fees	$3,060	$ 510

Financial Aid Available	Deadline (fall starts)	Awarded to Full-Time	Part-Time
Gift Aid		No	No
Federal College Work-Study		No	No
Federal Perkins Loans	NA	Yes	No
Federal Stafford Loans	NA	Yes	Yes
School-Based Loans	NA	Yes	No
Outside and Private Loans	NA	Yes	Yes
Graduate Assistantships			

Percentage of Students Receiving Aid	Full-Time	Part-Time
All students	0%	1%
Minority students	0%	0%
Women students	0%	1%
International students	0%	0%

WEST GEORGIA COLLEGE
School of Business

Carrollton, Georgia 30118
Telephone: 404-836-6467

Total Enrollment (1993-94)	Full-Time	Part-Time
	40	21

Cost of Attendance (1993-94)		
Academic Year		
Standard Course Load per Semester/Term		
(credit hours/units)	10	5
Semesters/Terms per Academic Year	3	3
Tuition and Fees		
Resident	$1,539	$ 579
Nonresident	$3,849	$1,734
Living Expenses	$3,375	$3,375
Summer Term		
(R = Required, O = Optional, N = None)	R	R
Standard Course Load	10	5
Tuition and Fees		
Resident	$ 513	$ 193
Nonresident	$1,283	$ 578

Financial Aid Available	Deadline (fall starts)	Awarded to Full-Time	Part-Time
Gift Aid	August 1	Yes	
Federal College Work-Study	NA		
Federal Perkins Loans	NA		
Federal Stafford Loans	NA		
School-Based Loans	NA		
Outside and Private Loans	NA		
Graduate Assistantships	August 1	Yes	

Percentage of Students Receiving Aid	Full-Time	Part-Time
All students	25%	0%
Minority students	14%	0%
Women students	29%	0%
International students	63%	0%

WEST TEXAS A&M UNIVERSITY
T. Boone Pickens College of Business

WTAMU Box 768
Canyon, Texas 79016-0001
Telephone: 806-656-2730

Total Enrollment (1993-94)	Full-Time	Part-Time
	99	274

Cost of Attendance (1993-94)		
Academic Year		
Standard Course Load per Semester/Term		
(credit hours/units)	9	6
Semesters/Terms per Academic Year	4	4
Tuition and Fees		
Resident	$1,166	$1,094
Nonresident	$2,970	$2,626
Living Expenses	$3,160	
Summer Term		
(R = Required, O = Optional, N = None)	O	O
Standard Course Load	3	3
Tuition and Fees		
Resident	$ 439	$ 439
Nonresident	$ 847	$ 847

Financial Aid Available	Deadline (fall starts)	Awarded to Full-Time	Part-Time
Gift Aid	April 30	Yes	Yes
Federal College Work-Study		Yes	Yes
Federal Perkins Loans		Yes	Yes
Federal Stafford Loans		Yes	Yes
School-Based Loans		No	No
Outside and Private Loans		No	No
Graduate Assistantships		Yes	Yes

WEST VIRGINIA UNIVERSITY
College of Business and Economics

Graduate Programs
P.O. Box 6025 - MP
Morgantown, West Virginia 26506-6025
Telephone: 304-293-5408

Total Enrollment (1993-94)	Full-Time	Part-Time
	37	130

Cost of Attendance (1993-94)

Academic Year		
Standard Course Load per Semester/Term		
(credit hours/units)	15	8
Semesters/Terms per Academic Year	3.5	Variable
Tuition and Fees		
Resident	$ 4,228	$ 90/cr.hr.
Nonresident	$11,490	$313/cr.hr.
Living Expenses		
Summer Term		
(R = Required, O = Optional, N = None)	R	O
Standard Course Load	12	8
Tuition and Fees	Included above	

Financial Aid Available

	Deadline (fall starts)	Awarded to Full-Time	Part-Time
Gift Aid		Yes	No
Federal College Work-Study	March 1	Yes	No
Federal Perkins Loans	March 1		
Federal Stafford Loans	Open	Yes	Yes
School-Based Loans		No	No
Outside and Private Loans		No	No
Graduate Assistantships	March 15	Yes	No

Percentage of Students Receiving Aid	Full-Time
All students	68%
Minority students	
Women students	
International students	

WESTERN CAROLINA UNIVERSITY
Graduate Programs in Business

Forsyth Building
Cullowhee, North Carolina 28723-9033
Telephone: 704-227-7401

Total Enrollment (1993-94)	Full-Time	Part-Time
	78	75

Cost of Attendance (1993-94)

Academic Year		
Standard Course Load per Semester/Term		
(credit hours/units)	9-15	3-6
Semesters/Terms per Academic Year	2	2
Tuition and Fees		
Resident	$1,395	$ 246-$ 401
Nonresident	$7,461	$1,793-$2,675
Living Expenses	$5,000	
Summer Term		
(R = Required, O = Optional, N = None)	O	O
Standard Course Load	3-6	
Tuition and Fees		
Resident	$ 79/hr.	
Nonresident	$247/hr.	

Financial Aid Available

	Deadline (fall starts)	Awarded to Full-Time	Part-Time
Gift Aid - Fellowship	April 15	Yes	Yes
- Study Grant	May 5		
Federal College Work-Study	March 31	Yes	No
Federal Perkins Loans	March 31	Yes	No
Federal Stafford Loans	March 31	Yes	Yes
School-Based Loans		No	No
Outside and Private Loans		No	No
Graduate Assistantships	April 1	Yes	No

Percentage of Students Receiving Aid	Full-Time
All students	45%
Minority students	100%
Women students	40%
International students	15%

WESTERN NEW ENGLAND COLLEGE
School of Business

1215 Wilbraham Boulevard
Springfield, Massachusetts 01119
Telephone: 413-782-1305

Total Enrollment (1993-94)	Part-Time
	568

Cost of Attendance (1993-94)	
Academic Year	
Standard Course Load per Semester/Term	
(credit hours/units)	3
Semesters/Terms per Academic Year	3
Tuition and Fees	$813
Living Expenses	NA
Summer Term	
(R = Required, O = Optional, N = None)	O
Standard Course Load	3
Tuition and Fees	$813

Financial Aid Available	Deadline (fall starts)	Awarded to Part-Time
Gift Aid	NA	No
Federal College Work-Study	NA	No
Federal Perkins Loans	NA	No
Federal Stafford Loans	NA	Yes
School-Based Loans	NA	No
Outside and Private Loans	NA	
Graduate Assistantships	NA	No

Percentage of Students Receiving Aid	Part-Time
All students	NA
Minority students	NA
Women students	NA
International students	NA

WESTERN WASHINGTON UNIVERSITY
College of Business and Economics

Bellingham, Washington 98225-9072
Telephone: 206-650-3898

Total Enrollment (1993-94)	Full-Time	Part-Time
	18	34

Cost of Attendance (1993-94)		
Academic Year		
Standard Course Load per Semester/Term		
(credit hours/units)	16	8
Semesters/Terms per Academic Year	4	4
Tuition and Fees		
Resident	$1,046	$ 840
Nonresident	$3,179	$2,544
Living Expenses	NA	NA
Summer Term		
(R = Required, O = Optional, N = None)	R	R
Standard Course Load	12	8
Tuition and Fees		
Resident	$1,778	$ 914
Nonresident	$1,828	$ 964

Financial Aid Available	Deadline (fall starts)	Awarded to Full-Time	Awarded to Part-Time
Gift Aid	May 1	Yes	No
Federal College Work-Study	February 28	Yes	No
Federal Perkins Loans	NA		
Federal Stafford Loans		Yes	No
School-Based Loans	NA		
Outside and Private Loans	NA		
Graduate Assistantships	May 1	Yes	Yes

Percentage of Students Receiving Aid	Full-Time	Part-Time
All students	23%	10%
Minority students	0%	5%
Women students	13%	2%
International students	8%	0%

THE WHARTON SCHOOL
(University of Pennsylvania) Graduate Division

102 Vance Hall
Philadelphia, Pennsylvania 19104-6361
Telephone: 215-898-6182

Total Enrollment (1993-94)	Full-Time	Part-Time
	1,525	NA

Cost of Attendance (1993-94)

Academic Year
Standard Course Load per Semester/Term
(credit hours/units)
Semesters/Terms per Academic Year   First year, 4 terms
                                     Second year, 2 semesters

Tuition and Fees	$19,928
Living Expenses	$11,572

Summer Term

(R = Required, O = Optional, N = None)	NA	O
Standard Course Load		
Tuition and Fees		$2,541/course

Financial Aid Available

	Deadline (fall starts)	Awarded to Full-Time	Part-Time
Gift Aid	March 30	Yes	NA
Federal College Work-Study	NA	No	NA
Federal Perkins Loans	March 30	Yes	NA
Federal Stafford Loans	June 15	Yes	NA
School-Based Loans	None	Yes	NA
Outside and Private Loans	July 1	Yes	NA
Graduate Assistantships	None	Yes	NA

Percentage of Students Receiving Aid	Full-Time	Part-Time
All students	65%	NA
Minority students	80%	
Women students	65%	
International students	5%	

THE WICHITA STATE UNIVERSITY
W. Frank Barton School of Business

Box 48-201 Clinton Hall
Wichita, Kansas 67260-0048
Telephone: 316-689-3230

Total Enrollment (1993-94)	Full-Time	Part-Time
	82	466

Cost of Attendance (1993-94)

Academic Year
Standard Course Load per Semester/Term

(credit hours/units)	9	3-6
Semesters/Terms per Academic Year	3	3
Tuition and Fees		
Resident	$1,800	$1,800
Nonresident	$5,650	$5,650
Living Expenses	$8,600	$8,600

Summer Term

(R = Required, O = Optional, N = None)	O	O
Standard Course Load	6	3
Tuition and Fees		
Resident	$ 600	$ 600
Nonresident	$1,800	$1,800

Financial Aid Available

	Deadline (fall starts)	Awarded to Full-Time	Part-Time
Gift Aid		No	No
Federal College Work-Study		No	No
Federal Perkins Loans	March 15	Yes	Yes
Federal Stafford Loans	March 15	Yes	Yes
School-Based Loans	1 month before beginning of academic year	Yes	Yes
Outside and Private Loans	Determined by student and lending agency	Yes	Yes
Graduate Assistantships	4-6 weeks before semester	Yes	Yes

WIDENER UNIVERSITY
School of Management

One University Place
Chester, Pennsylvania 19013
Telephone: 215-499-4305

Total Enrollment (1993-94)	Full-Time	Part-Time
	60	800

Cost of Attendance (1993-94)		
Academic Year		
Standard Course Load per Semester/Term		
(credit hours/units)	9	6
Semesters/Terms per Academic Year	3	3
Tuition and Fees	$9,450	$6,300
Living Expenses	NA	NA
Summer Term		
(R = Required, O = Optional, N = None)	O	O
Standard Course Load	Included above	
Tuition and Fees	Included above	

Financial Aid Available	Deadline (fall starts)	Awarded to Full-Time	Part-Time
Gift Aid	NA		
Federal College Work-Study	April 1	Yes	Yes
Federal Perkins Loans	April 1	Yes	Yes
Federal Stafford Loans	April 1	Yes	Yes
School-Based Loans	NA		
Outside and Private Loans	NA		
Graduate Assistantships	April	Yes	No

Percentage of Students Receiving Aid	Full-Time	Part-Time
All students	30%	10%
Minority students		
Women students		
International students		

WILLAMETTE UNIVERSITY
Atkinson Graduate School of Management

900 State Street
Salem, Oregon 97301
Telephone: 503-370-6167

Total Enrollment (1993-94)	Full-Time	Part-Time
	133	52

Cost of Attendance (1993-94)		
Academic Year		
Standard Course Load per Semester/Term		
(credit hours/units)	15	6
Semesters/Terms per Academic Year	2	2
Tuition and Fees	$11,800	$4,680
Living Expenses	$ 8,035	
Summer Term		
(R = Required, O = Optional, N = None)	O	O
Standard Course Load	3-6	3-6
Tuition and Fees	$1,170-$2,340	$1,170-$2,340

Financial Aid Available	Deadline (fall starts)	Awarded to Full-Time	Part-Time
Gift Aid	March 31	Yes	No
Federal College Work-Study	None	Yes	
Federal Perkins Loans	NA	No	No
Federal Stafford Loans	None	Yes	Yes
School-Based Loans	NA	No	No
Outside and Private Loans	None	Yes	Yes
Graduate Assistantships	June 30	Yes	No

Percentage of Students Receiving Aid	Full-Time	Part-Time
All students	80%	50%
Minority students	100%	
Women students	70%	
International students	50%	

WILLIAM CAREY COLLEGE
Graduate Center for Professional and Executive Development

1856 Beach Drive
Gulfport, Mississippi 39507
Telephone: 601-865-1513

Total Enrollment (1993-94)	Full-Time	Part-Time
	30	45

Cost of Attendance (1993-94)		
Academic Year		
Standard Course Load per Semester/Term		
(credit hours/units)	6	3
Semesters/Terms per Academic Year	4	4
Tuition and Fees	$3,360	$1,440
Living Expenses	$5,200	NA
Summer Term		
(R = Required, O = Optional, N = None)	O	O
Standard Course Load	6	3
Tuition and Fees	$ 960	$ 480

Financial Aid Available	Deadline (fall starts)	Awarded to Full-Time	Part-Time
Gift Aid	July 1	Yes	No
Federal College Work-Study	July 1	Yes	No
Federal Perkins Loans		Yes	Yes
Federal Stafford Loans		Yes	Yes
School-Based Loans			
Outside and Private Loans			
Graduate Assistantships		Yes	No

Percentage of Students Receiving Aid	Full-Time	Part-Time
All students	100%	100%
Minority students	100%	100%
Women students	100%	100%
International students	100%	100%

WOODBURY UNIVERSITY
Master of Business Administration Program

7500 Glenoaks Blvd.
Burbank, California 91510-7846
Telephone: 818-767-0888

Total Enrollment (1993-94)	Full-Time	Part-Time
	78	53

Cost of Attendance (1993-94)		
Academic Year		
Standard Course Load per Semester/Term		
(credit hours/units)	6	6
Semesters/Terms per Academic Year	3	3
Tuition and Fees	$7,560	$3,960
Living Expenses	$8,166	$7,962
Summer Term		
(R = Required, O = Optional, N = None)	O	O
Standard Course Load	6	3
Tuition and Fees	$1,920	$1,020

Financial Aid Available	Deadline (fall starts)	Awarded to Full-Time	Part-Time
Gift Aid	NA		
Federal College Work-Study	NA		
Federal Perkins Loans	NA		
Federal Stafford Loans	August 1	Yes	Yes
School-Based Loans	NA		
Outside and Private Loans	NA		
Graduate Assistantships	NA		

Percentage of Students Receiving Aid	Full-Time	Part-Time
All students	14%	9%
Minority students	40%	75%
Women students	10%	14%
International students	0%	0%

WORCESTER POLYTECHNIC INSTITUTE
Graduate Management Programs

100 Institute Road
Worcester, Massachusetts 01609
Telephone: 508-831-5218

Total Enrollment (1993-94)	Full-Time	Part-Time
	45	154

Cost of Attendance (1993-94)		
Academic Year		
Standard Course Load per Semester/Term		
(credit hours/units)	12	6
Semesters/Terms per Academic Year	2	2
Tuition and Fees	$12,218	$3,042
Living Expenses	$ 5,882	NA
Summer Term		
(R = Required, O = Optional, N = None)	O	O
Standard Course Load	6	3
Tuition and Fees	$ 3,042	$1,521

Financial Aid Available	Deadline (fall starts)	Awarded to Full-Time	Awarded to Part-Time
Gift Aid		No	No
Federal College Work-Study		No	No
Federal Perkins Loans		No	No
Federal Stafford Loans	July 15	Yes	Yes
School-Based Loans		No	No
Outside and Private Loans	July 15	Yes	Yes
Graduate Assistantships		Yes	No

Percentage of Students Receiving Aid	Full-Time	Part-Time
All students	NA	NA
Minority students	NA	NA
Women students	NA	NA
International students	0%	0%

WRIGHT STATE UNIVERSITY
College of Business and Administration

110 Rike Hall
Dayton, Ohio 45435
Telephone: 513-873-2437

Total Enrollment (1993-94)	Full-Time	Part-Time
	115	425

Cost of Attendance (1993-94)		
Academic Year		
Standard Course Load per Semester/Term		
(credit hours/units)	12	6
Semesters/Terms per Academic Year	3	3
Tuition and Fees		
Resident	$3,894	$2,214
Nonresident	$6,975	$3,960
Living Expenses	$5,400	
Summer Term		
(R = Required, O = Optional, N = None)	O	O
Standard Course Load	12	6
Tuition and Fees		
Resident	$1,298	$ 738
Nonresident	$2,325	$1,320

Financial Aid Available	Deadline (fall starts)	Awarded to Full-Time	Awarded to Part-Time
Gift Aid	April 1	Yes	Yes
Federal College Work-Study	April 1	Yes	Yes
Federal Perkins Loans	April 1	Yes	Yes
Federal Stafford Loans	NA	Yes	Yes
School-Based Loans	April 1	Yes	Yes
Outside and Private Loans	NA	Yes	Yes
Graduate Assistantships	NA	Yes	

Percentage of Students Receiving Aid	Full-Time
All students	89%
Minority students	4%
Women students	
International students	

XAVIER UNIVERSITY
MBA Program

3800 Victory Parkway
Cincinnati, Ohio 45207-3221
Telephone: 513-745-3525

Total Enrollment (1993-94)	Full-Time	Part-Time
	70	1,020

Cost of Attendance (1993-94)		
Academic Year		
Standard Course Load per Semester/Term		
(credit hours/units)	9-12	6
Semesters/Terms per Academic Year	2	2
Tuition and Fees	$325/cr.	$325/cr.
Living Expenses	NA	NA
Summer Term		
(R = Required, O = Optional, N = None)	O	O
Standard Course Load	6-9	6
Tuition and Fees	$325/cr.	$325/cr.

Financial Aid Available	Deadline (fall starts)	Awarded to Full-Time	Awarded to Part-Time
Gift Aid	May 31	Yes	Yes
Federal College Work-Study		No	No
Federal Perkins Loans	April 15	Yes	Yes
Federal Stafford Loans	None	Yes	Yes
School-Based Loans		No	No
Outside and Private Loans	None	Yes	Yes
Graduate Assistantships	March 31	Yes	No

Percentage of Students Receiving Aid	Full-Time	Part-Time
All students	10%	2%
Minority students		
Women students		
International students		

YALE UNIVERSITY
Yale School of Organization and Management

Box 1A
New Haven, Connecticut 06520
Telephone: 203-432-5932

Total Enrollment (1993-94)	Full-Time
	420

Cost of Attendance (1993-94)	
Academic Year	
Standard Course Load per Semester/Term	
(credit hours/units)	5
Semesters/Terms per Academic Year	2
Tuition and Fees	$20,785
Living Expenses	$11,075
Summer Term	
(R = Required, O = Optional, N = None)	N
Standard Course Load	
Tuition and Fees	
Resident	
Nonresident	

Financial Aid Available	Deadline (fall starts)	Awarded to Full-Time
Gift Aid	March 31	Yes
Federal College Work-Study	March 31	Yes
Federal Perkins Loans	March 31	Yes
Federal Stafford Loans	March 31	Yes
School-Based Loans	March 31	Yes
Outside and Private Loans	None	
Graduate Assistantships	NA	

Percentage of Students Receiving Aid	Full-Time
All students	58%
Minority students	77%
Women students	69%
International students	43%

YOUNGSTOWN STATE UNIVERSITY
Williamson College of Business Administration

Williamson Hall
Youngstown, Ohio 44555
Telephone: 216-742-3069

Total Enrollment (1993-94)	Full-Time	Part-Time
	20	190

Cost of Attendance (1993-94)

Academic Year		
Standard Course Load per Semester/Term		
(credit hours/units)	12	4-8
Semesters/Terms per Academic Year	4	4
Tuition and Fees		
Resident	$ 85/qtr.hr.	$ 85/qtr.hr.
Nonresident	$138/qtr.hr.	$138/qtr.hr.
Living Expenses	$10,000	$8,000
Summer Term		
(R = Required, O = Optional, N = None)	O	O
Standard Course Load	8	4
Tuition and Fees		
Resident	$ 85/qtr.hr.	$ 85/qtr.hr.
Nonresident	$138/qtr.hr.	$138/qtr.hr.

Financial Aid Available

	Deadline (fall starts)	Awarded to Full-Time	Awarded to Part-Time
Gift Aid	Quarterly deadline	Yes	Yes
Federal College Work-Study	No deadline	Yes	No
Federal Perkins Loans	April 1	Yes	
Federal Stafford Loans	No deadline	Yes	Yes
School-Based Loans	No deadline	Yes	Yes
Outside and Private Loans		Yes	Yes
Graduate Assistantships	Quarterly deadline	Yes	No

15
Scholarship Opportunities

The following pages list organizations that provide scholarship, fellowship, and grant opportunities for graduate business students. Information for this section was provided by the organizations in early 1994. Check the listings for programs that match your qualifications and needs and then write to the addresses provided in these listings for current information or an application. For further reference, a bibliography appearing at the end of this chapter lists other sources of scholarship, fellowship, and grant information.

Alexander Graham Bell Association for the Deaf

College Scholarship Program

Eligibility: Severe or profound hearing loss, either from birth or before language developed; uses oral communication methods as customary form of communication; attending regular hearing college full time

Basis for Award: Scholarship, activities, some emphasis on financial need, recommendations

Amount of Award: $250 to $1,000

Application Deadline: April 15

Application Information: Scholarship Awards Committee
c/o Alexander Graham Bell Association for the Deaf
3417 Volta Place, N.W.
Washington, DC 20007

American Association of University Women Fellowships and Grants

Selected Professions Fellowships

Sponsor: American Association of University Women Educational Foundation

Eligibility: Women who are citizens or permanent residents of the United States in designated fields where female participation has traditionally been low

Basis for Award: Focus professions group fellowships awarded to women from ethnic minorities historically under-represented in business administration (M.B.A., two-year programs only); special consideration given to applicants who demonstrate professional promise in innovative or neglected areas of research and/or practice in public interest concerns

Amount of Award: $5,000 to $9,500

Application Deadline: February 1

Application Information: AAUW Educational Foundation
1111 Sixteenth Street N.W.
Washington, DC 20036-4873

International Fellowships

Sponsor: American Association of University Women Educational Foundation

Eligibility: Women of outstanding academic ability who are not citizens or permanent residents of the United States; must hold the equivalent of a U.S. bachelor's degree before December 1

Basis for Award: Applicants judged on their professional potential and on the importance of their projects to their country of origin; preference given to women whose credentials prove prior commitment to the advancement of women and girls through civic, community, or professional work

Amount of Award: $14,850

Application Deadline: December 1

Application Information: AAUW Educational Foundation
1111 Sixteenth Street N.W.
Washington, DC 20036-4873

Career Development Grants

Sponsor: American Association of University Women Educational Foundation

Eligibility: Women who are U.S. citizens or permanent residents, who hold a baccalaureate degree, and who have received their last degree on or before June 30, 1987

Basis for Award: Women who are reentering the work force, changing careers, or advancing their current careers and who are in the early stages of their programs; special consideration given to qualified AAUW members; preference given to women pursuing degrees in nontraditional fields

Amount of Award: $1,000 to $5,000

Application Deadline: January 3

Application Information: AAUW Educational Foundation
1111 Sixteenth Street N.W.
Washington, DC 20036-4873

The American Institute of Certified Public Accountants (AICPA)

Scholarships for Minority Accounting Students

Eligibility: Must be a minority graduate student who is in a five-year accounting program or who was an undergraduate accounting major and is presently accepted in a master's-level accounting, business administration, finance, or taxation program, or who had any undergraduate major and is presently accepted in a master's-level accounting program; must be enrolled as a full-time student (nine semester hours or equivalent); must be a citizen or permanent resident of the United States

Basis for Award: Primarily merit; financial need evaluated as a secondary criterion

Amount of Award: Up to $5,000

Application Deadline: July 1

Application Information: Minority Scholarships Programs
American Institute of Certified Public Accountants
1211 Avenue of the Americas
New York, NY 10036-8775

The American-Scandinavian Foundation (ASF)

Awards for Study in Scandinavia

Eligibility: Open to United States citizens and permanent residents who have completed under-graduate studies; outstanding proposals from all fields encouraged and carefully considered; other factors being equal, priority given to candidates at the dissertation level; candidates expected to have undertaken appropriate correspondence with institutions and scholars in Scandinavia; competence in the language of the country expected

Basis for Award: The significance and feasibility of the proposal, the qualifications of the applicant to pursue the program, and the special merit of pursuing the program in Scandinavia

Amount of Award: $2,500-$15,000

Application Deadline: November 1

Application Information: The American-Scandinavian Foundation (ASF)
Exchange Division
725 Park Avenue
New York, NY 10021

Appraisal Institute Education Trust Scholarship

Sponsor: Appraisal Institute

Eligibility: United States citizens, graduate students majoring in real estate appraisal, land economics, real estate, or allied fields

Basis for Award: Academic excellence

Amount of Award: $3,000

Application Deadline: March 15

Application Information: Appraisal Institute Education Trust
c/o Appraisal Institute
875 North Michigan Avenue, Suite 2400
Chicago, IL 60611-1980
Attn: Jennifer Schless, Project Coordinator

Association of School Business Officials International Exhibitor Scholarships

Sponsor: Annual Meeting Exhibitors

Eligibility: Must be a member of ASBO for at least 36 consecutive months before January 1 of the year in which the application is made; be employed on a full-time basis in a school business management position for 36 consecutive months immediately prior to January 1 of the year in which application is made; be recommended for the scholarship by the chief school administrator(s) for whom the applicant has served for the past 12 months (Other factors include professional achievements and activities, community and civic activities, aims and goals, and professional references.)

Basis for Award: Recognizes individuals who are employed in school business management and who are improving their technical skills and competence by pursuing further academic training

Amount of Award: $1,200

Application Deadline: August 1 of the year for which the application is being made

Application Information: Exhibitor Scholarship Coordinator
ASBO International
11401 North Shore Drive
Reston, VA 22090

Bush Leadership Fellows Program

Sponsor: The Bush Foundation

Eligibility: Must be a U.S. citizen or permanent resident between the ages of 28 and 54 at the application deadline date; must have worked or lived for at least one continuous year immediately prior to the application in Minnesota, North Dakota, South Dakota, or the following 26 counties of northwestern Wisconsin: Ashland, Barron, Bayfield, Buffalo, Burnett, Chippewa, Douglas, Dunn, Eau Claire, Florence, Forest, Iron, La Cross, Lincoln, Oneida, Pepin, Pierce, Polk, Price, Rusk, St. Croix, Sawyer, Taylor, Trempleau, Vilas and Washburn; must be employed full time, with a minimum of five years experience including some experience in a policy-making or administrative capacity; must have baccalaureate degree or equivalent in educational and work experience

Basis for Award: To prepare men and women at mid-career for greater leadership roles within their professions and communities; (Recent award winners include those who have distinguished themselves as leaders either in their careers or communities or both.)

Amount of Award: Monthly stipend and 50 percent of tuition expenses plus travel expenses up to fixed maximum amounts

Application Deadline: Completed applications are accepted between September and December depending on the current year's application deadline.

Application Information: Bush Leadership Fellows Program
E-900 First National Bank Building
332 Minnesota Street
St. Paul, MN 55101

Business and Professional Women's Foundation Educational Programs

The Avon Products Foundation Scholarship Program for Women in Business Studies

Sponsor: Avon

Eligibility: Must be a woman 25 years of age or older and a citizen of the United States; must be officially accepted into an accredited program or course of study at a United States institution, including institutions in Puerto Rico and the Virgin Islands; must be graduating within 12 to 24 months from September 1 of the application year; must be studying in a business-related field such as management, business administration, marketing, sales, or accounting

Basis for Award: Applicant must have a definite plan to use the desired training to upgrade skills for career advancement, to train for a new career field, or to enter or re-enter the job market

Amount of Award: $1,000

Application Deadline: April 15

Application Information: Scholarships
BPW Foundation
2012 Massachusetts Avenue, N.W.
Washington, DC 20036
(Include enrollment verification with request)

Canadian Federation of University Women

Fellowships and Awards

Sponsor: Canadian Federation of University Women

Eligibility: Women university graduates who have been accepted into the proposed place of study, and are Canadian citizens or have held landed immigrant status for at least one year

Basis for Award: Varies; write to address below for specific information about each award

Amount of Award: Ranges from $1,000 to $9,000

Application Deadline: November 30

Application Information: Canadian Federation of University Women
55 Parkdale Avenue
Ottawa, Ontario
K1Y 1E5
Canada

Charles R. Drew Memorial Scholarship Commission

District and National Scholar of the Year Awards

Sponsor: Omega Psi Phi Fraternity, Inc.

Eligibility: District—Omega Psi Phi Fraternity college senior in good financial standing with an average of "B" or above
National—chosen District Scholar of the Year who plans to enroll in graduate or professional school within two years after graduation from an undergraduate school

Amount of Award: District—varies among districts; Drew Commission matches award up to $750
National—District award plus $1,000

Application Information: Charles R. Drew Memorial Scholarship Commission
Omega Psi Phi Fraternity, Inc.
International Headquarters
2714 Georgia Avenue, NW
Washington, DC 20001

Undergraduate and Graduate Scholarship Grants

Sponsor: Omega Psi Phi Fraternity, Inc.

Eligibility: Member of Omega Psi Phi Fraternity in good financial standing with an average of "B" or above who can demonstrate financial need

Amount of Award: Up to $500

Application Deadline: May 15

Application Information: Omega Psi Phi Fraternity, Inc.
International Headquarters
2714 Georgia Avenue, NW
Washington, DC 20001

Chase Manhattan Scholarship

Sponsor: Financial Women International

Eligibility: Must be a member of Financial Women International (to be a member, must be employed within the financial industry in a managerial or supervisory capacity)

Basis for Award: Competitive

Amount of Award: Varies; usually about $2,000 per year

Application Deadline: Generally, May 1

Application Information: Chase Manhattan Scholarship
7910 Woodmont Avenue
Suite 1430
Bethesda, MD 20814-3015

Congressional Fellowships on Women and Public Policy

Sponsor: Women's Research and Education Institute (WREI)

Eligibility: Must be currently enrolled in a master's or doctoral program at an accredited institution in the United States; strongly recommended that applicants have completed at least nine hours of graduate course work and have a demonstrated interest in research or political activity related to women's social and political status

Basis for Award: Academic performance, work with community groups, and interest in analyzing the effect of gender differences on laws and lawmaking

Amount of Award: Stipend of $9,500 for the academic year; $500 provided for the purchase of health insurance; reimbursement of up to $1,500 for the cost of six hours of tuition at home institutions directly related to the fellowship experience

Application Deadline: Mid-February

Application Information: Women's Research and Education Institute
Congressional Fellowship Program
1700 18th Street, NW Suite 400
Washington, DC 20009

Consortium for Graduate Study in Management

Eligibility: Must be a U.S. citizen certifying membership in one of the following minority groups: African American, Native-American, or Hispanic; must qualify for admission to a Consortium MBA program

Basis for Award: Applicant's desire to study management; proven aptitude, ability, and scholarship

Amount of Award: Full tuition plus stipend of $2,500 per year; second-year support contingent upon satisfactory progress in the first year

Application Deadline: December 1, early decision;
February 1

Application Information: Consortium for Graduate Study in Management
12855 N. Outer 40 Drive, #100
St. Louis, MO 63141

Corporate Executive Fellows Program

Sponsors:	Columbia Business School, Stanford Graduate School of Business, John D. and Catherine T. MacArthur Foundation, corporate participants, and National Urban Fellows, Inc.
Eligibility:	Minority men and women who are U.S. citizens, meet the requirements for admission to Columbia Business School or Stanford Graduate School of Business, have significant work experience, and have demonstrated excellent ability, maturity, and leadership potential, and are willing to relocate for the duration of the fellowship, which includes a nine-month mentorship assignment at a major corporation
Basis for Award:	Serious commitment to a management career in the corporate sector; must meet the criteria of the Corporate Executive Fellows Program (Write to the address below for details.)
Amount of Award:	Full tuition, stipend of $16,000 during mentorship assignment, relocation allowance of $1,000 and reimbursement of travel costs
Application Deadline:	Applications accepted year round
Application Information:	Corporate Executive Fellows Programs National Urban Fellows, Inc. 55 West 44th Street New York, NY 10036

The Educational Foundation of the National Restaurant Association

Graduate Fellowship

Sponsor:	H. J. Heinz Company Foundation
Eligibility:	Currently be a full-time teacher or administrator of a food service/hospitality program; be accepted in a graduate degree program on a full time or substantial part-time basis, beginning or continuing in the upcoming fall term; be pursuing a course of study designed to improve skills in teaching or administering food service/hospitality courses, or food service/hospitality career education
Amount of Award:	$1,000 to $2,000
Application Deadline:	December 31
Application Information:	Scholarship Department The Educational Foundation of the National Restaurant Association 250 South Wacker Drive, Suite 1400 Chicago, IL 60606

Electrical Women's Round Table, Inc.

Julia Kiene Fellowship
Lyle Mamer Fellowship

Sponsor:	Electrical Women's Round Table, Inc.
Eligibility:	Applicant must be graduating senior or have a degree from an accredited institution pursuing a master's or Ph.D.
Basis for Award:	Applications judged on the basis of scholarship, character, financial need, and professional interest in electrical energy
Amount of Award:	Julia Kiene Fellowship—up to $2,000 Lyle Mamer Fellowship—up to $1,000

Application Deadline:	March 1
Application Information:	Electrical Women's Round Table, Inc.
	P.O. Box 292793
	Nashville, TN 37229-2793

Freethought Essay Competition

Sponsor:	Freedom From Religion Foundation, Inc.
Eligibility:	College student, graduate or undergraduate
Basis for Award:	Themes are separation of church and state; rejecting religion; contest announced February of each year
Amount of Award:	Saul Jakel Award $1,000; other cash awards of $500, $200 (also honorable mentions of $100, at judges' discretion)
Application Deadline:	August 1
Application Information:	Send self-addressed stamped envelope to:
	FFRF, Inc.
	P.O. Box 750
	Madison, WI 53701

Government Finance Officers Association of the United States and Canada

Daniel B. Goldberg Scholarship

Eligibility:	Currently a full-time student in a graduate program that prepares students for careers in state and local government finance and expecting to be enrolled in the spring 1995 semester (including spring 1995 graduates); baccalaureate degree or its equivalent; legal resident of the United States or Canada; recommendation by the dean of the graduate program
Basis for Award:	Plans for pursuit of a career in state or local government finance; strength of past course work and present plan of study; letters of recommendation from the dean of the graduate program and others; undergraduate and graduate grade-point averages
Amount of Award:	$3,500
Application Deadline:	Generally, mid-February
Application Information:	Government Finance Officers Association
	Scholarship Committee
	180 North Michigan Avenue
	Suite 800
	Chicago, IL 60601-7476

Public Investor Scholarship

Sponsor:	Fidelity Investments Institutional Services Company
Eligibility:	Must have been admitted on a full- or part-time basis to a graduate program in public administration, finance, business administration, or social sciences; must hold a baccalaureate degree or its equivalent; must be a legal resident of the United States or Canada; must present a letter of recommendation from the dean of the graduate program
Basis for Award:	Past academic record and experience; strength of past graduate course work and present plan of study; letters of recommendation from the dean of the graduate program and others; grade-point average; must plan to pursue a career in state or local government

Amount of Award:	$3,000
Application Deadline:	Generally, mid-February
Application Information:	Government Finance Officers Association
	Scholarship Committee
	180 North Michigan Avenue
	Suite 800
	Chicago, IL 60601-7476

Graduate Fellowships for American Indians

Sponsor:	American Indian Graduate Center
Eligibility:	Must be an enrolled member of a federally recognized American Indian tribe or Alaska Native group, or possess one-fourth degree (federally recognized) Indian blood; pursuing a master's or doctorate degree as a full-time graduate student at an accredited graduate school in the United States; in need of financial aid after exhausting available aid at the college financial aid office
Basis for Award:	Applicant's unmet financial need as verified by the applicant's college financial aid office
Amount of Award:	Range from $250 to a maximum of $10,000
Application Deadline:	April 30
Application Information:	American Indian Graduate Center
	4520 Montgomery Boulevard NE, Suite 1-B
	Albuquerque, NM 87109-1291
	(505) 881-4584

IAFUS Graduate Study Fellowship

IAF Field Research Fellowship Program at Doctoral Level
IAF Field Research Fellowship Program at Master's Level

Sponsor:	Inter-American Foundation
Eligibility:	Must be enrolled in U.S. academic institution at master's or doctoral level; focus of thesis on elimination of poverty
Basis for Award:	Budget must be submitted for field research in Latin American country
Amount of Award:	Ph.D. — Average $14,000-16,000 for a maximum period of 18 months
	Master's — Average between $2,000-3,000 for a maximum period of six months
Application Deadline:	Ph.D. — December 1
	Master's — early March
Application Information:	IAF Fellowship Program, Dept. 555
	901 North Stuart Street, 10th floor
	Arlington, VA 22203

Institute of International Education

Fulbright British-American Chamber of Commerce Award

Sponsor:	U.K. Fulbright Commission and British American Chamber of Commerce
Eligibility:	U.S. citizen with a bachelor's degree
Basis for Award:	Grant tenable for graduate study in business for a one-year M.B.A. in the United Kingdom
Amount of Award:	Covers round trip travel to the United Kingdom, maintenance allowance for 12 months, tuition, and allowance for in-country travel

Application Deadline: October 31

Application Information: U.S. Student Programs
Institute of International Education
809 U.N. Plaza
New York, NY 10017

Fulbright U.S. Graduate Study Program for Study or Research Abroad

Sponsor: Institute of International Education

Eligibility: U.S. citizen with a bachelor's degree

Basis for Award: Selection made on the basis of the applicant's academic or professional record, language preparation, and the feasibility of the proposed study project and personal qualifications

Amount of Award: Varies; grants cover travel, living expenses, tuition waivers, if applicable

Application Deadline: October 31

Application Information: U.S. Student Programs
Institute of International Education
809 U.N. Plaza
New York, NY 10017

Japanese American Citizens League

Sponsor: Japanese American Citizens League

Eligibility: JACL member or American citizen of Japanese ancestry; must be currently enrolled or planning to enter an accredited Graduate School in the following semester

Basis for Award: Scholastic achievement, extracurricular activities, community involvement, personal statement or essay, letters of recommendation

Amount of Award: $1,000-$5,000

Application Deadline: March 1

Application Information: JACL National Headquarters
1765 Sutter Street
San Francisco, CA 94115
(send self-addressed, stamped, legal-sized envelope)

The Kosciuszko Foundation Tuition Scholarships

Eligibility: Full-time graduate students in the United States; U.S. citizens of Polish descent; Poles who are permanent residents of the United States; Americans of non-Polish descent who are pursuing studies/research relating to Polish subjects

Basis for Award: Academic excellence; evidence of identification with Polish American community; financial need.

Amount of Award: Varies up to a maximum of one year's tuition

Application Deadline: January 15

Application Information: The Kosciuszko Foundation
Domestic Grants Office
15 East 65th Street
New York, NY 10021

Lady Davis Graduate Fellowships

Sponsor: Eldee Foundation, Montreal, Canada

Eligibility: Completion of their bachelor's studies with excellent marks
Award tenable at the Technion-Israel Institute of Technology in Haifa, Israel

Basis for Award: Distinction in chosen field of specialization as well as qualities of mind, intellect, and character

Amount of Award: Reasonable living expenses plus travel and tuition

Application Deadline: November 30

Application Information: Executive Secretary
The Lady Davis Fellowship Trust
P.O.B. 1255
Jerusalem 91904
Israel

McKnight Doctoral Fellowship

Sponsor: Florida Education Fund

Eligibility: Must be African-American, U.S. citizen, and have obtained bachelor's degree

Basis for Award: Must be admitted into *doctoral* program at one of the 11 participating institutions in Florida

Amount of Award: $11,000 annual stipend and up to $5,000 fees/tuition annually

Application Deadline: January 15

Application Information: Florida Education Fund
210 East Kennedy Boulevard #1525
Tampa, FL 33602

Minorities in Government Finance Scholarship

Eligibility: Applicants must be full- or part-time students of public administration, (governmental) accounting, finance, political science, economics, or business administration (with a specific focus on government or nonprofit management); plan to pursue a career in state or local government finance; be Black, Indian, Eskimo or Aleut, Asian or Pacific Islander, or Hispanic; be a citizen or permanent resident of the United States or Canada

Basis for Award: Plans to pursue a career in state and local government finance; past academic record and experience; strength of past course work and present plan of study; letters of recommendation from the dean of the graduate program and others; grade point average

Amount of Award: $3,500

Application Deadline: February 18

Application Information: Government Finance Officers Association
Scholarship Committee
180 North Michigan Avenue
Suite 800
Chicago, IL 60601-7476

National Association of MBA Women (NAMBAW) Scholarships

Sponsor: National Association of MBA Women

Eligibility: Must be enrolled in an M.B.A. program; must be a member of the association (For details on membership, write to the address below.)

Basis for Award: Grades; essay on future use of M.B.A. education (career); extracurricular activities related to intended business career

Amount of Award: $250-$1,000

Application Deadline: Traditionally, September 15 or October 15

Application Information: National Association of MBA Women
7701 Georgia Avenue, NW
Washington, DC 20012

The National Black MBA Association, Inc. (NBMBAA)

MBA Scholarship Program

Sponsors: Anheuser-Busch; Avon Products; Coca-Cola Company; Connaught Labs; Eastman Kodak; Earl G. Graves Publishing; Ford Motor Company; General Electric Company; General Motors Corporation; Hewlett Packard; Marriott Corporation; National Basketball Association; Prudential Company

Eligibility: Minority students enrolled in full-time graduate business management program

Amount of Award: $3,000

Application Deadline: March 31

Application Information: National Black MBA Association, Inc.
National Headquarters
180 N. Michigan Avenue, Suite 1515
Chicago, IL 60601

Doctoral Fellowship Program

Sponsors: Anheuser-Busch; Avon Products; Coca-Cola Company; Connaught Labs; Eastman Kodak; Earl G. Graves Publishing; Ford Motor Company; General Electric Company; General Motors Corporation; Hewlett Packard; Marriott Corporation; National Basketball Association; Prudential Company

Eligibility: Minority students enrolled in full-time doctoral business or related field program

Amount of Award: $5,000

Application Deadline: March 31

Application Information: National Black MBA Association, Inc.
National Headquarters
180 N. Michigan Avenue, Suite 1515
Chicago, IL 60601

National Council of Farmer Cooperatives Graduate Awards

Edwin G. Nourse Award

Sponsor: The National Council of Farmer Cooperatives

Eligibility: Any graduate student in economics, business, communications, sociology, or other relevant field who has an agricultural vocational objective

Basis for Award: Best doctoral dissertation on some aspect of economics, finance, operations, or structure of American agricultural cooperatives

Amount of Award:	$1,000
Application Deadline:	April 15
Application Information:	National Council of Farmer Cooperatives Graduate Awards 50 F Street, N.W., Suite 900 Washington, DC 20001

Kenneth D. Naden Award
E. A. Stokdyk Award

Sponsor:	The National Council of Farmer Cooperatives
Eligibility:	Any graduate student in economics, business, communications, sociology, or other relevant field who has an agricultural vocational objective
Basis for Awards:	Two best master's theses on some aspect of economics, finance, operations, or structure of American Agricultural cooperatives
Amount of Awards:	Kenneth D. Naden Award — $800 E. A. Stokdyk Award — $600
Application Deadline:	April 15
Application Information:	National Council of Farmer Cooperatives Graduate Awards 50 F Street, N.W., Suite 900 Washington, DC 20001

National Hispanic Scholarship Fund

Eligibility:	Must be a United States citizen or permanent resident of Hispanic parentage; must have completed at least 15 units/credits prior to fall registration; must be enrolled in college for the fall and spring semester of each year on a full-time basis (full-time graduate student must be carrying minimum of six units); must attend an accredited college or university in one of the 50 states or Puerto Rico
Basis for Award:	Available on a competitive basis to graduate students of Hispanic background
Amount of Award:	$500 to $1,000
Application Deadline:	June 15
Application Information:	National Hispanic Scholarship Fund Post Office Box 728 Novato, CA 94948

The National Italian American Foundation

FBI Honors Internship Program

Sponsor:	Federal Bureau of Investigation
Eligibility:	Must have one year of academic work left in any major to enhance their area of study and research
Basis for Award:	Academic achievement, community involvement, and financial need
Amount of Award:	Approximately $4,800 (50-75 students selected per year)
Application Information:	The National Italian American Foundation 666 Eleventh Street, N.W. Suite 800 Washington, DC 20001-4596

A.P. Giannini Scholarship

Eligibility: Students with concentrations in banking or international finance

Basis for Award: Academic achievement, community involvement, and financial need

Amount of Award: $1,000

Application Information: The National Italian American Foundation
666 Eleventh Street, N.W.
Suite 800
Washington, DC 20001-4596

E.D. Stella Scholarship

Sponsor: NIAF in conjunction with the Detroit Chamber of Commerce

Eligibility: Undergraduate and graduate business majors

Basis for Award: Academic achievement, community involvement, and financial need

Amount of Award: $1,000

Application Information: The National Italian American Foundation
666 Eleventh Street, N.W.
Suite 800
Washington, DC 20001-4596

Bolla Wines Scholarship

Sponsor: Bolla Italian Wines

Eligibility: At least 21 years of age, a grade point average of 3.0 or higher, and a background in International Studies with an emphasis on Italian business or Italian-American history

Basis for Award: Essay about "The Importance of Italy in Today's Business" (approximately 1,000 words)

Amount of Award: $1,000

Application Information: The National Italian American Foundation
666 Eleventh Street, N.W.
Suite 800
Washington, DC 20001-4596

National Society of Hispanic MBAs

Eligibility: Must be of Hispanic descent and enrolled in a full-time MBA program

Basis for Award: Need, essay, grades

Amount of Award: Varies—$1,000 to $3,000

Application Deadline: Varies by chapter

Application Information: National Society of Hispanic MBAs
P.O. Box 685007
Austin, TX 78768-5007

National Society of Professional Engineers (NSPE) Education Foundation

Professional Engineers in Government Management Study Fellowship

Sponsor: The Professional Engineers in Government

Eligibility: Must be an engineer-in-training or registered professional engineer from any discipline pursuing advanced study in management; must be U.S. citizen or current NSPE member

Basis for Award: Professional activities; community activities; essay; undergraduate final GPA; GRE/GMAT scores; NSPE membership; PEG membership; government employee

Amount of Award: $2,000

Application Deadline: January 14

Application Information: NSPE Education Foundation
1420 King Street
Alexandria, VA 22314

Schinnerer/Pepp Management Study Fellowship

Sponsors: Victor O. Schinnerer & Company, Inc.
Professional Engineers in Private Practice (PEPP)

Eligibility: Must be a registered professional engineer employed by a consulting engineering firm prior to graduate study and an NSPE and NSPE/PEPP member either before or after the fellowship award; must be pursuing an M.B.A. in management, master's in engineering management, or master's in public administration

Basis for Award: Professional activities, community activities, essay, undergraduate final GPA, GRE/GMAT score

Amount of Award: $3,000

Application Deadline: January 14

Application Information: NSPE Education Foundation
1420 King Street
Alexandria, VA 22314

Orville Redenbacher's Second Start Scholarship Program

Sponsor: Orville Redenbacher

Eligibility: Adults over the age of 30 who have decided to go back to college or pursue a college degree for the first time at accredited college or university

Basis for Award: Not solely on need; 500-word essay required

Amount of Award: $1,000

Application Deadline: May 1

Application Information: Orville Redenbacher's Second Start Scholarship Program
P.O. Box 39101
Chicago, IL 60639

Patricia Roberts Harris Fellowship Program

Sponsor: U.S. Government

Eligibility: Preference given to minority group and women graduate students; must be U.S. citizen; must attend school full time

Basis for Award: Designed to increase professional opportunities for those underrepresented in certain fields and for students choosing to enter careers in the public interest

Amount of Award: Annual stipend of $14,000 plus $9,000 institutional allowance

Application Deadline: Non-competing for 1994; specific information available from school financial aid office

Application Information: U.S. Department of Education
Division of Higher Education Incentive Programs
Patricia Roberts Harris Fellowship
400 Maryland Avenue
Washington, DC 20202

PRA-Fellowships

Sponsor: Organization of American States (OAS)

Eligibility: Must be a citizen or permanent resident of an OAS member country with a university degree or must have demonstrated ability to pursue advanced studies in the field chosen; fellowships for advanced study or research in any field, with the exception of the medical sciences; must know the language of the study country

Award tenable in any of the member countries of the Organization of American States (Antiqua and Barbuda, Argentina, Bahamas, Barbados, Belize, Bolivia, Brazil, Canada, Chile, Columbia, Costa Rica, Dominica, Dominican Republic, Ecuador, El Salvador, Grenada, Guatemala, Guyana, Haiti, Honduras, Jamaica, Mexico, Nicaragua, Panama, Praguay, Peru, Saint Christopher and Neves, Saint Lucia, Saint Vinvent and the Grenadines, Suriname, United States, Trinidad and Tobago, Uraguay, and Venezuela) with the exception of the country of which the candidate is a citizen or in which a permanent residence is maintained

Basis for Award: Evidence of having had advanced training in the field for which the fellowship is requested

Amount of Award: Provides funds sufficient to cover, as a maximum, and in accordance with the circumstances, travel expenses, tuition fees, study materials, and subsistence allowance (which varies from country to country)

Application Deadline: March 1

Application Information: General Secretariat of the OAS
Department of Fellowships
Washington, DC 20006-4499

Rotary Foundation Ambassadorial Scholarships

Sponsor: The Rotary Foundation of Rotary International

Eligibility: Bachelor's degree or equivalent prior to commencement of scholarship studies

Basis for Award: Multi-year grant to assist students with the cost of pursuing a degree in another country

Amount of Award: $10,000 or its equivalent per year for two to three years

Application Deadline: July 1

Application Information: Local Rotary Club
OR
The Rotary Foundation
One Rotary Center
1560 Sherman Avenue
Evanston, IL 60201

BIBLIOGRAPHY

A Selected List of Fellowship Opportunities and Aids to Advanced Education for United States Citizens and Foreign Nationals, 1988, The National Science Foundation, 4201 Wilson Blvd., Room 907, Arlington, VA 22230

Annual Register of Grant Support, 1993 edition, ($165), Reed Reference Publishing Co., 121 Chanlon Road, New Providence, NJ 07974

Bureau of Indian Affairs Higher Education Grants and Scholarships, (free), Office of Indian Education Programs, Code 522, Room 3516, 18th and C Streets, N.W., Washington, DC 20240

College Costs and Financial Aid Handbook, 1994, ($16.00), College Board Publications, Box 886, New York, NY 10101-0886

Directory of Financial Aids for Minorities, 1993-95, Gail A. Schlachter, ($47.50 plus $4 postage), Reference Service Press, 1100 Industrial Road, Suite 9, San Carlos, CA 94070

Directory of Financial Aids for Women, 1993-95, Gail A. Schlachter, ($45.00 plus $4 postage), Reference Service Press, 1100 Industrial Road, Suite 9, San Carlos, CA 94070

Don't Miss Out, 1994, 19th edition, Robert Leider, ($7.00), Octameron Associates, Inc., P.O. Box 2748, Alexandria, VA 22301

Earn & Learn: Cooperative Education Opportunities Offered by the Federal Government, 1994, 15th edition, Joseph Re, ($4.00), Octameron Associates, Inc., P.O. Box 2748, Alexandria, VA 22301

Federal Benefits for Veterans and Dependents, Fact Sheet IS-1, 1993, ($3.25), Superintendent of Documents, U.S. Government Printing Office, Washington, DC 20402

Financial Aid Fin-ancer, 1994-95, 5th edition, Joseph M. Re, ($4.00), Octameron Associates, Inc., P.O. Box 2748, Alexandria, VA 22301

Financial Aid for Graduate and Professional Education, 1993 edition, ($2.35), Peterson's Guides, Inc., P.O. Box 2123, Princeton, NJ 08543-2123

Financial Aid for Minorities in Business, ($4.95), Garrett Park Press, P.O. Box 190B, Garrett Park, MD 20896

Financial Aid for Study and Training Abroad, 1992-94, ($40.00), Reference Service Press, 1100 Industrial Rd., Suite 9, San Carlos, CA 94070

Financial Aid for the Disabled and Their Families, 1992-94, ($37.50 plus postage), Gail Ann Schlachter and R. David Weber, Reference Service Press, 1100 Industrial Road, Suite 9, San Carlos, CA 94070

Financial Aid Officers: What They Do To You and For You, 1993-94, 7th edition, ($4.00), Donald Moore, Octameron Associates, Inc., P.O. Box 2748, Alexandria, VA 22301

Financing Graduate School, 1993, ($14.95), Patricia McWade, Peterson's Guides, Inc., P.O. Box 500, Englewood Cliffs, NJ 07632

Foundation Grants to Individuals, 8th edition, ($55.00 plus postage), Foundation Center, 79 Fifth Avenue, 8th Floor, New York, NY 10003

Free Money for Graduate School, 1993, ($35.00), Laurie Blum, Henry Holt and Company, Inc., 115 West 18th Street, New York, NY 10011

Funding for U.S. Study—A Guide for Foreign Nationals, ($39.95), Institute of International Education, 809 United Nations Plaza, New York, NY 10017

Getting Yours: The Complete Guide to Government Money, 3rd edition, ($11.95 plus postage), Penguin Publications, 375 Hudson Street, New York, NY 10011

Graduate Guide to Grants, 1993, ($25.00), Harvard University, Byerly Hall, 8 Garden Street, Cambridge, MA 02138

Grants for Graduate Study, 1991, 3rd edition, ($59.95), Andrea Leskes, ed., Peterson's Guides, Inc., P.O. Box 500, Englewood Cliffs, NJ 07632

Grants Register 1993-95, 1993, ($89.95 plus postage), St. Martin's Press, 175 Fifth Avenue, New York, NY 10010

Higher Education Opportunities for Minorities and Women, 1991, ($8.00), U.S. Government Printing Office, Washington, D.C.

How to Find Out about Financial Aid, 1987, ($35.00), Gail Ann Schlachter, Reference Service Press, 1100 Industrial Road, Suite 9, San Carlos, CA 94070

Internships and Fellowships, 1991, (free), Smithsonian Institute, Visitor Information and Associates' Reception Center, 1000 Jefferson Drive SW, Room 153 MRC 010, Washington, DC 20560

Loans and Grants from Uncle Sam, 1994-95, ($5.00 plus postage), Octameron Associates, Inc., P.O. Box 2748, Alexandria, VA 22301

Need a Lift?, ($2.00), National Emblem Sales Division, American Legion, Box 1050, Indianapolis, IN 46206

Student Aid Annual, 1994, ($22.47 plus postage), Chronical Guidance Publications, P.O. Box 1190, Moravia, NY 13118-1190

The Black Collegian's Guide to Graduate Fellowships for Minority Students, 1992, 4th edition, ($10.00), Renee Carrere, Black Collegiate Services, Inc., 1240 S. Broad Street, New Orleans, LA 70125

The College Blue Book: Scholarships, Fellowships, Grants and Loans, 1993, 24th edition, ($48.00), Macmillan Publishing Co., Inc., Attn.: Order Dept., 100 Front Street, Box 500, Riverside, NJ 08075

The Federal Student Aid Factsheet, 1991, (free), U.S. Department of Education, 7th and D Streets, SW, Washington, DC

The Graduate Scholarship Book: The Complete Guide to Scholarships, Fellowships, Grants, and Loans for Graduate and Professional Study, 1993, 2nd edition, Daniel J. Cassidy, ($19.95), Prentice-Hall, Inc., P.O. Box 500, Englewood Cliffs, NJ 07632

The Individual's Guide to Grants, 1983, Judith B. Margolin, ($19.95), Plenum Publishing Company, 233 Spring Street, New York, NY 10013, Attn: Order Department

The International Scholarship Directory, 1993, ($24.95 plus postage), Daniel J. Cassidy, National Scholarship Research Service, 2280 Airport Blvd., Santa Rosa, CA 95403

The Scholarship Guide for Hispanics, 1994, (free), a VISTA Scholarship Guide, Montemayor y Asociados, 70 N.E. Loop 410, Suite 870, San Antonio, TX 78216

The Student Guide, 1993-94, Federal Student Aid Programs, P.O. Box 84, Washington, DC 20044

U.S. Student Fulbright Grants and Other Grants, 1994-95, (free), Institute of International Education, 809 United Nations Plaza, New York, NY 10017-3580

Appendix A
Sources of Additional Assistance

Academic Management Service (AMS)

50 Vision Boulevard
East Providence, RI 02914

Telephone: 800-635-0120

- government-backed loans

- academic credit line to $25,000

- budget tuition payment plan if school participates in program

- application deadlines open for loans and credit line

Business and Professional Women's Foundation

Loan Programs
2012 Massachusetts Avenue, NW
Washington, DC

- jointly sponsored by the BPW Foundation and the Sears-Roebuck Foundation

- applicant must be a U.S. citizen

- applicant must have written notice of acceptance for enrollment at a school accredited by the American Assembly of Collegiate Schools of Business (AACSB)

- must have academic and/or work experience records showing career motivation and ability to complete course of study

- loans up to $2,500 for an academic year; interest rate at 7 percent; repayment begins 12 months after graduation

- application deadline April 15

ConSern Loans for Education

205 Van Buren Street
Suite 200
Herndon, VA 22070

Telephone: 800-SOS-LOAN

- private loans available for employees and relatives of sponsor companies (approximately 800)

- U.S. Citizen attending accredited institution

- $1,500–$25,000

- based on creditworthiness

- variable interest rate — 15-year repayment with interest payable immediately

The Education Resource Institute (TERI)

330 Stuart Street, Suite 500
Boston, MA 02116

Telephone: 800-255-TERI

- private loans available for full- or part-time study at any accredited institution in any state

- applicant or co-signer to demonstrate credit worthiness and be a U.S. citizen or permanent resident

- twenty five-year repayment period (dependent on amount borrowed)

- loans from $2,000 up to the cost of education

Hattie M. Strong Foundation

1735 Eye Street, N.W.
Suite 705
Washington, D.C. 20006

Telephone: 202-331-1619

- private loans for American students studying in the U.S. or abroad and entering their final year of study in a baccalaureate or graduate degree program

- applicants to be enrolled full-time

- interest-free maximum of $2,500

- repayment based on income

- applications available January 1–March 31

Knight College Resource Group

855 Boylston Street
Boston, MA 02116-2611

Telephone: 617-267-1500
          800-225-6783

- private loans for creditworthy applicants

- tuition payment plans

MBA LOANS

2400 Broadway, Suite 230
Santa Monica, California 90404

Telephone: 800-366-6227

- Federal Stafford Loans and private Tuition Loan Program (TLP) available to students enrolled in a graduate business program at an accredited, degree-granting college or university

- TLP based on being credit-ready (i.e., the absence of adverse credit information)

- loan consolidation program available for federal loans

- payment options available

(refer to more detailed information provided in Chapter 6)

Executive MBA LOANS

2400 Broadway, Suite 230
Santa Monica, California 90404

Telephone: 800-366-0603

- Executive MBA (EMBA) LOANS available to students enrolled in an executive M.B.A. program at an accredited, degree-granting college or university

- EMBA LOANS based on being creditworthy

- payment options available

(refer to more detailed information provided in Chapter 6)

New England Education Loan Marketing Corporation (Nellie Mae)

50 Braintree Hill Park, Suite 300
Braintree, MA 02184

Telephone: 800-634-9308

- private and federal loans

- GradShare loans available to students attending any member school of the Consortium on the Financing of Higher Education (COFHE) (32 schools)

- GradExel loans available to students attending any accredited, degree-granting college or university in the U.S.

- loan eligibility based on projected future earnings rather than current income

- loan consolidation program for federal loans

- payment options

Option 4 Loan Program

Telephone: 800-635-3785

- applicant or co-sponsor must be a U.S. citizen and demonstrate creditworthiness

- loan amounts from $2,000 to $15,000, not to exceed the cost of attendance less other aid

- repayment begins 45 days after loan disbursement

- interest rate is variable

- maximum repayment period is 15 years

P.L.A.T.O.

205 Van Buren Street
Suite 200
Herndon, VA 22070

Telephone: 800-SOS-LOAN

- same criteria as ConSern loan except do not have to be employee or relative of sponsor company

Smart Loan Consolidation

P.O. 1304
Merrifield, VA 22116-1304

Telephone: 800-524-9100

- minimum $7,500 debt

- consolidation dependent upon ownership of loan, i.e.,
  SALLIE MAE

- term of payment tied to indebtedness

- spousal consolidation

U.S. Department of Education

Office of Student Financial Assistance
400 Maryland Avenue
Washington, D.C. 20202

Telephone: 800-433-3243 (Federal Student
Aid Information Center)

- distributes applications for federal assistance and
  provides assistance with completion

- information on federal financial aid

Appendix B
Sample Loan Application and Promissory Note

The sample loan application and promissory note shown on the following pages was in use for the 1994-95 award year. This sample will give you an idea of what information is requested on a loan application and what promissory notes include. You should read your own loan application(s) and promissory note(s) carefully to insure that you understand all the terms and conditions of your loan(s).

MBA LOANS
A Program of the Graduate Management Admission Council

Tuition Loan Program — Application and Promissory Note — 1994-95

A. **BORROWER**

1. Legal Name
Last _____
First _____ M.I. _____

2. Social Security No.

3. TLP Loan Amount Requested
$ _____ .00

4. Birthdate
Month | Day | Year

5. Driver's License Number
State of Issuance:

6. Will your TLP be cosigned?
☐ No ☐ Yes
If yes, complete Cosigner Application on last page of this application packet and submit with TLP application.

7. Have you requested or been granted credit under another name?
☐ No ☐ Yes (list name)
Last _____
First _____
Middle _____

8. Address While in School
Street _____
City _____
State _____ Zip _____
Telephone ( ) _____

9. Permanent Home Address
Street _____
City _____
State _____ Zip _____
Telephone ( ) _____

10. Total undergraduate/graduate student educational loan debt. (Do not include TLP Loan Amount Requested in question #3 or other loans for this loan period.)
Stafford $ _____ Perkins $ _____
SLS $ _____ Other $ _____

11. Citizenship (check one)
☐ U.S. Citizen or National
☐ Permanent Resident or other Eligible Alien
If you checked the 2nd Box, you must attach a copy of the front/back of your registration card. A credit-worthy U.S. citizen cosigner is required to complete enclosed Cosigner Application.

12. Have you ever defaulted on a Stafford (GSL), SLS, or other educational loan?
☐ No ☐ Yes
If Yes, submit documentation regarding current status of the loan with your application.

13. For Future Use

14. Enrollment Period - not to exceed 12 months (e.g. From 08-94 To 05-95).
From _____ _____
To _____ _____
Month | Year

THE FOLLOWING 3 REFERENCES MUST BE COMPLETED WITH EVERY ITEM FILLED IN OR YOUR APPLICATION WILL BE REJECTED!

15. Consumer Credit Reference (Do not list student loans)
Creditor's Acct. # _____
Creditor's Name _____
Street _____
City/State/Zip _____
Phone ( ) _____

Personal References: You must provide two different names, U.S. addresses, and telephone numbers.

16. Parent or Guardian:
Name _____
Street _____
City/State/Zip _____
Phone ( ) _____

17. Adult Relative: (Not at same address given in 16)
Name _____
Street _____
City/State/Zip _____
Phone ( ) _____

18. **SIGNATURE(S):** I reviewed the information I have presented in the "Borrower" section of this Application and Promissory Note and certify that it is true and accurate to the best of my knowledge and belief. I have read, understand and agree to the terms of the Application and Promissory Note and the "Borrower's Certification" printed on the back of this Application and Promissory Note. I understand and agree that my lender will be Norwest Bank South Dakota, N.A., and you are authorized to check my credit and employment history and to answer questions about your credit experience with me.

Signature of Student Borrower | Date
Cosigner 1's Signature (if any) | Date
Cosigner 2's Signature (if any) | Date

B. **SCHOOL**

19. DOE School Code
Branch Code (if any)

20. Grade Level

21. Enrollment Status
☐ Full Time
☐ Half Time

22. Anticipated Graduation
Month | Day | Year

23. Loan Period (e.g. August 15, 1994 = 08 15 94)
From _____ Month | Day | Year
To _____ Month | Day | Year

24. Cost of Attendance for Loan Period
$ _____ .00

25. Estimated Financial Aid (do NOT include the TLP amount requested in question #3).
$ _____ .00

26. Other Loans For This Loan Period. (do NOT include the TLP amount requested in question #3).
Stafford $ _____
Perkins $ _____
Other $ _____

27. Authorized TLP Disbursement Amount(s) and Date(s):
	Amount	Month	Day	Year
1st	$			
2nd	$			
3rd	$			

28. I hereby certify that the student named in Section A is accepted for enrollment or is enrolled and in good standing as at least a half-time student and is making satisfactory progress in an educational program determined to be eligible for the TLP program, and that the student is eligible for the TLP loan. I further certify that this institution will comply with all applicable TLP policies and provisions, and that information provided in Sections A and B is true, complete and correct to the best of my knowledge and belief. ☐ EA

Signature of School Official: _____ Date: _____
School: _____ Phone: _____

In this Note the words "I", "me", "my" and "mine" mean the above signed borrower and cosigner(s), unless the language specifically refers to only one or the other. If more than one person signs this Application and Promissory Note, "Promissory Note", each person will be liable for the full amount of the loan. "You", "your" and "yours" mean Norwest Bank South Dakota, National Association, and any other holder of this Promissory Note.

C. PROMISE TO PAY

I promise to pay to the order of Norwest Bank South Dakota, N.A., Sioux Falls, South Dakota, or to a subsequent holder, according to the terms below: the sum of the Loan Amount Requested to the extent it is advanced to me, or on my behalf, which includes an amount equal to the insurance premium described below in paragraph H. (the "Loan Amount"); interest on the Loan Amount; late charges; and, in the event of default, costs of collection and reasonable attorneys' fees.

D. DEFINITIONS

1. **Interim Period** - The "Interim Period" will begin on the date my loan is disbursed and will end on and include the last day of the calendar quarter following the earliest of the following dates:

   (a) Six months after I, the above signed borrower, cease to be enrolled (for any reason other than graduation) in at least half-time study at the graduate business school named above or any other graduate business school participating in the MBA LOANS program; or

   (b) Six months after I, the above signed borrower, graduate from the graduate business school listed above or any other graduate business school participating in the MBA LOANS program; or

   (c) Three years after the date of my first disbursement of any Tuition Loan Program (TLP) loan.

2. **Repayment Period** - The "Repayment Period" will begin on the day after the Interim Period ends and will continue for 144 months.

3. **Statement Period** - I, the above signed borrower, will receive statements on my loan at the address shown on your records (see paragraph L. Notices). The period of time covered by a statement is called a "Statement Period". During the Interim Period, I will receive quarterly statements on my loan. The quarterly statements will cover Statement Periods beginning on the first day of each January, April, July and October. During the Repayment Period I will receive monthly statements on my loan. The monthly statements will cover Statement Periods beginning on the first day of the Repayment Period and on the same day of each following month.

E. INTEREST

1. **Accrual of Interest** - Interest will accrue from the date of disbursement until payment in full at the Variable Rate described in paragraph E.2. below.

2. **Variable Rate** - During the Interim Period, the Variable Rate is the annual rate equal to 3.25% plus the Current Index, rounded to the nearest one-eighth (.125) of one percent. During the Repayment Period, the Variable Rate is the annual rate equal to 3.4% plus the Current Index, rounded to the nearest one-eighth (.125) of one percent. The Variable Rate will change quarterly on the first day of each January, April, July and October (the "Change Date(s)") if the Current Index changes. The "Current Index" for any calendar quarter beginning on a Change Date (or for any shorter period beginning on a disbursement date and ending on the first Change Date) is the previous calendar quarter's average of the Index rounded to the nearest one-hundredth (.01) of one percent. The Index is the rate published weekly in The Wall Street Journal, "Credit Markets" section, in the table that quotes the result, as the "coupon equivalent" rate, of the most recent auction of the 13-Week U.S. Treasury Bills. If the Index is no longer available, you will choose a comparable substitute.

F. TERMS OF REPAYMENT

1. **Interim Period** - I am not required to make payments during the Interim Period. You will add unpaid accrued interest to the principal balance of the loan at the commencement of the Repayment Period.

2. **Repayment Period Statements** - I will make consecutive monthly payments during the Repayment Period in the amounts and on the payment due dates shown on my monthly statements until I have paid all of the principal and interest and any other charges I may owe under this Promissory Note.

3. **Standard Repayment Terms** - Subject to the terms of paragraph F.4., below, I will repay my loan in consecutive monthly installments of principal and interest calculated each Change Date to equal the amount necessary to amortize the unpaid principal balance of my loan (as of the date of calculation) in equal monthly installments of principal and interest at the Variable Rate then in effect over the number of months remaining in the Repayment Period.

   If I have an outstanding TLP loan under which I have elected the option of a Fixed Rate at repayment on that loan, I may elect to have interest accrue under this Promissory Note during the Repayment Period at the same rate as the Fixed Rate on my outstanding TLP loan. If I do not have an outstanding TLP loan with the Fixed Rate option, then this option is not available.

4. **Alternative Repayment Terms** - If I, the above signed borrower, graduate from a graduate business school participating in the MBA LOANS program, I may choose the following alternative repayment option. To exercise my right to convert to an alternative repayment option, I will notify you in writing after my graduation date and at least 60 days prior to the beginning of the Repayment Period.

   Variable Rate/12 Interest Only, 132 Principal and Interest Payments - Under this option, interest will

Lender Code: 831197

accrue during the Repayment Period at the Variable Rate. I will make 12 consecutive monthly payments of accrued interest only, followed by 132 consecutive monthly payments of principal and accrued interest calculated each Change Date to equal the amount necessary to amortize the unpaid principal balance of the loan (as of the date of calculation) in equal consecutive monthly installments of principal and interest at the Variable Rate then in effect over the number of months remaining in the Repayment Period.

Any cosigner(s) of this Promissory Note agrees that the above signed borrower may elect any alternative repayment option without notice to or consent from the cosigner(s) and such election shall not affect or release the cosigner(s) from cosigner's obligations under this Promissory Note.

5. **Amounts Owing at the End of the Repayment Period** - Since interest accrues daily upon the unpaid principal balance of my loan, if I make payments after my payment due dates, I may owe additional principal and interest and late charges at the end of the Repayment Period. In such case, I shall pay the additional amounts and you will increase the amount of my last monthly payment to the amount necessary to repay my loan in full.
6. **Minimum Repayment** - Notwithstanding paragraphs F.3. and F.4., I agree to pay at least $600.00 each year (principal and/or interest) or the unpaid balance, whichever is less.
7. **Payment** - Payments will be applied first to accrued interest, then to late charges, and the remainder to principal.

G. LATE CHARGES

I will pay a late charge if I fail to make any part of an installment payment within 15 days after it becomes due. A late charge may not exceed $5.00, or 5% of the installment, whichever amount is greater.

H. FINANCE CHARGES

1. **Insurance Premium** - You will charge me and I will pay an amount equal to the insurance premium which you will pay to HEMAR Insurance Corporation of America (HICA) for its insurance on this Promissory Note which is equal to 7.5% of the Loan Amount Requested to the extent it is approved. This amount will be identified on my Disclosure Statement. If I do not have a cosigner, I will pay an additional amount equal to the premium which you paid to HICA which is equal to 2.5% of my loan balance (principal plus capitalized interest) at the beginning of the Repayment Period.
2. **Deducted from Disbursements** - At the time you issue any disbursement, you will deduct 7.5%, an amount equal to the insurance premium, from the disbursement. I will not be entitled to any reimbursement of insurance premium after I cash my disbursement check.
3. **Added to the Principal** - If I, the above signed borrower, do not have a cosigner, I will pay you the additional amount equal to the insurance premium described above in paragraph H.1. at the earlier of the beginning of the Repayment Period or upon default as defined in paragraph J. below. This amount will be added to my loan balance at the beginning of the Repayment Period. This amount will be identified on my Disclosure Statement given to me shortly before the beginning of the Repayment Period.

I. RIGHT TO PREPAY

I have the right to prepay all or any part of my loan at any time without penalty.

J. WHOLE LOAN DUE

I will be in default and you have the right to give me notice that the whole outstanding principal balance, accrued interest, and all other amounts payable to you under the terms of this Promissory Note are due and payable at once and to cease to make any further disbursements to me, if:

1. I fail to make any monthly payment to you when due; or
2. Any payment has not reached you within 15 days after it is due; or
3. I fail to notify you of a change in my name, address, or school enrollment status within ten days after a change occurs; or
4. I break any of my other promises in this Promissory Note; or
5. Any bankruptcy proceeding is begun by or against me, or I assign any of my assets for the benefit of my creditors; or
6. I make any false written statement in applying for this loan or at any time during the Interim or Repayment Periods; or
7. I die; or
8. I am in default on any loans I may already have with you, or on any loans I may have with you in the future.

My failure to receive a coupon book or a statement does not relieve me of my responsibility and obligation of making my required loan payments in accordance with the terms and conditions of this Promissory Note. You may report my payment history to credit reporting agencies.

If I default, I will be required to pay interest on this loan accruing after default at the same rate of interest applicable to this loan prior to my default. The interest rate after default will be subject to adjustment in the same manner as before default.

K. COLLECTION COSTS

I agree to pay you reasonable amounts permitted by law, including reasonable attorneys' fees and court costs, which you incur in enforcing the terms of this Promissory Note if I am in default.

L. NOTICES

1. I will send written notice to you, or any subsequent holder of this Promissory Note, within ten days after any change in my name, address, or school enrollment status.
2. Any notice required to be given to me by you will be effective when mailed by first-class mail to the latest address you have for me.
3. The lender and/or HEMAR Insurance Corporation of America (HICA) may report the status of this loan to a credit bureau. Therefore, in order to maintain a good credit rating, it is to my advantage to comply with all the terms of the loan agreement and to meet my responsibilities as a borrower under this program.
4. CALIFORNIA RESIDENTS ONLY: A married applicant may apply for a separate account. MAINE RESIDENTS ONLY: Consumer reports (credit reports) may be obtained in connection with this application. If I request 1) I will be informed whether or not consumer reports were obtained, and 2) If reports were obtained, I will be informed of the names and addresses of the consumer reporting agencies (credit bureaus) that furnished the reports. NEW YORK RESIDENTS ONLY: A consumer credit report may be requested in connection with updates, renewals or extensions of any credit as a result of this application. If I subsequently ask for this information, I will be informed whether or not such a report was requested and, if so, the name and address of the agency that furnished the report. OHIO RESIDENTS ONLY: The Ohio laws against discrimination require that all creditors make credit equally available to all credit-worthy customers, and that credit reporting agencies maintain separate credit histories on each individual upon request. The Ohio Civil Rights Commission administers compliance with this law. WISCONSIN RESIDENTS ONLY: For married Wisconsin residents, my signature confirms that this loan obligation is being incurred in the interest of my marriage or family. No provision of any marital property agreement (premarital agreement), unilateral statement under Section 766.59 of the Wisconsin Statutes or court decree under Section 766.70 adversely affects the interest of the lender unless the lender, prior to the time that the loan is approved, is furnished with a copy of the marital property agreement, a statement, a decree or has actual knowledge of the adverse provision. If the loan for which I am applying is granted, my spouse will also receive notification that credit has been extended to me.

M. ADDITIONAL AGREEMENTS

1. The proceeds of this loan will be used only for the educational expense of the above signed borrower at the graduate business school listed above. I understand that when you accept this signed Promissory Note, you are not agreeing to lend me money. You have the right to lend an amount less than the Loan Amount Requested or to accept or reject my cosigner(s). I will be required to repay only the amount you actually lend to me. If more than one person signs this Promissory Note, each person will be liable for the full amount of the loan.
2. If the HEMAR Insurance Corporation of America is required under its insurance contract to repay my loan, the HEMAR Insurance Corporation of America will become the owner of this Promissory Note and as my creditor will have all the rights of the original lender to enforce this Promissory Note against me.
3. This Promissory Note shall be governed by the laws of South Dakota.
4. Upon receipt of the Disclosure Statement, I will review it and if I am not satisfied with the terms of my loan as approved, I may cancel this Promissory Note and all disbursements. To cancel this Promissory Note, I will contact you within three days of receipt by me of the loan check and I will not cash any loan checks.
5. By accepting past due payments you do not waive or affect any right to accelerate this Promissory Note. I waive any notice of dishonor, notice of protest, presentment, demand for payment, and all other notices or demands in connection with this Promissory Note and consent to any and all extensions, renewals, or releases of any party liable upon this loan or any other loans I have outstanding under the MBA LOANS program, or waiver or modification that may be granted by you, all without affecting or releasing the borrower or the cosigner(s) from such loans.
6. If any provision of this Promissory Note is held invalid or unenforceable, that provision shall be considered omitted from this Promissory Note without affecting the validity or enforceability of the remainder of this Promissory Note.
7. Any provision of this Promissory Note may be modified if jointly agreed upon in writing by you and me. Any modification will not affect the validity or enforceability of the remainder of this Promissory Note.
8. I understand that this loan is an educational loan and is made under a program which is funded in part by a non-profit organization and as such, is not dischargeable in bankruptcy during the first seven years of repayment.
9. I will not sign this Promissory Note before reading both sides of it, including the Notice to Cosigner(s), even if otherwise advised. I acknowledge that I have received an exact copy and that I have the right at any time to pay in advance the unpaid balance due under this Promissory Note without penalty.

N. BORROWER'S CERTIFICATION

I declare that the following is true and correct. I, the borrower, certify that the information contained in my Promissory Note for the TLP is true, complete and correct to the best of my knowledge and belief and is made in good faith. I hereby authorize the school to pay to the lender any refund which may be due me up to the amount of this loan. I certify that the proceeds of this loan will be used for educational expenses at the school named for the loan period stated on the Promissory Note. I further authorize any school that I may attend to release to HICA, the lending institution, subsequent holder, U.S. Department of Education, or their agents or guarantor, any requested information pertinent to this loan (e.g., employment, enrollment status, current address). I also authorize HICA, the lender, subsequent holder, their agent or guarantor to check my credit and employment history, answer questions about their credit experience with me, and to release any information gathered in the credit review process. For the purpose of learning my current address and telephone number, I authorize HICA, the lender, subsequent holder, their agent or guarantor to release information and make inquiries to the individuals I have listed on my Promissory Note as references. I further authorize any lender or holder of any of my outstanding educational loans to release any information on any of my outstanding educational loans to any other lender or holder of any of my other educational loans. I understand that I must immediately repay any funds that I receive which cannot reasonably be attributed to meeting my educational expenses related to attendance at the school named on the Promissory Note for the loan period requested. At my lender's option, I understand that my lender may either electronically transmit funds to the school to be applied to my account or if my lender issues check(s), I authorize my lender to issue a check made payable to me, or jointly payable to me and the school, and send it to the school. I understand that I will receive a Disclosure Statement that identifies my loan amount (as determined by the lender), fee amounts and rates. I understand and agree that if the information on the Disclosure Statement conflicts with the information on this Promissory Note, the information on the Disclosure Statement applies. I also certify the following: I have read the materials explaining the loan program that have been provided to me; I understand the provisions of the program, my responsibilities and my rights under this program; and that the MBA LOANS program is funded in part by a non-profit organization.

O. NOTICE TO COSIGNER(S)

For the purposes of this notice, the words "you" and "your" refer to the cosigner(s), not the lender. You are being asked to guarantee this debt. Think carefully before you do. If the borrower doesn't pay the debt, you will have to. Be sure you can afford to pay if you have to, and that you want to accept this responsibility. You may have to pay up to the full amount of this debt if the borrower does not pay. You may also have to pay late charges and/or collection costs, which increase this amount. The lender can collect this debt from you without first trying to collect from the borrower. The lender can use the same collection methods against you that can be used against the borrower, such as suing you, garnishing your wages, etc. If this debt is ever in default, that fact may become a part of your credit record. This notice is not the contract that makes you liable for the debt.

Lender Code: 831197

Appendix C
Borrower's Rights and Responsibilities

When you take out a student loan, you take on certain rights and responsibilities. Understanding these rights and responsibilities will help you be a successful borrower.

The Loan Application Certification, Promissory Note, and Notice of Disclosure that you will receive when your loan is guaranteed provide a complete listing of your rights and responsibilities as a borrower. You should read these documents carefully before signing them.

The following are some important facts about your student loans that will help you understand your rights and fulfill your obligations.

Entrance and Exit Counseling

If you borrow money through the Federal Perkins or Federal Stafford loan programs, an entrance interview with a financial aid administrator is required before you can receive your loans. Exit counseling, either in the form of an interview or in some cases a letter, is required when you leave school. During the interviews or in the letter, the financial aid administrator will provide loan repayment information to you and will go over your rights and responsibilities as a borrower.

Federally Guaranteed Student Loans

A federally guaranteed student loan is money you borrow from a bank or other lending institution to help you pay for your education; the loan is guaranteed by the federal government through a guarantee agency.

The Promissory Note

- When you receive a loan, you must sign a promissory note. The promissory note is your promise to repay the loan.

- You must meet all the terms of the promissory note.

- Read and keep your copy of the signed promissory note, as well as the borrower's rights and responsibilities sheet you receive.

- When you have repaid your loan, the lending institution must return your original promissory note or give you a paid-in-full notification.

- A sample promissory note is included in Appendix B.

The School's Payment and Refund Policies

- The Federal Stafford Loan checks are generally made out jointly to the borrower and the school and sent directly to the school or transferred electronically.

- You must make arrangements with the school for the disbursement of loan funds to pay for tuition and fees and to receive the balance, if any, for your living and other expenses.

- You have a right to know about any financial aid that has been paid to the school on your behalf. You also have a right to the timely payment of money that the school owes you. Ask the school about its payment and refund policies and how you will be paid money from each type of aid program received through the school.

When You Must Repay Your Loan

- If you leave school early or cease to be at least a half-time student, you must contact your lender to set up a repayment plan.

- Your student loan is a debt and must be repaid. If you wish, you may repay your loan early without penalty.

Loan Repayment Terms

- When you receive a loan, it is your responsibility to understand and follow all repayment terms.

- The guarantor may charge an insurance premium to guarantee your loan against default. The insurance premium will be deducted proportionally from each disbursement and does not reduce the amount you are obligated to repay.

- An origination fee will be deducted from the proceeds of your Federal Stafford Loans. This fee is determined by federal law and does not reduce the amount you are obligated to repay.

- Federal Stafford Loans have a grace period before you have to begin repayment of principal and interest. The grace period starts when you leave school or drop below half-time attendance. The grace period on all variable interest rate loans or loans with an applicable interest rate of 8 percent or higher is six months; 7 percent loans have a nine-month grace period. Federal SLS loans have no grace period, but you may delay repayment for six months if you also have a Federal Stafford Loan.

- You must contact your lender to make repayment arrangements no later than 90 days before your grace period ends.

- Your lender must give you a repayment schedule before you begin paying back the loan. This schedule must conform to the repayment provisions in your promissory note.

- The amount of your monthly payment will be equal to the amount necessary to amortize the unpaid principal balance of your loan, including capitalized interest if applicable, over the length of the repayment period.

- You will be required to make payments of at least $50 per loan per month unless your lender agrees to a lower amount.

- You must pay back your loan in accordance with the repayment schedule.

- You are responsible for repayment of all loans, including interest and any fees, even if you do not finish school.

- You have a right to repay part or all of the loan ahead of schedule without penalty.

Loan Repayment Period

You may take at least 5 years, but no more than 10 years, to repay your Federal Stafford (GSL) or Federal SLS loans. The following are exceptions to this rule:

- You can repay your loan in full at any time.

- If your loan is small enough that by paying the minimum of $50 per month it will be paid off in less than five years, you will not be permitted to take five years.

Delaying Loan Repayment

- Under certain conditions, such as unemployment, you may be able to defer (delay) repayment of your loan. Interest may still accrue for some loans during the deferment period.

- Your promissory note will contain a complete listing of the conditions under which you may qualify for a deferment.

- Deferments will not be included in determining the 5- to 10-year repayment periods mentioned above.

Other Loan Repayment Options

- If you are in your grace period or in repayment, you may be eligible for the Federal Loan Consolidation Program.

  - You can combine or consolidate any or all of your loans into a single, new loan. This new loan will have a repayment period of from 10 to 30 years.

  - You can consolidate debts from the following types of loans:

    Federal Stafford Loans

    Federal Supplemental Loans for Students

    Federal Perkins Loans (National Direct Student Loans)

    Health Professions Student Loans (HPSL)

  - You may not wish to consolidate lower interest loans if the rate on the consolidation loan is higher.

- If you have Federal SLS loans, the following are three refinancing options that may be available to you.

  - Refinancing to secure combined repayment: The holder of your SLS loans may consolidate those loans to allow you to make a single monthly payment of principal and interest.

  - Refinancing to secure a variable interest rate: If you borrowed at a fixed interest rate, the holder of your SLS loan(s) may reissue your loan(s) at a variable interest rate. Depending on when you first borrowed, the interest rate, which will change each July 1, will have a maximum of 11 or 12 percent.

  - Refinancing to discharge previous loans: If the holder of your SLS loan(s) denies you the option of refinancing to secure a variable interest rate, you may apply to another lender to refinance your SLS loan(s) at a variable interest rate.

If you use one of these refinancing options, the refinancing lender will disclose to you the repayment terms and the amount of any charges applicable to each option.

- Under certain circumstances, individuals who enlist in the military may have their loans repaid by the Secretary of Defense, in accordance with Section 902 of the Department of Defense Authorization Act, 1981 (P.I. 96-342, 10 U.S.C. 2141, note). Questions concerning the program should be addressed to your local recruiter. The program described is a recruiting program for the service involved and does not pertain to prior service by an individual or those not eligible for enlistment in the armed forces.

If You Are in Trouble with Your Loan

- If you are financially unable to make payments, you have a right to ask your lender for any of the following:

  - A short period during which you make no payments on principal

  - An extension of time to make payments

  - The option to make smaller payments

  Your lender is not required to approve your request.

- Keep in contact with your lender if you are having financial problems. Your lender will work with you in maintaining your credit standing. This is the best way to stay out of default.

Changes in Status

- Notify your lender and guarantor immediately if you do any of the following:

  - Fail to enroll for the period for which the loan was intended

  - Leave school for any reason

  - Cease to be enrolled in school at least half time

  - Transfer from one school to another

  - Graduate

  - Change your name or address

- If you received a deferment, notify your lender when the reason for the deferment no longer exists.

- If your lender sells your loan(s) to another bank, it must tell you in writing.

Defaulting on a Loan

- If you fail to meet your loan repayment terms, you are delinquent.

- Your lender will give you a written notice of your failure to repay before declaring your loan in default.

- If you continue to be delinquent, you default on the loan, and the entire balance becomes due.

- If you do go into default, you may be sued.

What Loan Default Will Mean to You

- If you fail to repay your loan and go into default, your default will be reported to a credit bureau. Being in default means you may:

  - Lose your federal and state income tax refunds,

  - Face legal action,

  - No longer be eligible for student aid,

  - Find it difficult to obtain other credit.

- Defaulting on a student loan will damage your credit rating.

- Defaulting could prevent you from getting a credit card, a car loan, a tax refund, or additional financial aid if you decide to either continue or go back to school.

Appendix D
Checklist for Applying for Admission and Financial Aid

Following is a checklist of tasks that you will need to accomplish as you apply for admission and financial aid at various graduate schools of management. This checklist assumes that you are applying for admission in the traditional fall term and that you will be beginning your efforts approximately 12 months in advance. If you will be applying for admission mid-year or if you are beginning the process later in the cycle, you will probably need to vary the steps and compress the process. You should also be aware that mid-year and late applicants may have fewer financing options open to them.

Summer
- Write draft statement of purpose.
- Start browsing through graduate school catalogs and source books such as the GMAC's *Official Guide to MBA Programs* (see order form at the back of this book).

September
- Meet with advisors and faculty members to discuss statement of purpose.
- Ask advisors and supervisors for letters of recommendation.
- Sign up for the Graduate Management Admission Test (GMAT) (see order form for registration materials and schedule of test dates at the back of this book).
- Study for the GMAT using GMAC's *Official Guide for GMAT Review* (see order form at the back of this book).

October
- Take the GMAT.
- Request application materials from graduate management schools.
- Read all materials and determine all admissions and financial aid deadlines.
- Determine which financial aid application(s) are required by each school.

October/November
- Attend a GMAC MBA Forum (see schedule on inside back cover) to talk with graduate management school representatives.

November
- Decide where you will apply.
- Order grade transcripts from every college you ever attended to be sent to each school to which you are applying.
- If you are currently enrolled in college, ask if your records office can send a transcript with your fall term grades in time to meet the deadlines of programs to which you are applying.

December
- Complete all admissions applications (do a draft on a photocopy of the form first).
- Give your recommenders the forms to fill out or the addresses to which they should send their letters. Also provide them with a copy of your statement of purpose or your responses to specific questions asked by the school(s).

- Obtain the appropriate financial aid application(s).

- Research the availability of private scholarships for which you may be eligible.

- Investigate the availability of tuition assistance from your own or your parents' employer.

December/January
- Mail admissions applications. Even if deadlines are later, it is good to get the applications in early. Keep copies of the applications for your records.

January
- Gather your financial records for the previous year.

- Complete and send in your financial aid application(s), using estimates if necessary. Keep copies of the applications for your records.

- Request financial aid transcripts from all institutions you attended previously; have them sent to all schools to which you are applying for financial aid.

February
- Contact schools about the possibility of visiting. Make trips, if possible.

March
- If schools request additional information or documentation, send it in promptly.

April
- If requested, send a copy of your federal income tax form to the financial aid office at each school to which you have been admitted.

- If you submitted estimates on your financial aid applications, submit actuals now.

- Review award letters, compare offers, and select a school to attend.

May
- Submit loan applications.

August/September
- Receive first loan disbursement, pay tuition, enroll in school.

- Apply for in-school deferments of any previous educational loans.

Appendix E
Guarantee Agencies

Alabama
Alabama Commission on Higher
    Education
3465 Norman Bridge Road
Montgomery, Alabama 36105
(205) 269-2700

Alaska
Alaska Commission on
    Postsecondary Education
Alaska Student Loan Corp.
3030 Vintage Boulevard
Juneau, Alaska 99801-7109
(907) 465-2854

Arizona
Arizona Educational Loan Program
United Student Aid Funds, Inc.
USA Group
P.O. Box 3028
Tempe, Arizona 85244
(602) 814-9988

Arkansas
Student Loan Guarantee Foundation
    of Arkansas
219 South Victory
Little Rock, Arkansas 72201-1884
(501) 372-1491

California
California Student Aid Commission
P.O. Box 510845
Sacramento, California 94245-0845
(916) 445-0880

Colorado
Colorado Guaranteed Student Loan
    Program
One Denver Place
999 18th Street, Suite 425
Denver, Colorado 80202-2471
(303) 294-5070 (status check)
(303) 294-5050 (main number)

Connecticut
Connecticut Student Loan
    Foundation
525 Brook Street
P.O. Box 1009
Rocky Hill, Connecticut 06067
(203) 257-4001

Delaware
Delaware Higher Education Loan
    Program
Carvel State Office Building
820 North French Street
4th Floor
Wilmington, Delaware 19801
(302) 577-6055

District of Columbia
American Student Assistance
330 Stuart Street
Boston, Massachusetts 02116
(617) 426-9796

Florida
Florida Student Financial Assistance
    Foundation
Office of Student Financial
    Assistance
325 West Gains Street
1344 Florida Education Center
Tallahassee, Florida 32399-0400
(904) 488-4095

Georgia
Georgia Student Finance
    Commission
Suite 200
2082 East Exchange Place
Tucker, Georgia 30084
(404) 414-3000

Hawaii
Hawaii Education Loan Program
United Student Aid Funds, Inc.
P.O. Box 22187
Honolulu, Hawaii 96823-2187
(808) 536-3731

Idaho
Student Loan Fund of Idaho, Inc.
P.O. Box 730
Fruitland, Idaho 83619
(208) 452-4058

Illinois
Illinois Student Assistance
    Commission
1755 Lake-Cook Road
Deerfield, Illinois 60015
(708) 948-8550

Indiana
State Student Assistance
  Commission of Indiana
Loan Division
150 West Market Street
Suite 500
Indianapolis, Indiana 46204-2811
(317) 232-2366

Iowa
Iowa College Student Aid
  Commission
914 Grand Avenue
Suite 201
Des Moines, Iowa 50309
(515) 281-3501

Kansas
United Student Aid Funds, Inc.
USA Group
11100 USA Parkway
Fishers, Indiana 46038
(800) 824-7044

Kentucky
Kentucky Higher Education
  Assistance Authority
1050 U.S. 127 South
Frankfort, Kentucky 40601
(502) 564-7990

Louisiana
Louisiana Student Financial
  Assistance Commission
P.O. Box 91202
Baton Rouge, Louisiana
  70821-9202
(504) 922-1011

Maine
Finance Authority of Maine
Maine Educational Assistance
  Division
State House Station 119
Augusta, Maine 04333
(207) 287-2183

Maryland
Maryland Higher Education Loan
  Corporation
2100 Guilford Avenue, Room 305
Baltimore, Maryland 21218
(410) 333-6555

Massachusetts
American Student Assistance
330 Stuart Street
Boston, Massachusetts 02116
(617) 426-9434

Michigan
Michigan Guarantee Agency
P.O. Box 30047
Lansing, Michigan 48909
(517) 373-0760

Minnesota
Northstar Guarantee, Inc.
440 Cedar Street
Suite 210
St. Paul, Minnesota 55101
(612) 290-8795

Mississippi
Mississippi Guarantee Student Loan
  Agency
3825 Ridgewood Road
Jackson, Mississippi 39211
(601) 982-6663

Missouri
Coordinating Board for Higher
  Education
3515 Amazonas Drive
Jefferson City, Missouri 65109
(314) 751-3940

Montana
Montana Guaranteed Student Loan
  Program
P.O. Box 5209
Helena, Montana 59604-9947
(406) 444-6594

Nebraska
Nebraska Student Loan Program
P.O. Box 82507
Lincoln, Nebraska 68501
(402) 475-8686

Nevada
United Student Aid Funds, Inc.
USA Group
11100 USA Parkway
Fishers, Indiana 46038
(800) 824-7044

New Hampshire
New Hampshire Higher Education
  Assistance Foundation
44 Warren Street
P.O. Box 877
Concord, New Hampshire 03302
(603) 225-6612
(800) 235-2577 (within New
  Hampshire)
(800) 525-2577 (outside New
  Hampshire)

New Jersey
New Jersey Higher Education
  Assistance Authority
Guaranteed Student Loan Program
4 Quakerbridge Plaza
Trenton, New Jersey 08625
(609) 588-3200

New Mexico
New Mexico Student Loan
  Guarantee Corporation
P.O. Box 27020
Albuquerque, New Mexico
  87125-7020
(505) 345-8821

New York
New York State Higher Education
  Services Corporation
99 Washington Avenue
Twin Towers
Albany, New York 12255
(518) 474-5592

North Carolina
North Carolina State Education
  Assistance Authority
P.O. Box 2688
Chapel Hill, North Carolina
  27515-2688
(919) 549-8614

North Dakota
North Dakota Guaranteed Student
  Loan Program
P.O. Box 5509
Bismarck, North Dakota
  58502-5509
(701) 224-5600

Ohio
Ohio Student Aid Commission
309 South 4th Street
Columbus, Ohio 43215
(614) 644-6549

Oklahoma
Oklahoma State Regents for Higher
  Education
500 Education Building
State Capitol Complex
Oklahoma City, Oklahoma
  73105
(405) 524-9100

Oregon
Oregon State Scholarship
   Commission
1500 Valley River Drive
Suite 100
Eugene, Oregon 97401
(503) 687-7400
(800) 452-8807 (within Oregon)

Pennsylvania
Pennsylvania Higher Education
   Assistance Agency
1200 North 7th Street
Harrisburg, Pennsylvania
   17102-1444
(717) 257-2850

Rhode Island
Rhode Island Higher Education
   Assistance Authority
560 Jefferson Boulevard
Warwick, Rhode Island 02886-1320
(401) 277-2050
(800) 922-9855 (outside Rhode
   Island)

South Carolina
South Carolina Student Loan
   Corporation
Interstate Center, Suite 210
P.O. Box 21487
Columbia, South Carolina 29221
(803) 798-0916

South Dakota
Education Assistance Corporation
115 First Avenue, S.W.
Aberdeen, South Dakota 57401
(605) 225-6423

Tennessee
Tennessee Student Assistance
   Corporation
404 James Robertson Parkway
Suite 1950, Parkway Tower
Nashville, Tennessee 37243-0820
(615) 741-1346
(800) 342-1663 (within Tennessee)

Texas
Texas Guaranteed Student Loan
   Corporation
P.O. Box 15996
Austin, Texas 78761
(512) 835-1900

Utah
Utah Higher Education Assistance
   Authority
P.O. Box 45202
Salt Lake City, Utah 84145-0202
(801) 321-7200

Vermont
Vermont Student Assistance
   Corporation
Champlain Mill
P.O. Box 2000
Winooski, Vermont 05404-2000
(802) 655-9602
(800) 642-3177 (within Vermont)

Virginia
Virginia State Education Assistance
   Authority
411 East Franklin Street
Suite 300
Richmond, Virginia 23219
(804) 792-5626

Washington
Northwest Education Loan
   Association
500 Coleman Building
811 First Avenue
Seattle, Washington 98104
(206) 625-1283

West Virginia
Pennsylvania Higher Education
   Assistance Agency
John F. Kennedy Center
Room 512
734 Schuylkill Avenue
Philadelphia, Pennsylvania 19146
(215) 735-2877

Wisconsin
Great Lakes Higher Education
   Corporation
2401 International Lane
Madison, Wisconsin 53704
(608) 246-1800

Wyoming
United Student Aid Funds, Inc.
USA Group
11100 USA Parkway
Fishers, Indiana 46038
(800) 824-7044

Puerto Rico
Puerto Rico Higher Education
   Assistance Corporation
P.O. Box 42001
Minillas Station
San Juan, Puerto Rico 00940-2001
(809) 763-3535

Trust Territories
Hawaii Education Loan Program
United Student Aid Funds, Inc.
1314 South King Street
Suite 961
Honolulu, Hawaii 96814
(808) 536-3731

Virgin Islands
Virgin Islands Joint Boards of
   Education
P.O. Box 11900
Charlotte Amalie
St. Thomas, Virgin Islands 00801
(809) 774-4546

GLOSSARY

Academic Year: A period of time of study that typically consists of two semesters or three quarters.

Acceptable Documentation: Written documents that substantiate the information reported on a student aid application. Includes the U.S. income tax return, bank statements, and signed statements from the applicant and the applicant's family. Federal regulations list documents that are acceptable proof of the accuracy of applicant data.

Accrued Interest: Interest on loans that accumulates and must be paid at a later date, usually when the principal becomes due. Interest can either be simple or compound.

Adjusted Gross Income (AGI): The income figure taken from the federal income tax form. The AGI typically is the total of wages and interest and dividend income minus certain adjustments (i.e., IRA contributions).

AFDC (Aid to Families with Dependent Children): Federal grant money administered by state Departments of Social Services, often referred to as "Welfare." Also called ADC (Aid to Dependent Children).

Allowances: Financial modifications included in the need analysis formula to allow for a family's non-discretionary expenses or to shelter assets or income for retirement or emergency purposes.

Asset Protection Allowance: In the federal need analysis formula, an allowance against assets based on the student's age and marital status.

Assets: Financial holdings such as cash on hand in checking and savings accounts, stocks, bonds, trusts and other securities, loan receivables, home equity, other real estate equity, business equipment, and business inventory.

Award: A specific amount of financial assistance offered to a student through financial aid programs to pay for educational costs.

Award Letter: Notification to students about whether they have qualified for financial aid. The award letter usually gives information on the types and amounts of aid offered, specific program information, responsibilities of the student, and the conditions that govern the award.

Award Year: The period of time the financial aid award covers. The award year may be the academic year or 12 months.

Base Year: The 12-month period ending on December 31 preceding the award year. For example, calendar year 1994 is the base year for the 1995-96 award year.

BIA (Bureau of Indian Affairs): A federal agency that handles American Indian affairs and that administers grants to students who are at least one-fourth American Indian.

Campus-based Programs: The term applies to three federal Title IV student aid programs administered by eligible schools. The programs are the Federal Perkins Loan, Federal College Work-Study, and Federal Supplemental Educational Opportunity Grant programs. Only the first two are available to graduate students.

Cancellation of Loan: A portion or all of some student loans can be cancelled (no repayment required) if the borrower performs service in certain geographic areas or academic fields. Some loans will be cancelled upon the death of the borrower. Promissory notes define the special circumstances under which a loan can be cancelled.

Capitalizing Interest: Adding any accrued interest to the principal of a loan prior to repayment. Once interest is capitalized, the amount of the loan principal increases, and the payments also increase.

Collection Agency: A business that specializes in collecting payment on defaulted or delinquent loans. Collection agencies usually receive a percentage of the amount they collect from borrowers whose payments are overdue.

Collection Costs: The reasonable costs incurred by a lender in using a commercial skiptrace agency (an agency that locates people who have moved without leaving a forwarding address) or collection agency in an attempt to recover loan funds.

Compound Interest: Interest computed on the sum of an original principal and accrued interest.

Co-signer or Co-maker: One of two individuals who are joint borrowers on a loan and who are equally liable for repayment of the loan.

Cost of Attendance (COA) or Cost of Education: The costs that are typically associated with attending school for one academic year. Costs are established by the institution and generally include tuition and fees, room and board, books and supplies, transportation, personal and miscellaneous expenses, child care, and disability-related expenses.

Debt Management Counseling: Counseling for students on the subject of assuming debt and accumulated indebtedness. It includes a projection of the expected monthly payments and the length of repayment for student loans.

Default: A loan is in default when the borrower has failed to make payments for a certain period of time or has failed to comply with other terms of the promissory note.

Deferment: A specified period of time during which the repayment of the principal amount of a loan is suspended. Depending on the type of loan, interest may or may not continue to accrue. Deferments are typically granted during enrollment in a degree program and during periods of unemployment or economic hardship. Borrowers whose first loan was disbursed prior to July 1, 1993, may be eligible for deferments not only under these conditions but also under other conditions.

Delinquency: A loan is delinquent when the borrower has failed to make an installment payment on its due date.

Disbursement: The process by which financial aid funds are made available to students who have applied and are eligible for them. Disbursements can be made in a variety of ways including crediting the student's account or issuing a check made payable to the student or made payable jointly to the student and the institution.

Disclosure Statement: A statement that the lender must send to the borrower either before or at the time they disburse a loan, as well as at the beginning of the repayment period. The purpose is to provide borrowers with information about the terms of the loan and the definition and the consequences of default. The statement includes items such as: amount of the loan, interest rate, fee charges, length of the grace period (if any), the maximum length of repayment, the minimum annual repayment, and deferment conditions.

Due Diligence: Full and timely disclosure to student borrowers of their rights and obligations. The use of extensive, persistent, and forceful procedures for the making, servicing, and collection of student loans.

Earned Income: Income received for work performed, including wages, salaries, and tips.

Eligible Noncitizen: A student aid applicant who is not a U.S. citizen, but is eligible to receive Title IV financial assistance (permanent resident; noncitizen national; and certain residents of the Trust Territory of the Pacific Islands and Micronesia).

Enrollment Status: Describes the number of credit hours for which the student is enrolled: full time, half time, part time, etc.

Entrance Interview: The 1986 Amendments to the Higher Education Act require schools to perform loan entrance interviews. Before a loan is approved, the institution must inform students about their borrower rights and responsibilities.

Exit Interview: Each school participating in the Federal Perkins, Federal Stafford, and Federal SLS Loan programs must offer special counseling, often called "exit counseling," to review the student's loan obligation and related information.

Family Contribution (FC): The figure that indicates how much of a family's (including the student's) financial resources should be available to help pay for educational expenses. This figure is determined according to statutory formulas.

Federal College Work-Study: A federal program that provides funds for jobs for students who demonstrate financial need. The school awards College Work-Study funds to a student and then assists the student in locating a job where those funds can be earned.

Federal Consolidation Loan: A program offered by some lenders that allows borrowers to combine loans from Federal Perkins, Federal Stafford, Federal Supplemental Loans for Students (SLS) and the Health Professions Student Loans (HPSL) into a single loan at a single rate of interest with a single periodic payment. Under loan consolidation, the consolidating lender pays off the original lenders and issues a consolidation loan in the amount of the outstanding principal and accrued interest of all loans that are to be consolidated.

Federal Direct Stafford Loans: A loan program similar to the Federal Subsidized Stafford Loan Program and the Federal Unsubsidized Stafford Loan Program. The federal government provides funds to schools to lend directly to students.

Federal Methodology (FM): The need analysis formula established by Congress to determine a student's family contribution (FC). The FC is used to determine eligibility for federal aid, which includes the campus-based and Federal Stafford Loan programs. FM measures a student's financial resources, taking into consideration the income and assets of the student, student's spouse, and if applicable, student's parents.

Federal Perkins Loan Program: Formerly called National Direct Student Loans (NDSL), and renamed the Federal Perkins Loan to honor Congressman Carl Perkins. The program provides low-interest student loans to both undergraduate and graduate students. Schools make loans to their students from a fund composed of federal and institutional contributions.

Federal PLUS: Federal Parent Loan for Undergraduate Students. Parents may borrow on behalf of their children who are dependent students. Loans are made by lenders, such as banks, credit unions, or savings and loans. Graduate students are no longer eligible for PLUS loans.

Federal Subsidized Stafford Loan Program: Formerly the Guaranteed Student Loan (GSL) and renamed for Senator Robert T. Stafford, this loan program provides federally subsidized, low-interest loans to students. Loans are financed by lenders such as banks, savings and loans, and credit unions, and are insured by the federal government.

Federal Supplemental Loans for Students (SLS): A Title IV aid program that provided loans to students who did not meet the need criteria for a Federal Stafford Loan or who qualified for further assistance beyond the funds available to them through the Federal Stafford Loan Program. This program is no longer available; it has been replaced by the Federal Unsubsidized Stafford Loan Program.

Federal Unsubsidized Stafford Loans for Middle Income Students: A Title IV aid program that provides loans to students who do not meet the criteria for a Federal Subsidized Stafford Loan or who qualify for further assistance beyond the funds available to them through the subsidized program. Unlike the subsidized program, the borrower must either pay interest during periods of enrollment or request an in-school deferment; deferred interest accrues and is capitalized.

Fellowship: This term is often used interchangeably with scholarship and grant. The term refers to awards paid to students either toward the cost of tuition or for living expenses. Fellowships may be outright gift aid or may be given in return for services performed.

Financial Aid Application: The document(s) that must be completed by the applicant (and possibly the applicant's parents). These documents provide the financial data that will allow the school to determine the family's financial contribution and the student's aid eligibility.

Financial Aid Form (FAF): A need analysis form processed by the College Scholarship Service to determine financial aid eligibility of students for certain non-federal aid programs.

Financial Aid Office: The office that administers various forms of financial aid. A student may need to deal with a central university financial aid office, a business school financial aid office, or both.

Financial Aid Package: An offer by an institution to a student aid applicant of one or more forms of financial aid (loans, grants and/or scholarships, College Work-Study).

Financial Aid Transcript (FAT): A form used by educational institutions to collect data about Title IV and other financial aid received by a student at previously attended educational institutions.

Financial Need: The difference between the school's cost of attendance and the family's ability to pay (the Family Contribution).

Forbearance: For Federal Stafford, Federal SLS, or Federal PLUS borrowers, the lender may agree to grant a temporary suspension of payments, to allow an extension of time for making payments, or to accept smaller payments than were previously scheduled. Forbearance may be granted for circumstances that are not covered by deferments, and is usually given in situations where personal problems, such as hospitalization or short-term unemployment, affect the borrower's ability to meet loan payment obligations.

Free Application for Federal Student Aid (FAFSA): A free need analysis service of the U.S. Department of Education. All students applying for federal aid must file the FAFSA.

Full-time Student: In general, one who is taking a minimum of 12 semester or quarter hours per academic term in institutions with standard academic terms.

Gift Aid: Student financial aid such as scholarships, fellowships, and grants that do not have to be repaid.

Grace Period: The period of time that usually begins when a loan recipient ceases to be at least a half-time student and ends when the repayment period starts. The loan principal and interest need not be paid by the student during the grace period. Depending on the type of loan, interest may not accrue during this period.

Graduate and Professional School Financial Aid Service (GAPSFAS): A centralized application and needs analysis service used to determine the financial aid eligibility of graduate and professional students for certain non-federal aid programs. GAPSFAS is administered by Educational Testing Service for the Graduate and Professional School Financial Aid Council. The service is available for the 1994-95 award year, but will discontinue operations on May 1, 1995.

Grant: A form of financial aid that does not require repayment and does not require that work be performed.

Guarantee Agency: A state agency or private, non-profit institution or organization that administers the Federal Stafford Loan and Federal PLUS programs. Guarantee agencies insure lenders against losses due to a borrower's default, death, disability, or bankruptcy, and are involved in the process of locating capital to finance student loans.

Guarantee Fee: An insurance fee that the guarantee agency charges the lender. The fee is usually passed on to the borrower. In most cases, the lender reduces the amount of the borrower's loan disbursement by this amount.

Guaranteed Student Loan (GSL): Former name of the Federal Subsidized Stafford Loan Program.

Half-time Student: The definition of this term is determined by the institution, but generally equals 6 semester, trimester, or quarter hours per academic term or 12 semester hours or 18 quarter hours per academic year.

Higher Education Act: In 1965, this act permanently established the U.S. government's role in providing grants and loan programs to ensure access to higher education.

Immigration and Naturalization Service (INS): Federal agency responsible for verifying citizenship and immigration status on the Student Aid Report.

Income Protection Allowance: In the federal need analysis formula, an allowance against income for basic living expenses not included in the standard student budget.

Interest Subsidy: Interest payments by the federal government to the lender on a Federal Subsidized Stafford Loan while the borrower is enrolled on at least a half-time basis or is in a grace period.

Internal Revenue Service (IRS): Federal agency responsible for collecting taxes. Student aid application data are verified using IRS information and forms.

Loan: An advance of funds that is evidenced by a promissory note requiring the recipient to repay the specified amount(s) under the prescribed conditions.

Merit-based Assistance: Any form of financial aid awarded on the basis of personal achievement or individual characteristics and not based on demonstrated financial need.

National Direct Student Loan (NDSL): Former name of the Federal Perkins Loan Program (see Federal Perkins Loan Program). First established as the National Defense Student Loan program.

Need Analysis: The calculation used to determine a student's financial need.

Need-based Assistance: Any form of financial aid awarded on the basis of demonstrated financial need.

Office of Student Financial Assistance (OSFA): The branch of the Department of Education having overall responsibility for administering federal student financial aid programs and for developing policies and procedures to meet the objectives of those programs.

Origination Fee: A processing fee calculated on the amount borrowed for a loan and charged to the borrower by the lender. This fee, like the guarantee fee, is subtracted from the amount of the loan proceeds.

Overaward: The situation that occurs when the student's family contribution plus financial aid exceed the cost of attendance. Overawards result most often when a student's enrollment status is reduced or when additional resources become available to the student after the award offer has been made.

Parent Contribution (PC): The amount of money that the parents are expected to contribute to the student's educational expenses.

Payment Period: An institutionally defined length of time over which financial aid funds will be disbursed to a student.

Principal and Interest: Principal refers to the amount of loan funds borrowed; interest refers to the amount charged for the use of the money over a period of time. Interest is usually stated as a percent.

Professional Judgment: The law allows financial aid administrators to determine whether the expected family contribution derived from the Federal Methodology (FM) is correct or whether revisions should be made based upon information or circumstances known to the aid administrator. Administrators may make discretionary changes to individual data elements. Professional judgment is used to make a more accurate assessment of the family's financial condition. Professional judgment decisions must be made on an individual, case-by-case basis, and the reasons must be documented in the student's file.

Projected Year: A 12-month period consisting of either the summer prior to the academic year and the academic year or the calendar year in which the academic year begins. For example, calendar year 1995 is the projected year for the enrollment period beginning in September 1995.

Promissory Note: The legal document a borrower signs when obtaining a loan. It lists the conditions under which the loan is made and the terms under which the borrower agrees to pay back the loan.

Reauthorization: A term used in the U.S. government to denote the renewal of an existing act of Congress.

Repayment Period: The period during which the borrower repays a loan.

Repayment Schedule: A plan that sets forth the interest rate on a loan, the frequency of payments, the principal and interest due in each installment, the number of payments required to pay the loan in full, and the due date of the first payment.

Satisfactory Academic Progress: This term, as defined by each institution, is used to describe a satisfactory rate of course completion as well as individual term performance. Regulations require that a student be making satisfactory academic progress to receive Title IV aid.

Scholarship: A form of financial assistance that does not require repayment or employment. A "merit-based" scholarship may be made to a student who demonstrates or shows potential for distinction, usually in academic performance. Some scholarships require both academic proficiency and demonstrated financial need.

Secondary Markets: Institutions that buy loans from lenders, providing more capital to make additional loans. Once the loans are purchased, the secondary market is responsible for managing and servicing them. Some contract with a servicer to perform these duties. The sale of a loan does not effect the borrower since the terms of the loan remain the same after it is purchased.

Selective Service System: Federal agency responsible for verifying selective service status on the Student Aid Report (see Statement of Registration).

Self-help Expectation: The principle that students have an obligation to help pay for a portion of their education. A standard self-help expectation is frequently computed in the analysis of student resources.

Self-help Programs: Funds from work and loan sources. Title IV self-help programs include Federal Perkins Loan, Federal Stafford Loan, Federal PLUS, and Federal College Work-Study. Graduate students are no longer eligible for PLUS.

Servicer: A business organization that specializes in managing, billing, and collecting loans for lenders or secondary markets.

Servicing: The activities involved in managing and collecting loans. Includes keeping track of borrowers while in school, billing borrowers when the loan is due, and carrying out collection activities to ensure continued payment.

Simple Interest: Interest computed solely on the original principal of a loan.

Simplified Needs Test: A formula under the Federal Methodology for calculating a student's family contribution for those whose adjusted gross income is equal to or less than $50,000 and who file or are eligible to file either the 1040EZ or 1040A tax form. When using this formula, a family's assets are not included.

Skiptracing: The attempt to find a valid address for a borrower who cannot be located. Any information on the borrower's loan application (i.e., references), from the alumni or registrar's offices, from the U.S. Department of Education, or from a commercial skiptracing service may be used.

Statement of Educational Purpose/ Certification Statement on Refunds and Default: Students must sign this statement each year in order to receive federal student aid. By signing, students agree to use the funds solely for educational purposes and certify that they are not in default on any educational or Title IV loan and do not owe any repayment on funds they received for which they were not eligible.

Statement of Registration: In order to be eligible for Title IV aid, students must certify that they have registered for selective service or are not required to do so because they are female, in the armed services on active duty, have not reached their eighteenth birthday, were born before 1960, or are citizens of the Federated States of Micronesia or the Marshall Islands or a permanent resident of the Trust Territory of the Pacific Islands (Palau).

Student Aid Report: The document that the federal government sends to the student reporting the information the student submitted on the FAFSA and indicating the calculated family contribution. The student must send this document to school(s) so that the school(s) can determine federal aid eligibility.

Student Budget: See Cost of Attendance.

Student Contribution: The calculated amount a student is expected to contribute toward educational costs based on an analysis of income and assets.

Subsidized Loan: A loan for which the borrower is not responsible for all of the interest payments. In the Federal Subsidized Stafford Loan program, the government makes interest payments to the lender on behalf of the borrower while the student attends school on at least a half-time basis, and during approved grace or deferment periods. Some institutions subsidize their own loans by not charging interest while a student is in school.

Taxable Income: Income earned from wages, salaries, and tips as well as interest income, dividends, alimony, estate or trust income, business or farm profits, and rental or property income. These types of income are usually reported on an IRS tax form.

Title IV: Refers to federal student financial aid programs for students attending postsecondary educational institutions. The programs are authorized under Title IV of the Higher Education Act of 1965, as amended, and administered by the Department of Education. The programs are Federal Pell Grants, Federal Supplemental Educational Opportunity Grants (SEOG), Federal College Work-Study, Federal Perkins Loans, Federal Stafford Loans, Federal Supplemental Loans for Students (SLS), PLUS Loans, and State Student Incentive Grants. Graduate students are only eligible for Federal College Work-Study, Federal Perkins Loans, and Federal Stafford Loans.

Undergraduate: A postsecondary student who does not have a baccalaureate degree.

Unmet Need: The situation in which a student's financial aid package does not meet the calculated need (the difference between the cost of attendance and the student's and parents' expected contribution).

Untaxed Income: Income received that is not taxed. Examples are some Social Security benefits, welfare benefits, interest on tax-free bonds, some unemployment compensation, military and other subsistence and quarters allowance, and contributions to retirement funds.

Verification: The process of substantiating the data that a student has provided on the financial aid application when applying for Title IV aid.

Verification Items: Specific applicant (and family) information that must be checked for accuracy in the verification process. These may include income and assets. Verification may also extend to other items at the discretion of the institution.

This is your mailing label. Type or print clearly.

Order Form for Official GMAC Publications

For fastest service, call **800-982-6740** Monday through Friday, 8:00 a.m. to 4:30 p.m. Eastern time (outside the U.S. or Canada, call **609-771-7243**). Ask for **Department G36**. Or mail this order form with your payment or credit card information to the address at the right. Prices are effective through August 31, 1995. *NOTE: The special telephone numbers above are for publications credit card orders only; for other GMAT services or information, call 609-771-7330.*

Payment Method: ☐ VISA ☐ MasterCard ☐ Check/Money Order (in U.S. dollars, payable to ETS/GMAT)

Credit Card Number _____ Expiration Date ___/___

Cardholder's or Authorized User's Signature _____

Daytime Telephone Number _____

		U.S. Delivery*	Foreign Delivery*	Price
The Official Guide for GMAT Review	238409	☐ $13.95	☐ $23.95	$ _____
The Official Software for GMAT Review**	238558	☐ $59.95	☐ $74.95	_____
Special Value! GMAT Review Set** (GMAT book and software)	238356	☐ $65.00	☐ $85.00	_____
The Official Guide to MBA Programs	238333	☐ $14.95	☐ $29.95	_____
The Official Guide to Financing Your MBA	238336	☐ $12.95	☐ $22.95	_____
Special Value! MBA Planning Set (MBA book and financing book)	238357	☐ $24.00	☐ $45.00	_____
			SUBTOTAL	_____
		In California, add 8.25% sales tax		_____
		In Canada, add 7% GST R131414468		_____
		TOTAL ORDER		$ _____

 * See shipping information on reverse side.
** See hardware requirements on reverse side.

TO _____

GRADUATE MANAGEMENT ADMISSION TEST 696-01
EDUCATIONAL TESTING SERVICE
P.O. BOX 6108
PRINCETON, NJ 08541-6108
GMAC
GUIDES
G-96

This is your mailing label. Type or print clearly.

Order Form for Official GMAC Publications

For fastest service, call **800-982-6740** Monday through Friday, 8:00 a.m. to 4:30 p.m. Eastern time (outside the U.S. or Canada, call **609-771-7243**). Ask for **Department G36**. Or mail this order form with your payment or credit card information to the address at the right. Prices are effective through August 31, 1995. *NOTE: The special telephone numbers above are for publications credit card orders only; for other GMAT services or information, call 609-771-7330.*

Payment Method: ☐ VISA ☐ MasterCard ☐ Check/Money Order (in U.S. dollars, payable to ETS/GMAT)

Credit Card Number _____ Expiration Date ___/___

Cardholder's or Authorized User's Signature _____

Daytime Telephone Number _____

		U.S. Delivery*	Foreign Delivery*	Price
The Official Guide for GMAT Review	238409	☐ $13.95	☐ $23.95	$ _____
The Official Software for GMAT Review**	238558	☐ $59.95	☐ $74.95	_____
Special Value! GMAT Review Set** (GMAT book and software)	238356	☐ $65.00	☐ $85.00	_____
The Official Guide to MBA Programs	238333	☐ $14.95	☐ $29.95	_____
The Official Guide to Financing Your MBA	238336	☐ $12.95	☐ $22.95	_____
Special Value! MBA Planning Set (MBA book and financing book)	238357	☐ $24.00	☐ $45.00	_____
			SUBTOTAL	_____
		In California, add 8.25% sales tax		_____
		In Canada, add 7% GST R131414468		_____
		TOTAL ORDER		$ _____

 * See shipping information on reverse side.
** See hardware requirements on reverse side.

TO _____

GRADUATE MANAGEMENT ADMISSION TEST 696-01
EDUCATIONAL TESTING SERVICE
P.O. BOX 6108
PRINCETON, NJ 08541-6108
GMAC
GUIDES
G-96

This is your mailing label. Type or print clearly.

Order Form for Official GMAC Publications

For fastest service, call **800-982-6740** Monday through Friday, 8:00 a.m. to 4:30 p.m. Eastern time (outside the U.S. or Canada, call **609-771-7243**). Ask for **Department G36**. Or mail this order form with your payment or credit card information to the address at the right. Prices are effective through August 31, 1995. *NOTE: The special telephone numbers above are for publications credit card orders only; for other GMAT services or information, call 609-771-7330.*

Payment Method: ☐ VISA ☐ MasterCard ☐ Check/Money Order (in U.S. dollars, payable to ETS/GMAT)

Credit Card Number _____ Expiration Date ___/___

Cardholder's or Authorized User's Signature _____

Daytime Telephone Number _____

		U.S. Delivery*	Foreign Delivery*	Price
The Official Guide for GMAT Review	238409	☐ $13.95	☐ $23.95	$ _____
The Official Software for GMAT Review**	238558	☐ $59.95	☐ $74.95	_____
Special Value! GMAT Review Set** (GMAT book and software)	238356	☐ $65.00	☐ $85.00	_____
The Official Guide to MBA Programs	238333	☐ $14.95	☐ $29.95	_____
The Official Guide to Financing Your MBA	238336	☐ $12.95	☐ $22.95	_____
Special Value! MBA Planning Set (MBA book and financing book)	238357	☐ $24.00	☐ $45.00	_____
			SUBTOTAL	_____
		In California, add 8.25% sales tax		_____
		In Canada, add 7% GST R131414468		_____
		TOTAL ORDER		$ _____

 * See shipping information on reverse side.
** See hardware requirements on reverse side.

TAKE THE NEXT STEP TOWARD YOUR MBA.

The Official Guide for GMAT Review, 7th Edition
- contains three *actual* tests plus samples of each question type — 900 questions in all!
- gives answers and explanations by GMAT test authors
- includes exclusive information about the *new* Analytical Writing Assessment
- includes comprehensive math review

The Official Software for GMAT Review, Version 5.0
- interactive tutorials with examples of each question type and step-by-step explanations
- two *actual* tests (different from those in the *GMAT Review* book) with on-screen timer, automatic scoring, and individualized feedback
- includes exclusive information about the *new* Analytical Writing Assessment
- includes two sets of disks (four 5^1/$_4$″ and two 3^1/$_2$″)
- **Hardware requirements:** IBM PC, XT, AT, PS/2 or 100% compatible computer; hard disk with 4.0 megabytes of free space; 512K; DOS 2.0 or higher; CGA, EGA, VGA, Hercules Graphics, or 100% compatible graphics card and monitor (A printer is optional.)

The Official Guide to MBA Programs, 7th Edition
- profiles and compares more than 600 graduate management programs worldwide
- offers advice on choosing a school and handling the application process
- examines management careers and gives sources for more information

The Official Guide to Financing Your MBA, 2nd Edition
- suggests ways to pay for your MBA
- includes information on loans, scholarships, work-study, etc.
- compares financial aid packages
- provides information on specific schools

Ordering Information: To order, see reverse side. The books are also sold in many bookstores.

Shipping Information: Orders sent to the U.S., Guam, Puerto Rico, U.S. Virgin Islands, and U.S. territories are shipped by first class mail or UPS (*street address required*). Allow two to three weeks from time of order receipt for delivery. Orders shipped outside the U.S. are sent airmail; allow four to six weeks from time of order receipt for delivery. *Rush delivery is available with most telephone orders.*

TAKE THE NEXT STEP TOWARD YOUR MBA.

The Official Guide for GMAT Review, 7th Edition
- contains three *actual* tests plus samples of each question type — 900 questions in all!
- gives answers and explanations by GMAT test authors
- includes exclusive information about the *new* Analytical Writing Assessment
- includes comprehensive math review

The Official Software for GMAT Review, Version 5.0
- interactive tutorials with examples of each question type and step-by-step explanations
- two *actual* tests (different from those in the *GMAT Review* book) with on-screen timer, automatic scoring, and individualized feedback
- includes exclusive information about the *new* Analytical Writing Assessment
- includes two sets of disks (four 5^1/$_4$″ and two 3^1/$_2$″)
- **Hardware requirements:** IBM PC, XT, AT, PS/2 or 100% compatible computer; hard disk with 4.0 megabytes of free space; 512K; DOS 2.0 or higher; CGA, EGA, VGA, Hercules Graphics, or 100% compatible graphics card and monitor (A printer is optional.)

The Official Guide to MBA Programs, 7th Edition
- profiles and compares more than 600 graduate management programs worldwide
- offers advice on choosing a school and handling the application process
- examines management careers and gives sources for more information

The Official Guide to Financing Your MBA, 2nd Edition
- suggests ways to pay for your MBA
- includes information on loans, scholarships, work-study, etc.
- compares financial aid packages
- provides information on specific schools

Ordering Information: To order, see reverse side. The books are also sold in many bookstores.

Shipping Information: Orders sent to the U.S., Guam, Puerto Rico, U.S. Virgin Islands, and U.S. territories are shipped by first class mail or UPS (*street address required*). Allow two to three weeks from time of order receipt for delivery. Orders shipped outside the U.S. are sent airmail; allow four to six weeks from time of order receipt for delivery. *Rush delivery is available with most telephone orders.*

TAKE THE NEXT STEP TOWARD YOUR MBA.

The Official Guide for GMAT Review, 7th Edition
- contains three *actual* tests plus samples of each question type — 900 questions in all!
- gives answers and explanations by GMAT test authors
- includes exclusive information about the *new* Analytical Writing Assessment
- includes comprehensive math review

The Official Software for GMAT Review, Version 5.0
- interactive tutorials with examples of each question type and step-by-step explanations
- two *actual* tests (different from those in the *GMAT Review* book) with on-screen timer, automatic scoring, and individualized feedback
- includes exclusive information about the *new* Analytical Writing Assessment
- includes two sets of disks (four 5^1/$_4$″ and two 3^1/$_2$″)
- **Hardware requirements:** IBM PC, XT, AT, PS/2 or 100% compatible computer; hard disk with 4.0 megabytes of free space; 512K; DOS 2.0 or higher; CGA, EGA, VGA, Hercules Graphics, or 100% compatible graphics card and monitor (A printer is optional.)

The Official Guide to MBA Programs, 7th Edition
- profiles and compares more than 600 graduate management programs worldwide
- offers advice on choosing a school and handling the application process
- examines management careers and gives sources for more information

The Official Guide to Financing Your MBA, 2nd Edition
- suggests ways to pay for your MBA
- includes information on loans, scholarships, work-study, etc.
- compares financial aid packages
- provides information on specific schools

Ordering Information: To order, see reverse side. The books are also sold in many bookstores.

Shipping Information: Orders sent to the U.S., Guam, Puerto Rico, U.S. Virgin Islands, and U.S. territories are shipped by first class mail or UPS (*street address required*). Allow two to three weeks from time of order receipt for delivery. Orders shipped outside the U.S. are sent airmail; allow four to six weeks from time of order receipt for delivery. *Rush delivery is available with most telephone orders.*

Order Form for *GMAT Bulletin of Information*

Applicants to schools requiring the Graduate Management Admission Test (GMAT) may arrange with Educational Testing Service (ETS) to take the test on one of four dates. If you wish to receive free of charge a *Bulletin of Information* describing arrangements for taking the test, the nature of the exam, and scoring procedures, complete the address label at the right and mail it to:

**Graduate Management Admission Test
Educational Testing Service
P.O. Box 6101
Princeton, NJ 08541-6101**

To order a *GMAT Bulletin of Information* by telephone, call (609) 771-7330.

A registration form and return envelope accompany each *Bulletin of Information*.

Depending on where and when you want to take the test, your completed registration form and fee must be received by the date indicated on the Registration Calendar (see reverse side) for the test date you select (requests for supplementary and Sabbath observer centers have earlier deadlines). It is to your advantage to send for your *Bulletin* and complete your registration form as early as possible. (Processing of registrations for 1994-95 will begin in late August 1994.)

*Please note that, although you may receive order forms from several schools, you need only one **GMAT Bulletin** and registration form.*

This is your mailing label. Type or print clearly.

TO

**GRADUATE MANAGEMENT ADMISSION TEST   666-17
EDUCATIONAL TESTING SERVICE
P.O. BOX 6101
PRINCETON, NJ 08541-6101
GMAT BULLETIN**

Order Form for *GMAT Bulletin of Information*

Applicants to schools requiring the Graduate Management Admission Test (GMAT) may arrange with Educational Testing Service (ETS) to take the test on one of four dates. If you wish to receive free of charge a *Bulletin of Information* describing arrangements for taking the test, the nature of the exam, and scoring procedures, complete the address label at the right and mail it to:

**Graduate Management Admission Test
Educational Testing Service
P.O. Box 6101
Princeton, NJ 08541-6101**

To order a *GMAT Bulletin of Information* by telephone, call (609) 771-7330.

A registration form and return envelope accompany each *Bulletin of Information*.

Depending on where and when you want to take the test, your completed registration form and fee must be received by the date indicated on the Registration Calendar (see reverse side) for the test date you select (requests for supplementary and Sabbath observer centers have earlier deadlines). It is to your advantage to send for your *Bulletin* and complete your registration form as early as possible. (Processing of registrations for 1994-95 will begin in late August 1994.)

*Please note that, although you may receive order forms from several schools, you need only one **GMAT Bulletin** and registration form.*

This is your mailing label. Type or print clearly.

TO

**GRADUATE MANAGEMENT ADMISSION TEST   666-17
EDUCATIONAL TESTING SERVICE
P.O. BOX 6101
PRINCETON, NJ 08541-6101
GMAT BULLETIN**

Order Form for *GMAT Bulletin of Information*

Applicants to schools requiring the Graduate Management Admission Test (GMAT) may arrange with Educational Testing Service (ETS) to take the test on one of four dates. If you wish to receive free of charge a *Bulletin of Information* describing arrangements for taking the test, the nature of the exam, and scoring procedures, complete the address label at the right and mail it to:

**Graduate Management Admission Test
Educational Testing Service
P.O. Box 6101
Princeton, NJ 08541-6101**

To order a *GMAT Bulletin of Information* by telephone, call (609) 771-7330.

A registration form and return envelope accompany each *Bulletin of Information*.

Depending on where and when you want to take the test, your completed registration form and fee must be received by the date indicated on the Registration Calendar (see reverse side) for the test date you select (requests for supplementary and Sabbath observer centers have earlier deadlines). It is to your advantage to send for your *Bulletin* and complete your registration form as early as possible. (Processing of registrations for 1994-95 will begin in late August 1994.)

*Please note that, although you may receive order forms from several schools, you need only one **GMAT Bulletin** and registration form.*

This is your mailing label. Type or print clearly.

TO

**GRADUATE MANAGEMENT ADMISSION TEST   666-17
EDUCATIONAL TESTING SERVICE
P.O. BOX 6101
PRINCETON, NJ 08541-6101
GMAT BULLETIN**

Registration Calendar

Test Dates	DOMESTIC REGISTRATION GMAT administrations in the U.S., Guam, Puerto Rico, U.S. Virgin Islands, and U.S. Territories			INTERNATIONAL REGISTRATION GMAT administrations in all other countries (including Canada)	
	REGULAR REGISTRATION	LATE REGISTRATION & CENTER CHANGE	SPECIAL REQUESTS	FINAL REGISTRATION & CENTER CHANGE	SPECIAL REQUESTS
	Registration forms **received** after this date must be accompanied by the late registration fee.	Add the late registration fee. Registration forms **received** after this period will be returned.	Last **receipt** date for supplementary centers and Saturday-Sabbath observer administrations*	Registration forms received after this date will be returned.	Last date for receipt of requests for supplementary centers† and Saturday-Sabbath observer administrations*
	Deadline Dates				
Oct. 15, 1994*†	Sept. 16	Sept. 17-23	Aug. 30	Sept. 2	Aug. 19
Jan. 21, 1995*	Dec. 16	Dec. 17-23	Dec. 6	Dec. 9	Nov. 25
Mar. 18, 1995*	Feb. 17	Feb. 18-24	Jan. 31	Feb. 3	Jan. 20
June 17, 1995*	May 19	May 20-26	May 2	May 5	April 21

*Administration dates for observers of the Saturday Sabbath are Monday, October 17, 1994; Monday, January 23, 1995; Monday, March 20, 1995; and Monday, June 19, 1995.

†No supplementary centers will be established for foreign registration for the October 1994 test date.

Test Disclosure is not available for the October 1994 test date.

Scores are reported approximately *four* weeks after the test date.

Registration Calendar

Test Dates	DOMESTIC REGISTRATION GMAT administrations in the U.S., Guam, Puerto Rico, U.S. Virgin Islands, and U.S. Territories			INTERNATIONAL REGISTRATION GMAT administrations in all other countries (including Canada)	
	REGULAR REGISTRATION	LATE REGISTRATION & CENTER CHANGE	SPECIAL REQUESTS	FINAL REGISTRATION & CENTER CHANGE	SPECIAL REQUESTS
	Registration forms **received** after this date must be accompanied by the late registration fee.	Add the late registration fee. Registration forms **received** after this period will be returned.	Last **receipt** date for supplementary centers and Saturday-Sabbath observer administrations*	Registration forms received after this date will be returned.	Last date for receipt of requests for supplementary centers† and Saturday-Sabbath observer administrations*
	Deadline Dates				
Oct. 15, 1994*†	Sept. 16	Sept. 17-23	Aug. 30	Sept. 2	Aug. 19
Jan. 21, 1995*	Dec. 16	Dec. 17-23	Dec. 6	Dec. 9	Nov. 25
Mar. 18, 1995*	Feb. 17	Feb. 18-24	Jan. 31	Feb. 3	Jan. 20
June 17, 1995*	May 19	May 20-26	May 2	May 5	April 21

*Administration dates for observers of the Saturday Sabbath are Monday, October 17, 1994; Monday, January 23, 1995; Monday, March 20, 1995; and Monday, June 19, 1995.

†No supplementary centers will be established for foreign registration for the October 1994 test date.

Test Disclosure is not available for the October 1994 test date.

Scores are reported approximately *four* weeks after the test date.

Registration Calendar

Test Dates	DOMESTIC REGISTRATION GMAT administrations in the U.S., Guam, Puerto Rico, U.S. Virgin Islands, and U.S. Territories			INTERNATIONAL REGISTRATION GMAT administrations in all other countries (including Canada)	
	REGULAR REGISTRATION	LATE REGISTRATION & CENTER CHANGE	SPECIAL REQUESTS	FINAL REGISTRATION & CENTER CHANGE	SPECIAL REQUESTS
	Registration forms **received** after this date must be accompanied by the late registration fee.	Add the late registration fee. Registration forms **received** after this period will be returned.	Last **receipt** date for supplementary centers and Saturday-Sabbath observer administrations*	Registration forms received after this date will be returned.	Last date for receipt of requests for supplementary centers† and Saturday-Sabbath observer administrations*
	Deadline Dates				
Oct. 15, 1994*†	Sept. 16	Sept. 17-23	Aug. 30	Sept. 2	Aug. 19
Jan. 21, 1995*	Dec. 16	Dec. 17-23	Dec. 6	Dec. 9	Nov. 25
Mar. 18, 1995*	Feb. 17	Feb. 18-24	Jan. 31	Feb. 3	Jan. 20
June 17, 1995*	May 19	May 20-26	May 2	May 5	April 21

*Administration dates for observers of the Saturday Sabbath are Monday, October 17, 1994; Monday, January 23, 1995; Monday, March 20, 1995; and Monday, June 19, 1995.

†No supplementary centers will be established for foreign registration for the October 1994 test date.

Test Disclosure is not available for the October 1994 test date.

Scores are reported approximately *four* weeks after the test date.

A Program of the Graduate Management Admission Council

The Best Way to Finance Your Graduate Management Education

How you finance your graduate business education is an important decision. Recognizing the vital link between finances and access to graduate management education, the Graduate Management Admission Council, a not-for-profit association of business schools, has established the MBA LOANS programs. In this way we can make the benefits of an MBA degree available to the greatest number of people.

Economy	Focus	Access	Response
You can save thousands of dollars with MBA LOANS low interest rates and low fees. Capitalization of your MBA LOANS interest occurs only when you begin repayment, another economical feature of the program. MBA LOANS and EXECUTIVE MBA LOANS were designed by business schools to meet the special needs of full-time and executive graduate business students.	A complete portfolio of federal and private loans is available through MBA LOANS. This single source gives you access to all Federal Stafford Loans and to our unique Tuition Loan Program. You can also use the MBA LOANS consolidation program for all your outstanding federal student loans. Our exclusive EXECUTIVE MBA LOANS program offers generous loan limits that can provide all the funding needed for executive business education.	Easy qualifying is an important part of the MBA LOANS programs. No in-school loan payments, no cosigner, and no collateral are required. Our credit guidelines are flexible, no additional credit application is necessary, and our programs are available to borrowers of all income levels. The EXECUTIVE MBA LOANS program requires a credit evaluation.	The MBA LOANS programs are committed to providing the highest level of responsive service. Our quick loan processing assures you of a prompt decision on your loan application. Most questions can be answered with a single call to one of our toll-free numbers. Please call for information or for an application packet. **MBA LOANS 1-800-366-6227** **EXECUTIVE MBA LOANS 1-800-366-0603**